Redeeming Objects

Redeeming Objects

A West German Mythology

Natalie Scholz

THE UNIVERSITY OF WISCONSIN PRESS

Publication of this book has been made possible, in part,
through support from the George L. Mosse Program in History at the University of Wisconsin–Madison and the Hebrew University of Jerusalem.

The University of Wisconsin Press
728 State Street, Suite 443
Madison, Wisconsin 53706
uwpress.wisc.edu

Gray's Inn House, 127 Clerkenwell Road
London EC1R 5DB, United Kingdom
eurospanbookstore.com

Printed in the United States of America
This book may be available in a digital edition.

Library of Congress Cataloging-in-Publication Data

Names: Scholz, Natalie, 1972– author.
Title: Redeeming objects : a West German mythology / Natalie Scholz.
Other titles: George L. Mosse series in the history of European culture, sexuality, and ideas.
Description: Madison, Wisconsin : The University of Wisconsin Press, 2023. |
Series: George L. Mosse series in the history of European culture, sexuality, and ideas |
Includes bibliographical references and index.
Identifiers: LCCN 2023006024 | ISBN 9780299344306 (hardcover)
Subjects: LCSH: Consumer goods—Germany (West) | Consumers—Germany (West)—History. | National socialism. | Germany (West)—Economic conditions—20th century.
Classification: LCC HC286.5 .S394 2023 | DDC 338.943—dc23/eng/20230526
LC record available at https://lccn.loc.gov/2023006024

In loving memory of my father

Bruno Franjo Scholz

(1933–2021)

To articulate the past historically does not mean to recognize it "the way it really was" (Ranke). It means to seize hold of a memory as it flashes up at a moment of danger.

—WALTER BENJAMIN, "Theses on the Philosophy of History"

Encountering a ghost or approaching a subject in this way is never quite as easy as Benjamin might be taken to suggest. It takes some effort to recognize the ghost and to reconstruct the world it conjures up.

—AVERY GORDON, *Ghostly Matters*

Myth deprives the object of which it speaks of all History. In it, history evaporates. It is a kind of ideal servant: it prepares all things, brings them, lays them out, the master arrives, it silently disappears: all that is left for one to do is to enjoy this beautiful object without wondering where it comes from. Or even better: it can only come from eternity.

—ROLAND BARTHES, *Mythologies*

Agreed: post-war Germany is a miracle. But it is a very queer miracle. There is a superb frenzy of life on the surface; but at the heart, there is queer stillness.

—GEORGE STEINER, "The Hollow Miracle"

CONTENTS

ILLUSTRATIONS

ACKNOWLEDGMENTS

The scholarly work that ended up producing this book is inextricably interwoven with my professional path in academic life and with the opportunities and challenges this path had in store for me. Most importantly, it is interwoven with the luck of meeting people whose inspiration, advice, and support made all the difference in the world. It is impossible to trace all the conversations that had an influence on my reflections. Nor is it possible to properly give credit to what happens when two minds intertwine their thinking, sending observations and ideas back and forth. In such conversations, where do the thoughts of one person end and the ideas of the other begin? But all these inspirations could only flourish because those I trusted were equally generous with their empathy and reliable support when I suddenly found myself on the threshold of leaving academia. I have written elsewhere about the experiences that pushed me to that threshold. That I ended up staying was in many ways improbable and a testament to these academic friendships that were sustaining me. This left me with an enormous gratitude and an emboldened sense that when it comes to my scholarly work, I must follow my own intuitions even if that means sidestepping some of the current logics of academic life.

While I chose at one point to—half-seriously, half-jokingly—call myself a "slow professor," actually doing "slow scholarship" requires the kind of time that the normal institutional demands do not allow for. I want to thank those institutions that put faith in my project by generously funding it and thereby giving me the invaluable gift of time. The first expeditions into the territory of postwar popular culture were made possible by a Feodor Lynen Research Fellowship from the Alexander von Humboldt Foundation and a Lise Meitner Postdoctoral Fellowship from the North Rhine–Westphalian Ministry for Science and Research.

Later on, research fellowships at the Institute for Advanced Study Konstanz and the Netherlands Institute for Advanced Study provided me with both time and an environment that encouraged me to venture further into the unsettling territory of redeeming objects. During the last few years, colleagues in the Department of History at the University of Amsterdam worked at ensuring that faculty had at least one teaching free period in the course of an otherwise long academic year. Without the beneficial effects of this collective effort, I would not have been able to finish the book.

The late Hayden White once said at a public event in Amsterdam that "writing is a fear-producing activity." Sharing not only my ideas and findings but at times also the emotional challenges I experienced in the writing process was a crucial part of the journey that resulted in this book. My thanks go to everyone who listened to what I had to say and reacted with genuine interest and often attentive questions or comments. I cannot list all of these encounters here, but I can say that every single one of them mattered, that many fed me with new thoughts, and that they all helped me to keep going.

I want to thank Margit Szöllösi-Janze for welcoming me as a scholar with an interesting project when I still felt like an inexperienced postdoc; Rudolf Schlögl for staying true to being my earliest mentor; Matthijs Lok for asking me to work with him on the theme of "forgetting," which paved the way for chasing the Volkswagen's ghosts; Carola Dietze for telling me that "the Volkswagen needs to be in the book"; Bernd Stiegler for his hospitality as the owner of a historical collection of private photographs; Anne Gerritsen, Florence Bernault, Laura Fair, and Kenda Mutongi for showing me the magic and fun of female writing companionship; George Blaustein for always reminding me that it matters how we write; Leora Auslander for her encouraging comments and for inviting me to write a piece that gave me the chance to find a new writing voice; Alon Confino for believing in my project and for showing me how to dwell with great humanity in the uncomfortable realms of the past; Liz Buettner for saying precisely the right thing in our very first conversation and for supporting me ever since in so many ways; Paula Diehl for sharing her indomitable spirit at the right moments; Boris Schafgans for the creativity that always sparkles in his presence; Gudrun Brockhaus for modeling how to hold on to one's own thinking against sometimes scary odds; Dimitri Roudenko for helping me to find my way through those spheres where history "out there" and "in here" converge; Ana Dragojlovic for feeding me with the kind of anthropological theory and for always inspiring the kind of self-reflection that the book needed; Carolyn Birdsall, Guy Geltner, and Markus Stauff for being the best collegial supporting team anyone could ever wish for; Marieke Bloembergen for introducing me to colonial and subaltern history, for showing me how to be an empathic and strong-willed female academic, and for standing at my side in the maze of Dutch academia; Till van Rahden for sharing his rich intellectual universe with me, for his generous guidance on so many matters, and for everything else; Sheryl Kroen for letting me in on her journey "from the rubble to the end of history," for our amazing never-ending conversation about the emotions writing can produce, for being the first reader of the book manuscript, and for everything else.

I also want to thank Kerstin, Heike, and Nicola for never ever doubting that I would finish the book and Robère and Agnieszka for all the times they invited me to babble on about it at their kitchen table. To my parents, Bruno and Hanne, I owe a confidence that has also helped to carry me through the bumpy stages of my writing process. Their own paths through the period that this book covers were always present in my mind. Josef has been at my side through it all, tirelessly encouraging me to defend the space I needed for the book against the other demands of life. It is impossible to imagine this journey without him.

Redeeming Objects

INTRODUCTION

A West German Mythology and the Ghosts of the Past

On a Thursday in May 1949 a photo appears in a West German illustrated magazine. A young woman stands next to a shiny Mercedes convertible. She smiles and raises her hand in a presenting gesture. The text begins with the words: "Nobody can tell . . ." and "There it is: The new Mercedes!"

On the following Monday, the Parliamentary Council in Bonn signs the German Basic Law, and the western occupation zones become the Federal Republic of Germany.

Four days earlier, the German Werkbund opened an exhibition of modern furniture in Cologne.

A week earlier, the Berlin blockade ended.

Two weeks earlier, the first foreign presentation of German industrial products since the end of the war concluded in New York.

In April and May an export exhibition took place in Hannover. The posters showed Christopher Columbus and his ship in front of a globe.

The first meaning of "mythology" in the *Oxford English Dictionary* reads: "The exposition of a myth or myths; the interpretation of fables; a book of such expositions." In this nowadays rarely used sense of the word, this book is a mythology. It traces how, during the first fifteen years after the Second World War, a powerful myth emerged about West German society and about its place in history. At the center of this myth is a belief that the consumption and export of industrial commodities distanced and redeemed West Germany from the Nazi past and placed the country squarely within the present of an evolving postwar West. This belief has influenced both collective memory and historical scholarship and is not coincidentally compatible with a Cold War framework of scholarly interpretation that glued together Western consumer culture and democratic freedoms, contrasting them with the totalitarianism both of the Communist East and of the former Third Reich.[1]

The chapters of this book do not attempt to grasp, let alone present, the whole of postwar West German culture and society nor the whole of West German consumer and material culture. Rather, they try to shine a light on specific structures of feeling and perception that crystallized in widespread public discourses around certain consumer objects or certain ways of presenting them that were heavily charged with symbolic and political meaning. The underlying scholarly work of mythology that has brought these structures to the surface was set in motion when, more than fifteen years ago, I began to dig through material of the postwar period and was confronted with subtle yet clear-enough references to the Nazi past where I had never expected them. Neither examining the available literature nor growing up and living in (West) Germany during the 1980s and 1990s had prepared me for stumbling upon the most troubling aspects of the German past while studying iconic consumer objects of the 1950s. What I found, without looking for it, mirrored back to me in unsettling ways the limitations of the framework within which my thoughts had unfolded until then.

The 1948 currency reform, the shop windows filling up again with merchandise, the boom of the West German economy in the early 1950s, and the accompanying export successes of West German industrial products are *narrative* pillars of the "economic miracle," a mythical story about the historical event—stretched out for a decade—that marks postwar West Germany's rebirth as a Western nation. The Volkswagen and modern design interiors are *symbolic* pillars of one of this story's core messages, namely, that in this economic miracle Germany was reborn as a better Germany, a country that stood in sharp contrast to the Nazi past, a Germany that had learned its historical lessons.

In recent decades a plethora of scholarly books and articles on the history of the Federal Republic have substantially complicated and even decomposed this mythical miracle story. On the one hand, we know a great deal about the many continuities between the Nazi era and the early Federal Republic, from the large numbers of former Nazis in high positions in the country's major institutions to longer-lasting influences of the Nazi concept of a *Volksgemeinschaft* (racial community). After the equality of man and woman was included in the new Basic Law, the patriarchal family was reconceived as the "key building block" of West German society.[2] It is very clear by now that the postwar transformation was much more messy and took much longer than the economic miracle narrative implied. On the other hand, historians have begun to shed light on various activities of Germans who, after 1945, engaged in rethinking and remaking the social and political life with the aim of creating a more open and democratic society: from the early years' discussions about which consequences to draw from Germany's descent into tyranny to vivid conversations during the 1950s about education, family structures, gender relations, and sexuality as essential terrains for building a viable democracy.[3] Yet when a younger generation articulated a more radical desire to democratize society in the 1960s, they were driven by a deep-seated unease with the mentalities of their parents, which these previous efforts had not alleviated.

In between these two big themes—the continuities with the Third Reich and collective efforts to forge a democratic society—historians have asked how West Germans dealt with the horrors of the Nazi past while the new West German state undid the Allies' denazification program. The long collective process to confront the mass violence of the Holocaust only truly began in the early 1960s with Adolf Eichmann's trial in Jerusalem, which was intensely reported on in West German media, and with the subsequent Auschwitz trials in Frankfurt. During the Federal Republic's first decade there was not exactly silence about the Third Reich but rather a way of speaking and remembering in which Germans positioned themselves as victims of a manipulative dictator and of the cruelties of war.[4]

Contestations over the idea of Germany's 1945 "zero hour," or *Stunde Null*, capture the difficulties of comprehending the chaotic and centrifugal forces and attitudes characterizing West Germany's postwar moment. There is a consensus, however, about at least one lesson that Germans were forced to learn by the end of the war: that the war defeat had been comprehensive and definitive and, as a consequence, that the new sovereign power lay in the hands of the Allies, who had the authority to decide on Germany's future.[5] These new power relations, a widespread aversion to warfare, and, induced by the Western Allies, the democratic institutional structure of the Federal Republic, founded in 1949, constitute an incontestable historical break with the Nazi period. We can only appreciate this break, however, with the hindsight knowledge that this new democratic polity would go on to have a long and peaceful future, something that appeared far from obvious to many contemporaries inside and outside Germany during the 1950s.

In spite of this complex and paradoxical historical image of the period, the economic miracle still exerts imaginative power, providing a popular narrative about West Germany's postwar rebirth as a nation. The emergence of this miracle myth cannot be understood without the transnational context of its beginnings. After the Marshall Plan was launched in 1947, West Germany not only received economic support but also became an important focal point of transnational propaganda efforts, orchestrated by the United States, to praise the workings of industrial productivity and a free circulation of commodities as the ultimate remedy for the crisis of war-torn Europe. These propaganda efforts went on to strongly influence a popularized image of "the West" as a whole. As the geopolitical tensions of the dawning Cold War intensified, the revival of West Germany's economy became a foundational success story of this postwar West.[6]

Working within this framework, historians have interpreted the rising consumer culture of the 1950s in West Germany as an element of postwar "modernization," "liberalization," and "Westernization" that went hand in hand with the political and moral conservatism of the era, a combination sometimes summarized with the metaphor of a "motorized Biedermeier." The cover of Axel Schildt's 1999 historical essay on the "success story of the Federal Republic," entitled *Ankunft im Westen* (Arrival in the West), captures this perspective visually by showing a photo of Volkswagen director Heinrich Nordhoff standing proudly in front of a parade of Volkswagen Beetles at the monumental plant in Wolfsburg. Other accounts modified this interpretation by highlighting the role women were assigned as consumer citizens of the Federal Republic's social market economy and by revealing how young German consumers appropriated American popular culture, thereby inciting both moral and racial anxieties in the German public.[7] In spite of the diversity and depth of its insights, however, the scholarship on postwar consumer culture usually assumes that commodities paved the way into West Germany's future and led the country away from its Nazi past.[8]

In 2001, however, Alon Confino and Rudy Koshar formulated the opposite idea of this assumption: given the strong public taboo on National Socialism in the Federal Republic, it would be particularly productive to look for the Nazi past's traces where they are not "directly discernible," especially around material objects and mass consumption.[9] Nevertheless, scarcely any scholars have seriously explored the question of if and how postwar consumer objects, which became so important for the country's new self-understanding, echoed or evoked the Nazi past. This refusal to approach postwar consumption as a terrain that not only projects a future but also reflects and produces forms of social memory has to do, I suggest, with the *ongoing* symbolic power of the period's consumer objects to denote a new postwar era of West Germany and the West at large.[10]

The field of material culture studies has produced a sharpened understanding of the unique ways in which the world of material objects acquires political meaning and mediates between the past and the present. Many scholars have analyzed the ways in which movable and especially immovable material relics were bound together with various German pasts and how contemporaries made sense of or reacted to them.[11] Yet where material objects that exist for a longer stretch of time are linked to the past in a concrete and tangible way, newly produced commodities do not have such a physical connection to former times. The idea that commodities, especially industrially manufactured ones, are simply "new" and as such oriented toward a desired future therefore holds a strong plausibility. In a way, this notion is already at the heart of what Karl Marx called the fetish character of the commodity. This fetish character not only makes the material conditions of production magically disappear from consciousness but also thereby creates its own phantasmagoria about the relations between people in space and time.[12] Since at least the late nineteenth century, commodity culture's phantasmagorias have connected mass-produced objects with fantasies of exotic settings and of earlier historical epochs. For obvious reasons, *explicit* nostalgia of the Nazi past was unacceptable in postwar West Germany and therefore absent in the commercial imaginary. However, in the words of Walter Benjamin, when it comes to mass consumption the new is not only the ever same but also "the source of that illusion which is inseparable from the dream-images of the collective."[13] This book tries to disentangle the historicity of the postwar era's collective dream images from mass consumption's illusion of "the new."

If one starts leafing through the illustrated magazines of the 1950s hoping to understand the contemporary meanings attached to consumption and commodities, one encounters an atmosphere intensely focused on the present: messages to consumers circulated around the "modern" and the "new." After a first unexpected and disturbing discovery in the historical material, I hesitatingly began to ask how precisely this dreamscape of commodities that promised a better future on magazine pages and in feature films related to the Nazi past. Seriously considering this question made it necessary to selectively expand my view from the postwar into the National Socialist period itself. After all, to delineate and understand historical change we must take into account the whole period in which we assume this change occurred. In areas like constitutional history, the innovations of the Federal Republic are obvious. In the wide field of collective ideas and imaginations, change is much harder to identify clearly.

Minds and hearts, beliefs and perceptions, moral convictions, intuitions, and worldviews rarely transform overnight. Often they do not even register as "old" or as anything that demands reflection. A sociological study conducted in the early 1950s by the Frankfurt Institute for Social Research and recently published for the first time impressively confirms this point. Based on organized group discussions among ordinary Germans, the study shows a "political culture" that becomes intelligible "only in its continuity to National Socialism," a continuity that happened in the latent sphere "of affects and the unconscious."[14] While attempting to shuffle off the burden of guilt imposed on them by the Allies and the new political order, the participants established mutual understanding among themselves by resorting to a language that was still strongly shaped by National Socialism.

The vague term "structure of feeling" is well suited to delineate those parts of a culture that are often unconscious yet also particularly characteristic and omnipresent. A structure of feeling points to "the deep community that makes the communication possible," but it "can fail to be fully understood even by living people in close contact with it."[15] The term "structure of feeling" marks Raymond Williams's attempt to conceive of culture as something that can never be fully grasped, something that encompasses the full richness and complexity of social life, including gestures, styles and ideas, and assumptions or intuitions that cannot or need not be spoken. Precisely these aspects often end up being perceived as strange by a younger generation with different historical experiences. Williams reminds us that the work of understanding cultures requires an intense effort to imagine realities beyond the documents' obvious surface meanings. It demands that we try to see and think together contradictory elements such as the parallel existence of incompatible structures of feeling.

If this is true for any historical period, the first two postwar decades in Germany confront us with a particularly challenging blend of disparate perceptions and perspectives. While historians have to categorize and separate aspects of social life from each other, in the reality of lived experience they are, as Williams emphasizes, "an inseparable part of a complex whole."[16] One story from my own family history illustrates the capacity of the postwar period to astonish when elements that are usually separated in historical consciousness appear together. A few years ago, my father suddenly mentioned to me how Germans frequently reacted during the 1950s and 1960s when he told them the year of his birth, which was 1933. After he said "1933" they would reply: "Ah, the good year!" When that happened, my father sometimes pretended not to understand them and asked: "Why the good year?" Then his interlocutors clarified that it was "the good year" because of Hitler's rise to power. Because my father has the German name Scholz and spoke German well, Germans could not know that he was the child of two Yugoslavian parents who had joined the partisan movement in 1941 and that he had been on the run from the German Wehrmacht with his whole family during the war.

This memory sheds light on the unexpected ways in which an intuitive and affective perception—"the good year"—could collide with a radically different one, in this case, the perception of a young Yugoslavian engineer hopefully beginning a professional career in West Germany made possible by the economic miracle and the fact that the Federal Republic was *not* Nazi Germany. How often, one wonders, might similar situations have occurred between people who had radically different experiences of and views on the war and the Nazi period? According to the official raison d'être of the Federal Republic, 1933 was not supposed to be remembered as a "good year" by its citizens. Based on the available historical knowledge about the period, however, it should be far from surprising that it still was so by enough West Germans to incite a casual remark uttered with the expectation of being understood by a "deep community." My own surprise is probably related to the imprint that the official character of the Federal Republic as a polity founded *against* the Third Reich has had on the collective self-perception and memory that evolved from it. A similar kind of tension seems to have already played a role when the Institute for Social Research found it difficult to publish monographs that had resulted from the said group discussions because their content "caused too great a shock."[17]

George Steiner, who had escaped the Nazis by emigrating with his family, once described the articulations of the "myth" that emerged after the 1948 currency reform in West Germany as the "acrobatics of oblivion." At the "center of the miracle of Germany's material resurrection" he observed "a profound deadness of spirit" and an "inescapable sense of triviality and dissimulation" created by a language still "injected with falsehood."[18] It was a period of historical denial and of a "busyness" that, as Hannah Arendt observed, had become Germans' "chief defense against reality."[19] It was also the period from which emerged a new national identity built on the pride about the country's economic achievements and renewed international recognition. At this very moment Germans began to call the unexpected postwar ascent of their country the "German miracle" or the "economic miracle." This language of the miraculous was, as this book argues, more than a suitable metaphor for unexpectedly good economic developments. Rather, it is a historically meaningful element of the cultural repertoire that created West Germany's postwar myth by placing at its center the magical capacity of commodities to create a fantasy of renewal. The first "falsehood" of the miracle language consists of concealing the term's own historicity. It connotes a wondrous national regeneration through economic success in a distinctly post-Fascist mode while reusing the vocabulary of the German miracle or the economic miracle that had already been introduced and popularized by the National Socialists to convey a wondrous national regeneration through economic success.[20]

The West German idea of experiencing an economic miracle became popular shortly after the intense moral and spiritual crisis that pervaded postwar German society had reached a peak. This crisis, as Monica Black's work has recently shown, expressed itself around 1948–49 in strong apocalyptic fears, which also filled the popular press, the widespread belief in a wonder healer, and a wave of accusations about so-called evil spirits. Black argues convincingly that these phenomena were fueled by a deep-seated wish to be redeemed from a vague and not necessarily articulated perception of being haunted by something from the past that ultimately resisted being fully understood.[21] While this moral crisis certainly occurred in reaction to the official collapse of the Third Reich's value system, it was also still shaped by the same value system's ongoing influence. When postwar Germans spoke about the "evil period," they often meant the horrors of the occupation and *not* those of the Nazi regime. To the extent that Germans felt—and repressed—guilt or shame about the war, these feelings might have been not only about the mass crimes committed by Germans but also about losing the war in the first place; the latter was, after all, the ultimate shameful event in a Nazi worldview.[22] How did the need for redemption that resulted from the downfall of Nazi Germany relate to a past in which Germans had sought redemption by becoming Aryan rulers of a world purified from all "evil"?[23] Although such a question must remain unanswerable, it invites us to take the gray and murky area of human experience seriously, an area that does not neatly map onto well-defined political and social orders and their presumably clear place in historical time.

In their nonlinguistic capacity to absorb and channel different symbolic contexts and affects, material objects in particular inhabit this gray and murky realm, whether they are old objects that survived the end of Nazism or newly produced commodities that invaded the public realm long before most Germans could actually purchase them. A close observation of how contemporary discourses developed around these different materialities reveals a convoluted reality of moral, political, emotional, and historical contexts of belonging. This reality was shaped decisively by West Germany's real and perceived dependence on how the country was seen and judged by the Western Allies, which formally held sovereign power over West Germany until 1955. Feelings of resentment, or *ressentiment*, toward the occupation powers as well as toward the victims of the Nazi rule formed, in Anna Parkinson's words, "less obvious yet paradigmatic postwar affective communities."[24] The currency reform in 1948 and the founding of the Federal Republic in 1949 marked the birth of West Germany as a new political and economic entity and the moment when such resentment began to be replaced by a new self-confidence. The commodities that West Germany produced and started to export again immediately were viewed as enabling and embodying this successful transformation.

"Nobody can tell . . . There it is: The new Mercedes!" With these words an illustrated magazine celebrated the new Mercedes 170 S in May 1949 (fig. I.1).[25]

I.1 Item on the new Mercedes 170 S. *Neue Illustrierte*, May 1949. Reproduced from Staatsbibliothek Berlin.

The image and the short accompanying text exemplify what Roland Barthes has described as essential in the workings of myth. Myth, according to Barthes, "transforms history into nature." It presents reality in a way that lets its historical dimension evaporate. In myth "things lose the memory that they once were made." Myth also "depoliticizes" speech. It talks about things in a way that makes them inaccessible to political or intellectual debate because they appear natural, obvious, and "innocent." Their meaning seems to come self-evidently out of themselves, so there really is nothing that one could question or think about. Myth thereby gives things the "blissful clarity" of a "statement of fact." *There it is: The new Mercedes!* While Barthes's *Mythologies* were a "synchronic sketch" about his own time and place (France in the 1950s), he conceded the alternative of a "diachronic study" of myth that would track down a myth's historical genealogy or would observe how old myths evolved into the present.[26] This book probes the possibilities of a genealogical approach that goes back in time, from various starting points in the postwar period, to the Nazi era, and sometimes beyond. Doing so regularly also implies the opposite movement: following the evolution of some elements of Nazi culture into the postwar period.

That the introduction of a new Mercedes on the West German market in May 1949 supposedly had nothing to do with Germany's *political* present or past is the most obvious meaning of the item published only days before the founding of the Federal Republic. En passant, the text refers to the fact that the new model was "outwardly unchanged," meaning with respect to its predecessor model, which had, in fact, been used by the German Wehrmacht. This is a "new Mercedes," but what is new about it (its technical innovations) is hidden ("nobody can tell") underneath an already well-known shape. The continuity is half-exposed, half-concealed. It does not immediately register for most twenty-first-century readers, but it is formulated clearly enough to be understood by the period's deep community.

That some Mercedes cars indeed carried a heavy political significance due to their Nazi past had been obvious only eight months earlier. In August 1948 the same magazine published another photo with a Mercedes convertible and someone smiling and waving at the camera (fig. I.2). That someone was an American businessman, and the car was a bullet-proof Mercedes from Hitler's motor pool. The spectacle of this car being exhibited in New York as a kind of war booty aroused the bitterness of the author, who wrote with biting irony that the "clueless owner on the 'führer's seat'" did not quite know what to do with the vehicle and that he had been warned that "Hitler's ghost would doubtlessly haunt the car." In August 1948 Hitler's Mercedes in New York embodied Allied denazification in a material and symbolic form. Accordingly, its spectacle was surrounded by feelings of resentment poured into irony and subliminal aggression: a neurologist supposedly wanted to use "Freudian methods" to examine the Mercedes (or its new owner—the formulation is ambiguous), and a production company planned to film the car while it was being fired at "under the condition that the unhappy owner sits in the car himself."[27]

The specter of a vehicle that embodies, through its direct connection with Hitler, Nazi Germany's recent grandiosity and power as well as, through the car's changed ownership and situation, Germany's subsequent downfall incited an irritated reaction. The American ownership of Hitler's Mercedes and its journey as a traveling exhibit through "Western European countries" confronted

HITLERS GEISTERAUTO

Der ratlose Besitzer auf dem „Führersitz". Ein amerikanischer Geschäftsmann, Christopher G. Janus, hat den 230 PS starken Mercedes-Benz-Wagen Hitlers erworben, der eine Panzerung von 60 mm Dicke, kugelsichere Scheiben und Pistolen- und Maschinengewehrfächer hat. Mr. Janus weiß im Grunde nicht, was er mit dem Wagen anfangen soll. Er bekam die merkwürdigsten Angebote. Man warnte ihn, der Geist Hitlers würde zweifellos im Wagen spuken. Ein Nervenarzt will ihn nach Freudschen Methoden untersuchen. Eine Filmgesellschaft will den Wagen beschießen lassen und darüber einen Film drehen — unter der Voraussetzung, daß der unglückliche Besitzer selbst im Wagen sitzt!

I.2 Item on Hitler's Mercedes in New York. *Neue Illustrierte*, August 1948. Reproduced from Staatsbibliothek Berlin.

West German readers in a materially mediated way with the Western world's perception of their country's recent past. A moral asymmetry between victorious and defeated country was inscribed in the object's fate and countered by the text's abrasive efforts to expose the businessman himself as ridiculous and worthless.

If the item about a Mercedes carrying "Hitler's ghost" was thus full of the ghosts of a past that was not yet history, the introduction of the Mercedes 170 S less than a year later reflected the principle of a mass consumption that presents the ever same as ever new. These two different ways of relating to the world of objects in the context of West Germany's political transition from war to postwar demarcate the cultural space that this book explores. In between the two, the Western Allies' relationship to West Germany changed from an emphasis on denazification to one on integration into a world of commodity and trade relations. This world and its political imaginary were shaped in important ways by European imperialism. The larger postwar reality of a self-identified "Western" world whose imperial and colonial ambitions were for the most part not yet abandoned, let alone fundamentally questioned, emerges in this book as a crucial context for West German society's reinvention of itself as a member of this "West." Without questioning the unique character of the Third Reich's catastrophic imperial and genocidal project on the European continent, it is important to note that the international condemnation of Nazism did not simultaneously engender a similarly radical reckoning with other regimes of violence that were legitimized on the basis of racist paradigms, even though international discussions about such issues certainly entered into a new phase at this time.[28] Yet the ideas that had underpinned and legitimated the European colonial projects continued to permeate Western culture at large when West Germany was welcomed back as a member of the Western community. Together with the emerging Cold War, this postwar context of what Stuart Hall has called a "colonizing culture" shaped what the Allies regarded as a sign of West Germany's renewal, which, in turn, provided a decisive framework for West Germany's "redeeming objects" to do their mythical work.[29]

Working through a vast amount of both popular and highbrow publications as well as films, the following pages bring to light how the period's iconic redeeming objects became prime carriers of the miracle myth. This myth produced and mediated a consciousness in which the collective experience of a historical break subsided into the vague sense of a modernity that was both timeless and timely and both German and Western. Even though the miracle myth did not preclude cultural change, it lastingly loaded its redeeming objects with an ambivalent, opaque, and highly problematic political legacy.

Chapter 1, "Stranded Objects," steps into the topic by exploring the role material objects played in the period of political limbo between 1945 and 1949. The chapter resorts to the anthropological concept of a "make-believe space" (Yael Navaro-Yashin's term) to grasp the political meanings of material culture during Germany's postwar moment by analyzing personal diary entries and private photo albums next to published material. "Stranded objects" stand for the material legacy from the Nazi past—from Nazi symbols to the problem of dispossessed Jewish property—and this legacy's connection to the psychological aspects of political transition. Stranded objects reminded Germans of how the Third Reich's racially informed phantasmagorias of time and space had violently shaped the relationship between people, places, and objects in an expanding German Empire. While often defying the capacities of language, these objects' uncomfortable presence pervaded early postwar texts and films before fading from view in subsequent years.

The objects that are the focus of chapter 2, "Miraculous Objects," chapter 3, "Timeless Objects," and chapter 4, "Expanding Objects," did not carry that same burden because they were industrially produced commodities that were not regarded as being implicated in the Nazi past. These redeeming objects entered the public realm as constitutive elements of an emerging myth about West Germany's new beginning. As such, however, they did *not* leave the past behind. Instead, they helped cast out the specter of national shame, which in 1948 loomed in the spectacle of Hitler's Mercedes being showcased by an American businessman. The myth of redeeming objects, while being invested above all in creating a future, produced a West German make-believe space that allowed political imaginaries and cultural patterns from the Nazi past to find their way across the rupture of 1945. The paradoxical unity of these two movements—beginning the new, continuing the old—and the tensions and contradictions this unity generated pervades these three core chapters of the book. The Volkswagen (chapter 2), the interior of modern homes (chapters 3 and 4), and German commodities as tokens of West Germany's export successes (chapters 4 and 2) were imagined as redeeming objects and thereby enabled old ways of interpreting the world to hide inside the emphatically new. Redeeming objects became the iconic nodal points of a culture in which codes from the Nazi past constantly impregnated the underbelly of a discourse that set itself apart from the same past on the surface.

What the book deals with therefore cannot be sufficiently grasped with the binary concepts of continuity and break. Rather, the cultural significance of redeeming objects is about *suspending* historical consciousness. These objects became the center of a mythical realm in which history itself was an absence. That absence was filled with a political imaginary of the new West German polity in relation to space *and* time through miraculous, timeless, and globally expanding objects. This imaginary had a dreamlike or phantasmagoric character befitting the consumerist paradigm while at the same time manifesting an elective affinity to the previous era's Fascist dreamworld, which itself had been built on many already existing cultural patterns from German nationalism and imperialism.[30]

This myth of postwar modernity has enabled and at the same time obfuscated continuing structures of feeling. It has created an atmosphere of latency ripe with public secrets, which are hidden in plain sight, and their accompanying web of cultural allusions evoking the intuitive and often unconscious knowledge of an affective community of postwar Germans who had lived through the Nazi years as adults. This latent character, together with various changes in the discourse that began to occur at the end of the 1950s, made it next to impossible for younger generations to properly understand how precisely the central icons of West Germany's renewal had continued to be implicated in the very culture they purportedly helped to leave behind.

The book dissects the multilayered character of the miracle myth of redeeming objects, it examines how the myth developed during the first fifteen years after the war, and it maps the myth's intricate relationship to the paradoxes of the postwar period. In doing so, finally, the book attempts to comprehend to a certain extent its long-term cultural resonance. I could only embark on this endeavor by considering the historical, cultural, and social position from which I have necessarily approached the topic.[31] Reflecting on how this generated emotional responses in myself eventually turned into a form of methodology where I treated my own uneasy reactions to historical material as relevant information. Out of this process evolved the decision to give special attention to textual or visual modes of expression that did not fit into the prevalent interpretive paradigms, to chase the "ghosts," as it were, and find out more about their place in the postwar discourse and how this place had come about. By becoming attentive to my own affective reactions, I learned to trace how certain objects had historically acquired specific cultural and affective qualities and to ask difficult questions about the relation of these qualities to West Germany's past and to the country's postwar present in a Western world still shaped very much by the colonial paradigm.

The mythical character of the ideas, images, and worldviews that I explore in the following pages will become visible as a truth generator in the Foucauldian sense, which, as a consequence, has created blind spots, especially for the generations of Germans who were still children or not yet born at the end of the war. These blind spots produced a legacy of "blind eyes" that has continued into the present and that still often shapes our understanding of the past and determines what we are able to see in the archives and what we overlook. As Catherine Hall has reminded us, being able to reflect on one's own "blind eyes" is only possible because the present has already changed, and new experiences, debates, voices, and ways of seeing have already modified the embodied position from which one's "blind eyes" can be noticed.[32] The process that has generated an awkward, often anxious, and never fully finished oscillation between "blind" and "seeing" eyes was intimately interwoven with the kind of reading, thinking, discussing, and writing that produced the following pages. This process is a necessary element of the challenge to study a myth that is not yet (completely) history.[33] Through the whole book runs an awareness that the culture of the past, which I try to study critically by pushing the boundaries of its dominant understanding, has also shaped my own thinking in a way that cannot simply be put aside. To an extent, the structure of each chapter reflects my own intellectual journey. My hope is that readers are willing to stumble through the thicket of the archives with me and will relate to my moments of hesitation and astonishment as well as to how the view of the past that I propose here has come into being.

1

Stranded Objects

The Political beneath the Rubble

The Make-Believe Space

There is a wall cupboard in my study. It stores a mishmash of things: archival material from my PhD, exercise books from school, puppets from my childhood, an old computer, and a sleeping bag. Then there is Hitler's *Mein Kampf*. It is a copy from 1942 that my husband's father, who was a soldier in the war, had received from one of his superiors. A small swastika is printed in gold on the cover. The symbol is so worn out that it has become nearly indiscernible. When I discovered the book in a bookshelf together with other political literature that had ended up in our small guest room, I was not comfortable with it. I opened the book with a strange feeling and decided to store it where nobody else would be able to see it: in my cupboard. This copy of *Mein Kampf* belongs in an awkward category of things that are there yet not *supposed* to be there. The book's existence connects our Amsterdam home to my husband's childhood home in lower Bavaria as well as to his father's time in the war.

In 1945 the book, because of its content and because of the swastika on its cover, counted among the objects removed from the German public sphere by the Allied military government, together with other Nazi literature, portraits and busts of Hitler, and swastika flags. The private sphere, though, remained untouched by these efforts. My husband's father, whom I never met, passed away a long time ago, and like so many other German men, he never talked much about the war or Hitler to his family. His relationship to National Socialism probably resembled that of many Wehrmacht soldiers: he was neither an opponent nor a fervent Nazi. He probably would have preferred not to go to war and not to lose his brother in the war. He probably would also have preferred Germany to win the war once it had started.[1] For whatever reason, he kept *Mein*

Kampf. After his death it became a random heirloom, a historical object, potential material for critical scholarship, and now it silently and awkwardly lies in the darkness of my cupboard. In my own family there are no family heirlooms that could connect me and my brother back to a longer family history and incite possibly uneasy questions about our ancestors' experience of the Third Reich. My mother and her family fled from Danzig (today Gdansk, Poland) at the end of the war, bringing with them only a handful of photos.

Objects can connect us with the past in a way we don't even understand. Their physical quality undermines the clear distinction between past and present. Even the absence of objects can have such effects. While doing research for this book, I spent some time looking through German family photo albums from the middle of the century, especially from the first ten years after 1945.[2] In albums that covered the Nazi period, there was sometimes a void where a photo had been ripped out. I often wondered what that absent photo had depicted. Had the photo disappeared because it had revealed a family member's involvement in the Nazi movement? One of these photo albums includes portraits of a well-situated middle-class family taken every Christmas. The couple and their son always stand in the same way in front of the Christmas tree, the presents neatly arranged on a table. In one year, a relief portrait of Hitler stands on the table next to the Christmas tree, towering above all the other presents (fig. 1.1).

When I saw this photo, my spontaneous reaction was a minor reality shock. I was confronted with the kind of evidence that had been largely absent from the German public since the end of the war as Germans tried to prove that they had never been Nazis. In front of me was evidence of how one family had embraced the Nazi movement and given one of its prime material manifestations—a portrait of Hitler—a central position in their private lives. In front of me was also evidence that this family saw no reason to tear this photo out of the album, to tear this part of their past out of their family memory. Something in me indignantly thought that this photo shouldn't be there. Then I was surprised that I was so surprised.

Leafing through more photo albums, I found more Nazi symbols and references to the Nazi regime: a photo from a local Nazi Party meeting with swastika flags in the background, a photo from an official Nazi commemoration event, a photo from a visit to the German pavilion at the world's fair in Paris, photos from streets decorated with Nazi flags, a private photo series "Unsere schönen Reichsautobahnen" (our beautiful imperial highways) followed by photos from a Nuremberg party rally, many photos from urban places flooded with swastika flags in an album entitled "vacation 1938," photos from Nazi monuments, a snapshot of a man on a boat who is smiling into the sun and whose Nazi Party pin

1.1 Portrait of Hitler on a table next to a Christmas tree, private photo album, undated. Photographer unknown. Reproduced from Bernd Stiegler private collection.

is visible.[3] The Christmas photo was merely special in that it was the only evidence of a Nazi symbol's presence in a private home. Yet the very existence of those other photos also testifies to the continued presence of Nazi symbols, even if only in a photograph, in those private homes where the albums had been kept. Oddly, this discovery produced a sense of disorientation in me.

My surprised reaction illustrates an unintelligible chasm that the end of the war and the Third Reich in 1945 has produced. Such an abrupt change of political order creates a sense of disorientation precisely because there is no such thing as an abrupt change of political order. After all, such an order does not exist only in the form of institutions, rules, and laws. A political order is also a social form that has to be imagined, believed, and enacted by its members. The political philosopher Claude Lefort has called this the social form's "mise-en-sense," a combination of its staging and its meaning.[4] In a similar vein, the anthropologist Yael Navaro-Yashin defines a social form as a "make-believe space" that comes into being through the interaction of discourses, imagination, fantasies, and "the tangible."[5]

When a social form ceases to exist as a set of institutionalized rules and is replaced by a different set, this does not merely require a new work of "make-believe"; the social form of the past will linger on by way of its ongoing material and linguistic presence. The materiality of objects and the built environment play a special role in exerting such a presence due to their entanglement with the affects residing in the bodies of the humans who daily interact with this material world. In our experience, we do not control material objects' affective meanings. Instead, the objects store and radiate those affects back to us. Knowing an object's past can induce the impression that it resists voluntary acts of reinterpretation. The object, then, has acquired a life of its own whose change necessitates physical interventions.[6] This is why in times of revolution people feel the necessity to destroy the symbols and monuments of the old regime in order to break their power. This is also why we need the material reality around us to understand our role in the world and to relate to the past, the present, and the future in a meaningful yet often unconscious way. Our unspoken feelings indicate how the material and the imaginative, that is, objects, images, and words, converge in order to generate what we call culture. The political order is a vital ingredient of that culture because it provides its framework, its omnipresent and at the same time mostly subliminal basis.

I was surprised about my findings in the photo albums just as I was about the copy of *Mein Kampf* in my hands because I had, unconsciously, imagined the "normal" postwar German household to be free of such material remnants from the Nazi past. This tells us something about the make-believe space of the

Federal Republic of Germany that I was born into and its accompanying structures of feeling. I had learned early on what this space looked like and incorporated this knowledge into my conception of the self-evident reality in which I lived. This West German make-believe space, however, was established after the war by Germans who had for the most part lived through the National Socialist rule in German territory and had thus been enclosed for twelve years by the radically different make-believe space of Nazi Germany. In his postwar reflection on the language of the Third Reich, Victor Klemperer, a Jewish-born scholar who had escaped deportation by going into hiding, gives a vivid account of how the reality of a homogenized Nazi cultural space had colonized the thoughts not only of those Germans who belonged to the Nazi racial community but even of Jews and other excluded groups.[7] For the philologist Klemperer, who focused on linguistic style, it was clear that the "language" he tried to describe encompassed images, material objects, and the built environment as well as bodily gestures and habits.

As a consequence of Germany's total defeat, both the Federal Republic and the German Democratic Republic were created in outspoken opposition to the Third Reich. This meant that the Nazi make-believe space was supposed to be a thing of the past. This thing of the past, however, continued to be present in different forms. For the generation of Germans who were born after the war or who were too young to remember the Nazi rule, this could be confusing. In his 2013 book *After 1945*, the literary scholar Hans Ulrich Gumbrecht, born in 1948 in Bavaria, reflects on how his generation experienced a world that was infused with the latent and opaque presence of their parents' past. This "presence of the past," he states, "was and is at the same time, troubling and inaccessible." Writing about his teachers Gumbrecht specifies: "More than in direct descriptions, then, the 'real' world from 'before the war' was made present—in latent form—through various kinds of allusions, most of which escaped unnoticed."[8]

In a postscript to the German version of the book, the material and spatial character of this experience is captured in a typewritten facsimile of a paper that Gumbrecht had written as a student in the winter term of 1972–73 for a seminar on "collective memory." In this paper he explored how "probable fragments" from the Third Reich appeared in his childhood consciousness. He was confused about the street names of his home town once he started to read the street signs in the early 1950s. What he had known as Horst-Wessel-Strasse was in reality the Welzstrasse. What he thought to be the Adolf-Hitler-Strasse was in fact the Theaterstrasse. When he visited Munich he learned that "Hitler gave speeches in front of the Feldherrnhalle," and when his family drove to Nuremberg, he was told that this was "the Autobahn that 'he' had built." At home, he spotted a swastika in a photo album of the "cigarette service" about the 1936 Olympic games. Later he discovered a similar album on Adolf Hitler at his grandfather's place. He started to suspect that his grandfather had removed images from their family photo albums "because of the Americans."[9]

As a child, Gumbrecht grew up in a world that was pervaded by the persisting framework of the Third Reich, although it had officially ended before his birth. This frame was inscribed in the streets through the Nazi names used by his parents. The landscape and the cityscapes were blotched with sights that were meaningful because of their origin in that Nazi past. Seemingly innocent albums that the young boy explored turned out to be incarnations of the same social form "Third Reich." Gumbrecht the university student looked back in bewilderment at the once-inscrutable codes of his childhood. In *After 1945* he presents his generation's intellectual journey as evolving around precisely this bewilderment about the chasm between two worlds whose mysterious and ungraspable coexistence had deeply marked their youth. While the Federal Republic was supposed to replace the Third Reich and make it disappear, the Nazi make-believe space instead continued to overlap with the postwar make-believe space. This coexistence of two make-believe spaces left behind inscrutable traces of itself, "allusions and insinuations" emerging around material objects whose meanings oscillated between the Nazi past and the postwar present.

The material "order of things," the way people and objects interacted, was transformed in manifold ways during the National Socialist regime, the war, and its aftermath. It was aesthetically politicized through redesigning public and private spaces and spreading their meaning in mass media; it was loaded with affects through a myriad of meticulously planned audiovisual public stagings; it was violently reorganized through the dispossession and redistribution of property as well as through the exclusion, deportation, and murder of Jews and other ostracized people; it was disturbed through wartime deprivations and the black market economy; it was cut off through displacement; and it was destroyed by the bombings.[10] The aim of this chapter is to understand the transitional rubble moment by concentrating on the relationship between people, things, and the political. Although we know a great deal about the Nazis' enormous efforts to reshape the material order of things in Germany, it remains a challenge to comprehend the effects of this endeavor on Germans' structures of feeling. In Nazi Germany the experience of political power and ideology was closely intertwined with the everyday experience of material culture. What happened to this nexus after Germany's defeat? What can accounts of the everyday after the war tell us about the ways in which the political was present through objects stranded beneath and within the rubble?

"When the humans remain silent, we must listen to the rubble."[11] Marie Luise Kaschnitz, the author of this sentence, lived in Frankfurt am Main from 1941 onward. Between December 1944 and June 1945 she wrote a series of essays that were published in the magazine *Die Wandlung* (The change). When Kaschnitz started to write these texts Frankfurt's Jewish population had been diminished from approximately thirty thousand in 1933 to practically none in 1945.[12] Like all big cities in Germany, Frankfurt had witnessed major Allied bombings; the biggest ones, in March 1944, destroyed large swaths of the city center. In 1946 Kaschnitz's essays were published as a book with the title *Von Menschen und Dingen* (On people and things).[13] Kaschnitz attempted to grasp the immensity of the experiences—the loss of life and well-being, the moral and material destruction, the dissolution of identity—by focusing on the relationship between human beings and their material world: houses and the things inside them, as well as houses turned into things (i.e., bricks) in the rubble landscape of 1945. Kaschnitz was horrified by the stoicism with which Germans talked about their loss of loved ones, home, and health: "The enormity is hushed up, so thoroughly that . . . whoever lets oneself be shaken by it, resembles a lunatic." Her suggestion to listen to the city rubble's "nightly chant" reacts to this inability to adequately acknowledge a disorienting and painful reality. This included the loss of objects one had lived with and that had made possible the personal sense of self.[14] Insisting on the challenge this loss created for any authentic new beginning, Kaschnitz admitted that the end of the "old" material culture may have been for the better. The human relationship to the world of things was so strongly influenced by the past "experience of power" that she could not imagine a future of rebuilt "theatres, department stores, villas, fast trains, smooth highways, schools," since anything begun again "in the old way" would also be doomed in just the same way.[15]

In their famous 1967 book *Die Unfähigkeit zu trauern* (The Inability to Mourn), the German psychoanalysts Alexander and Margarete Mitscherlich formulated their impression that the first loss most Germans were unable to deal with was the loss of their former, grandiloquent German identity, linked to the Third Reich and to their narcissistic love of the führer.[16] The Mitscherlichs asserted that many Germans were in a certain way still living in the past, whose loss they were unable to process and accept appropriately. Eric Santner's 1990 study *Stranded Objects*, on memory and film in 1980s Germany, takes the Mitscherlichs' analysis as a starting point. In Santner's view, postwar Germans' pain about their personal losses, as well as feelings of guilt and shame, were closely intertwined with, as well as numbed, masked, or silenced behind, the difficulty of accepting the death of their former identity as Germans.[17] The concept of "stranded objects" stems from Donald Winnicott's "transitional objects," which help infants learn to accept the reality of living in a world they cannot control. Transitional objects are experienced neither as internal nor as external but help the infant to understand the difference between the two and to give up the illusion of omnipotence. When the infant experiences a traumatic separation from the caregiver, the transitional object can change its function and transform into a means of denying the loss or separation.[18] Santner sees a similar dynamic at play in 1980s West German culture, where stranded objects, with their poisoned cultural repertoire, still transmitted the legacy of the Nazi past in a ghost-like fashion to the following generations.[19]

What concerns us here, in psychoanalytic language, is the original moment of separation. Adult Germans experiencing National Socialism were not infants, but they lived in a culture that constantly promised them collective omnipotence while threatening their livelihood if they fell outside the Nazi definition of racial community or chose to reject this definition openly. For Santner, stranded objects were not necessarily material. Focusing on material objects, however, allows for specific insights into how people perceived their world and tried to make sense of it in the wake of the Third Reich's breakdown. The Nazi regime had provided Germans with an abundance of objects and urban spaces that manifested their newly defined identity as "Germans."[20] As the regime collapsed, this materiality abruptly lost its original context and could appear as an uncanny material relic stranded beneath the rubble and in the limbo before a new political order took shape.

The chaos of the material world resulting from the war was about more than material hardship, including traumatic loss of one's belongings and habitual urban environment. In the midst of the rubble, where did the political begin, and where did it end? Being confronted with one's destroyed home was usually experienced as something private and individual.[21] For Dorothea Klein, by contrast, the bombing of her hiding place was "like an enormous liberation" that catapulted her out of a separate "Jewish fate," as she wrote in 1946.[22] She felt relief not only because the chaos provided some protection from being deported. As a Jew, she had already lost all her belongings. Now the bombings moved her closer together with her non-Jewish friends who were also thrown into homelessness and poverty. In her eyes, the shared human experience of loss interfered with the grim reality of the Third Reich's exclusionary politics.

Many things carry their political meanings silently and unnoticed until they come to the surface in times of political change. But even then these meanings are not necessarily registered in language. As the Third Reich broke down, the temporal and spatial coherence of everyday life's material rituals was shattered as well. When the "Aryan race" ceased to exist as a reality that was put into practice by the state, the relationship between people and the spaces they inhabited changed, too. With the occupation, a new political authority established itself and decided who was allowed to do what, when, and where. What the end of the war meant, individually and collectively, could only be experienced in one moment and in one place at a time, while the political situation continued to be fluid and changing. Some dimensions of postwar Germans' experiences left their traces only in the seemingly unimportant and weird details of how people described their way through the rubble. If we put material objects at the center of attention, the pervasive entanglements between the outspoken and the latent come into full view. In many texts material objects radiate a troubling indeterminacy between the intimate and the political, guilt and innocence, past and present, around which language encountered its own limits.

The Disorder of Things

The general disorder of the war's immediate aftermath manifested itself in many ways as a disorder of material things.[23] The destruction of homes and infrastructure and the ensuing hardship had started in many places long before the end of the war. For Germans who were considered members of the racial community, or *Volksgemeinschaft*, this hardship had been tempered for a while by the Nazi Empire's system of exploitation.[24] When Saul Padover entered the city of Aachen with the American forces, he was surprised to find German middle-class homes equipped with "labor-saving devices . . . and massive furniture. . . . [T]he closets bulged with excellent clothes."[25] Julius Posener, a German architectural historian who came back to Germany with the British army, was equally surprised that the outward appearance of Germans did not match the destruction around them. They looked "bright, well-groomed and quite well-dressed" thanks to an "economic system kept up by millions of foreign hands and through the robbery of the whole continent until the end."[26] In his postwar diary, Paulheinz Wantzen, a journalist for the local newspaper in Münster, angrily remembered that during the war "every stable girl ran around in a fur coat that was stolen in France, Holland, or Belgium, [and] countless apartments are full of the most unbelievable booty." Wantzen, a fervent Nazi supporter, was appalled to see these same people now kissing up to the occupation forces. Such frankness about the presence of war booty in Germans' private homes was rare.[27] Instead, there are many descriptions of how occupation soldiers, especially Russians, looted German houses after the defeat. The opposite reality of Germans' own acts of looting only occasionally entered accounts of the war.[28]

In January 1941 the author Erich Kästner, whose books had been banned by the Nazis, wrote down the story of a German soldier who reported that Holland looked as if it had suffered an "invasion of locusts" because of the plundering by German soldiers.[29] In February 1943 he noted that someone had described the "shootings of Jews in the East," including an SS guard who "pulls the rings and earrings" from the Jews he is about to murder.[30] When the end of the war approached, Kästner chronicled the stories and rumors spreading throughout the Austrian countryside where he was staying. People warned each other that the Russian and American soldiers took "watches and rings," especially from German soldiers who returned from Italy.[31] Only later, in the reworked version of his diary, published in 1961 under the title *Notabene*, did Kästner put the two phenomena together: "[Some victors] search German soldiers for weapons, they requisition on their own account rings and watches and trade their booty for booze from the farmers. I wouldn't be surprised if among the valuables there were also rings and watches that had originally been owned by an Italian."[32]

The chaotically changing political order manifested itself regularly in a politically reversed relationship between people and things. The mass rape of German women, committed most of the time but not exclusively by Russian occupation soldiers, temporarily turned German women's sexualized bodies into another form of war booty. In Hertha von Gebhardt's perception of the first chaotic week of mass rapes, the event of rape blended into an evolving black market economy. The fifty-year-old Berliner described how a friend was first raped by a Russian soldier and subsequently given food as a reward. Gebhardt commented on this event with survivalist humor: "I would never have dreamt of finding myself marching from Breitenbach to Rüdesheimer Platz with a beef leg on my shoulder that had cost nothing, except for a woman's threefold willingness for cohabitation."[33]

Her statement not only expresses the difficulties of women's everyday life in a destroyed and conquered city but also registers how the shift of political authority over the city changed the relationship between people, places, and objects. "Marching" is used as a colloquial expression for walking in a decided and vehement manner, but the term simultaneously evokes soldiers' physical way of walking and performing their power over space. In Gebhardt's formulation, a stubborn and proud act of independence—marching on the street with an enormous food supply—is combined with its very opposite when she recalls that the beef leg was a "thank you" for a woman who had been raped by an occupation soldier. The expression that she "would never have dreamt" of finding herself in such a situation demonstrates how difficult it was for her to grasp the reality of this violently altered order of things.

In September 1945 the journalist Ursula von Kardoff summarized the new political situation in Berlin by describing the radically changed correlation of ethnically defined bodies, objects, and spaces. "How improbably fast the roles have been reversed," she noted in her diary. "The Russians occupy half-empty train carriages in clean (if not very becoming) uniforms, and on the carriage roofs sit the ragged Germans and duck their heads when a tunnel approaches."[34] The accustomed order of things, this passage implies, would have Russians sitting in ragged clothes on the roofs of the railroad cars, whereas Germans would occupy the comfortable carriages. Accordingly, Kästner had heard from a friend who was in Poland in 1943 that "the tram has compartments for Germans and others for Poles, and that the German compartments are often half-empty, whereas the Polish are overcrowded."[35]

Former Wehrmacht soldiers' experience of conquering other countries would necessarily impact how they perceived the physical spectacle of an occupied and destroyed Germany around them. On the bank of the Rhine in Cologne, Karl Zimmermann stumbled upon a tent camp of British soldiers playing jazz music and warming themselves with a fire in a barrel. He described the scene in May 1946 in the cultural magazine *Die Gegenwart* (The present): "It was like in the wilderness, like anywhere out there, it was like on the earliest morning of our times. No: it was late in the evening, it was the evening after a false feast at the end of a day that you will never forget. It was like it had been in many places in Russia: The battleground unattended, the ruins completely neglected, and those who want to live zealously go along."[36]

Time and space have lost their clarity, and the author moves around in his thoughts to see if he can find any time or place that might correspond with this experience. "The earliest morning of our times" refers to an evolutionary model of civilization in which Germany was thrown back into a primitive past. The other temporal suggestion, "late in the evening," corrects this idea and places the scene back into a late stage of a civilization that somehow has taken a bad turn after a "false feast," presumably Germany's. Finally, Zimmermann compares the spectacle with a different, recently lived through time and space, namely, the Russia of Germany's eastern campaign. At this point, his personal war memories superimpose the image he is confronted with in Cologne. What he saw "was like" what he had seen in Russia. However, since the roles were changed, it was not only "like" it but also its opposite. And it is this opposition that seems to make it so difficult for Zimmermann to get a grip on this reality.

In the popular press, too, a sentiment of disorder regarding the place of Germans in their own dismantled country came to the surface. In October 1946 the *Neue Illustrierte* showed a photo of a boy picking up the butt of a cigarette in order to sell it on the black market. The caption commented: "The youth in Germany's major cities trade in a way that used to be common only in eastern and southern areas."[37] A year later, the magazine published an article about the ongoing deprivation of most Germans' existence: "No, no: The man in the street . . . is not a nihilist. As a German, he does not consider adapting to the standard of living of the inhabitants of cities in the Balkan."[38] A sense of nationalist and racial entitlement pervades these efforts to understand the dire circumstances of postwar everyday life as a reversal of Germany's recent domination and exploitation of geographic regions deemed inferior.

Experiencing the material reality of the postwar moment was thus connected with the need to orient oneself in a new cultural and political geography. This orientation necessarily referred to existing frameworks of perception. A caricature in the satirical magazine *Der Simpl* showed five people living together in one room in a half-destroyed building. Its title, "Bei Ortsgruppenleiters," refers to local Nazi Party leaders. The text asks: "Is this the *Lebensraum* that the führer had promised us?"[39] The continuing relevance of concepts stemming from the Nazi project of geographic expansion thus collides with the postwar reality of a reduced and destroyed Germany. The war photo album of former Wehrmacht soldier Hans Mäder illustrates in another way the difficulty of comprehending the new political reality's inscription in the material reality of postwar life. When Mäder put together his album years after the end of the war, he started with idyllic images of his Thuringian home village, Crawinkel. At the end of the war and of the album, the village returned on the pages, this time in ruins. Beneath these photos, Mäder added the accusatory or desperate-sounding comment: "And that is how I found my homeland [*Heimat*]."[40] The first photographed ruins of his album, however, are those of Rouen and appear among Mäder's otherwise tourist-like images from his service in France. In 1941, when his unit was sent to the East, he included rubble images of Lida and Vitebsk in Belarus. His comment indicates that Mäder probably never expected to see the home that he left in order to take part in Germany's war being destroyed by the same war.[41] It was not merely the rubble that was the scandal for Mäder but rather that *this* rubble physically accentuated the fact that the roles had indeed been reversed improbably fast, as Kardoff had put it.[42]

These inverted roles included occupation forces that redefined Germany's geographic space. As millions of displaced people moved around the country, the occupation zones created a new split between people and their personal belongings.[43] Refugees from the East found themselves separated from their belongings, which ended up in a region that had suddenly ceased to be Germany. In February 1945 Erich Kästner marveled at the "countenance and patience of the people" when he wrote about a woman who had fled from Gnesen. Gnesen (Gniezko) belonged to the Polish territories that were occupied by German troops in September 1939. The woman regretted that she had to leave behind "the new dining room, the vacuum cleaner, the sewing machine, and the boxes with the good clothes." In the published version of 1961 the text has been modified: "One must marvel at the resignation of *those people* who are so much more attached to their belongings than the likes of *us*" (my emphasis). This formulation distanced Kästner from the normality of the expanded German Empire that had shaped the original text.[44] As Dolf Sternberger described how American soldiers cooked their breakfast among the rubble of the Kassel train station in the summer of 1945, he compared the city to a "steppe that grows over a former empire." A banal signpost on a door declaring that "this restaurant is open again" disoriented him. Is this a new sign, he wondered, or a remainder of the earlier reconstruction phases announced by the Nazis after every air raid? If it was new, the signpost would fulfill its role in helping the tired and hungry Germans. If it was a remnant from the past, it would lead "into emptiness."[45] The disorienting materiality of everyday life interfered with Sternberger's sharp consciousness of the political moment. The empire is gone, the state of the rubble testifies to it, yet at the same time, the rubble contains objects whose position in time is questionable, holding present the precarious position of Germany as a whole.

A Material Transition

In one way, the postwar disorder of things was reordered quickly. The Allied occupation decided immediately to remove all Nazi symbols and even Nazi art from German public spaces. While photos of Allied soldiers in command of major Nazi monuments documented the victory symbolically in the media, American GIs took pictures of themselves with seized Nazi flags and other Nazi symbols (fig. 1.2).[46] Occupation troops and German officials began to remove swastikas, Nazi monuments, and other Nazi symbols from the public space even before the Third Reich's surrender. As Kathleen Nawyn points out in her study on demilitarization in Württemberg-Baden, many GIs took Nazi flags and German military medals as souvenirs. Some Germans took away such objects even before the Allied soldiers arrived at their city. Removing military and Nazi symbols was initially part of establishing the occupation forces' political authority; later on it was aimed at reshaping German society away from militarism and Nazism. In July 1945 the US military government prohibited "the use of military or Nazi . . . flags, banners or tokens." The other Allies approached the issue in a similar way. The Soviets, however, also targeted private German homes. The Americans and the British were more cautious in this regard, which was in turn

1.2 US soldiers with Nazi flag, Lauingen, Germany, 1945. Reproduced from the 12th Armored Division Memorial Museum, The Portal to Texas History.

appreciated by many Germans.[47] How did Germans experience this material aspect of their society's transition from war to postwar?

Kästner's diary contains an exceptionally rich account of how the inhabitants of the village of Mayrhofen in the Austrian region of the Zillertal reacted to the change of national authority and political symbols. One and a half months after US soldiers entered the Zillertal, Kästner's self-perception was shaken by their early denazification efforts. American army officers interrogated him on June 18, 1945, about his activities during the Third Reich: "Shortly after their departure they came back again and wanted to inspect the living space, asking if there were Hitler portraits in the house!" In the 1961 version he emphasizes his astonishment even more: "So much naivety could hardly be real! Did they seriously expect to find pictures of Hitler on the walls at the end of June?" Being targeted by denazification efforts clearly contradicted Kästner's own self-understanding as a silenced opponent of the regime. The issue was emotionally charged. As it turns out, however, it was in no way an absurd idea to enquire about Hitler portraits in the house where he stayed.[48]

At the end of the war, Kästner and his partner lived in the home of a farmer's family. In March 1945 he described how the family's mother reacted to the news of her second son's death in the war. She "tore the picture of Hitler from the wall and wanted to throw it in the garden and crush it. She was prevented from doing so." There was no need to introduce the fact that there was a picture of Hitler on the wall. Instead, it is noteworthy that the mother wanted to destroy the portrait. In the 1961 version this constellation is reversed. The text draws attention to the presence of a portrait of Hitler in the host's house as something memorable and thereby puts this presence at a critical distance from Kästner himself: "When we sit in the warm parlor and listen to the radio news, Mrs. Steiner keeps us company. The photograph of the dead soldier is not the only decoration in the room. A carved crucifix and a colored image of Hitler hang opposite each other on the walls."[49]

The differences between the original and the published diary shine a light on the political iconoclasm of the postwar moment as an important yet ambivalent act of self-cleansing. On May 4, 1945, the "Ostmark," Austria's name as a region inside the Third Reich, had become "Austria" again. In the original diary, this regime change appears as the change of various materialized political symbols pervading everyday life: people were ordered to fly new flags in the red-and-white colors of Austria, and the inhabitants responded quickly by using white bed sheets. In the same night "the images of Hitler disappeared. The burden of bondage writhed from the soul, and many wheeled instead a new burden on their breast."[50] While Kästner linked the presence of portraits of Hitler to being oppressed by a violent regime, he also associated the subsequent absence of these images with, presumably, the "burden" of a bad conscience.

In his 1961 book it is the swastika, never mentioned in the original diary, that takes center stage. Kästner describes in detail how he witnessed the women of the neighborhood transforming the Nazi flag into the Austrian flag: "Everywhere the swastika was separated from the Hitler flags. Everywhere white bed sheets were cut. Everywhere the peasant women sat at their sewing machines and neatly sewed the red-and-white panels of fabric together."[51] This transformation left material traces. The following day one could see on the red panels "circles and segments in unfaded red that until yesterday had been protected from the weather by the swastika." Peering into his neighbors' homes, Kästner also noticed "rectangles in saturated color" that "told us how easily wallpaper becomes pale and how big the Hitler portraits had been."

The German soldiers who retreated from Italy via the Alps after the defeat of the German army simply left "cockades, ribbons, and so on" on the path.[52] That most of these decorations would contain the swastika is absent from Kästner's account. For contemporary readers, this fact must have been self-evident, but for a younger generation reading Kästner's *Notabene*, it was not necessarily self-evident anymore. In *Notabene* the discarded military insignia are even idyllically compared to mountain flowers. At this point in the diary the material transition is complete. It will only be disturbed one more time when the American officer searches for portraits of Hitler in Kästner's provisional home.

Whereas Kästner was scandalized by the Americans' idea that they would find any symbols of the defeated Nazi regime weeks after the capitulation, an American report from June 1946 described precisely such a situation in the mayor of Neckartailfingen's home: "On the walls behind the [mayor's] desk there were on the left a picture of the crucifixion and on the right a document stating 'In the name of the Führer and Supreme Commander I bestow upon you the Iron Cross First Class.' On the opposite wall there was a picture of two young men in uniform, the mayor's sons. The mayor did not quite understand interrogator's [*sic*] surprise at seeing the wall decorations. He told with great pride that the son who had received the Iron Cross First Class always had been a *Draufgänger* [go-getter]."[53] Although private homes were not purged of Nazi and military symbols, there was still an expectation among American officials that Germans would willingly discard all references to the Nazi regime. The mayor's reaction shows that he did not count military memorabilia among the objects that might offend the new government, even though Wehrmacht medals like the Iron Cross contained the swastika and thus testified to the entanglement of the German army and the Hitler regime.

In spite of the fact that many Germans removed Nazi symbols on their own initiative or complied willingly with the orders to remove them, the perspectives of the military government and the German population were very different, especially regarding military emblems. Yet even the American military government struggled with the distinction between nazified army medals and non-Nazi medals. Eisenhower decided in May 1945 that "*Hoheitsabzeichen*" [national insignia] and other army insignia "of [a] Nazi nature" were banned; however, "medals and decorations" were allowed if "all Nazi emblems, e.g., [the] *Hakenkreuz* [swastika]," were "obliterated or removed."[54] The swastika therefore proved to be the feature that was used for an otherwise difficult distinction.

Three years later, on June 11, 1948, the *Neue Illustrierte* published a photo of a boy standing in front of the Reich Chancellery in Berlin and holding a military badge in his right hand (fig. 1.3). The boy intended to sell this Iron Cross on the

1.3 Boy holding an Iron Cross in front of the Reich Chancellery in Berlin. *Neue Illustrierte*, June 1948. Reproduced from Staatsbibliothek Berlin.

black market for a pack of American cigarettes. "The boy doesn't know whose medal this is," the text states. "He only knows that the medal features a small swastika, a sign that it was newly endowed by a man who declared millions of men to be heroes because he needed them for his purposes."[55] Hitler, unnamed, is described as "a man" who, standing on the balcony of the Reich Chancellery, "got drunk from the jubilance of the crowd." The photo with the boy in front of Hitler's Reich Chancellery brings all three elements together: the boy, the Iron Cross, the chancellery. It demonstrates that the past is present through these material remnants while evoking ongoing anxieties about German youth.[56] The text defines the Iron Cross as a Nazi symbol and explains why it was not suited for a democracy. While Kästner avoided mentioning the swastikas on military medals, the *Neue Illustrierte* pointed to the swastika on the Iron Cross as evidence of its perverted meaning. This testifies to the ongoing urgency of such a clarification. When the debate about German rearmament began some years later, it was accompanied by a discussion about Wehrmacht medals. Whereas many Germans were critical of the prospect of a new German army, some former Wehrmacht soldiers now demanded that they be permitted to wear their war decorations. In a 1951 survey of two thousand people, half of the men said they had kept their war decorations, and an equal number favored granting permission to wear them. Only a quarter of them thought that the presence of the swastika was a reason to deny the request.[57]

The continuing presence of Nazi symbols in the private sphere was not a topic often written about during the immediate postwar years. An exception is the satirical magazine *Der Simpl*, which regularly pointed to material remnants of the Nazi past in private German homes as a sign of Germans' ongoing support for National Socialism. In October 1947 the magazine printed a caricature entitled "The old lady's secret," which depicts an old woman who takes a portrait of Hitler out of her drawer and looks at it tenderly (fig. 1.4).[58] In September 1947 a poem entitled "Shortsightedness" by Heinz Hartwig questioned the extent to which Germans had changed their political attitudes. It listed acts of destructing politically problematic material whose occurrence the author ironically assumed to have happened but had not witnessed himself because of his bad eyesight:

I didn't see the pyres
with all the books on combat and war
and didn't see that from the bourgeois house
the smoke of burned pictures rose.[59]

1.4 "Das Geheimnis der alten Mamsell" (The old lady's secret), caricature, *Der Simpl*, October 1947. Artist: Fr. Bilek. Reproduced from Universitätsbibliothek Heidelberg.

The poem also addressed material expressions of militarism, such as "the Prussian soldier's haircut" worn by some Germans. When Hartwig wrote that he "didn't see the slamming / of certain records on certain heads," he could mean recordings of Hitler's or Goebbel's speeches as well as military music.[60]

The poem reflects on Germans' flawed attitudes toward a democratic system through various objects closely related to the Nazi past. Doubting that people had thrown away their copies of *Mein Kampf* or their portraits of Hitler, Hartwig feared that Germans would not "stand together to defend freedom."[61] The text points to an unsolvable dilemma. The absence of visible acts of material iconoclasm incites the idea that these objects are still in German homes, that they continue to embody a frame of mind heavily permeated by Nazism. This, however, remains a suspicion, creating a painful uncertainty about which nothing can be done.

The uncanny enters the public realm where uncertainty reigns about what belongs to the past and what belongs to the present political order. Material objects are privileged embodiments of this kind of uncertainty. Such an uncertainty emerged repeatedly in early postwar accounts of the disorder of things in the rubble. Destroying Nazi symbols in the public sphere amounted to the occupation forces' most resolute measure to lay the material grounds for a new make-believe space, confirming their awareness of these objects' political power. But there were limits to this reordering. The Nazi regime had infiltrated public and private spaces to such a degree that complete destruction was impossible and not even attempted in the private realm. Critics such as those writing for *Der Simpl* regarded the ongoing presence of Nazi symbols in the private home as a nagging problem and thus perceived these objects to have a dangerous political power. The Nazi politicization of the material environment left behind an uncanny legacy that was not dissolved by the transition from war to postwar.

A sequence in the film *Deutschland im Jahre Null / Germania Anno Zero* (*Germany Year Zero*, Italy, 1948, directed by Roberto Rossellini) captured this problem. In the ruins of the Reich Chancellery, young Edmund tries to sell a recording of a speech by Hitler to two British soldiers. In order to convince them, he plays the record on a record player. The subsequent shots from inside the empty halls of the chancellery show a father and his little son wandering around, accompanied by Hitler's voice.[62] While Hitler talks agitatedly about Germany's coming victory, father and son wander through the ruins, followed by images of Berlin's destroyed streets while the crowd on the record screams and applauds triumphantly. The juxtaposition of sound and image conjures the uncanny presence of that which is defined as belonging to the past. How sure could one be about this delineation between past and present? How much did the material remnants from the Third Reich still contain and store the spirits of the past?

The Nazi Past: Nowhere and Everywhere

The presence of the Nazi past could hide itself not only in the obvious political symbols but also in the most banal objects: a restaurant's sign in the rubble, an officer's boots, a hotel with a history, a conspicuous gap in a shop sign. The more references I have tracked in postwar publications, the more obvious it became that these references are only the tip of the iceberg. To acknowledge that such objects were meaningful because they were remnants of the Nazi past was not very common, maybe because many objects silently carried the past into the present in a way that made a clear-cut division between past and present and the political and nonpolitical impossible. In an uncomfortable way, such remnants could complicate Germans' efforts to pull themselves out of the rubble and reconstruct an identity. An officer's boots were not only symbols of militarism that carried the sound and the habitus of the Wehrmacht into the postdefeat era but also just boots, needed in the harsh material conditions of the early postwar years. If they incited men to walk in a certain proud way, who could help it? Yet Karl Zimmermann, writing in April 1946, saw German men with those boots as enjoying precisely this aspect of wearing them.[63]

By contrast, some material remnants of the Nazi regime might not have been perceived as such at all. In March 1947 the *Neue Illustrierte* lamented the disappearance of "a Berlin landmark" that "rose above the Olympic Stadium for ten years: The clock tower, built in 1936." A photo of the blast and another photo of the clock lying in the rubble were accompanied by the headline "It Called the Youth." Although it mentioned the date of the tower's construction, the magazine did not count the Olympic Stadium among the buildings that would represent the Nazi past.[64] That the Olympic Games in Berlin were a huge national and international propaganda effort for the new Nazi Germany and that the architecture, captured and distributed in countless photo reports as well as on film, had played a crucial role in this effort did not make its way to the surface of public expression.[65] The clock tower, the building, and, by extension, all the memories attached to them were kept seemingly innocent and nonpolitical.

This is all the more noteworthy, given that the *Neue Illustrierte* generally showed considerable interest in the problem of urban remnants from the Nazi past. A good example is a photo report on Munich that the magazine had published three months earlier and that paid special attention to the legacy of Nazism inscribed in Munich's built environment. On a double page it presented Munich as the former "Hauptstadt der Bewegung" (capital of the movement) with its many representative Nazi buildings and sites. A big photo on top of the page showed the Königsplatz, which had served as a site for Nazi Party gatherings and public rituals. In the foreground of the photo construction workers demolished one of the Ehrentempel (temples of honor). On another image the shop sign of a local savings bank had a conspicuously large void right between the words "savings bank of the capital" and "Munich." The caption stated sarcastically that the savings bank had "noticed the new time" and "removed two words from the old sign, 'capital of the movement.'"[66] The report revisited some of the main sites that had taken on a sacred character for the Nazi movement and left a deep mark in the texture of Munich's urban environment. The savings bank sign points to the way in which a nazified self-understanding had pervaded even the most profane aspects of life.[67] The examples, however, were restricted to sites that were actually demolished or denazified. Places that were similarly imbued with Nazi meanings but were reused for other purposes were lost from sight.

An omnipresent and indestructible material remnant from the Nazi past were the air-raid bunkers.[68] Since they had been built in large quantities during the war and were the places in which many Germans suffered through the bombardment of their cities, these bunkers had mostly negative memories attached to them. In the immediate postwar period, many bunkers were transformed into hospitals, jails, schools, hotels, or other "places of peaceful industry."[69] Such employments were presented as emblems for a successful conversion from war to peace. Yet the transformed bunkers still served as reminders of the war itself, although not necessarily as reminders of the totalitarian practices of control the Nazis had used them for.[70] In the case of a new bunker hotel in Düsseldorf, however, the connection between the bunker and the Nazi rule was at the same time more evident and more complicated than usual.

In July 1948 the women's magazine *Constanze* published an article on a new hotel installed in a transformed underground air-raid bunker. The hotel was built by a German Jew who had come back from Britain, where he had emigrated during the war. He transformed the bunker that had been built on the site of the former synagogue, which had been "destroyed by the Nazis' fire." *Constanze*'s bunker story was thus a story about the postwar relationship between Jewish and non-Jewish Germans. Readers learned that a German Jew with the name Karl Marx had opened the hotel "as a symbol of racial tolerance." The magazine emphasized that this hotel's reasonable offers ("meant for normal economic circumstances") were the opposite of any racketeering, thereby both counteracting and inadvertently reproducing antisemitic stereotypes of Jewish profiteering. What the magazine quotes as Marx's motivation resembles findings about the self-image of returning German Jews as a "gift" to the Federal Republic.[71] Marx wanted to "prove" that "we Jews do not know racial hate and do not want any revenge." He wanted to do "something useful and constructive" in Germany, hoping for positive reactions. The latter did not happen, however, which left him so disappointed about the prevailing antisemitism that he decided to leave Germany again, leaving his hotel behind "as a monument of our good will."[72]

The article constructed its narrative by working with the site itself as a carrier of meaning both through its history and through its aesthetic transformation.[73] It declares decidedly that "only a Jew could use again the place of the former Jewish Synagogue." The appropriation of the place by the Nazis was thus reversed, even if the article did not mention the controversial question of restitution. Remarkably, the bunker appeared less as a memory site for the war than as a memory site for the crimes against Jews. The war only comes into view again when the transformation of the "useless bunker into a light and modern hotel" is described in detail: "The lower staircases, which the tired and chased Germans climbed hastily during the air raids, were covered with carpets and converted into a terraced restaurant." The place is even presented as a "heaven" for every visitor "regardless if they were Jewish or pagan."[74] The text thus imagined the site as a place that could be redefined by the presence of both Jewish and non-Jewish Germans. Unfortunately, the announced departure of a frustrated Karl Marx seriously undermined this vision.

The article was exceptional in that it called to mind a connection between the inscription of the National Socialist rule into the urban space, on the one hand, and the former presence of Jews as well as their exclusion, deportation, and eventual murder, on the other. As one might suspect, it was very rare to formulate such a connection, even in the early postwar cultural magazines that engaged in serious soul-searching about the Nazi past. Karl Zimmermann's report on Düsseldorf, published in April 1946 in *Die Wandlung*, is one of the rare examples in which an author wrote about his impressions of a destroyed city and, in doing so, included a reflection on sites and places closely connected to the National Socialist regime and its crimes. To be clear, Zimmermann's aim was to record the evidence of new civic activities proving that Düsseldorf's "genius loci" still existed. The passage on the military boots mentioned above is just a side note in parentheses within the description of the positive developments of a reawakening city life.

Zimmermann observed that "the spell of the war" and its accompanying "unspeakable trepidation" had disappeared from the city, a spell that he remembered as having infiltrated the experience of the urban space even before the war had started. He referred to aircrafts that left "from dawn to dusk" from Düsseldorf airport in 1937 and 1938.[75] As he confronted the past whose memory is stored in urban spaces, he also announced that this past had disappeared. In doing so, Zimmermann resorted to a nebulous language, conjuring up a vague consciousness rather than a distinct memory. The Düsseldorf airport was indeed used by the German air force, namely for the disastrous German bombings of Spanish cities during the Spanish Civil War in the late 1930s. This concrete context remains unspoken. Was it meant to invisibly hover between the lines, noticeable only for those who knew and dared to look that way?

Among the things that had already vanished from the urban space the author also named the "dark November days of the evil acts of 1938 committed against Jews." To this memory he added another one, which he called "the ghostly spook" of the burial of a murdered "legation counselor" in the city's planetarium.[76] Contemporaries might have known that Zimmermann referred to the bombastic funeral of the German legation counselor Ernst Eduard von Rath in Düsseldorf, whose murder in Paris had been used by the Nazis to justify the pogroms.[77] The long sentence on the 1938 pogrom and the spooky burial ends with an acknowledgment of the fact that "many, many of those . . . who have applauded the crime and the thoughtlessness" still exist, "and even more than that."[78] The paragraph starts by evoking an urban atmosphere that is liberated from the specter of war, and it ends by alluding to the still-powerful presence of the Nazi past and its crimes. Even though Zimmermann attempted to acknowledge the full scope of the Third Reich's presence in the built environment of Düsseldorf's ruined cityscape, he simultaneously struggled with his own ability to do so. The emergence of the Kristallnacht pogrom is the one disturbing memory that eventually inhibits the intended narrative of postwar cultural liberation.

After giving a detailed account of the economic hardship and the inhabitants' efforts to rebuild their city, Zimmermann's walk led him to the "exhibition area of 1937," the district of the big Nazi exhibition *Schaffendes Volk* (Toiling Volk). He registered as "still standing" the "close-packed iron flagpoles" and the "steed riders," which are characterized by a "rough monumentality that was rare in those times." He also noticed that the monument for Albert Leo Schlageter—a political martyr in the eyes of the Nazis—"still looms" across the street.[79] In this overview of the major urban sights of Düsseldorf's Nazi past, the absences are noteworthy, too, the first one being that the Nazi connection itself remains unnamed.[80] Like Hans Ulrich Gumbrecht's seminar paper from the 1970s, Zimmermann's text lists the materialized remains of the Nazi past, thereby evoking an uncanny atmosphere. Yet Zimmermann did not name the beast that haunted him. The absence of a framework with which to make sense of these impressions and transform them into a coherent narrative is palpable.

Many reports and reflections on German cities that had been destroyed by the bombings did not mention Nazi sites at all or other memories of Nazi activities, let alone atrocities that might have been associated with certain places. When Josef Dünninger recalled in August 1946 in the *Frankfurter Hefte* memories of his last visit to the still-undestroyed city of Würzburg in 1943, he produced a dizzying account soaked with nostalgia, a dreamlike memory of a "timeless image" in which the different "layers of time" and history "flowed together in a basic mood," where everything was "woven into a seamless order." He summarized this experience with the sentence "And so we strolled through the city as if through a timeless feast." As he acknowledged that "the feast is over," he had trouble finding any sense in this cruel end. He and his friend had forgotten, he wrote, that their romantic city experience was "pressed from the blood and the tears of history."[81]

Was it all deceit then? In the end, Dünninger resorted to the metaphor of being a guest: "We had crept into a feast, to which we hadn't been invited, and our hearts were not armed, when a horrible signal chased the unsolicited guests from the tables."[82] Dünninger, who had worked as a German ethnologist in Würzburg before the war, disavowed the fact that, during National Socialism, mystical ideas about old cities had converged with Nazi ideas and spread through all the channels of propaganda.[83] The author imagined himself and his friend to stand outside of a "feast" to which they had, in fact, been constantly invited on the basis of an ideology that excluded and eventually annihilated those who were *not* invited. Accordingly, the bombings marked the moment when a very positive and fascinating experience ended. In this article, the Nazi past is so successfully hidden in the urban space that it is rendered neither noticeable nor noteworthy.

As a German Jew living in the Third Reich while being somewhat protected through her marriage to an "Aryan," Lotte Paepcke remembered walking through a German city in a very different way than Dünninger did. In her book *Unter einem fremden Stern* (Below a foreign star), published in 1951, she described in general terms how Jews experienced moving to a new city: "The people who have built all the houses and have erected all the monuments ostracize and proscribe the foreign Jew who stands for the first time in front of all these constructions as if he is in a hostile fortress." When she came out of hiding at the end of the war and for the first time since 1933 walked on the street again as a free citizen not threatened by exclusion, deportation, and murder, she had a short moment of triumph. The fear came back when she realized that her former enemies populated these streets and that they were supposed to live together again "as if everything didn't happen. As if they had not risen from their office desks and as if they had not stepped out of the doors of their living rooms in order to sweep the sidewalk clean from us."[84]

Many intellectuals struggled with their attempts to recover parts of the urban culture for the necessary new beginning in postwar Germany.[85] This was particularly difficult in cities that were marked especially strongly by the National Socialist regime, as was the case in Munich. In an article published in July 1947, Wilhelm Hausenstein tried to figure out which part of Munich's history and heritage could be revived for the future. Diving into the long pre-Nazi past, he came up with three elements: first, the splendidness of the city's art; second, the city's Christian religion and catholic culture; third, the city's liberality. Hausenstein dealt with the Nazi years, the war, and their effects on the city by directly addressing the reader: "You know how much or how little of such a Munich character has remained."[86]

While the bombings had spared more of Munich than of other cities, the twelve years of Nazi "art politics" had deeply compromised its heritage, even if "the exhibitions are over." The Nazi building that represented this compromised past for Hausenstein was the Haus der deutschen Kunst (House of German art), which he merely called "an arthouse": the monumental building built by the Nazis as the main sight for exhibiting "German art." Hausenstein emphasized above all its mediocre architectural quality: "But an arthouse has remained whose pillars are rather posts or poles." He decidedly did not ponder the issue that this building was but one of many massive Nazi buildings in Munich whose presence was a reminder of how thoroughly Munich's urban space had been nazified.[87]

Hausenstein did, however, mention that before 1933, when the Nazi movement was formed in Munich, the Nazis filled "halls, streets, and squares with their arrogant stupidity and their boring noisiness." The relative silence on the infiltration of city space during the Third Reich, whether through its public political rituals and festivals or through its crimes against the Jewish community, only becomes more conspicuous with this remark. Instead, Hausenstein formulated a strange observation about the relationship between the people of Munich and their built environment. There was a "nearly metaphysical" cause for the collapse of the city: "A city, in order to survive, has to be looked at, daily and by the hour, with the eyes of love. . . . [T]he built brick is dependent on this gazing human eye. It will always be one of my worst memories that one day in the old city center, *in November 1939*, I suddenly understood: the houses are scarcely looked at with a loving gaze—and that is why they are redundant, that is why they will fall . . . they who should have been looked at with twice as loving eyes!"[88]

The most emotional passage in the whole text is an enigma. Two months after the beginning of the war, a year after the Kristallnacht and its destruction of Jewish-owned buildings and synagogues in the city, Hausenstein remembered having been shocked by the urban citizens' lack of a loving gaze for Munich's "houses." Why should the buildings have been loved even more than usual at this specific moment? Hausenstein, an art historian and art critic, not only had been an "inner emigrant" banned from publishing during the Third Reich but also had stayed married to his Belgian Jewish wife throughout the regime.[89] It is difficult not to speculate that this peculiar passage carries the weight of hidden and possibly unspeakable memories. A desperate wish to build a new live and save the city from its own past permeates the whole article. "I will be happy," Hausenstein concluded, "if I could give the impression that, from yesterday and today, there is a Munich of the spirit, that is worth preserving for tomorrow."[90]

Dolf Sternberger, who was also married to a Jewish woman, is the only writer I have encountered in early postwar Germany who put into words how the exclusion of and the violence against the Jewish population had changed the meaning of the urban landscape itself. In the very first text that he published in the magazine *Die Wandlung*, he mentioned being surprised that his eyes filled with tears when he first looked upon the destroyed city of Frankfurt. His tears, he felt, would have seemed more appropriate in other moments, when he and his wife had to flee from the city, when they hurried through "cold and empty streets" and sat in the train compartment, fearing that a "henchman with high boots" would ask for their papers. Sternberger asked himself: "Should I not hate it, this city, that has tortured us in this way? Was it not destroyed already from inside long before the bombs fell and the fires spread?"[91]

Two years later, in the context of the debate on the reconstruction of the Goethehaus in Frankfurt, Sternberger turned again to this theme.[92] The initiative to rebuild Goethe's birthplace in the original way was part of efforts to reappropriate the nineteenth-century writer as a major ingredient of a German culture on which the new postwar Germany could be founded. The reconstruction of the Goethehaus became one of the most important debates on the moral questions involved in the rebuilding of Germany's cities.[93] The journalist Walter Dirks famously argued that there was a logic to the wartime destruction of the Goethehaus that should be respected: Germany had left Goethe's path of humanism; therefore, it was a deserved and meaningful consequence that his birthplace had been destroyed, too.[94] Dolf Sternberger did not argue strictly against a reconstruction; instead, he argued for prioritizing the housing needs of the people. Before doing so, however, he formulated his general reservations in a way that inserted a different urban experience of Nazi politics into the debate on this major heritage site.

The director of the Goethehaus had addressed Sternberger in a letter as an "old Frankfurter" and had asked him to support the reconstruction of the building. The formulation "old Frankfurter" triggered Sternberger's hesitation. Did "the old Frankfurt," Sternberger asked himself, really collapse on the day of the fatal bombings? In his answer, he reiterated that Frankfurt had been "destroyed and ruined a hundred times and a thousand times before its crackling collapse." Sternberger filled this statement with concrete meaning by rendering a long and vivid line of memories from Frankfurt during the Third Reich, beginning with the "alarming, unending, uncanny, screaming tinkling of the firefighters." This was *not* the noise of the bombing nights but had occurred "earlier, much earlier, it is long ago already, nearly nine years." In remembering "the night of 8 November 1938," Sternberger evoked how he, "scared stiff," had listened behind the window to the sound of motorbikes, "evil noises, pervading everything," how he had seen the "glow of fire stemming from the nearby synagogue," how he had anticipated "unprecedented violence."[95]

Sternberger described "fellows in high boots" who "silently and methodically" destroyed shop windows "with an iron rod," unhindered by callous spectators; men entering his apartment building searching for his neighbors; big guys on motorbikes who "hunted people, neighbors, citizens"; a shivering woman who said that "the Jews had been rounded up in the festival hall" and were being humiliated by SA men; a family that "stood densely packed with a few suitcases" in the entrance of their house, with "baggage vouchers hanging from the lapels of their coats as if they were cargo ready to be shipped." This painful enumeration ends with a short summary of the ensuing horrors of fear, of fleeing, and of "the walk to the station, uncertain of the end." The city of Goethe, Sternberger concludes, had been "destroyed inside without a war, suffocated, squeezed to death, hollowed out." The spirit of Goethe had been "cast out of the air of this city." "What happened afterward was only the aftermath, the execution. It only regarded a scenery, lifeless shells."[96]

This is an extraordinary text. Although he knew that "nobody wants to hear these things anymore," Sternberger chose to make present "the memories of an old Frankfurter," not merely the experience of suffering from persecution and violence but also the fact that such experiences stuck to the materiality of the urban landscape.[97] The city itself, the houses and the streets, had taken on a new meaning as a result. A new order had been established in which a group of people was deprived of the right to walk the streets as citizens. They had lost the right to stay safe in the city's private or public spaces. A new order had been established that wiped this group's holy places of worship, the synagogues, out of the urban space. A new order had been established in which the property of these people had lost any protection and was demolished or taken away, an order in which they themselves became a form of property. The relationship between people, places, and objects had defined the city life of "the old Frankfurt." This city, with its age-old Jewish community, had fundamentally changed before it was destroyed by the bombings. By telling this story, Sternberger reclaimed the city for himself and for all those who had been excluded and persecuted. Implicit in his text is the bitter realization that denying this part of the city's history came close to repeating the former exclusion.

Sternberger's text is important because it throws light on what is usually absent, even in texts by people who had similar experiences in the Third Reich. If I turn back to Wilhelm Hausenstein's reflection on Munich, I cannot help but notice the complete absence of any mention of the Kristallnacht pogrom and the destruction of Munich's synagogues.[98] This is not to assume that Hausenstein's personal way of relating to these events would necessarily have been similar to Sternberger's. But the consciousness that "nobody wants to hear these things anymore" has probably prevented many from pulling to the surface of explicit public discourse their most painful memories and the consequence of these memories for the relationship not only between Jewish and non-Jewish Germans but also between all Germans and their urban space in the wake of the Nazi terror.[99]

Marie-Luise Kaschnitz's postwar essays on "people and things" showed a strong sensitivity to the way in which the materiality of everyday life was a fundamental aspect of people's experiences. Like Sternberger, Kaschnitz had lived in Frankfurt during the Third Reich, and she published her essays in Sternberger's *Die Wandlung*. Her texts, however, completely omitted any concrete reference to the fate of Jews or their buildings and belongings. Her style of writing in a rather abstract mode accommodated such omissions. But those omissions were common also when people wrote in a much more concrete way on their memories and experiences. For Germans who did not belong to those formerly excluded from the *Volksgemeinschaft*, it was one thing, and obviously already difficult, to acknowledge the reality of the murder of Jews explicitly; it was another thing, however, for these Germans to relate it back to their own everyday life. Memories attached to the physical manifestations of the city had the capacity to do just that. Even if many instances of Nazi violence and persecution of Jews and other excluded groups may have happened outside of the everyday realm of "Aryan" Germans, other instances clearly did not, which is especially true of the pogroms on November 9, 1938, and of the destruction of major urban sites of Jewish life.[100] It is also true of the dispossession and redistribution of Jewish property.

The Unspeakable Legacy of Aryanization

The Nazis redefined and reordered the country's material culture on an unprecedented scale. This process included violently disrupting the order of things by first destroying Jewish property, then seizing what remained, and finally redistributing it among Aryan Germans after the Jews themselves were arrested and deported from German territory.[101] German men and women took part in the National Socialists' violent Germanization policy in the Reich's new territories, which included demolishing buildings and cities, appropriating apartments, and redistributing objects, as well as making themselves a proper German home in occupied foreign countries.[102] All of these massive interferences in the relationship between the people and the material world they inhabited were part of the Nazi undertaking to build a German Empire and transform it into an Aryan space, of imagining and creating "a world without Jews" (Alon Confino). What was the moral and emotional legacy that the politicized material culture of this Nazi policy left behind for postwar Germans? What was the effect of the massive, violent, and politically induced transfer of objects from Jews to Aryans on Germans' relationship to their past and to each other, including to the survivors of the Third Reich?[103]

Franziska Becker's oral history study on the southern German village of Baisingen has demonstrated that the process of Aryanizing Jewish property worked in two ways. First, the act of buying Jewish property for a low price and thereby benefiting from the Jews' deportation established a materially mediated complicity with their mass murder. Second, this process linked both groups through the resulting presence in Aryan households of objects formerly owned by Jews. With the end of the war and the breakdown of the Nazi order it became much more difficult to rationalize buying what had belonged to one's deported Jewish neighbors as merely a "legal" acquisition. The return of a Jewish survivor to Baisingen who reclaimed his property that was spread among the population resulted in a cascade of denial, outright lying, or distortion of the facts by his former neighbors. These defensive reactions are strong testimony to the huge problem embodied by those objects for postwar Germans.[104]

Because guilt, shame, and complicity were at stake, there was virtual silence regarding the legacy of Aryanization in the postwar published sphere.[105] It is only in reports on everyday conversations that we can catch a glimpse of the problem. A Jewish merchant from Hamburg wrote in early 1945 in his diary that "many who took Jewish apartments and Jewish things are now in great fear that the Jews could come back, reclaim their property, and bring the people eventually to justice for robbery and theft."[106] And a young German businessman told an American officer at the end of 1944: "At least eighty percent of the Germans have sinned against the Jews. They have robbed and murdered the Jews, not out of conviction, but for profit, the most heinous of sins. Now they are troubled in their consciences and a great fear is among them."[107] The Norwegian author Sigrid Undset expressed herself bluntly in public on the topic of Germans' moral burden connected with acts of dispossession in the context of the war. Having been forced to flee Norway after the German occupation, Undset wrote in October 1945 in the American German paper *Die Neue Zeitung* that German mothers were as guilty as German fathers, as they took over "homes and properties of people in occupied territories, even keeping family portraits which they occasionally offered to sell back to their owners at a high price!"[108] With a candor that was unusual, Undset laid bare the humiliating and denigrating effect at the core of these acts.

The casual way in which the topic surfaces in Clemens Münster's reflections on the return of art exhibitions after the war seems more typical. A coeditor of the *Frankfurter Hefte*, Münster wrote in May 1946 about the absence of paintings from the public sphere for "nearly seven years" and described the disappearance of art in Nazi Germany: "The last visit to a museum before the war, then still one or the other auction ('from private property in Berlin'—do you remember what that meant?), a visit to some friends' country house, apart from that, old paintings existed only as reproductions."[109] The generalizing way in which Münster postulated a total absence of "old paintings" from both the public and private spheres during the war contradicts the cultural reality of the Third Reich, where museums, including historical art museums, were open long after the war had begun.[110] Münster hinted at the auctioning of artworks stemming from dispossessed Jewish collectors by asking readers if they remembered what the phrase "from private property in Berlin" meant. This arguably established a community of insiders who shared a knowledge that they neither wanted nor had to spell out in order to understand each other.[111] Remembering these auctions implies, at the very least, Münster's knowledge of people who benefited from art bought from Jews who were excluded and dispossessed. At the same time, this memory itself contradicts his stern statement that art was nowhere to be found after 1939.

The satirical magazine *Der Simpl* perhaps most acutely sensed and expressed the moral problem the dispossession of Jews had left behind. In January 1947 the magazine published a caricature entitled "Das Gewissen" (The conscience) (fig. 1.5) depicting a man who walks through the rubble at night, looking fearfully

1.5 "Das Gewissen" (The conscience), caricature, *Der Simpl*, January 1947. Artist: K. H. Böcher. Reproduced from Universitätsbibliothek Heidelberg.

over his shoulder at a passerby. The caption delivered his thoughts: "Will anyone really remember the small Aryanization deal from the year 38?"[112] Some months later, a short text entitled "Schweigen ist—verfluchtes Gold" (Silence is—cursed gold), a variation of the German proverb "talking is silver, silence is gold," followed up on the theme:

> Back then, when the glass cascades of "non-Aryan" shop windows fell onto the street and monstrosities were allowed to happen, many, a great many, stayed silent. Back then the silence transformed itself into gold, just like the talking, if it was "conform." Laces, braids, stars, golden rims, and emblems. For some people, it slipped into the wallet—the gold of silence or of the hoarse talking. Depending. It is long ago since the gold sank.
>
> And today?—Yes, they are staying silent again. Many, a great many. It is frightening: those who should be silent, talk—those who should talk, stay silent. In a time in which you can rely neither on proverbs nor on people.[113]

Aryanization appears here as a prime example of how Nazi Germany had reversed common morality. While the Kristallnacht was perceived by many Germans as a transgression, acquiring dispossessed Jewish property was not. The text merges uniforms and symbols, on the one hand, and the dispossession of Jewish property, on the other, into one and the same nazified moral and material universe casting its heavy shadow on the postwar world.[114]

Two years later, in April 1949, *Der Simpl* published a fake letter written by a certain Colonel von Klug who called the attention of "all owners of Aryanized houses" to the approaching deadline for registering "Aryanized real estate," as well as to the right for restitution, which was included in the new Bavarian constitution. The colonel regretted that the American authorities failed to recognize why restitution claims were "mean-spirited." He explained that "these assets were ceded completely voluntarily and some of them without any compulsion even after the so-called 'Kristallnacht 1938.'" In the second part of the letter he gave advice on how to sabotage the restitution: "Don't return the house that you once captured quietly to its former Jewish owner! Spoil it for them! We will find ways and means to legally take away his pleasure in interfering in your current property situation." He signed the letter "with the German salute."[115]

The text reflects the growing agitation, especially by home owners, against the restitution regulations, an agitation that would accelerate after the transfer of power from the Allies to the West German government.[116] Such a sharp satirical critique of the Nazi mentality and the poisonous antisemitism behind this kind of agitation was a very marginal position in a public sphere increasingly dominated by a discourse that focused on German victimhood. The Nazi Aryanization of Jewish property had left behind a legacy that could uncomfortably remind many postwar Germans of their complicity in the crimes against the Jews. While this came to the surface only very occasionally, even in a publication like *Der Simpl*, it usually remained utterly absent from the pages of the German press.

Objects Stranded On-Screen

If written documents of the time tend not to speak about the difficult legacy of Aryanization, then we have to turn to other sources. Films both invest material objects with affect and render the phenomenal world to the viewer. Material objects on-screen can be a nearly invisible part of a self-evident material environment, but they can also become central to the cinematic production of meaning. The material world captured on-screen always has a history of its own that can inform this meaning. In the last sections of this chapter I approach objects on-screen as "tangible events" relating to the complex reality of material culture, in this case, the challenge posed by the disrupted order of things in postwar Germany.[117] German rubble films, the main genre of the early postwar period, focus on the moral crisis that Germany's historic rupture produced. The two films *Zwischen gestern und morgen* (*Between Yesterday and Tomorrow*, 1947, directed by Harald Braun) and *Die Mörder sind unter uns* (*The Murderers Are among Us*, 1946, directed by Wolfgang Staudte) tell stories in which material objects and the built environment silently embody the moral burdens that the Nazi past has left behind.[118] Through their specific use of material objects, both films bring the problem of dispossession and the legacy of Aryanization to the cinematic surface.

The viewer enters both films by looking through the eyes of two formerly excluded persons at ruined cityscapes with isolated icons of an idyllic prewar Germany and with wandering ragged people. A woman who was in a concentration camp arrives at a station in the city rubble of Berlin, walks to the building in which she used to live, talks to the old optician in his shop, climbs the stairs, enters her old apartment, and discovers that it is occupied by a stranger. This is the opening of *The Murderers Are among Us*. A man who was forced to emigrate to Switzerland arrives at Munich central station, strolls through the rubble of Munich, and enters the half-destroyed Palasthotel, only to find a pile of stones behind the facade in which a woman searches for something. This is the opening of *Between Yesterday and Tomorrow*.

There is a third entrance, happening in the narrated time of March 1938.[119] A woman enters the lobby of the Palasthotel through the revolving door, steps out of the shadows, pauses, looks around anxiously, and approaches the reception desk to ask for "a nice room, with bathroom, for just one night." The hotel manager hesitatingly refers to the "stipulations" but complies with her request. Shortly afterward, the woman stands in the doorway of an elegant hotel room. She takes deep breaths, walks across the carpet toward the window and turns on a light, walks toward the desk and turns on another light, sits down at the desk and smiles, walks into the bathroom, looks around smiling, turns on the water faucet, puts her hand under the water, dries her hand, and then sits down on the edge of the bathtub, taking it all in. Placed in the middle of the film *Between Yesterday and Tomorrow*, these moments are part of a flashback memory of the Palasthotel's manager that unravels the central problem of its plot.

All three entrances show people who are coming back into a world that has excluded them, encountering a material environment from which they were separated by force some years earlier. Only one of these entrances takes place during the Nazi regime and involves mortal danger. The appearance of the Jewish woman Nelly Dreyfuss in the space of the hotel has a ghostlike quality. The carpet she walks on and the desk she sits at are not intended to be used by her.[120] As she connects again with these material surroundings, it becomes obvious that the place and the objects within it have already silently registered the *absence* of Jews. Her presence disturbs the unspoken rules by which people and things interact. This entrance thus performs how, in March 1938, the whole material environment was already defined by the exclusion of Jews. Dreyfuss will die the night after she enters the hotel, throwing herself from the top of the staircase, choosing death in order to escape her imminent arrest by the Gestapo.

The main storyline of *Between Yesterday and Tomorrow* begins with the return of the exiled caricaturist, Michael Rott, who searches for the woman, Annette Rodenwald, with whom he was in love when he learned that the Gestapo was after him and he had to leave the country in March 1938. In the hotel he encounters unfriendliness, evasion, and mistrust from the people he meets: the concierge, the manager, and Rodenwald herself, who, after having had no further news of Rott, married the hotel manager, Ebeling. What does this story about a returning émigré's experience have to do with material culture? An object or rather its absence functions as a central mnemonic site. The flashback that introduces Dreyfuss also introduces the reason for the mistrust Rott encounters: a necklace that belonged to Dreyfuss disappeared on the same night Dreyfuss died and Rott left. Ebeling assumes Rott betrayed Dreyfuss to the police in order to steal her necklace. Rott, who himself had to flee from the Gestapo, thus finds himself accused of being complicit in the persecution and dispossession of a Jewish woman.

1.6 Two screenshots from *Between Yesterday and Tomorrow* (1947): Kat finds the jewelry in the rubble. Reproduced from NDF Neue Deutsche Filmgesellschaft.

In fact, the necklace in question has already appeared on-screen before the flashback introduces Nelly Dreyfuss. Kat, the young woman whom Rott encounters at the very beginning, was looking for it in the rubble. In a scene preceding the flashback, she discovers a box in a steel locker and opens it. A close-up shot of the jewelry in the box accompanied by dramatic music accentuates the moment of her triumph (fig. 1.6). As a single mother living in meager circumstances, she intends to sell the jewelry on the black market. This is the first scene in which the necklace becomes the central object of attention. the second scene follows in the flashback: Dreyfuss entrusts the manager with her necklace, explaining why she had to come out of hiding to see her former husband, an actor named Corty. While she describes how she feels being banished from everything that used to be her life, she constantly touches and moves the necklace in her hands (fig. 1.7): "For once I needed to relive my life for a bit, I needed to be surrounded by light, . . . I needed to wear my clothes, I needed to feel carpets under my feet and . . . see my husband."

In such moments the necklace is imbued with meaning through the bodily interaction between the object and the characters, through the emotions that inform this interaction, and through close-ups and music. The necklace thereby

1.7 Screenshot from *Between Yesterday and Tomorrow* (1947): Nelly Dreyfuss holding her jewelry. Reproduced from NDF Neue Deutsche Filmgesellschaft.

turns into a silent witness testifying not only to Dreyfuss's suffering, exclusion, and death but also to the problem of complicity and guilt that the other characters of the story face in relation to this object's history. The necklace embodies a material legacy around whose disturbing presence the whole story of the film is organized.[121]

Once Kat learns that Rott is suspected of stealing the necklace, she gets the jewelry back and proves Rott's trustworthiness by placing it in the hands of Rott's former lover. This act foregrounds Kat as the innocent female character who takes things pragmatically into her own hands to build a new life. In doing so, she opens up the path to a better future for both of them. At the same time, nothing is solved by this act. The viewer knows that the necklace itself carries a moral burden, and in the hands of Rott's former lover it has certainly not arrived where it belongs. In fact, it belongs to no one anymore. Troubled by her own involvement, Kat says, "You get into something, and suddenly you are in it, but now I know that it was wrong," and runs to the steel locker in the rubble of the hotel where she had found the jewelry. In the last shot she leans over the locker, crying desperately as Rott approaches to console her. Kat's desperation seems to be about the impossibility of disentangling the hopelessly entangled constellation of loss, survival, and guilt in a world in which both the material and the moral order of things has been catastrophically disrupted. In the last moments of the film both the music and the couple's demeanor change from dramatic to more cheerful, hinting at the possibility of their future life together.

When Michael Rott and Nelly Dreyfuss reenter the spaces they were forced to leave they both experience social rejection due to the way National Socialism had reshaped the relationship between people, places, and objects. Susanne Wallner, the concentration camp survivor of *The Murderers Are among Us*, faces another kind of rejection. Hans Mertens, a former Wehrmacht soldier, lives in Wallner's disheveled and partly damaged but still fully furnished Berlin apartment. The two main characters meet for the first time when she attempts to reappropriate her living space. In the long sequence that follows, the relationship between Mertens and Wallner is negotiated through their relation to the space of the apartment. But first, Mertens appears alone, nervously searching for something in a cupboard among women's scarves. Finally, he pulls a camera out of a chest of drawers. While he holds the camera in his hands, a close-up shot, he hears a knock at the door. He stops and looks for a short moment directly into the film camera as if to implicate the viewer in his moral conflict (fig. 1.8). Then he lets the camera slide into the pocket of his jacket and opens the apartment door. The Dutch angle used in the shot underlines the moral dubiousness of his action.[122] As the door opens, wind blows through the shattered windows of the apartment, rendering present the disrupted barrier between inside and outside as an effect of the bombings. At the end of the following dialogue, Mertens pulls the camera out of his jacket pocket and places it on a cabinet in the corridor before leaving the apartment. The film camera then zooms in on the photo camera on the cabinet. In the subsequent scene we learn that Mertens wanted to sell the camera to a girl at a nightclub so that he could buy liquor.

In both films, the moment in which the main characters reenter the space they had been forced to leave during Nazism is linked to another main character searching for an object that belongs to a victim of the regime. They are about to sell these objects on the black market but reverse their intended action due to a guilty conscience. The ambivalent ownership status of these stranded objects is related to the problem of poisoned social relationships in the aftermath of the Third Reich's violent politics of exclusion. These stranded objects embody the material presence of relationships burdened by the past in an inscrutable way.

Standing in front of the opened apartment door, Wallner introduces herself as the "owner" of the apartment, to which Mertens replies confusingly that he

1.8 Screenshot from *The Murderers Are among Us* (1946): Mertens finds a camera in a chest of drawers. Reproduced from DEFA.

himself is the owner. She may only have been the tenant of a place that actually belongs to the landlord. When she insists that she has a "right" to live there, he invites her to look through the shattered window onto the rubble of the city, accusing her of having been absent when "all hell broke loose" and the victims were buried where they were found. When he asks her where she had been, suggesting she had been "in a safe place," Wallner answers, "Yes, I was in a safe place. If you want to call it that." In this moment, Wallner, the unspecified victim (we don't know if she is Jewish or maybe a Communist), accepts Mertens's language and does not talk about her experience of being imprisoned in a concentration camp.[123] Pragmatically, she suggests that she could move into a small room, allowing Mertens to stay for a while. Wallner will eventually help Mertens overcome his war trauma and start working as a physician again. Starting out as a possibly Jewish victim of the regime, anxiously facing a new beginning, she turns into a practical and selfless woman through the process of negotiating the right to use her own space and property.[124] As her victimhood is effaced from the screen, what remains is the presence of the furnished apartment itself with its unclear ownership status.

In both films, the female act of cleaning up the material remnants of the past in order to turn them into tools for creating a newly ordered and morally redeemed life is also shown to be mixed up with the legacy of the Nazi past. Kat morally "soils" her hands by selling the necklace to build a better home for herself and her son, unknowingly repeating the act of dispossession. Wallner's actions become associated with the Nazi past in a very different way. Her obsessive cleaning might be interpreted as an effort not only to clear away the effects of the bombings but also to rub off the patina of her victimhood, to wipe away the presence of her past in the shared place. When she finds the letter of Mertens's supposedly dead former captain, Brückner, she takes it to Brückner's wife against Mertens's will. Brückner, who turns out to be alive, owns a factory that converts army helmets into cooking pots and has a perfectly ordered German home. He is also, as will become clear in the end, responsible for the war crime that torments Mertens. The film sets Wallner's domestic order in proximity to Brückner's home and thereby to the Nazi past: Wallner wearing a headscarf and cleaning the flat in a self-assured way is juxtaposed with Brückner's wife taking off her cleaning scarf in an annoyingly self-assured manner. Another parallel is produced through shots of both homes' dining tables laid with tablecloths and neatly arranged porcelain dishes. Mertens's complaints that Wallner has reestablished "bourgeois order" in his apartment and that "everything is always perfect at a philistine's place" contrast with Brückner praising his own apartment as "absolutely perfect."

Last but not least, Mertens's final confrontation with Brückner is triggered through a symbolically charged object inside the new domestic order: the Christmas tree. A single shot of the Christmas tree, standing on the chest of drawers (fig. 1.9), is followed by Mertens's odd question, whether the tree "is meant to stay in the room?" In the following flashback, Brückner's order for a mass killing of civilians on the eastern front is interwoven with the decoration of the company's Christmas tree. Brückner ignored Mertens's request to spare the civilians and instead commanded Mertens to organize the Christmas star for the tree. There follows the image of the group of civilians being shot. Then a man, presumably Mertens, is seen from behind, crumpling the Christmas star in his right hand and dropping it to the snowy ground. The subsequent close-up reveals on closer inspection that the Christmas star has the form of the Star of David (fig. 1.10).[125]

The Star of David, visible or not for the contemporary viewers, underlines the subliminal consciousness of the murder of the Jews, which pervades the film in other ways, too.[126] The obligation for Jews to wear the yellow badge in the shape of a Star of David marked a culmination in the history of the exclusion of the Jews from the Aryanized German space. Introduced in September 1941,

1.9 Screenshot from *The Murderers Are among Us* (1946): the Christmas tree on the chest of drawers. Reproduced from DEFA.

1.10 Screenshot from *The Murderers Are among Us* (1946): the Christmas star / Star of David in the snow. Reproduced from DEFA.

when mass deportations were well under way, the yellow badge made the practice of exclusion even more humiliating for the remaining Jews and at the same time more difficult to ignore for Aryan Germans.[127] The badge directly confronted the Germans defined as "Aryans" with their excluded Other in the public space. The Star of David in the snow, intended as a Christian star on a Christmas tree, completes the material constellation that incites Mertens to turn against Brückner. The Christmas tree on Wallner's chest of drawers brings back Mertens's memories of the mass killing and links this space directly to the army's version of building a proper German home in the occupied territories. Yet the chest of drawers on which the Christmas tree stands already filled the screen at the moment when Mertens was about to take Wallner's camera. Through this final sequence of scenes her apartment becomes once more invested with Mertens's feelings of guilt and shame.[128]

The ruined city landscape in rubble films served both as a metaphor for the breakdown of German society and as a stage for reconstruction.[129] The city rubble as an off-screen material reality captured on-screen was also an inescapable reminder of the experience of the bombings that Germans tried to make sense of, which included linking the bombings to the mass killings in the East. The German population viewed the bombings, in Frank Stern's formulation, "as terror from the skies, a response to terror against the Jews."[130] Both films contain a crucial scene in which the moral conflict about dispossessed property and its legacy of guilt is directly related to the experience of the bombings.

When Mertens and Wallner first meet and Wallner confirms that she was "in a safe place" during the bombings, her past as a victim of the Nazi rule disappears behind the theme of the bombings. The shift of attention from the apartment to the rubble alleviates Mertens's morally uncomfortable position as the occupant of Wallner's apartment and the thief of her property. It enables the plot to turn to his other problems with respect to the past, leaving the apartment as the silent and opaque background of his unease. In *Between Yesterday and Tomorrow* the equivalent scene takes place during a flashback explaining how Kat had learned about the necklace. On the night of the "great air raid" of Munich, Kat was working as a waitress in the bar of the Palasthotel when Dreyfuss's ex-husband, Corty, entered as a guest. As Kat enquires about the jewelry box protruding from his coat pocket, he opens the box, tenderly touches the necklace, and answers that he received the jewelry when he was in despair, sold it to start a new life, then bought it back in order to "never give it away again." With his hands resting on the jewelry box, Corty sits at exactly the place he had sat with Dreyfuss the night of her death. As the camera shows first the empty seat and then a close-up of Corty's face, dramatic music rises, emphasizing his inner affliction with respect to her absence and with respect to the necklace.

In a melodramatic mode, the scene turns the objective reality of the screen into the inner reality of the protagonist to become an emotional experience of the spectator.[131] The end of this moment is crucial for the relation between dispossession and bombings. Dramatic music fuses and eventually fades to the sound of the sirens announcing the air raid that will destroy the city, kill Corty, and bury the necklace under the rubble. The cinematic configuration of the necklace in Corty's hands, the empty seat, and the dramatic music transformed into sirens captures accurately how the intermingled experience of owning this dispossessed object, with its accompanying feelings of guilt, merges with the catastrophe of the bombings, in which Corty chooses to die by leaving the shelter. The iconic shot of the final scene of the film brings together both the problematic legacy of dispossession and the result of the bombings: Kat cries while leaning over the steel locker where she had found the necklace amid the rubble.

In both films the two female victims of the regime lose the unquestioned ownership of their possessions due to the way German society under Nazi rule treated them. Because of this background, their material objects—Dreyfuss's necklace and Wallner's furnished apartment—have a troubling material presence that infuses both cinematic stories in complex ways. This moral burden of postwar materiality on-screen has to be taken seriously as referring to an equally complex and troubling social reality in postwar Germany. The films use a gendered structure to cope not only with the challenge posed by the past crimes but also with the presence of these crimes in the form of dispossessed property. In these and the following years, women's own participation in the Nazi regime was systematically ignored. Instead, women were given the responsibility of cleaning up the mess, literally and figuratively, and of helping men to come to terms with *their* past.[132] As the problem of male guilt relates in these two films in a peculiar way to the dispossessed belongings of a female victim, the problem of dispossession and the related mass murder is intermingled with the issue of postwar gender relations. The woman's physical act of cleaning up and reordering is supposed to solve *both* problems but stays itself, as both films subtly indicate, problematically entangled in the legacy of National Socialist culture.

The Obliterated Link

In the movie *In jenen Tagen* (*In Those Days*, 1946–47, directed by Helmut Käutner), there is no attempt to reorder the rubble, there is only a peculiar form of clearing it both materially and morally.[133] The film, which, according to film scholars, had "the evident intention of conforming to the wishes of the audience and the occupation authorities alike," tells the stories of people who remained "humans in inhumane times."[134] Two men, one of whom wears a former Wehrmacht uniform whose military decorations have been removed, talk about the state of humanity while they dismantle a stranded automobile by stripping it of anything that could still be of use. The ex-soldier's view is bleak: "There are no humans anymore." At this point, the car wreck itself begins to talk (voice-over by Käutner) and offers a view stemming from its "objective" perspective as an inanimate object that has witnessed the stories of its different owners during the preceding twelve years. The stranded object's function is to give access to various personal experiences during the Third Reich and thereby assure the viewer that humaneness had not completely disappeared. The "unprejudiced" and "heartless" object connects the viewer to the trace of humanity, which in turn linked both people and objects to each other, thereby pointing toward a possible future. The film sets out to find worthy elements in the wreck that is the Nazi past, just as the men try to find useful parts in the car wreck. German cinemagoers seem to have been skeptical at first, but according to one report, after they saw the film they came to identify with its way of narrating the past.[135] The journal *Das Auto* was enthusiastic about the fact that a car had become a "film star" and attested to the movie's capacity to "open up the avenue out of the misery of our days to the hope of tomorrow!"[136]

The seven stories told in the film are all connected first through the car itself and then with an object that the two men find in the wreck. The car was mostly owned and used by Germans who were victims themselves, who supported someone who suffered from the regime, or who at least did nobody any harm. The only exception is a Wehrmacht officer on the eastern front whose callous attitude provoked the death of the German soldier driving him. Scholars have pointed out that the film serves postwar Germans' need to be released from guilt. Others have emphasized that the structure provides a complex narrative framework by bringing together historical and personal time in order to shape the notion of humaneness.[137] It has also been observed that *In Those Days* attempts to dissociate the automobile from its entanglement with Nazi modernity and imbue it with a "humanist inflection" even as it still resorts to the notion of a soulful technology central to Nazi ideology.[138] In all these interpretations, the car is seen either as a narrative device or as a symbol of technology without taking seriously its presence on-screen as a material object.

A focus on this materiality and its role in the narrative reveals how the film uses the intimate links between the car and its owners to show how people managed to preserve their moral integrity during the Third Reich. Serving as a guide through the past, the anthropomorphized vehicle presents the relationship between people, places, and objects as untainted by the Nazi past. Although the car connects every story and every character in the stories, there is no attention given to how the car changes its owners. *The Murderers Are among Us* and *Between Yesterday and Tomorrow* expose the difficult moral legacy associated with the manner in which material objects were redistributed in the Third Reich. *In Those Days*, by contrast, sanitizes precisely this aspect of the Nazi past's legacy. Moreover, both the first and the last episodes ambiguously conjure the political dreamscape invested in automobiles.

The film narrates the "birth" of the supposedly "objective" car in a way that marks it as a carrier of political meaning, yet the film then immediately neutralizes this notion. The date 30-1-33 (January 30, 1933), scratched into the windscreen, triggers the first episode (fig. 1.11). The flashback begins with pictures from the factory in which the Opel was produced. The voice-over comments: "When I was young I believed my life would last a thousand years and would be fabulous, but it was not so fabulous, and it only lasted twelve years." This statement, together with the date, implicitly marks the car as an embodiment of the Nazi regime itself. The episode, however, transforms the date into a symbol of harmlessness. A man, Peter, gives the car to a woman he loves, Sybille. That

1.11 Screenshot from *In Those Days* (1946–47): the date 30-1-33 scratched into the windscreen of the car. Reproduced from Camera-Filmproduktion.

same evening, they get mired in a crowd that has gathered to watch the torch parade on the occasion of Hitler's rise to power. Although they know what is going on, Peter trivializes the event's importance and is instead occupied by his love of Sybille. Using her ring, he scratches the date into the windscreen to produce a memento of his personal moment of happiness, thereby undermining any idea that the year 1933 might have been experienced as a "good year" for political reasons.

A surprising slip occurs in the cinematic narrative at precisely the point where the car's function as a soothing connection between people as human beings intersects with the legacy of Aryanization. It is through this narrative faux pas that this legacy is erased from the plot and the screen. The error appears at the logical conjunction between the third and fourth episodes. The third episode tells the story of a couple, Wilhelm and Sally Bienert, who own a picture frame shop. At the center of the story is Mr. Bienert's loyalty to his Jewish wife in spite of the regime's increasingly severe measures of exclusion. The redefinition of urban space in the context of racial exclusion first appears in the form of a new name, "Nathan Levy," in white letters replacing the original name on the window of the neighbor's shop. Mr. Bienert, however, does not want to comply

1.12 Screenshot from *In Those Days* (1946–47): the destroyed shop window of the Bienerts' picture frame shop. Reproduced from Camera-Filmproduktion.

with the new rule. When the Nazi hordes are throwing stones at all the shops "with the white letters," Wilhelm Bienert stands outside and stares into his own unmarked shop window. He then dispels the unbearable tension by throwing a stone into the window himself (fig. 1.12).[139] The next day, both he and his wife commit suicide.

A staple that affixes a small shred of paper to the dashboard of the car serves as the material link between the postwar rubble and this story from the Nazi past. At the end of the story the staple holds an important document: it is The police president's announcement that Mr. and Mrs. Bienert are no longer allowed to own and drive their car (fig. 1.13). The film thus gives ample cinematic attention to the state-sanctioned separation on racial grounds between this couple and the very object that connects all the characters of the film. This opens up the question, What happened to the couple's car after their death? A horseshoe pinned on the dashboard connects the car wreck with the next story and turns out to carry the unspoken answer to this question. In the next episode, the horseshoe reemerges on the dashboard as a picture frame holding the photograph of a woman. In the first scene of the episode, the same woman, Dorothea, drives the car along a street.[140] Dorothea is desperately looking for her missing husband, Jochen, who is the car's owner. Jochen was caught by the Gestapo because he had worked for the resistance. He also had a love affair with his wife's sister, Ruth, also a member of the resistance. The essence of this story is again a moral one: in spite of her sister's betrayal, Dorothea selflessly puts herself in danger in order to help Ruth get out of the country.

While the previous owners do not usually play a role in the following episodes, the photograph framed by the horseshoe carries a narrative slip with a Freudian load that subverts the seeming unimportance of how the car materially connects its various owners to each other. A close-up shot on the back of the photograph reveals a handwritten message: "For Jochen's car, until Dorothea comes back from Venice—September 1938" (fig. 1.14). The manifest significance of this message for the story becomes clear when Dorothea asks herself and eventually her sister if the affair had started while Dorothea was in Venice. But there is a second, latent significance. The written message establishes unequivocally that the car was already owned by Dorothea's husband in *September* 1938. In the previous episode, however, the spectator had learned that the car belonged to the half-Jewish couple on the night of the pogrom against the Jews

1.13 Screenshot from *In Those Days* (1946–47): the police announcement that withdraws the right to drive a car from the Bienerts pinned to the dashboard of the car. Reproduced from Camera-Filmproduktion.

1.14 Screenshot from *In Those Days* (1946–47): the message on the back of the photograph. Reproduced from Camera-Filmproduktion.

on 9 *November* 1938. The obvious meaning of the date is crucial for the story. In one scene, the voice of Dorothea's husband even reads the full note aloud to her. We are left to wonder if this slip carries a message about what many or most postwar Germans were not able to think or see.

An article on the film in the *Neue Illustrierte* summarized the plot of every episode, including the deadly fate of the Jewish owners of the car in the "fall of 1938" and the words and date "Aug. 1938" [*sic*] written on the back of the photograph in the following episode, thereby reiterating the mistake of the film without commenting on it.[141] This parapraxia erases any awareness of the car as a morally problematic connection between Dorothea and her husband with the Bienerts, who had been driven into suicide by the Nazi regime. In *The Murderers Are among Us* Susanne Wallner comes back and claims her property. Nelly Dreyfuss's exclusion and suffering pervade *Between Yesterday and Tomorrow* through the troubling and explicit presence of her necklace. Sally and Wilhelm Bienert, by contrast, disappear without disturbing those who take over their property. Their use and loss of the car, as well as their related suicide, do not haunt the object, neither its following owner nor, for that matter, the whole storyline of the film, but it haunts the film itself in the form of this enigmatic mistake.

By introducing a different former owner, the same episode is, conspicuously, the only one that shows in a concrete way how the car physically linked its owners to each other. While Dorothea talks to her sister in a phone booth, a Wehrmacht soldier discovers the date "30-1-33" on the windscreen. He introduces himself to Dorothea as her car's former owner. It is Peter from the first episode of the film. In a monologue, during which he bends down to see the inscription, he reflects on what it means to him to "see one's car again," thereby performing the ongoing connection between an object and whoever had owned it before. The date in the windshield represents the idea that such a connection is "inscribed" into the object's material surface, while the whole scene demonstrates how this establishes a bond between the different owners. Since the date January 30, 1933, becomes associated with the military uniform that Peter wears, it acquires an even more ambiguous meaning. That January 30, 1933, was the happiest day of Peter's life, and the fact that he thinks that he "looks great" in his Wehrmacht uniform seems to make him the perfect supporter of the Third Reich. Supposedly, however, he is speaking ironically and actually means the opposite by these remarks. The car, the date in the car, Peter's uniform, and Dorothea's presence all underline that both owners are caught up in the same materially mediated social order. This constellation, together with the erroneous date on the back of the photograph, obliterates what could have linked the Bienerts' fate to that of the other owners of the car. Unwittingly or not, the appearance of Peter highlights the car as an object that connects only its Aryan owners to each other.

At the end of the episode this transformation is completed through the "conscription" of the car itself to military service. Both this anthropomorphization and the visual merging of (ex-)soldier and car at the beginning of the Wehrmacht episode echo aspects of the Nazi Volkswagen propaganda, discussed in the next chapter. At the end of the film's last episode, Josef, a soldier, and Maria, a woman refugee from the East who has a baby girl, drive the car together while Josef enthusiastically declares that they should go to Egypt. The couple conjures up a strong association with Jesus's birth and thereby with the promise of a future built on the basis of Christian and humane values. Once they are driving, however, they revel in a fantasy that calls to mind Germany's recent war of expansion and enthusiasm for the Volkswagen's successes in General Erwin Rommel's campaign in North Africa.

This chapter has observed how in private accounts of the early postwar period, published reflections, and films Germans struggled to make sense of various kinds of stranded objects and the heavy moral burden they inadvertently carried. *In Those Days* marks a deviation from this struggle. With the film's insistence that its central stranded object embodies a message that leads into a morally redeemed future, the film arguably anticipates what the following chapters interpret as the miracle years' myth of redeeming objects. The film intended to present the remnants of an Opel as a redemptive connecting link between humans in order to gloss over the moral abyss that the Nazi past had inserted into the car, even if this entailed tampering with the logic of diegetic chronology in a way that reproduced the very problem the film tried to hide: that the objects of the Nazi past were inextricably entwined with the violent creation of a racial community. In the following years certain categories of objects would become prominent symbols of West Germany's morally redeemed new beginning by glossing over the burden of the past in a similar way. Just as a subliminal presence of the Third Reich's make-believe space crisscrosses the screen of *In Those Days* and interferes with the outspokenly humanist message of the narrative, this presence would continue to haunt the shiny world of West Germany's redeeming miracle objects and eventually end up blurring our own memory of them.

2

Miraculous Objects

The Volkswagen as Imperial Debris

Getting the Joke

How many Jews fit in a Volkswagen?

Five hundred. Two in the front, three in the back, and the rest in the ashtray.

I remember this joke. Someone at school told it to me during my schooldays in Westphalia, West Germany. The memory is both distinct and vague. I suppose it happened in the early 1980s, when I was around ten years old. I had all but forgotten about the joke until a few years ago. It popped into my mind again like a ghostly apparition after I had begun to study the cultural meaning of the Volkswagen during the 1950s in West Germany.[1]

"To study social life one must confront the ghostly aspects of it," writes the sociologist Avery Gordon. "This confrontation requires (or produces) a fundamental change in the way we know and make knowledge." Gordon contends that an uncanny feeling stirred by a surprising encounter in the archive should be taken seriously as important information to be pursued. The feeling contains a raw form of knowledge both about what we study and about ourselves. *Ghostly Matters*, the title of Gordon's book, are ghostly because they emerge insisting that they encapsulate something difficult, painful, and essential to what we study, yet they cannot be captured adequately with any of the conceptual frameworks that we have at our disposal. Confronting the ghostly means starting "with the marginal, with what we normally exclude or banish, or . . . never even notice."[2] *How many Jews fit in a Volkswagen?*

There is a longer historiographical tradition that has taken its clues, just as Gordon does, from anthropological insights about the importance of the marginal and of the odd detail as a starting point for studying hidden cultural structures and codes.[3] Robert Darnton famously illuminated eighteenth-century print culture in Paris by attempting to "get the joke" of "the great cat massacre."[4] In such studies, the importance of starting with the odd detail derives at least in part from the fact that the cultural reality studied is quite far away from the historian's own reality and therefore requires such a method to make sense of it.[5] But where does it lead us if we try to "get" the Volkswagen joke in a similar way? Where does it lead us if we take the joke seriously as an apparently marginal element that possibly holds the key to "knowing" differently and, perhaps better, an aspect of contemporary history that is all too well-known? A contemporary historian who decides to start exploring a culture "where it seems to be most opaque" enters a particularly strange terrain.[6] The most opaque may turn out to be the most familiar; the most familiar may turn out to be the most obscure.

We usually assume that bizarre phenomena either are rare in contemporary European history or can merely be found on the "margins" of society.[7] In that respect, "our" extended present often begins shortly after 1945, closely linked to the establishment of "the West" as the dominant political and geographic framework of thinking. It is no coincidence that scholars of postcolonial history have been attuned to the dimensions of estrangement in contemporary history, to the difficulty of recognizing the familiar when it bears the traces of that which a society does not want to know about itself. Ann Stoler has coined the term "colonial aphasia" to grasp how already widespread insights about colonial and postcolonial history are systematically forgotten again, dissociated from the national histories, and excluded from the prevalent narratives.[8] The Volkswagen's symbolic meaning in contemporary Germany is, as I want to argue, an example of a similar phenomenon.

The Volkswagen started out in 1938 as one of the Third Reich's most heavily propagated people's products. Hitler promised a "people's car" to every family within the racially defined German *Volksgemeinschaft*. The promise was received with overwhelming enthusiasm by the German population. For years, the car was omnipresent in propaganda publications, various forms of public exhibitions, and press coverage. Yet it was never produced in large numbers in the newly built huge factory and city east of Hannover. From 1939 onward the Volkswagen factory produced weapons instead, as well as around fifty thousand Kübelwagen (bucket-seat car), a military version of the Volkswagen delivered to the German Wehrmacht. At the end of the war the production at the Volkswagen factory stopped.[9] When it started again in 1946 and increased after 1948, it was the first time that the car as it was originally conceived became a mass-produced reality populating German streets. Through its enormous success both in Germany and abroad the Volkswagen developed into a symbol of West Germany's successful new beginning: the "economic miracle." Eventually, it became "one of West Germany's few largely uncontested collective symbols."[10]

The latter, post-1945 part of this story constitutes the basis of the established Volkswagen narrative in Germany. This narrative rests on the assumption of a clear-cut cultural dissociation between the Volkswagen's existence before and after 1945. Yet how could the Volkswagen in the 1950s so successfully come to symbolize the new, post-Fascist Germany when it started out being so closely connected to the Germany of the Third Reich? If we limit ourselves to the framework of interpretations developed in recent decades to better understand postwar West German history, it is far from obvious how to address this question. Neither the rise of consumer culture and the various societal efforts to establish a viable democracy nor the persistent reality of Nazi tendencies, *Volksgemeinschaft* mentality, and the dominant culture of German victimhood suffice as interpretive schemes to grapple with the challenges this question raises. Few scholars have brought up the larger historical problem lurking behind this question, namely, the relationship between the political meanings of mass consumption under Nazism and during the early Federal Republic.[11]

As an iconic commodity, the Volkswagen epitomizes this problem in a unique way. To this day, it embodies Germany's successful transformation from the rubble of the Third Reich into a consumer-democratic model of the West. Yet how did this transformation from the Volkswagen's meanings during the Third Reich to its postwar status as political symbol take place? The success of this transformation entailed burning down the bridges that we would need to properly see its genesis. Making a genesis invisible in turn is how "miracles" come into being. Material from the margins is needed to better understand the historical emergence and establishment of Germany's "miracles." Trying to get the Volkswagen joke means confronting ghosts that are lurking behind the trope of miracles that worked to make them invisible.[12]

How many Jews fit in a Volkswagen? Five hundred. In the introduction to the edited collection *The Miracle Years*, historian Hanna Schissler mentions that she and other historians of her age remember a version of the joke from their childhood in 1950s West Germany.[13] In 1983 the playwright and director George Tabori gave the Volkswagen joke a central function in his play *Jubilee* (*Jubiläum*). The play premiered on January 31, 1983, in Bochum on the fiftieth anniversary of Hitler's rise to power, to which its title refers. The main characters are ghosts of dead people who were victims either of the Nazi regime or of postwar National Socialist attitudes.[14] They talk about their suffering in surreal and heartbreaking scenes that expose the ways in which the Nazi past and its afterlife still haunt German society. The Volkswagen joke is uttered three times during the play, haunting and torturing three of those characters.[15] It is a central motif that serves to enact onstage the presence of the Nazi past in West German everyday life. Tabori was born in 1914 into an assimilated Jewish family in Budapest and had lived in Germany since 1968. His father had died in Auschwitz. Did he see and articulate something in public that usually remained unspeakable?

About the time Tabori wrote his play, the American anthropologist Alan Dundes and the German ethnologist Thomas Hauschild collected the Volkswagen joke with other so-called Auschwitz jokes in the city of Mainz and published their findings in an English academic journal.[16] In order to publish a German version of the article four years later, they had to overcome their own reluctance, as well as their tendency to minimize the scope of what they first thought to be marginal but eventually identified as a common linguistic practice in German everyday life. They articulated "serious doubts" about publishing, fearing "the danger of popularizing jokes whose viciousness and cynicism cannot be outdone."[17]

How did the joke work, and what can it tell us about the Volkswagen? The joke connects the car that has become a symbol of postwar West Germany and a group of Jews, the very people whom the Federal Republic's predecessor polity, the Third Reich, had set out to annihilate. *How many Jews fit in a Volkswagen?* Why ask this question? Would Jews fit differently in the car from other people? The first part of the answer is a surprise: the number of Jews is much higher than the spatial dimensions of the Volkswagen would allow. The second part of the answer resolves the surprise first by reducing the number to the usual five and second by transforming the remaining Jews from living human passengers into the dead material of ashes, which fit perfectly in the car's ashtray.

From a psychological perspective, one could say that the joke manages antisemitic aggression and feelings of superiority as well as a German consciousness of the Holocaust—possibly accompanied by feelings of shame. Following psychological and sociological theories of humor, it seems appropriate to assume that the Volkswagen joke, when it "works," releases those impulses and feelings normally repressed due to a social taboo into their expression in the form of laughter.[18] This effect requires the joke to build and dissolve a tension through some form of witty joke-work. In this case, the joke is constructed around the Volkswagen. The Volkswagen joke, like any joke, uses the tension between the normal and the forbidden. It evokes something that was well-known and recognizable and at the same time unspeakable. The joke does not just connect the mass murder of the Holocaust directly to the object of this specific car. More importantly, it expresses the broken relationship between Germans and Jews through the object of the Volkswagen.

Such a reading, however, seems to contradict the existing Volkswagen historiography as well as all those stories about and images of the car that were widespread in West Germany after 1948. We are used to detecting in these images and stories the following messages: The production and export success of the Volkswagen turned Germany into a once-again-accepted and even respected member of the Western world. Its ubiquity on West German streets marked the end of postwar misery and life in the rubble and the beginning of economic recovery. For millions, the car represented the promise of a better life. It epitomized the feelings of freedom and the joy of driving through West Germany's rebuilt cities and idyllic landscapes, of going on a weekend trip with the family, or even of traveling to foreign countries. The Volkswagen imaginary, in short, made Germany a radiant modern society for which the past of the lost war became almost as elusive as a bad dream or as unoffending as a challenge that was successfully overcome.

How do all those well-known meanings of the postwar Volkswagen relate to the past of a Germany remodeled as a racial community? How do they relate to the past of a greater German Reich that was imagined in many ways as "a world without Jews" long before it put this imagination into the practice of mass murder?[19] The postwar success of the Volkswagen represents in both collective memory and historiography the development of West Germany into a Western, consumer-oriented society.[20] But something is missing from this story that has never been seriously addressed.[21]

By using the joke and an advertisement as my entry points to follow the traces of the ghostly in texts and images about the Volkswagen during the 1950s, I encountered a different meaning of the car. This meaning was both obvious and not obvious at the same time and is therefore captured by what the anthropologist Michael Taussig has named a "public secret," defining it as "that which is generally known but cannot be articulated."[22] Although public secrets can emerge in many forms, their characteristics match what scholars of material culture have claimed about the specific ways in which material objects can be invested with a highly affective value deriving both from linguistic and visual discourses about them and from the bodily interactions between people, places, and objects.[23] As Daniel Miller has put it, "Objects are artful; they hide their power and determine the way you feel."[24] In this way, a material object can incorporate conflicting and even contradictory meanings without difficulty. In other words, it lends itself to creating the silent presence of "that which is generally known but *cannot* be articulated" next to and possibly contradicting that which is generally known and *can* be articulated. The Volkswagen, this mass-produced material object, was the vehicle by which millions of postwar Germans imagined driving away from their past. But they were also driving "debris" from the Nazi Empire.[25]

Genealogy of an Advertisement

This Volkswagen advertisement was published in October 1960 in the high-brow cultural magazine *magnum* (fig. 2.1). The text says: "Young people—'critical generation'—chrome-sparkling catchwords and mere promises ceased to impress them long ago. They try to find the meaning behind the things; they ask—and expect clear answers; they calculate—and expect a reasonable, reliable value. Young people (of every age) examine the Volkswagen—and then drive the Volkswagen again and again."[26]

2.1 Volkswagen advertisement, *magnum*, October 1960. Reproduced by permission from Staatsbibliothek Berlin / Volkswagen Aktiengesellschaft.

The photo shows a group of young people inspecting the Volkswagen from different angles. The text presents the young generation as rational consumers who choose the Volkswagen for its reliable value for money. The ad gives the already existing meaning of the Volkswagen as a symbol of West Germany's economic recovery a twist by associating it with an informed approach to things that is necessary for a functioning democracy. It shows the Volkswagen as a central element of the new, economically successful, consumer-oriented, and democratic West German society. Germans' capacity to dispassionately scrutinize and subsequently choose the Volkswagen becomes a proof of the vehicle's good quality. Or is it the other way around? Does the ad promote the quality of the car, or does it promote the quality of the German people?

These young people are different from how people used to be, the text tells us, because "chrome-sparkling catchwords and mere promises *ceased* to impress them *long ago*." This sentence evokes a change of mentality. The "long ago" leaves the earlier mentality in a foggy past, but in order to make sense of the sentence the reader probably had to assume that this past is situated prior to May 1945. The text therefore conveys the idea that choosing the Volkswagen implies choosing a Germany different from the Germany of the Nazi past. The image seems completely situated in the timeless presence of a rational modernity, or does it? This effect suddenly appears in a different light when we juxtapose the photo with a series of other photos stemming from 1938 and from the following years of the Nazi regime's intensive propaganda for the Volkswagen, or KdF-Wagen, as it was also called after the leisure-time organization Kraft durch Freude (Strength through Joy).[27] A group of people surrounding and examining the Volkswagen was a standard motif of the campaign, starting with the presentation of the first small model to Hitler by Ferdinand Porsche in 1938 (fig. 2.2) and continuing with photos of the presentation of test cars all over Germany in subsequent years (fig. 2.3). These are the images of a German people who were developing a "KdF-Wagen psychosis," as the Social Democratic opposition described their reactions in one of its clandestine reports in 1939.[28]

A different interpretation of the advertisement now becomes plausible. The advertisement stages the car as an object that *manifestly* ensures the transformation of a society into a democracy by *latently* calling to mind its totalitarian past. The iconographic effect appears powerful not in spite of this second layer of meaning but precisely because of it. The question is, If the Volkswagen and its success in the early Federal Republic had all been about leaving behind the Nazi past, why would the Volkswagen company in the year 1960 have had any interest in publishing an advertisement whose text, even if implicitly, conjured up precisely this past?

2.2 Adolf Hitler receives a Volkswagen model for his forty-ninth birthday, April 1938. Reproduced by permission from bpk / Heinrich Hoffmann.

2.3 A Volkswagen in front of Sanssouci Palace in Potsdam, September 1938. Reproduced by permission from ANP / Scherl.

The car had obtained a nearly sacrosanct status as a national symbol in the course of the 1950s. This status reached a peak three months after the Allied occupation of West Germany officially ended and the Federal Republic became a sovereign state, when the production of the millionth Volkswagen was celebrated with great pomp at the factory in Wolfsburg on August 5, 1955. Yet in 1957 and in 1959 a curious thing happened. The Volkswagen was attacked in prominent periodicals. Less than a year before the *magnum* ad was published, *Der Spiegel*, the most important political magazine in West Germany, started a full-blown offensive against this most popular German symbol.[29] The magazine's cover story consisted of a long interview with Heinrich Nordhoff, director of the Volkswagen company.[30] Under the headline "Is the VW Outdated?" the interviewers confronted Nordhoff with their conviction that the existing Volkswagen model was decidedly behind the times both technologically and aesthetically. Nordhoff relied on the huge commercial success of the Volkswagen as his main argument against such criticism.

As the interview goes on tediously about technical details, there is a mismatch between this matter-of-fact content of the dialogue and the journalists' aggressive expression of dissatisfaction with the car. But then there is one short moment, appearing out of the blue, when the journalists of *Der Spiegel* articulated a very different form of discontent: "The automobile, as it is now, is, one could say, a homunculus, an artificial creation after a sociopolitical model—we all know after which one."[31] Nordhoff agreed with the claim but pushed it away by saying that "this is not important in this context," that it is "history," that they should stay "with the matter itself."[32]

In this passage, a problem comes to the surface that was obviously difficult to express openly, namely, the perception that, together with the Volkswagen, something of the spirit out of which it was born remained present. The Volkswagen embodies a "homunculus," an artificially created *human being* stemming from the Nazi past. As they tried to argue that this past was still relevant, and problematically so for the present Volkswagen, the journalists broke an unwritten rule. Nordhoff strived to reestablish the threatened division between past and present. The public secret—"we all know after which one"—was not to be voiced.

It had, however, already been written about two years earlier. In 1957 the illustrated magazine *Der Stern* published an article by the writer Alexander Spoerl, also under the title "Is the VW Outdated?"[33] "The Volkswagen," the author stated, "has long ceased to be an automobile. It is a catchword. Yet in everything that has to do with 'Volk,' catchwords are dangerous." Spoerl denounced the untouchable status of the car and formulated his own critique by presenting the Volkswagen as having an unusual "father": "His mother was a very sound construction idea. His father was faith," namely, the "unflinching faith" of the Germans who believed the promises of the Third Reich. The words "unerschütterlicher Glaube" (unflinching faith) are enclosed in quotation marks to identify them as Nazi language.[34]

In order to capture the true Nazi meaning of the car, the author told a joke about a worker in the Volkswagen factory of the Third Reich who stole all the pieces of the KdF-Wagen to put it together at home. When his friend asked him why he still hadn't assembled the car, he answered: "However I screw together the parts, it never becomes a car but always a cannon." These cannons, Spoerl claimed, were in reality Volkswagens, namely, the military Volkswagen-Kübel, which is then represented as an anthropomorphic entity living through recent German history: "The VW-Kübel became the most loyal comrade of the German soldier. Afterward he was the first 'war criminal' to be denazified. He put the sedan back on, the occupying soldiers fell in love with him, Wolfsburg received steel and the license for reconstruction. . . . His cross-country construction and the front-line experience made him well suited for the slightly uneven postwar Germany. That is how he acquired his steadfast reputation."[35]

Spoerl crossed the line of the usually unsaid by identifying the Volkswagen and the enthusiasm attached to it with the Germans' "faith" in the Nazi movement and its promises. He defended his self-proclaimed "sacrilege" by stating that "such reporting is needed in order to get a sober distance not only from the VW's deeds but also from one's own feelings."[36] The remainder of the article was dedicated to a technical critique of those aspects of the car that were indeed "outdated." The article apparently caused a great stir, but the resulting discussion left the political dimension in the realm of the unsaid. One automobile journalist reminded his readers in early 1959 of Spoerl's "strange chains of thought," which had "brought him much trouble."[37]

This is the context in which we must read the cover story interview in *Der Spiegel* in 1959. It is also the context in which we should place the *magnum* advertisement. Together, these three examples make it possible to expose the workings of the public secret. Spoerl and the journalists of *Der Spiegel* expressed an uneasiness about what the Volkswagen silently embodied in the German public sphere and thereby tried to expose the secret and undermine the car's sacred status. In 1960 the public secret was sufficiently exposed to publish an advertisement that both evoked it and at the same time covered it up with another layer of meaning in order to make it disappear again.

In 1962 Volkswagen started its very first big ad campaign in the postwar German press with the German branch of the New York agency Doyle Dane

Bernbach (DDB), which had promoted the VW in the United States from 1959 onward.[38] In view of the emerging discomfort about the Volkswagen at the end of the 1950s, the DDB campaign of the early 1960s can be interpreted as implicitly addressing the criticism that the car would be outdated. The image of a Volkswagen drawn onto an egg accompanied by the slogan "there are forms that cannot be improved" ironically turned the weak spot of a never-changing Volkswagen model into a strength by emphasizing the already iconic quality of the car's design (fig. 2.4). The brilliant irony and humor of the campaign prepared the car's appropriation by a younger generation that had not been exposed to Nazi Volkswagen propaganda. It still shapes the car's image in Germany today. The campaign brought about what the *magnum* ad of 1960 had attempted, namely, lifting the car's perception out of its still present but usually silenced implication in the Nazi project. It thus managed to transform the car's public secret of the 1950s, present for the older generation who had consciously lived through the Nazi years, into a different kind of secret, one that was unknowable for younger Germans who were never consciously exposed to Nazi propaganda, leaving a thread of strange and seemingly marginal traces in the historical archive.

The genealogy of the 1960 *magnum* ad can be taken farther back in time. Articles in *Der Spiegel* occasionally articulated a certain, yet always subliminal, discontent with the continuation and success of the Volkswagen. When reporting on the huge festivities of the production of the millionth Volkswagen in 1955, the magazine deemed the ongoing production of the same Volkswagen model problematic. Hitler's car was a perfect "timeless construction" that created the "vicious circle" of a self-reproducing success that unfairly falsified free market competition.[39] The Nazi legacy of the Volkswagen, however, was present in a different way when the article reproached director Nordhoff for creating an "esprit de corps" (*Korpsgeist*) among Volkswagen drivers and of committing Volkswagen workers to "conspiratorial loyalty" (*verschworene Gefolgschaft*), two expressions closely associated with both militarism and National Socialism.[40]

Two years before that, in January 1953, the Volkswagen played a curious role in an article by Jan Molitor in the weekly magazine *Die Zeit*.[41] Molitor (pseudonym for the journalist Josef-Müller Marein) reacted in a satirical mode to a recent survey by the High Commission for Occupied Germany (HICOG) exposing Germans' continuing support for National Socialism. The pollsters had asked twelve hundred people what they thought about the possibility that a party like the Nazi Party might come to power again. Twenty-six percent said they would not like to see it but would do nothing about it, 9 percent welcomed the possibility without supporting it actively, and 4 percent said they would support it. HICOG concluded that Nazism had begun to constitute a danger again in Germany.[42]

2.4 "There are forms that cannot be improved." Volkswagen advertisement, December 1962. Original in color. Reproduced by permission from Volkswagen Aktiengesellschaft.

Molitor criticized the polling method and called it "KdF," or "Krampf durch Fragen" (cramp through questions), alluding to the Nazi organisation Kraft durch Freude. He claimed to have tested the method himself both with Germans and with HICOG members. One question in this fake survey concerned the interviewees' opinion about the German highway system, or Autobahn. Result: 90 percent approval rate. "*Really* [English in the original]—they love Hitler's highways. Neo-Nazism is gaining ground even among the members of the occupation forces!" Another question asked the interviewees if they would like to buy a Volkswagen for 1,000 Deutsche Mark. This resulted in particularly enthusiastic reactions and brought about "a 98 percent rate of Nazis in West Germany," Germans and members of the occupying forces alike.

Molitor's message seemed to be that if the High Commission asked Germans about a possible new Nazi Party, then it might just as well have asked about their attitudes toward German highways and the Volkswagen. The high approval rate by Germans and occupiers of these modern achievements proves that everyone, regardless of nationality, is a Nazi, which is, of course, absurd. The article echoed widespread postwar German *ressentiment* in reaction to the Allied denazification efforts. In November 1948 German author and theater critic Hanns Braun captured his countrymen's problematic habit of pointing out that the Allies were not morally better than the Germans: "That which they blamed us for was . . . just the thing that 'everyone does'—the normal, quite simply, the usual."[43] Molitor indirectly claimed that if Americans shared Germans' views with respect to highways and the Volkswagen, they also, whether they liked it or not, shared their views with respect to the (not entirely bad) National Socialist past. Therefore, they should stop hypocritically unmasking Germans' Nazi affinities with the help of opinion polls. The author's pride as a citizen of a recovering postwar West Germany was hurt, and he shot back with the weapons of the economic miracle, the Volkswagen at the top of the list.

This rhetorical strategy, however, also shows a conflicting and uneasy consciousness not only about the truth that was discovered by the survey and widely discussed in the press but also about the close relationship between the economic miracle's objects of desire and the recent enthusiasm for the promises and offerings of National Socialism. The obscure logic of the article discloses a more coherent cultural meaning if we assume as general knowledge of the time that the Volkswagen was the epitome of a strong connection between the collective fantasies of pre- and post-1945 Germany. Because of the taboo on publicly expressing sympathy for (some aspects of) Nazism, this knowledge could not be articulated openly but only be uttered in a satirical code that makes it very difficult today to "get the joke."

2.5 "Der VW setzt sich durch" (VW prevails). Volkswagen advertisement, *Quick*, January 1952. Reproduced by permission from Staatsbibliothek Berlin / Volkswagen Aktiengesellschaft.

In January 1952 traces of this knowledge came to the surface in a different way. Volkswagen published a double-page ad in the illustrated magazine *Quick* under the heading "VW Prevails" (fig. 2.5). The ad elaborated on the theme of export with a long text and no fewer than sixteen photographs showing the factory in Wolfsburg and the Volkswagen or the VW van on German streets and in German landscapes, in the North African desert, on the Copacabana beach in Rio de Janeiro, in the virgin forest of the Belgian Congo, and in Egypt. The text declared in a long first sentence that "Two hundred and eighty thousand Volkswagens, all living beings that today conquer the streets in Germany and twenty-eight foreign countries in Europe and overseas, are the result of unwavering faith, tough perseverance, forward-looking pursuit, and tireless diligence" of "men . . . who were determined to achieve the Volkswagen's market success."[44] While these lines conjure up both the postwar recovery's language of work and achievement and the Nazi rhetoric of self-effacing endurance, the text went on to emphasize: "What has made it well-known and popular, what has made it the top-selling and most sought-after German car *is not its origin story* but the harmony of its technical and economical features and its value as a utility vehicle without unnecessary and expensive freight" (emphasis added). Why would Volkswagen advertisers deny explicitly, and thereby bring up, the idea that the (Nazi) origins of the Volkswagen had anything to do with its enormous postwar success? Did they react to a lingering disquiet that some must have felt about this success and its unspoken cultural meanings? Was this disquiet already similar to what Alexander Spoerl expressed five years later when he stated in *Der Stern* that the Volkswagen was a "catchword" that had to do with "Volk" and that such catchwords were in themselves "dangerous"?[45]

All the examples discussed so far bear witness to the presence of meanings associated with the Volkswagen that complicated the car's sleek integration into the evolving discourse about West Germany's rational and friendly renewal away from the Nazi past. Humor was often an important rhetorical device to accommodate this unmanageable presence of the past. In this vein, the first issue of the new magazine *Gute Fahrt*, launched in 1950 to be handed out gratis to owners of a Volkswagen, let the fictitious filling station attendant "Herbert" talk straight with his customers. He is enthusiastic about the prospect of the motorized future, when "every fourth federal citizen will own a Volkswagen." To evoke this future, "Herbert" employed a play on words based on the German word *Führerschein* (driver's license), claiming that in this bright future there will be "ein Volk, ein Reichtum, ein Führerschein" (one people, one affluence, one driver's license), which called to mind the famous Nazi slogan "Ein Volk, ein Reich, ein Führer."[46]

In the same year, a commercial Volkswagen film experimented with a mixture of humor and irony behind which lurked the vague impression that something odd was going on with the Volkswagen. The ten-minute film *Volkswagen-Geschichten* (Volkswagen stories) consists of a series of farcical commercials, some of which self-reflexively comment on the very act of filming the commercial.[47] In one sequence a voice-over explains: "Usually these film directors are quite ingenious people, in spite of their film tricks. But sometimes they overreach and only see a victim in every actor. See for yourself." In the next scene a film director explains to his actor "the role of his life": he has to lie down on the street and wait for a car to race toward him and suddenly stop just three meters in front of him. When the actor asks what would happen if the car's brakes did not work, the director replies: "You do not have to worry. In that case, the scene will certainly be cut out of the film." A third person calms the actor by stating that with *this* car nothing could happen to him because it is a Volkswagen.

The film shows a director willing to sacrifice the life of his actor in order to produce his message about the seemingly harmless Volkswagen. It thereby reveals hidden violence and brutality, as well as the concealment of that reality through propaganda techniques, while its humor transforms this atmosphere of danger into a distancing laughter.[48] The paradoxical message is that one should not trust the advertisement of the Volkswagen but that one can and should trust the quality of the car itself. Five years after the end of National Socialist propaganda, in which the Volkswagen had an important place, the central disorienting element in this film is the technique of advertising, or propaganda, itself.

On the genealogical journey back in time to disclose the presence of the public secret and the occasional expression of discomfort related to it we have nearly reached the endpoint. Before 1950 only one more example of uneasiness about how the car's National Socialist past also afflicted its present is discernible. In June 1948, when the car became available for West German customers for the first time, *Der Spiegel* picked on the factory's choice of continuing to produce the old model. The article author, however, explicitly identified the factory rather than the model itself with its beginnings as a Nazi project: "The Wolfsburg Volkswagen factory, the gigantic torso of the National Socialist economic hubris, has decided to follow the Porsche tradition. . . . It is Porsche's 1936 [Volkswagen] sedan that slides from the assembly line. In this way [the millions of Reichsmark previously invested in] the most powerful small car in the world have at least paid off."[49] The text is shaped by a difficult-to-untangle mixture of sober reporting, respect for the car's growing success (associated here with Porsche instead of Hitler), and sarcastic mockery about the whole enterprise's original political background. The article also refers to the factory's Nazi legacy of "DAF socialism" and "KdF cockiness" as a huge burden on the whole undertaking: "Everything is too big. . . . [T]he beauty of labor seems as if piled up with a dredger."[50] Presenting this burden as a purely economic one, these comments nevertheless reminded readers of the two Nazi organizations that had previously been responsible for the Volkswagen project and its propaganda: the Deutsche Arbeitsfront (German Labor Front, DAF), responsible for the program Beauty of Labor and its subdivision, Strength through Joy (KdF), which had given the car its Nazi name.

"What has made it well-known and popular, what has made it the top-selling and most sought-after German car is not its origin story" was the statement of the 1952 Volkswagen ad. The Volkswagen's origin story, which this ad tried to push away, consisted above all of the massive Nazi campaign for the Volkswagen, which continued even during the war. According to the historian Paul Kluke, writing in 1960, this Nazi Volkswagen propaganda had a "magic effect" and had "nearly" turned the Volkswagen into a "symbol of National Socialist propaganda technique" and "of the blind confidence of all German social classes."[51] This campaign had produced the "chrome-sparkling catchwords" that resonated so deeply into the postwar era that the postwar "critical generation" had to be declared immune to them in the well-crafted *magnum* advertisement that was published in the same year as Kluke's analysis.

Driving the Volkswagen through Space and Time

What were the narratives, metaphors, and images used in the postwar period that brought about the previously discussed expressions of discomfort? And what can those cultural scripts tell us about the hidden meanings of the Volkswagen that eventually transformed into ghostly apparitions? When Alexander Spoerl anthropomorphized the Volkswagen in 1957 to criticize its problematic legacy he took up an existing narrative. As early as November 1949 the car magazine *Motor-Rundschau* presented the vicissitudes of the Volkswagen since 1938 as the story of a young man named "Vinzenz" who should not be accused "of the bad manners of his past" if today he is "changed from the inside and the outside." Before the war he "bilked people out of their savings and made an enormous propaganda. During the war he became a soldier, proved himself a loyal comrade, and served in France, Russia, and Africa. Neither the cold in the East nor the heat in the desert sand harmed his primordially healthy constitution. After the war he ran around in a miserable state, the prototype of German postwar poverty. . . . Now, after the currency reform, the great miracle, he appears spick-and-span, with really good manners—therefore, a young man from a good family."[52]

The "bad manners" of the past exclusively regard the car's prewar existence and refer to the Volkswagen saving scheme during the Third Reich. In 1949 a court case began that had been initiated by a group of Volkswagen savers (*Volkswagensparer*) who had given money to the German Labor Front in order to later receive a Volkswagen for less than 1,000 Deutsche Mark. After the war these savers went to court, demanding that they receive the car under the terms they had been promised by the Third Reich.[53] The "bad manners" of the car's past are therefore not meant to be actions directed at persecuted victims of the regime or at populations of occupied territories but rather at those members of the former *Volksgemeinschaft* who had believed the Nazis' promises about a good postwar life. By conflating the car with the German soldier, the text claims that both have revealed their true, morally untainted, and resilient constitution during their war experiences. They suffered under the postwar occupation and then, after the "miraculous" currency reform, were transformed from formerly loyal and resilient soldiers into respected civilians. The anthropomorphized Volkswagen's name—Vinzenz—is derived from the Latin word for "winning."

The identification of the car, the German man, and the German soldier through the change of times implied a material continuity that included as one and the same car the Wehrmacht's Volkswagen, the so-called Kübelwagen, which had indeed "served in France, Russia, and Africa." The Kübel enabled the idea of a continuous physical existence of *the* Volkswagen across the 1945 divide. This conflation of Volkswagen and Kübelwagen was a common postwar theme that blatantly counteracts the idea of the Volkswagen as the symbol of a new beginning by harking back to a heroic image of the Nazi war and its conquering of geographic space. *Der Spiegel* resorted to a similar interpretive framework in 1950. Accompanied by photographs of the military Volkswagen's test rides, the article claimed that "these . . . Kübelwagens . . . proved themselves as the most magnificent military car that the world of mobile armament knew." It "did not turn too hot in Rommel's desert nor too cold in the half Arctic of Northern Norway and the Russian winter battles."[54]

The postwar habit of describing the Volkswagen Kübel as a "loyal comrade," of insisting that it was essentially the same car as the civilian Volkswagen, and of conflating it with the German soldier stemmed, in fact, directly from the Nazi war campaign for the Volkswagen. The military version was introduced as a by-product of the original KdF-Wagen. During the first year and a half after the beginning of the war, *Arbeitertum*, the central organ of the German Labor Front, concentrated on repeating its promises about the KdF-Wagen's delivery after the war.[55] From May 1941 onward the name KdF-Wagen was also used for the military Kübelwagen and its successful services for the German Africa Corps. An article stated that the KdF-Wagen was "on the road to victory." The text was accompanied by photos of the Kübelwagen in the desert, on a palm-fringed street, and next to a Bedouin with his camel. The two vehicles, the military and the civilian automobile, were merging into one.[56]

In March 1942 an article in *Arbeitertum* asserted that the "Volkswagen . . . stands his ground" in the field and "has exceeded all expectations" (fig. 2.6). While presenting the Volkswagen and the German soldier as "growing together," the text emphasized the car's physical reliability on any battlefront of the rapidly expanding Third Reich. "Quickly advancing to the enemy, versatile in combat," the Volkswagen was even more resilient than the German soldier. The anthropomorphized car conquered "the wide snow fields of Russia" and "the stony deserts of destroyed Soviet cities," and resisted "North Africa's glittering sun."[57] The article quoted from letters to the factory in which soldiers described their experiences and expressed their ardent desire to buy a Volkswagen after the German victory. Photographs showed soldiers in their Kübels in a landscape with a windmill and driving in muddy and bumpy terrain. One picture presented the civilian Volkswagen surrounded by leisurely dressed Germans in an idyllic mountain lake scenery: the "image of the future that every saver for a Volkswagen has in front of his eyes," while "the Volkswagen or, more precisely, the KdF-Wagen is 'conscripted to military service.'"[58]

In the postwar press a close association between the Volkswagen or the Volkswagen Kübel and a positive memory of the war popped up in different ways, often connected to the theme of traveling. In July 1951 the magazine *Der Stern* published an article about the journey of a reporter and his crew to Italy. These former Wehrmacht soldiers socialized with Italians and American GIs and visited both soldiers' and partisans' graves. One of the photos shows an Italian woman in a Kübelwagen next to several motor scooters. The woman reportedly referred to the Kübel as "a memory of your countrymen." The text also mentions that this "Volkswagen" enabled the German crew to "drive through Naples on a 'piece of Heimat (homeland).'"[59] In January 1951 *Quick* reported on the Africa journey that Hermann Schultze-Dewitz, Rommel's former colonel, undertook in his function as a representative of the German War Graves Commission. A photo shows him dressed in a civilian but uniform-like outfit standing next to the back end of a Volkswagen that carried the sign "German War Graves Commission" in German, Arabic, English, and French. Schultze-Dewitz emphasized that with his photo of Field Marshal Rommel he could "count on getting help everywhere," because the memory of the "Desert Fox" was very much alive among the Arabs. He added, "Besides, we are always here with our car." The journalist concluded his report by stating that with his remarks Schultze-Dewitz had given him "a nice feeling of security."[60]

Alon Confino has drawn attention to how West Germans' early postwar travels to foreign countries were often closely linked to German soldiers' war experiences in those countries.[61] These examples confirm this observation and give an idea of how smoothly the Volkswagen fit into an image of World War II as a good German war that included its efforts at imperialist geographic expansion. In a very specific way, the car—in either its civilian or its military version—was presented as giving German visitors abroad a cozy feeling of "security" by transporting them back home and back in time, transcending both space and time. This effect arguably ensued from a status of this material object as being situated somewhere outside or above the specific historical time and geographic space of postwar West Germany.

In a similar vein, the 1949 promotional film *"Kleiner Wagen . . . große Liebe": Ein Film für Autofreunde* (*Small Car . . . Big Love: A Film for Car Friends*) conveyed the joy and excitement of driving the Volkswagen as a form of conquering space and time.[62] The last minutes show a young couple driving for the first time in their Volkswagen through an idyllic German scenery of mountains, rivers, and fields, castles and old cities. In the final scene the couple and a hitchhiker savor the speed and wish they could drive around the world, singing cheerfully: "If the country passes by like in a fleeting dream, we feel divinely elevated above space and time."

Die Front bestätigt es:

DER *Volkswagen* HAT ALLE ERWARTUNGEN ÜBERTROFFEN

Aufnahme: von Stevenhagen (1), PK.-Aufnahmen: Bildberichter Baer, (P. Bildberichter Mengendorf (PBZ.) (

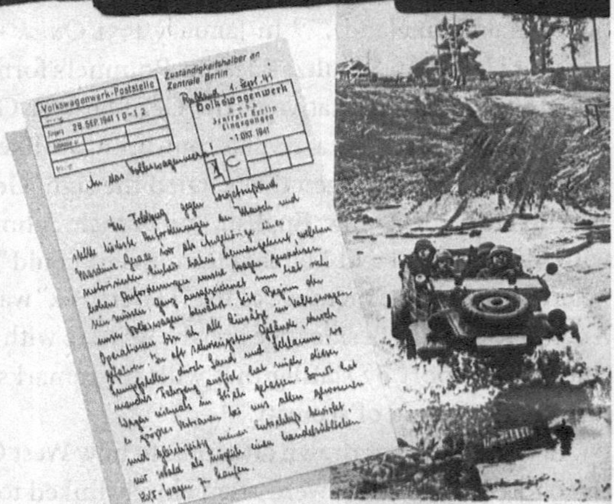

Unter der gleißenden Sonne Nordafrikas, im grundlosen gelben Sand der Wüste, unbeschadet von Hitze und Sandstürmen, flink im Vorstoß auf den Feind und wendig im Kampf, bewährt sich der Volkswagen. Die weiten Schneefelder Rußlands, steinige Wüsteneien zerstörter Sowjetstädte, den uferlosen Morast verschlammter Wege im Frühjahr und Herbst überwindet der Volkswagen, „unser *Volkswagen*". So denken stolz die Sparer überall im Deutschen Reich, wenn er in den PK-Berichten und im Rundfunk erwähnt wird oder die Soldaten in Feldpostbriefen von ihm berichten. „*Der Wagen, der dies alles leistet, der so unglaublich sich bewährt, wird mit allen diesen Vorzügen einmal mir gehören*", das ist die Freude jedes einzelnen.

Gewiß, es war bei Ausbruch des Krieges nicht leicht, sich umzustellen von einer Vorfreude auf so nahe Sicht — im Frühjahr 1940 sollte ja mit der Lieferung des Volkswagens begonnen werden — auf eine lange Wartezeit bis zum Ziel der Wünsche: der Fahrt im eigenen Wagen. Der Krieg überraschte eben auch hier wie auf so vielen Gebieten die absolut friedensmäßige Produktion, die friedlichen Hoffnungen und Gedanken der Volkswagensparer.

Man sah ohne weiteres ein, daß eine Umstellung von der Friedens- auf die Kriegsproduktion im Volkswagenwerk genau wie auf allen anderen Gebieten stattfinden mußte. Schließlich nähten ja auch die Schneiderateliers der Bekleidungsindustrie statt der Kleider und Anzüge Uniformen, und so war es nur folgerichtig, daß statt des Volkswagens für Privatzwecke nun erst einmal der kleine, leichte Geländewagen der gleichen Bauart als kriegswichtiges Fahrzeug hergestellt wurde. Schließlich weiß man ja ganz gewiß, daß diese Wartezeit über den Krieg hinweg nur ein Aufsparen der Hoffnung für die Zeit bedeutet, in der es wieder möglich ist, von der kriegsmäßigen auf die friedensmäßige Produktion zurückzukehren.

Der brave „Kamerad Volkswagen" tut im Kriege jetzt schon das Seinige. „*Beim Ausrücken aus Deutschland bekam ich einen Volkswagen*", schreibt einer aus Afrika. „*Diesen fahre ich bereits einige tausend Kilometer bei den denkbar ungünstigsten Verhältnissen und tollen Geländefahrten. Trotz allen Strapazen hatte ich bis jetzt noch keine Panne.*" Ist es bei dieser Glanzleistung ein Wunder, daß er sich hinsetzt und der KdF.-Dienststelle daheim seinen Entschluß mitteilt, sich nach der gesunden Rückkehr aus Afrika einen Volkswagen anzuschaffen?

Die Sicherheit des braven Wagens und seine Leichtigkeit (die ihm den Namen „*Wüstenfloh*" bei den Soldaten eingetragen hat), haben schon so manchem das Leben gerettet. Denn fünf Mann genügen ja, um den Wagen hochzuheben und an ihm bequem die notwendigen Reparaturen durchzuführen. „*Was ein Volkswagen hier zu leisten hat, kann sich in Deutschland bestimmt niemand vorstellen — und der Volkswagen hat alle Erwartungen übertroffen*", schreibt ein Afrikakämpfer an das Volkswagenwerk und bittet gleich mitten im Kriege darum,

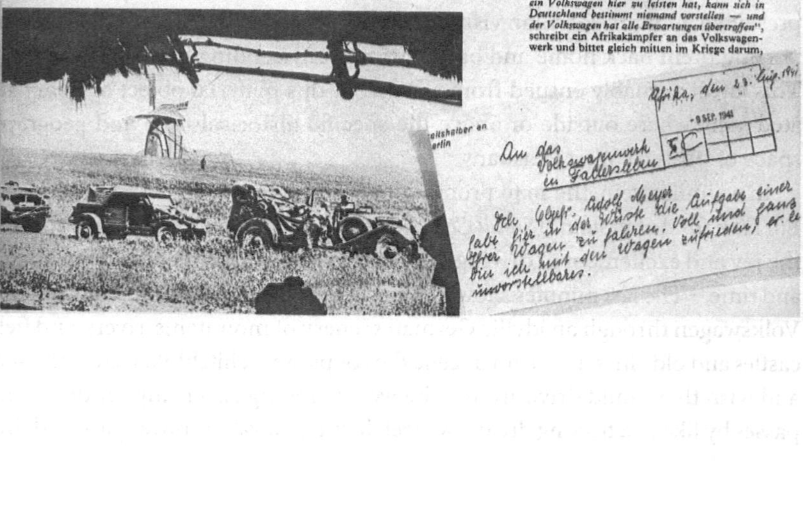

eine Sparkarte auf einen Volkswagen für ihn anzulegen. Was gäbe es für einen Soldaten, der während des ganzen Krieges mit seinem kleinen wendigen Wagen verwachsen ist, für eine schönere Vorstellung, als auch in Friedenszeiten in der Heimat so mit diesem Wagen verbunden zu bleiben, sich auch dort so schnell, sicher und unbeschadet auf schlechten Wegen, in Frost und Hitze fortbewegen zu können. *Denn gegen Frost und Hitze ist der Volkswagen gleichermaßen unempfindlich durch seinen luftgekühlten Motor.* Es gibt im heißen Afrika kein Kühlwasser, das in unbotmäßige Wallungen gerät und auch im kalten Osten keines, das gefriert und den Wagen vielleicht mitten im Kampf zum Stillstand verurteilt. *„Ja, auch im Osten steht er seinen Mann!“* So kann man getrost sagen bei diesem Wagen, der für den Soldaten ein richtiger Kriegskamerad geworden ist. Es gibt kaum eine Geländeschwierigkeit oder Unbill des Winters, die er nicht überwinden müßte und auch überwindet.

„Meine persönlichen Erfahrungen mit dem Wagen sind ziemlich die umfassendsten, die man machen kann“, schreibt einer der Kämpfer im Osten. *„Hier spricht man von Wegen und meint damit Wagenspuren durch knietiefen Staub und über Löcher und Höcker hinweg. Hier spricht man von Straßen und findet Schlaglöcher in solcher Lage, daß es unmöglich ist, sie zu umgehen. Das sind schwere Anforderungen hier an Fahrer und Fahrzeug. Ich habe so oft den Bruch der Achsen oder des Gestänges erwartet, wenn ich selbst zermürbt wurde von den harten Schlägen auf die Räder. Der kleine wendige Wagen aber ertrug sie widerstandsfähig wie ein schwerer Wagen.“*

Bei solchen Erfahrungen im schweren Gelände schlägt dem Soldaten das Herz nicht nur in militärischer Hinsicht höher. So mancher, der, ehe er den Soldatenrock anzog, Bauer oder Straßenarbeiter war, freut sich, daß er später einmal mit dem braven Wagen Geländeschwierigkeiten in unbebauten Gegenden der Heimat ebenso schnell und sicher wird befahren können. Der hohe Radstand, der hier so manchen grundlosen Sowjetmorast überwinden ließ, wird auch in der Heimat bei aufgeweichten Wegen und schlechtem Wetter oder auch im dicken Schnee des Winters ihm eine Hilfe sein.

Das aber, was die Soldaten an der Front mit dem Volkswagen erleben, hören auch die Sparer in der Heimat, und sie wissen es auch aus eigener Überlegung. Wenn sie auch schon vor dem Kriege *„ihren“* Volkswagen als vollausgereiftes Modell erwartet haben, so wissen sie jetzt, daß nach solcher unvorstellbaren Bewährung ihnen im Frieden ein Wagen in die Hand gegeben wird, der das Endergebnis aller nur möglichen Erfahrungen und Verbesserungen ist, die überhaupt einem Wagen mitgegeben werden können, und an dessen Verbesserung nicht nur die *Forschungsstätte im Volkswagenwerk*, sondern auch alle die Soldaten an der Front mitgeschafft haben.

Niemand hat das wohl mit so überzeugender Zuversicht und Siegesgewißheit ausgesprochen wie jener Oberleutnant, dessen Brief wir auf dieser Seite im Original wiedergeben, der aus der Kriegsgefangenschaft in Kanada an seine heimatliche Sparkasse den Auftrag zur Bestellung eines Volkswagens gibt. *„Die Lieferung des Wagens soll ab Werk erfolgen, wo ich ihn selbst nach meiner Rückkehr abhole.“* Kann man in wenigen Worten und sozusagen zwischen den Zeilen mehr aussprechen als in diesem Satz? Darin liegt jenes Bild beschlossen, das jeder Volkswagensparer für die Zukunft vor Augen sieht: ein eigener Volkswagen und eine Fahrt durch Berge, Sonne und Seen der schönen deutschen Heimat. Vorerst aber ist auch der Volkswagen, genauer gesagt: der KdF.-Wagen, „zum Heeresdienst einberufen“.

Dr. Haver

2.6 The Volkswagen "has exceeded all expectations." Article in *Arbeitertum*, March 1942.

In these scenes the film links the experience of driving the Volkswagen through the German landscape and cityscape to visions of an ideal Germany of social harmony and primordial culture without any trace of war destruction. Driving lifts the viewer above the concrete German postwar reality of a constricted and deformed national space. Similarly, the author of the illustrated book *Kleiner Wagen auf großer Fahrt* (Small car on a big journey), published in 1949, raves about his experience of finally driving the Volkswagen for the first time through the German landscape. He utters in astonishment: "It is not deformed and disfigured anymore, but it is familiar again—the face of the homeland [*Heimat*]."[63]

Nine years earlier, in December 1940, a cover article in *Arbeitertum* referred to the Nazi promise that after the war "every German worker will own his Volkswagen and drive on German highways from Klagenfurt to Narvik."[64] As a result, "the German worker will not have to deal with time and space—due to his social status he will own the world!"[65] This propaganda envisioned the postwar experience of owning and driving a Volkswagen as a form of conquering time and space. It transformed a harmless fascination with motorized mobility into an experience that was inextricably connected to the project and prospect of an expanded Nazi Empire. The promise that the Volkswagen would be available for every German worker was closely intertwined with the promise of a new European order under German leadership, including greater welfare within the racially defined *Volk*. The car functioned as a medium for imagining this future world in a concrete way: The German worker would drive his Volkswagen on the German Autobahn through the German Reich, from Klagenfurt in former Austria to Narvik in Norway. Driving the car meant belonging to the German people, being part of the "people's body," and dominating the world.[66]

What happened to this connection between the "people's body" and the "people's car" after the war? The future as it was envisioned by the Nazis clearly had not materialized. The postwar mass production of the civilian Volkswagen was in itself a new phenomenon and thereby also a reminder of the failure of Nazi politics and an indicator of the Federal Republic's success. The 1950s, however, lacked innovative Volkswagen advertising that could have clearly separated the meaning of the car from its Nazi legacy. There was nearly no Volkswagen advertising in the German press until the end of the decade. According to Michael Kriegeskorte, this absence was due to the fact that the car started its postwar career with an "image advantage that nearly placed it outside the competition."[67] The image of the car that already existed, however, was one that had been produced by the Nazi propaganda campaign.

The most important advertising activity of the Volkswagen company during the decade after 1949 consisted of producing and disseminating promotional films. Between 1949 and 1961 the company produced at least twenty-one of these films.[68] Through the middle of the decade, most of them used an audiovisual language that continued the aesthetics of the Weimar and the Nazi *Kulturfilme*.[69] The 1950 film *Amor am Steuer* (Cupid at the Wheel), for instance, reproduced both aesthetically and in terms of content many elements of the 1939–40 National Socialist film *Karlsbader Reise* (Karlsbader Journey), which had promoted the KdF-Wagen.[70] The Nazi film told the story of a couple's KdF-Wagen journey from Weimar to Karlsbad in the tracks of Johann Wolfgang von Goethe. In the 1950 film a young couple traveled in their Volkswagen convertible through Northern Germany following in the footsteps of the composer Carl Maria von Weber. At the heart of both films was the experience and visual spectacle of driving the car through German landscapes and cityscapes. While the Nazi film focused on a region recently incorporated into the Reich through the Munich Agreement and thereby linked the car to the project of an expanding empire, the postwar version's story was situated in the north of the Federal Republic. The geography changed, while the visual spectacle and way of narrating remained similar.

If the Nazi educational films "continued, perfected and infused" the avant-garde cinema of the 1920s "with new ideological meanings," then the early Volkswagen films transported many elements of this aesthetic into the postwar era.[71] What do these aesthetic similarities across the 1945 divide tell us about the postwar meanings of the Volkswagen? The most important feature-length postwar Volkswagen film, *Aus eigener Kraft* (literal translation: From one's own strength), from 1954, adopted the symphonic and rhythmic elements of Walter Ruttmann's avant-garde classic *Berlin: Die Sinfonie der Grosstadt* (*Berlin: Symphony of a Great City*) from 1927.[72] During the Third Reich, these elements were incorporated by Ruttmann and others into propaganda that produced a cinematic experience of what Jeffrey Herf has called "reactionary modernism," in which technology manifests the will of the superior people and has a metaphysical basis similar to nature. The Nazis believed they "had demonstrated that technology was not dead matter but a soulful cultural achievement that organically grew from the Volk."[73] At the automobile exhibition in 1939, whose centerpiece was the first public presentation of the Volkswagen, Goebbels explained that National Socialism understood how to "take the soulless framework of technology and fill it with the rhythm and hot impulse of our time."[74] Film was a particularly well-suited medium to capture the "synthesis of modern technical functionalism and organicist *Volksgemeinschaft*."[75]

The 1954 *Aus eigener Kraft* is a symphonic hour-long film in Agfacolor that stages city life, factory buildings, assembly line production, and industrious workers as a natural, flowing process of matter and bodies that magically engenders this hugely successful car "from" the people's "own strength." The film incorporates the city of Wolfsburg, still partly under construction, into this organic image of societal, technological, and natural wholeness built on the theme of dynamic movement. *Aus eigener Kraft* starts with traffic scenes in a big city, and among the vehicles are many, many Volkswagens. Accompanied by light and cheerful orchestral music, a male narrator's voice compares the movement of vehicles, the power of engines, and the human mastery of the machine to the primal forces of life. This movement, he claims, is based on a well-founded trust in the people "who built all this."

The film presents the Volkswagen factory as a "gigantic organism" and celebrates its success as a tale of West Germany's regained strength emerging from the power of its people and its technology. The Volkswagen is the product of a heroic achievement brought about by impersonal and powerful forces that orchestrate the interaction of people, machines, and space through organic motion. These forces operate in a timeless present without either a past or a future, while their outcome visibly consists of ever more motorization and ever more collective prosperity. In this perpetual present, the future is already there and can be observed in its endless self-creation, which is based on the natural principles of movement and power rooted in time immemorial.

The film presents a tale of self-creation out of nothing, "an example of the German reconstruction," as a preliminary text on-screen claims "the work of 20,000 people who have helped themselves." At the end of the film the director, Heinrich Nordhoff, speaks to his workers, claiming that "we have started from nothing to build this factory. Here . . . reconstruction happened with a clear plan, production was launched without the background of a tradition, without guarantee of success, solely trusting the superior construction of our car and our own capability. Now these gigantic halls stand again, belonging to the biggest and most beautiful industrial sites in Europe and the world."

One notes the contradiction of Nordhoff's claim that there was no tradition for the Volkswagen even as the factory halls now "stand again." A "clear plan" for mass-producing the Volkswagen had in fact been around since 1938.[76] The Nazi past of the Volkswagen is thus both inadvertently included in and at the same time written out of the story. This method effectively evokes a nebulously abstract presence that creates a mythical Volkswagen story that is dissociated both from its Nazi past and from its own concrete postwar genesis—a narrative accentuation of the preceding audiovisual spectacle.

This *dissociation*, however, cannot be separated from a simultaneous but silent *association* with some of the former Nazi project's ideals. As Nordhoff asserts that "the factory is the convincing proof that unity makes strong," the film shows the factory's monumental neoclassicist walls, constructed as the architectural manifestation of the Third Reich's most ambitious economic project. The description of the Volkswagen workers as "happy people who are self-assured and hopeful" is accompanied by shots of a stone relief showing a mother, a child, and a worker with a sturdy arm next to a gearwheel, an example of the heroic realism of Nazi art.[77] While the camera slowly moves up the facade Nordhoff summarizes: "That's how this factory and this car became the example of German diligence and German proficiency to the whole world."

At the end of the film, the Volkswagen operation is thus explicitly portrayed as representing the whole of German society. This identification rests on two maneuvers. On the explicit level, the Volkswagen appears as a phenomenon floating in the timeless space of an ideal modernity. On the implicit level, the film cinematically stages the transfiguration of the car's industrial production into a constitutive element of an organicist model of society, thereby continuing the connection of the Volkswagen to National Socialist fantasies of social harmony, racial exclusivity, and German superiority. It is the combination of both maneuvers, of the outspoken and the silent, that generates the mythical character of this miracle story about the people's and the car's regeneration from their own strength.[78]

The theme of export plays an important role in the film in a manner that echoes the Nazi campaign for the Kübelwagen. Due to its air-cooling system, the narrator explains, the car "is more independent and more versatile than we are ourselves," while images of the car crossing the desert and plowing through the snow appear on the screen. A sequence of animated scenes with stereotypical images of foreign countries illustrates the journey of a car "destined for the whole world" and driving "along the Andes, under Egypt's sun, to Java's virgin forests, and through the skyscrapers of the new world." As the narrator describes how "car and factory have grown into the world to be encountered everywhere, omnipresent," a world map appears with the shapes of various countries in Europe, North and South America, and Africa. All of them are illuminated by rays of light, while eastern Europe, the Soviet Union, China, and India remain in the dark. The rays originate from the spot in West Germany where the Volkswagen factory is situated (fig. 2.7).

This visualization of the Volkswagen export corresponds with a Cold War imagination of the Western Hemisphere as a community of countries connected by the free exchange of commodities. Yet the animated sequences also show a world benefiting from the export of the Volkswagen as a special form of German expansion, sending cars across the globe that were engendered by an organic

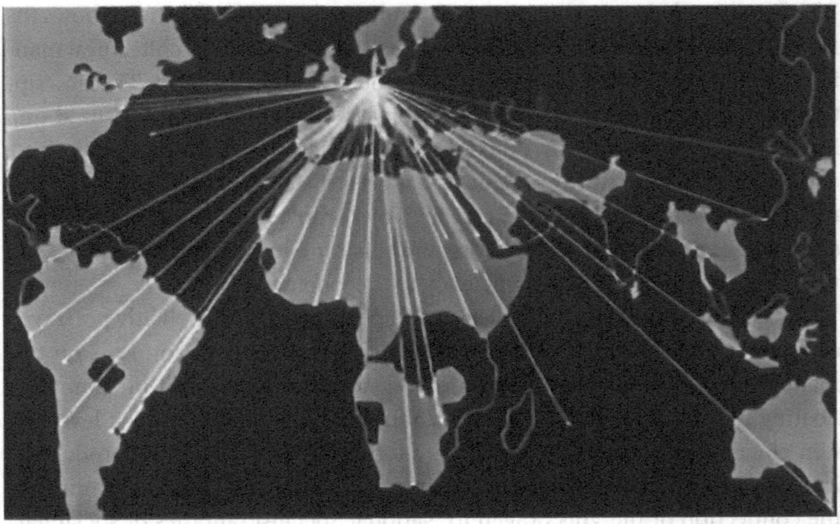

2.7 Screenshot from *Aus eigener Kraft* (1954): car and factory "have grown into the world." Original in color. Reproduced by permission from Volkswagen Aktiengesellschaft.

unity of factory, people, and car. The theme of the car that conquers the world is resumed again at the end of the film. As the last steps of the production process are shown and we finally see the finished car rolling off the assembly line and onto the streets, the narrator captures the moment with some pathos, accompanied by the crescendo of the symphonic music: "Here, finally, he can touch the earth. The earth has him, and he has the earth, the whole wide earth, for himself." With triumphant music, the camera moves past seemingly endless rows of Volkswagens parked in front of the factory building.

The spectacle of mass production's seriality and monotony comes across as timeless and without a past, yet it reverts to an aesthetic that had only very recently been used for the National Socialist message of a "people's body" able to conquer and control the world by means of its organic bond with matter and technology.[79] Earlier postwar Volkswagen films had staged how the car conquered the globe in a similar way. The ending of the 1949 film *Sinfonie eines Autos* (Symphony of a Car) shows Volkswagens rolling out of the factory followed by rows of VWs on a train and then a shot from a highway bridge of a long line of VWs on the Autobahn. In the last—animated—sequence, the viewer sees a globe from afar with Germany roughly in the middle of both screen and globe, while an endless number of Volkswagen cars stream out of Germany toward the viewer and into outer space (fig. 2.8).[80]

2.8 Two screenshots from *Sinfonie eines Autos* (1949): rows of Volkswagens on the Autobahn and Volkswagens streaming into outer space. Reproduced by permission from Volkswagen Aktiengesellschaft.

The theme of the car's export also dominated the scarce Volkswagen advertising activities of the decade. At the end of each year, ads informed readers about the previous twelve months' production and export numbers.[81] In January 1951 an ad with the tagline "Factory and car, the big success!" showed a white globe covered by a network of thin lines on which small Volkswagens drive around. At the top of the globe the silhouette of the Volkswagen factory comes into view.[82] While this early ad is similar to how the animated scenes in *Aus eigener Kraft* represented physical expansion across the globe, other examples of this series, which was continued until at least 1964, used a more abstract background that loosely evoked expansion in space.

The big celebrations organized in 1955 on the occasion of the millionth Volkswagen may have been the climax of this obsession with the car's export during West Germany's economic miracle. Volkswagen had invited twelve hundred journalists and representatives of the automobile industry in "all Western countries" for this three-day-long spectacle. More than one hundred thousand people filled the factory's stadium and witnessed a gigantic "peoples festival."[83] International brass bands and dancers from the UK, Sweden, Switzerland, the Netherlands, France, South Africa, and several South American countries marched into the stadium in a mixture of carnival and Olympic Games. "The world pays tribute to the Volkswagen" was the festival's central message.[84]

Given that the Third Reich was notorious for its excess of public rituals and mass events, the Federal Republic of Germany had good reason to act cautiously when it came to public presentations of itself. The excessive nature of this 1955 Volkswagen celebration, taking place in the same year that West Germany gained its status as a sovereign state, therefore exemplifies a symbolic transfer from the political to the economic sphere, from "Germany" to "the Volkswagen."[85] Such a transfer rested on the dual character of the Volkswagen as, on the one hand, a technical object that was situated outside the realm of history and politics and, on the other, a symbolic and material remnant from National Socialist fantasies of organic wholeness, omnipotence, and geographic expansion. It rested, in other words, on the Volkswagen as a polysemic object extending across the deep rupture in German history.

The Myth of the Miracle Car

> [Lizzy] had a keen sense of what held Hans here. . . . "[The factory] lies there above the water," she said, "and you cannot get away from it. *It has a power you have to comply with. Nothing can be changed about that. I think, because you feel that and because you cannot do anything against this order, that is why you can live and why it is good to live here and nowhere else.*"[86]

Lizzy is the British-born wife of the factory policeman Johann Schuckert in Horst Mönnich's novel *Die Autostadt*, published in 1951. Although Lizzy used to be a spoiled rich girl who embraced superficial consumer pleasures, life in the city changes her, and she understands that Wolfsburg and its factory are all about a social order that can only be apprehended through the mysterious interconnection between the people and the material world.

Mönnich's novel is arguably the most sophisticated attempt of the postwar period to renarrate the story of the Volkswagen and to escort the car, the factory, and the city of Wolfsburg from their Nazi past into the present. Mönnich, born in 1918 in Brandenburg, was a soldier during the war and had begun to experience the attraction of the Nazi movement as an adolescent orphan. In 1968 Mönnich summarized the 1945 moment of disillusionment with the question he pursued from then onward: "Where, if this, in which we had wrongly believed, had never been Germany—then where had Germany been?"[87] The answer given by the novel *Die Autostadt* was that the real Germany had been contained and had survived in the form of the Volkswagen and in the form of the city and factory that produced it.

The novel sold at least 110,000 copies and became so successful that it allowed Mönnich to build a career as a writer.[88] He had spent several months driving through the young Federal Republic in his Volkswagen and lived near the Volkswagen factory for a while so that he could interview people and collect material for the novel.[89] As a result, he applied a modernist style to convey the experiences, perceptions, and thoughts of the various people populating the novel. In 1951 Heinrich Nordhoff embraced the book in his foreword to the first edition as uncovering "truths" that "lie deeper than the visible, that touch the true core of events."[90]

Lizzy's words about the irresistible attraction of the city and the factory reflect much of how the novel as a whole depicts the meaning of the Autostadt Wolfsburg (formerly known as the Stadt des KdF-Wagen) after the war. Large parts of the novel convey a mystic link between the people, the place, the factory, and the car through organic metaphors: the masses pour into the factory like a "swelling vein," the organization of the city is compared to a human organism, the factory is "a being that has an autonomous life," the assembly line resembles a "stream." The people working there are all part of this miraculous organic structure that creates another living being: the Volkswagen. At the end of the assembly line the workers feed the car with gas just as a mother feeds her newborn baby with milk, inserting "a hose into the mouth of the creature" and letting "it drink the first food, some gulps of the liquid it will drink from now on."[91]

The text orchestrates the experiences of the German population during the Third Reich, the war, and its aftermath through the prism of the Volkswagen, the factory, and the city and thereby produces a complex and captivating postwar Volkswagen myth. The first quarter of the text is set in an unspecified postwar moment in which the factory is working and the inhabitants move from the provisional barracks into real houses. The city in reconstruction is filled by Germans from all parts of the former Reich, many of them refugees from the East. The rebuilt factory produces the postwar Volkswagen for the citizens of the Federal Republic and foreign admirers of the vehicle. Do we, as a consequence, also have to presume that the constellation of car, factory, and city as it is presented in the novel expresses a meaning consistent with the political form of the Federal Republic as a democracy? According to the French philosopher Claude Lefort, the unique feature of democracy as a form of society consists of the fact that it does *not* answer the question of power; hence, the symbolic locus of power remains empty. Lefort leaves us with the thought that a "democratic society emerges as a society without a body, a society that foils the representation of an organic totality."[92]

The Volkswagen as it is depicted in the novel *Die Autostadt* is, in fact, the linchpin around which society is presented precisely as a society with a body. The society of *Die Autostadt* is above all an organic totality. The machines, the factory, the streets and buildings of Wolfsburg, and the industrial technology that makes the city function form the glue that binds together the different German characters, all of whom have a vital role to fulfill in this living entity made of matter and human bodies merged into one strong and animated being. The novel produces a literary experience of such an organic totality of people and technology, including the built environment. At the beginning of the novel, a man enters a city on foot for the first time, a city that is being built in the middle of nowhere and that is still partly under construction. "What he sees here he has never seen in his life. There are streets like ribbons . . . that are as broad as highways. There are blocks of buildings that are symmetrically measured and aligned like soldiers." His experience takes on a mystical character when he starts encountering people:

> Footsteps.
> But not footsteps of a single person but of three, four.
> Of more people. Ten. Fifteen.
> Of more people. One hundred. Two hundred.
> Of more people. One thousand.
> Two thousand.
> Five thousand. He cannot count them. . . .
> The man . . . resembles a swimmer who is carried by and feels the support of a strange power and who only wants to use this power.

There are stairs, and behind them the horizon is filled with stones, building blocks, one next to the other.

The building blocks, the man notices, have a single sucking power. Therein the current of the vein hurls itself. . . .

The man turns and recognizes faces . . . all sorts of people that exist between Flensburg and Katowice. . . .

Then the man is alone. . . .

The building blocks have closed their suction cups.[93]

As an unspecified outsider, the man witnesses the power of the place. The rhythm of the language and the juxtaposition of numbers repeat the rhythm of the swelling mass of people, five thousand altogether, going to work in the Volkswagen factory. The "strange power" he perceives emerges from the bodily interplay between the buildings and the mass of people. The "building blocks" seem to have a forceful energy of their own, which becomes evident through the people being drawn toward them and past the visitor. The people have individual traits, but they move as one organic whole like a force of nature. Our outsider, and with him the reader, is overwhelmed by this experience, which points to greater realms beyond rational understanding. The long shots in *Aus eigener Kraft* showing the people pouring into the factory building seem like a perfect cinematic adaptation of these passages.

In the newly built city of Wolfsburg, Germans from all over the old Reich came together.[94] The novel gives voice to many of these refugees' stories and worries. They came "from Flensburg to Katowice" and thus represented ethnic Germans from all parts of the former Nazi Empire, such as Katowice in Silesia (which belonged to Poland before 1939 and after 1945), Transylvania (Romania), or simply "the East," that is, the Soviet occupation zone.[95] The City of the KdF-Wagen, founded in 1938, did not have a homegrown population extending into a pre-Nazi past, and the percentage of refugees was even larger than in other German cities.[96] This is an important background for the novel's depiction of a battered conglomerate of homeless people being merged as if by an invisible force into an ideal community of hard workers who believe in the material, technical, and social power of the city, the factory, and the miracle car that it produces. At an unspecified moment after Germany's supposed "zero hour" the city appears as an achievement-oriented society of social equality brought to perfection, where it mattered "much more than anywhere else how capable someone was and how well someone could use his own forces."[97]

The material symbiosis of the Volkswagen and its driver captures this fantasy of a perfect community. As a man enters his car, the vehicle's "gentle pulsing . . .

moved into his veins," and he feels liberated from everything that "profession, education, [and] reason and that pride, envy, jealousy, worry, and fear of losing his livelihood and all these things had cut into his face."[98] In such scenes, driving a Volkswagen becomes a social incarnation and enables a new vision of the future, the feeling of freedom and the perception of gliding "through space and time."[99] The novel conveys a transcendental worldview of organic wholeness related to the car, the factory, and the city that closely ties in with many elements of Nazi culture. It is the dream of a society without social differences, a redeemed organic entity realized through the workings of a soulful and animated technology embodied miraculously in the Volkswagen.

At the beginning of the novel, three consecutive scenes present the shift in the accepted narrative around the Volkswagen between the end of the war and the reconstruction period. Each time, a schoolteacher explains to her pupils the meaning of the Volkswagen and of the city, which was still under construction.[100] In the first passage, she tells them how the führer had the idea of creating a car that would no longer separate the working poor from the rich and how this led to the building of the city around them. A frame "with swastikas stamped into it" hangs on the wall, holding "the picture of the man with the hair falling above his forehead and with the little moustache." In the next scene, the teacher tells her students that an insane "dictator" had the idea of building a city and a factory in this place and that he was responsible for the "yoke of slavery" placed on foreign workers and for the flight of the children's parents from the East. The frame, now "sanded clean" of its swastikas, holds the image of a church in formerly German "Danzig" (Gdansk). In the third scene, the teacher describes how, after the war, masses of poor people came to the place with the factory because they believed in the value of the product it was meant to produce. Porsche is now the car's creator, and on the wall there is a "sanded" frame showing "the image of a car, and underneath is written in printed letters: THE GERMAN VOLKSWAGEN" (capitals in the original).

The sequence uses the picture frame as a central symbolic device. The same frame contains a picture of Hitler before 1945, then a church in Gdansk, and finally The German Volkswagen. This symbolism overtly indicates a shift of sovereign power from the führer to the Almighty to, eventually, the Volkswagen itself. There is a hint of sarcasm toward what is presented as a foolish admiration of the führer, a reference in line with the tendency of the times to ascribe all the problems of National Socialism solely to Hitler and his most important collaborators. No remark, however, relativizes the imagined power itself, a power that ends up inside the object of The Volkswagen while the frame, literally and figuratively, stays the same. In the course of this repetitive sequence, the car receives a renewed fetish-like magical quality that silently promises to finally realize the ideal community of workers and fulfill the societal vision of organic wholeness and harmony.[101]

When the novel narrates the end of the war, the symbiosis of city and factory, workers and machines becomes the very power that ensures the survival of the machines as the living heart of the whole organic system of power. The end of the war also brings to the surface the system of oppression and exclusion, the "yoke of slavery" on those who were placed at the exploiting edge of the organism. The novel mentions "fresh imports from Buchenwald" but compares the camps around the Autostadt favorably to the "much more miserable" ones that housed German prisoners in the East.[102] After the German defeat, the liberated Russian and Polish workers become "animals" who threaten to destroy the whole city. A racialized concept of the eastern enemy is very much intact in these passages and also informs how the text describes the emergence of a new "order" of "West and East."

As the Russians enter the factory, destroy, and take away as much as they can, the machines continue to work, miraculously protected and untouchable. In the chaos of early American occupation (later on replaced by the British), Mönnich depicts how German workers start to assemble the Kübelwagen on their own initiative. The naivety of the Americans and the pragmatism of the British allow the unexpected to happen: Kübelwagen production begins again and eventually transforms into the production of the first civilian Volkswagens rolling off the assembly line. This miracle can happen due to the Germans' slyness and their ability to outmaneuver the Allies.[103] A rising wave of admiration for the vehicle from the French and British follows.

Die Autostadt is, at its core, a founding myth that makes sense of Germany's historical rupture by presenting the Volkswagen as an object with magical qualities. The car, which is repeatedly referred to as "the miracle," bridges the gap between before and after and ensures the postwar resurrection of a West Germany rising from the ashes and ready to bring about its postwar economic recovery.[104] The military Volkswagen Kübel plays a key role in enabling this mythical transformation. The long section dedicated to the Kübel marks the transition from the verve of constructing the car, planning the city, presenting the Volkswagen to the world, and exciting global enthusiasm for it to the war successes, which eventually turn into war defeats.

The soldiers' experiences during the war with the Volkswagen Kübel are evocatively framed by a scene in which a Strength through Joy organizer who is also responsible for the Volkswagen savers reflects on the course of events, including the outbreak of the war (which he claims he does not like) and his personal involvement in keeping the war machinery going. While doing so he gazes at a globe. This object, moving slowly under a ray of sunlight, leads the narrator's gaze to the following war scenes: "The stripe of sun glimmered, and the terrestrial globe turned: mountains, deserts, seas. Now Africa wandered into the light."[105]

A private and his comrade, taking part in the Rommel campaign, are trapped in the dry course of a river, chased by enemy troops. They find their way out thanks to the "desert car," which is depicted as a living being with superhuman capacities: "At lightning speed . . . he had transported them as if he had wings. . . . He went on at any temperature. . . . He was the least demanding vassal the desert region had ever seen. . . . He was grateful and even-tempered."[106] As the globe turns, the Caucasus comes into view, where the German troops advance toward the mountains "with small cars that effortlessly swallowed the steppe-like plain. They were Volkswagens." The next turn of the globe reveals how this car "companion" conquered northern Russia and the ice zone near Narvik.[107] Finally, the globe turns back, and the sun shines on Leningrad (today Saint Petersburg). The approaching war defeat is captured in the form of a burned-out "skeleton of a car" with a dead driver in whose pocket the soldiers find a calculation of the monthly transportation costs of four workers in a car. The identity of the burned car is revealed at the very end: "It was a Volkswagen."

With this picture the scenery switches back to the organizer and his globe:

> Now the globe stood still. The stripe of sun seemed to hold it. Or did the two places it was resting between clamp it? The man approached.
>
> He saw that the stripe lay exactly between Hamburg and Brunswick. On the brink of the Lüneburg Heath.
>
> On the Autostadt.[108]

We can see now how the novel constructs what Nordhoff had called its "deep truth." Two material objects—the Volkswagen and the globe—mediate the metaphysical forces that assure that the essence of Germany does not die but is resurrected from among the dead. While the sun provides transcendental meaning, the globe starts moving by itself, following the progress of the German army and of the Volkswagen. When the globe turns back it reveals the moment of defeat embodied in the burned-out Volkswagen followed by the globe coming to a standstill. But this zero moment contains in itself the seed of rebirth. The sun shines its transcendental light on exactly the place that will induce the car's and the people's resurgence: The city in the north of Germany where the Kübelwagen was produced and where the civilian Volkswagen will soon follow in its military brother's footsteps, conquering the world once again, only this time as an export commodity.

In these scenes, the identity of the Kübelwagen and the Volkswagen is a core element of the Volkswagen's transfer from the Nazi world to the postwar world. The effect of these scenes is based on a rhetoric that was used by the Nazis, reappeared in car magazines after the war, and was criticized in 1957 by Alexander Spoerl. The novel *Die Autostadt* presents the beginning of the postwar mass production and export of the car as filling in the void created at the dark hour of Germany's defeat. The "miracle car" enables German superiority, seemingly destined for the dustbin of history at 1945's "zero hour," to transform itself from its military manifestation (back) into its civilian form of international trade relations.[109] The trail of destruction and suffering that the preceding version of German superiority had produced, if it is mentioned at all, is consigned to large collective forces beyond individual responsibility.[110] Jews are never mentioned.

Genesis of a Miracle

The trope of the miracle runs through Mönnich's novel like a leitmotif. It is directly linked to the unlikeliness of the Volkswagen surviving the war and coming out on the other side as the economic and symbolic foundation of a reborn Germany. In the novel this miracle story can happen because there is a miraculous strength situated *inside* the car stemming from the organic and magical connection between the workers, the machines, and the city. This miraculous version of a body politic that consists of both men and matter and survives its own death is a leftover, as we have seen, from National Socialism's ideas about an organic and romanticized bond between technology and the Aryanized German nation.

Mönnich's novel is disturbing. It presents the Volkswagen as being directly connected to a German body politic deeply shaped by fantasies of a racial community and its natural harmony and superiority. In 1945 Germany had lost the war and had ceased to exist in its previous political, geographic, and material form. Yet here is the story of the essential German body politic and its related make-believe space surviving the war in spite of this rupture. That is the main miracle the book unfolds. It does so in a compelling language whose pathos is at odds with the usually pragmatic and matter-of-fact public discourse about West German economic reconstruction in general and about the Volkswagen in particular.

The connection between the Volkswagen and a National Socialist body politic was a broader cultural phenomenon that left many traces in the archive. They can be found on the margins on those occasions when uneasiness about this connection was expressed explicitly. They can also be found in the way linguistic and aesthetic patterns were continued after 1945. These continuities pervade the archive of West German public discourse but have been pushed to the margins of our perception by the period's dominant narrative about the Volkswagen. The mismatch between these findings and the symbolic meaning of the Volkswagen as symbolizing a West Germany that was defined away from its own past created an interpretive void or, psychologically speaking, a cognitive dissonance. The concept of the miraculous seems to have filled this void by smoothing over the intrinsic cultural contradictions of West Germany's reconstruction.

If the Volkswagen became the most important symbol of the reemerging Federal Republic, the economic miracle became its most important catchword. Together, both incapsulate even today the birth of West Germany as a new entity, a new political, geographic, and economic being. Yet the Volkswagen was not the only debris of the Nazi Empire and its political fantasies. The miraculous as a political concept also played a critical role in the National Socialist worldview. The "German miracle" or "economic miracle" was a common expression used by the Nazi regime for the economic successes of the Third Reich.[111] Mönnich's novel about the miracle car was published in 1951. Around 1952 West Germans began to agree among themselves that the term "German miracle" or "economic miracle" was suitable to describe the economic and, by extension, the general development of their country after the currency reform.[112] Encapsulating the process of West Germany's postwar reconstitution, the German miracle redirected attention away from the concrete phenomena of cultural transfer and transformation, especially from those dissonant parts that would have disturbed the harmony and coherence of the narrative.

"Under the umbrella of the miracle term, the former supporters of the people's community imagined and enjoyed their uncanny status as the victors of history," writes Falko Schneider in his insightful account of the miracle as political concept in the twentieth century.[113] Schneider introduces the miraculous as a social-psychological concept able to mitigate the uncanny. The uncanny, in turn, is seen as a logical consequence of the postwar process that led the very country responsible for mass violence on an unprecedented scale into its quick economic recovery and redeemed status within the newly established Western international community. Remnants of the cultural framework of German society before 1945 were an unspoken yet constitutive part of this transformation. Referring to the economic boom and the success of the Volkswagen and other German commodities as a miracle both acknowledged and brushed aside the unlikeliness of a new West German identity built on these phenomena.

In order to better understand the genesis of the Volkswagen as this kind of miracle, we must revisit the postwar cultural transformation from a different angle. As Peter Fritzsche has put it, "the idea of Germany had been covertly Nazified as well as Aryanized" after January 1933.[114] The total defeat of National Socialism and the loss of state sovereignty resulted in a deep crisis of identity, a collectively shattered "unconscious self-confidence."[115] This experience followed twelve years of extreme collective self-aggrandizement at the expense of the Third Reich's proclaimed enemies and the racial community's "others." Before the war, an excess of national symbols, visualizations, and aesthetic and ritual materializations constantly provided the presence and thereby the "reality" of these ideas and imaginations in the public sphere. After the war, the state of Germany's national nonexistence was reflected in the destruction of German national symbols by the Allies and their subsequent absence from the public sphere, in which a different sovereignty ruled (see chapter 1).

A crisis of identity, a worldview in shambles, and the ensuing disorientation play out above all else on the emotional level. In the German case, the crisis was necessarily intensified by the Allies' efforts to denazify the population by confronting them with their collective responsibility for the mass murder committed in their name.[116] Collectivities need narratives and symbols to make sense of themselves, but the sense of self also depends on the acknowledgment an individual receives from other human beings. On the collective level of a society, this entails being recognized by other countries. After Germans embarked on coercing such "respect" from other nations through the brutal force of war and mass crime, they suddenly found themselves at the mercy of how the world in general and the occupation forces in particular looked at *them*.[117] The gradual genesis of the Volkswagen as a national symbol of West Germany is inextricably interwoven with such dynamics of real or imagined external perceptions and the emotional reactions evoked by them.

To understand how the Volkswagen became the symbol of the postwar economic miracle it is thus useful to pay attention to the affective sensibilities that emerged around this object in journalistic discourses from the years of Allied occupation onward. Any object's symbolic power derives from the affects it is able to provoke, affects that may spring from more complex narratives and interpretations and at the same time contain these (possibly contradictory) narratives in a condensed form.[118] If we follow the car in this way through its random occurrences in the press, the emotional reactions around the Volkswagen can roughly be summarized as an emotional journey from resentment to pride. The object of the Volkswagen served to mediate and embody the changing relationship between (West) Germans and "others," especially between

Germans and the occupation forces, as well as the larger Western world outside of Germany.

The first cars to come off the assembly line in 1946 and 1947 were not available for German private customers or German civilian authorities but were nearly exclusively delivered to the occupation forces.[119] In 1945 the car that the Nazis had previously made a symbol of the promised postwar affluence under the auspices of a greater Germany had fallen into the hands of Germany's former enemies. The earliest appearances of the Volkswagen in *Der Spiegel* testify to this situation's complicated constellation of sensibilities. In April 1947 the magazine reported on young people staging hunger riots in different cities of the British and American Bizone with attacks on British soldiers and the burning of cars. In Düsseldorf a Volkswagen was thrown into a pond, an incident illustrated with a photo whose caption read: "It did not end with the Volkswagen—adolescent evildoers."[120] The demonstration preceding these riots had been a major one, mobilizing eighty thousand to one hundred thousand people, according to the *Times* of London. The paper's account of the subsequent uproar captures the visceral rage present at the scene: "A *Volkswagen* in the service of the Military Government was pitched into a lake after the driver and passengers had been forced to get out, and another car in which foreign Press correspondents were travelling was stoned."[121]

In August 1947 *Der Spiegel* reported on the preparation of the export exhibition in Hannover, mentioning twenty-five new Volkswagens deployed as official taxis. The road traffic department had issued a decree that would prevent "the taxis [being] entered by foreigners full of calories and nicotine."[122] A month later, an article on the same exhibition stated sarcastically that the British representative had to be pushed to even take a look at the Volkswagen. Resentment also pervaded the writer's remark that German journalists were treated almost as "leprous people."[123] In January 1948 Jan Molitor wrote in *Die Zeit* about the celebration of the twenty thousandth Volkswagen. Summing up the disappointment of the workers about the fact that the Volkswagen was not available to them but only to the occupation forces, Molitor reported: "'The Volkswagen?' the workers say. 'The car runs and the people watch from the outside.'"[124] The workers' bad mood seemed to come from their bitterness about the war and the defeat caused by Hitler and from their disappointment about the foreign sovereignty over, as well as exclusive use of, the newly fabricated Volkswagen.

The currency reform marked a clear break with this early period of heightened resentfulness surrounding the postwar status of the car. Production of the Volkswagen increased, and more than half of all cars became available for Germans, mainly state officials and business owners.[125] From this moment onward, the attention of the public sphere shifted to the success of the car outside Germany. In October 1948 the magazine *Quick* printed a photo of a Volkswagen on the Dam Square in Amsterdam with a caption stating that "our small Volkswagen" could be found on every street corner in Holland (fig. 2.9). Two weeks later, another photo showed American workers at the port of Hamburg admiring a Volkswagen as a "nice little car" (fig. 2.10). This trend culminated in May 1949, right after the founding of the Federal Republic, with a headline about the big success of the German trade fair in New York accompanied by a photo of the Volkswagen surrounded by admiring visitors.[126]

2.9 "Our small Volkswagen" on the Dam Square in Amsterdam. *Quick*, October 1948. Reproduced from Staatsbibliothek Berlin.

2.10 Americans admiring the "nice little car" in Hamburg, *Quick*, October 1948. Photographer: Friedrich Bölt. Reproduced from Staatsbibliothek Berlin.

That a spectacle of national shame could still loom large behind the new spectacle of national pride became apparent in a report on the same event in the *Neue Illustrierte*. A photo of the admired Volkswagen was placed beneath an equally large one of protesters carrying banners with slogans such as "We don't want soap manufactured from Jewish bodies" and "Boycott this Nazi show." In the caption, the magazine informed its readers about another slogan: "Today the Volkswagen—tomorrow the death wagon."[127] The reader was thus confronted with the fact that presenting German commodities, especially the Volkswagen, in a city with a large Jewish community was not self-evidently generating enthusiasm but rather brought to the surface a reminder of the connection between German industrial production, in particular of this car, and the mass murder of Jews.

When the Spanish philosopher José Ortega y Gasset visited West Germany in September 1949, *Der Spiegel* reported proudly that the first thing he was interested in after crossing the border was a Volkswagen.[128] The magazine's first cover story on the Volkswagen from May 1950 confirmed this image of the car as an important source of a young West Germany's national pride. The view from the outside, in this case, the perception of the United States as the most important occupation power, proved to be a key element for this new meaning of the car. The first paragraph set the tone by citing a *Life* magazine story in which the Volkswagen was presented as a "symbol of German 'Reconstruction' [English in the original]: symbol of the sturdy German proficiency."[129]

Part 3 of this five-part series on the Volkswagen gave an account of the Nazi Volkswagen project, including a photo of Germans admiring a model of the KdF-Wagen. The article subsequently narrated the miraculous story of a Volkswagen Kübel that was found in southern Germany after the political "breakdown," brought to a garage, and afterward used by the mountain rescue service. Inexplicably, the car continued to run after falling into a twelve-meter-deep canyon.[130] This miraculous episode functions as a transition to the passage explaining how Volkswagen production started again under Allied control. The article clarifies that it was, above all, "the respect of the Allied soldiers" for the indestructible "Porsche-motor" that in the end assured the factory's postwar existence.[131]

American experts in New York, American soldiers in Hamburg, British soldiers, Dutch customers in Amsterdam, and a Spanish philosopher all entered the stage in 1948, 1949, and 1950 to affirm again and again to German readers that there were good reasons to be proud—of the Volkswagen in particular and of West Germany's steps toward economic and political recovery in general. Taken together, these examples indicate that the perception of Germany from the outside—whether real or imagined—fulfilled a crucial if not decisive role for the Volkswagen to emerge as *the* quintessential object of postwar national pride and as the center of the evolving miracle narrative.

What kind of perceptions from the outside were available to Germans in this period? *Der Spiegel*'s remark about *Life* magazine referred to a big photo report from May 1949 on West Germany after the Berlin blockade that was illustrated by a series of photographs from postwar life in many German cities. The report gave special attention to the Volkswagen with a full-page photo showing rows of Volkswagens in front of the factory in Wolfsburg. For *Life*, however, "German proficiency" was not the reason for the wondrous economic "recovery." Instead, the magazine referred to the currency reform and US aid as the main causes of the recovery.[132] The story in *Life* magazine is merely one reflection of a much larger effort from the outside to reinterpret Germany's position in the world. Between 1948 and 1952 the Marshall Plan, also known as the European Recovery Program, not only distributed economic aid but also created "the largest international propaganda operation ever seen in peacetime," with "a steady stream of press releases, pamphlets, radio shows, films, and traveling exhibits" all over Europe.[133] As Sheryl Kroen's work makes clear, this campaign established the most important features of the postwar political imaginary of the West. As a result it produced the staged event of western Europe's "recovery" based on the principles of free trade, productivity, and international cooperation.

In the context of this endeavor, Germany, the author of Europe's postwar crisis, was rebranded as a West Germany without history, a new entity rising out of the rubble, a model country of Western production and export, a country whose inhabitants were praised for their "almost fanatical reverence for toil."[134] This rebranding culminated in the 1950 Berlin Industries Fair, which was broadcast around the world.[135] In the exhibition, Germany's official appearance as a national entity happened in the form of a hand-drawn figure named "Herr X." The exhibition showed "the transformation of Herr X from a soldier in uniform, marching, creating destruction, annihilation, and extermination all over Europe, into a hard-working, vital participant in the recovery wearing a new suit."[136]

West Germans appropriated this Marshall Plan story of Germany's recovery and turned it into a popular narrative of national regeneration. In the West German version, the Western Allies were relegated to the sidelines, from which they were acknowledged as shouting approving remarks that confirmed a recuperated German self-confidence. Even before the term "German miracle" came into use, the 1948 currency reform had already been labeled "the great miracle" in Germany.[137] But it was not only the abundance of commodities suddenly filling German stores that was perceived as a miracle. The greatest miracle for postwar West Germans was the recognition of their country as a vital member of the Western community in the context of the emerging Cold War.

The Volkswagen stood not only for the proficiency and international success of German production but also for the blessings of an expanding mass consumption. German middle-class families bought the Volkswagen in rapidly rising numbers, from 60,000 in 1951 to around 150,000 in 1956. In July 1956 a third of all automobiles on German streets were Volkswagens. This situation did not change much until at least the early 1960s. In the course of the 1950s, the success of the Volkswagen thus resulted in its ubiquity on West German streets.[138] Taking pictures of people next to a car on the occasion of weekend trips and vacations was a common practice, and since many people bought a Volkswagen, the car figures prominently in private photo albums, especially during the second half of the decade.[139]

While it is impossible to know the meanings of such private manifestations of the car's importance, they were taking place within a culture that gave the car a central place in the public sphere and its new West German make-believe space. During the 1950s, the spectacle of the Volkswagen conquering the postwar West German cityscape and landscape often popped up in photo reports everywhere in the media, as well as in advertisements for various other commodities. Not surprisingly, the car was also very present in West German feature films. From a cheerful *Heimatfilm* about a female country doctor, to a comedy about a resentful policeman, Volkswagen drivers conspicuously populated the big screen. The car was used widely to support a fictional world in which social conflicts systematically resulted in the kinds of harmonious solutions that evoked the promise of an ideal community.[140]

What is more, owning the car was regularly referred to in the press as an indicator of being the right kind of German. On the one hand, it could be negative news if a famous person refused to be driven in a Volkswagen.[141] On the other hand, reporters frequently referred to driving a Volkswagen as a positive trait of people who belonged to the upper echelons of society. The choice of a Volkswagen made them appear as trustworthy people without false pretensions.[142] For director Heinrich Nordhoff, driving a Volkswagen was proof of the very best German virtues set against an allegedly amoral form of pretentious automobility. "I have no appreciation," he stated in 1954, "for those people who believe they have to present themselves with a big and expensive car. It must be a miserable self-confidence that needs such accessories to feel safe."[143] Such words reiterated ideas about the connection of German virtues with the simple and functional car that had already shaped the Nazi campaign.[144] While the export success and appreciation of the car in the United States were important sources of collective self-confidence after 1945, paradoxically, the specific superiority of the Volkswagen was also seen as sharply contrasting with American car culture, a view inherited from the past and in line with a broader postwar discourse on American superficiality and amoral capitalism.

The Volkswagen obtained its sacrosanct status as a national symbol of postwar West Germany in a transitional period when Germans started to reclaim a place in the world and to reactivate a sense of national pride. In 1955 both the German miracle and the Volkswagen myth had firmly established themselves, symbolizing a Germany that had regained its sovereignty by becoming a successful model economy of the West. When the production of the millionth car was celebrated that same year, it embodied the confidence of an intact German body politic. On the margins, however, the cracks in this fantasy soon began to show. Veiled in humor and sarcasm, writers in *Der Stern* and *Der Spiegel* attacked the Volkswagen as a problematic relict from the past. Beneath the surface of the outspoken, conscious or unconscious forms of uneasiness were continuously uttered. The 1958 satirical feature film *Wir Wunderkinder* (*We Children of the Miracle*) sharply points out the structural continuities between German society before and after 1945. The fervent Nazi, Tiches, reappears after the war as a black market dealer who owns a Kübelwagen. Later he drives a Volkswagen (fig. 2.11) before finally reappearing as a businessman driving a luxurious Mercedes.[145]

2.11 Three screenshots from *Wir Wunderkinder* (1958): Tiches in front of his Kübelwagen, Tiches driving a Volkswagen, a close-up of Tiches in his Volkswagen. Reproduced from Filmaufbau.

Fading out of Focus

In the course of this chapter I have woven together the loose threads of the marginal and uncanny that pop up in the archive around the Volkswagen in an attempt to create a connected but not entirely coherent web of readings. A physical activity such as weaving is perhaps a fitting metaphor for the work needed to understand "the 'unexpected capacity of objects to fade out of focus' as they 'remain peripheral to our vision' and yet potent in marking partitioned lives."[146] Ann Stoler aptly uses Daniel Miller's words to get to the core of what the study of "imperial debris" means. "Imperial formations," Stoler writes, are defined by racialized relations of force. Their "political forms ... endure beyond the formal exclusions." After an imperial formation has officially ended, much of its "rot" remains, defying the clear demarcation between before and after. Material objects in particular can become the carriers, "peripheral to our vision," of the still ongoing past. "Imperial debris" disobey a totalizing notion of continuity and rupture. They can only be "debris" because something has become past; they can only assert their power because something is still present. But they remain also, in spite of all their cultural force, a fragile phenomenon, an "ungraspable moment." Or rather, their force is in part due to the very fact that they "fade out of focus."[147]

Between 1946 and 1962 the Volkswagen became a sacrosanct national symbol through its capacity to silently transcend the 1945 divide. That capacity derived from the fact that it was not merely a symbol. The Volkswagen became a mass-produced material object that could be perceived and experienced as a physical embodiment of Germany's body politic. This body politic was the survivor of a polity and of a political imagination deeply shaped by National Socialism. The car was associated with dreams of a harmonious and superior people's community, it was linked to the desire and experience of belonging to an invincible people's body, and it combined promises of timelessness with imperialist fantasies of conquering and dominating exoticized geographic space. The Volkswagen could keep something alive that was supposed to be dead. It could bridge the gap between past and present, between the Germany before and after 1945. It could do all this not although but because it could simultaneously be the opposite, namely, an innocent technical commodity driving into the future and fading out of the political observer's focus.

How many Jews fit into a Volkswagen? Was the question meant as a provocation when it was asked during the 1950s? At the very least, the question must have reminded Germans of the fact that the postwar Volkswagen *was* different from the Volkswagen promised before 1945. Jews were now allowed to enter and drive the vehicle, something that was never intended by the Nazi regime.[148] Telling the joke, in any case, assumed a laughing audience of Aryan Germans. It thereby performed and repeated the act of exclusion.[149] As a speech act the joke painfully gives linguistic presence to the mass murder that had been the result of precisely the kind of body politic that the Volkswagen silently continued to manifest after the war.

Michael Geyer has thoughtfully stated that postwar West German culture was to a large extent shaped by what he calls "the imagined homecoming."[150] The imagined "home" of postwar Germans was reminiscent of the Nazi *Volksgemeinschaft* not least because of its racial exclusivity. If I put my findings about the Volkswagen next to Geyer's reflection, I see something similar. I can also see the occasional cracks in the supposedly safe cocoon of this unspoken fantasy. The imagined homecoming suffered, as Geyer emphasizes, from the "unexpected return of the dead" and eventually failed. The Volkswagen, however, was given a second postwar life in Germany that made the ghosts of the past, which used to live in its car body, utterly invisible. Due to the sweeping success of the DDB ad campaign that started in 1962, it soon became impossible to ask what the Volkswagen of the early Federal Republic had silently communicated about the relationship between Germans and Jews.

Paying attention to the uncanny has proved to be a helpful methodological tool for exposing the rarely acknowledged meanings of this powerful icon of postwar West Germany. It has enabled me to identify as a "ghost" a personal memory of the joke and an archival encounter with an advertisement that seemed to make no sense. Experiencing the ghostly aspects of these apparitions has meant recognizing their unique characteristic of lingering in a limbo between past and present, disrupting the usually unproblematic separation between a "then" and a "now," a disavowed and objectified past and a present that is owned as one's own. This is what makes the postwar Volkswagen "imperial debris," a manifestation of a disorienting and therefore a haunting cultural formation.[151]

3

Timeless Objects

Good Modernity and Its Other

"A Final Solution for Humanity"

> For the new houses one needed furniture, cutlery, vases, teacups. For them, too, the Bauhaus had found the definitive style-formula: . . . the good form. It was a late product of the Enlightenment and like all Enlightenment ideas a *final solution for humanity*. . . . It was said that more than an aesthetic solution depended on the "cleanliness" of form. The "good form" became an ethical category. Through it *our whole nature should be healed*.[1]

In April 1961 in the cultural magazine *magnum*, Karl Pawek reassessed the success of modern design in postwar West Germany. In order to develop a critical perspective on what he called the "Bauhaus myth," Pawek resorted to unusual expressions. The "good form" becomes a "final solution" (*Endlösung*) and is linked to a formulation that conjures up a famous slogan about German superiority ("*Am deutschen Wesen soll die Welt genesen*" / "The world shall be healed by German nature"). In the remainder of the article, Pawek, however, did not identify the Bauhaus in any way with National Socialism.

Why, then, does the Nazi expression for the genocide of European Jewry appear in Pawek's account? How can we grasp the contradiction between this choice of words and modern German design's dominant political interpretation, which was well established in 1961 and continues even today? This interpretation regards West Germany's iconic modern consumer objects as symbols of the Federal Republic's economic success, its integration into a Western international community, and its new political form as a liberal democracy. Within this framework Pawek's formulation appears nonsensical. The nonsensical, however, can point to a gap in our current understanding.

In recent years, scholarship on the postwar period in Europe has highlighted the extent to which the aesthetic shape of commodities became an important symbol of the new political, social, and geographic order that was established in western and eastern European countries with the onset of the Cold War.[2] Although modern design was presented in both West Germany and, somewhat later, East Germany as signaling a break with the Nazi past, the principles of functional simplicity developed by institutions such as the German Werkbund and the Bauhaus school had also been an essential aspect of the National Socialists' efforts to reinterpret and reshape the physical world in accordance with their racial concept of the German *Volk*.[3] Just as the Volkswagen was omnipresent in propaganda material after 1938, the dogma that simple, unadorned, and therefore "timeless" forms were the only proper way to furnish a truly German home was spread through many channels and media during the Third Reich.[4] After the war, the "good form" (gute Form) became the central catchword for modern design in postwar West Germany. But many of the forms, as well as the main ideas behind them, were already decades old. Different labels were used for this aesthetic scheme during the Third Reich, such as "new German living culture" (neue deutsche Wohnkultur) and "modern interior design," (moderne Innenarchitektur) alongside the term "good form." The headline of an article published in 1940 even proclaimed "the victory of the good form." The article described a furniture collection designed under the auspices of the Nazi organization Reichsheimstättenamt (Imperial Bureau of Homesteads) (fig. 3.1).[5]

Founded in 1907, the German Werkbund was the single most important German organization for the promotion of modern industrial design. After Hitler's rise to power, it quickly adapted to the new political context and enthused in April 1933 that "the great time of the Werkbund idea, the creative hour of the national form that conquers the world, has only just begun."[6] In June 1933 Theodor Heuss, secretary of the Werkbund and later to become the first president of the Federal Republic, conceded that the Werkbund's dedication to a "German style" harmonized well with the Nazi movement.[7] The Nazi office Schönheit der Arbeit (Beauty of Labor) recruited many former Werkbund members. Wilhelm Lotz, the former editor of Werkbund's main magazine, *Die Form*, became the principal editor of the Beauty of Labor's own periodical. The industrial designer Hermann Gretsch, a member of the Werkbund's executive committee since 1932, became head of the organization after it was overtaken by Nazi officials in 1935. He stayed in this position until the Werkbund was dissolved into the Third Reich's Chamber of Culture in 1938. With his continuing responsibility for major modern design exhibitions, Gretsch was probably the most influential designer of the

152 INNEN-DEKORATION

»EINFACHES WOHN- UND MUSIKZIMMER« KLAVIER DER FIRMA FERD. MANTHEY–BERLIN: KIRSCHBAUMHOLZ

ZUM SIEG DER GUTEN FORM

WK-VERBAND UND REICHSHEIMSTÄTTENAMT ALS WEGBEREITER

Geglückten und formvollendeten Neuerungen die Anerkennung und Begeisterung eines beschränkten Kreises zu erringen und ihnen hier den Durchbruch zu sichern, ist nicht das Schwierigste. Will man jedoch dem der Forderung der Zeit entsprechenden Stil des Gebrauchsmöbels Zugang in die große Menge und Allgemeinheit der Käufer und Verbraucher verschaffen, so muß sich der Eigenwilligkeit, Schönheit und Reinheit von Material und Form noch ein weiterer außerordentlich wichtiger Faktor zugesellen: der wohlfeile Preis, der den Erwerb auch dem mittelbegüterten Durchschnittskäufer möglich macht.

Die Lösung der Art, daß man nicht eines um des anderen willen, also: Idee und Preisgestaltung, schmälerte, war keine einfache. Sie erforderte viel Arbeit, Hingabe, Berechnung, Versuche und – Fehlschläge. In größtem Umfang glückte dieses lange und eifrige Bestreben dann doch in den stark beachtenswerten Erfolgen, die der »WK-« = »Wohnungskunst-Verband«, als Zusammenschluß der führenden Kräfte in der deutschen Möbelindustrie, und das Reichsheimstättenamt der DAF. in gemeinsamem Bemühen errungen haben. Sie entwickelten die »Zimmer unter 500 Mark«, Wohn-, Eß-, Schlafräume, in Edelhölzern und erlesener Verarbeitung. Jeder Zimmertyp ist in mehrfacher Ausführung wahlweise vertreten.

Um jenen in größten Mengen angestrebten Wohnungseinrichtungen aber jede Gefahr der Uniformierung und unpersönlichen Eintönigkeit zu nehmen, hat man unter gleichen Bedingungen Ergänzungs- und Einbaustücke geschaffen, die den Zimmercharakter beliebig abzuändern imstande sind. Es gibt Sitzbänke, zierliche Kommoden, zu mancherlei Zwecken abwandelbar, Gläser- oder Bücherschränke und

3.1 "Zum Sieg der Guten Form" (On the victory of the good form). *Innen-Dekoration*, no. 5, 1940. Reproduced from Staatsbibliothek Berlin.

Third Reich.[8] In spite of the closing of the Bauhaus school in 1933, the regime hired and cooperated with many designers influenced by both the Werkbund and the Bauhaus in order to standardize the production of consumer durables and to disseminate the idea of a timelessly good, simple, and honest form as the true expression of the *Volk*.

This chapter approaches modern design as an element of culture whose meanings in the public sphere exceed conscious intentions and thereby mold structures of feelings. The shape of everyday objects had already become part and parcel of a broader outlook on national life long before the advent of Nazism. These existing meanings were subsequently integrated into Nazi culture. Because the Nazis were keenly aware of the power of banal objects to embody ideas about nation and race, materiality played an important role in their various projects.[9] What happened to this cultural legacy after 1945? In his book *The Authority of Everyday Objects*, Paul Betts concisely compares the Third Reich's "effort to redeem the German object world" with how the Autobahn and the Volkswagen "revealed the Nazi conception of German mythical space." After the war, the same aesthetic principles that had promoted this "mythical space" reemerged in the young Federal Republic as a "distinctive postfascist aestheticization of everyday life" that cleansed "modernist goods of fascist contamination" and provided a "prime sphere of mythmaking" for the country's "moral regeneration."[10] Betts and others emphasize that modern design was successfully reframed after the war as a cultural good that distanced West Germany from the Nazi past and that was inextricably linked to the basic ideals of the postwar order in the West.[11] The same, however, was true for the Volkswagen. In both cases, historical interpretations have scarcely considered the presence of implicit meanings hidden behind the apparent transparency of discourses. It is only in those latent cultural realms that we can begin to see how historical relations between people and things create traditions of meaning that do not easily evaporate.[12]

Before and after 1945 a similar dreamworld of modern interiors was regarded as representing the essence of Germany as a social and political entity. To better understand the relaunch of the good form as a prime aesthetic marker of West Germany's body politic, I became curious about the nonsensical and the latent within a multitude of highbrow and popular texts, films, and advertisements that coproduced the postwar meanings of modern design in an atmosphere ripe with denial.[13] This critical work entailed taking seriously the silences, omissions, and discrepancies. It meant paying equal attention to what is said and what is not and to how meaning is created through the intermingling of both. It also required cutting across the 1945 moment by reading postwar material alongside cultural products and texts from the Nazi period.

Pawek continued his 1961 *magnum* article by stating that the Bauhaus had become the "mecca" of a "historical memory" that enabled the postwar "healing power" of modern design.[14] This statement not only exposes the catchword "Bauhaus" as a nearly sacred stand-in for the whole of Germany's "good" modern design tradition but also highlights modern design's ability to symbolically "heal" the republic of its tainted past.[15] By calling the Bauhaus tradition of the good form a "final solution for humanity," however, Pawek simultaneously disturbed and undermined the very idea of its "healing power."

Such uncanny remarks are an indication that the postwar political imaginary attached to modern design was charged with a more complicated relationship to the Nazi past than scholarship has so far acknowledged. It turns out that the coding of modern design as the redeeming shape of "the new" was precisely what made it possible to blur any clear understanding of how the same notions about everyday aesthetics had been intertwined with the organicist, metaphysical, and racially loaded ideas of the German people during the Third Reich. The postwar lure of what was often called the "timeless" modern depended to a considerable extent upon its capacity to obscure its own history and thereby this history's ongoing legacy.

Renarrating a German Tradition

Film ohne Titel (*Film without a Title*), directed by Rudolf Jugert and based on a screenplay by Helmut Käutner, was the most successful German film of 1948.[16] It tells the story of Martin (Willi Fritsch) and Christine (Hildegard Knef), who meet in Hannover during the war. Martin is the well-educated owner of an antique business in Berlin. Christine is a girl from the countryside who works as a maid in Martin's household. The social differences between them stand in the way of their romantic relationship against the backdrop of a German society in turmoil. The story is interrupted by the scriptwriter, the director, and the male star, who discuss which ending would be appropriate for postwar Germany. In the first version, a pessimistic rubble film, Martin gets lost in the black market and Christine marries a younger man. In the second version, a war-time comedy, Christine and Martin's love affair culminates in a traditional rural marriage. The third ending depicts the allegedly "true story" behind the film: Martin discovers the value of building "simple but honest furniture" and opens a workshop in Hannover. With the prospect of a shared future, he meets Christine again midway between Hannover and the countryside.

As Johannes von Moltke pointed out, *Film without a Title* negotiates "the tension between the city and the country" at the end of the war while hinting at "an emergent postwar consumer economy" transitioning "from antiquities to modern supply-and-demand commodity production."[17] A closer focus on the latter aspect reveals how the film prominently uses domestic material objects and their accompanying cultural convictions as central narrative elements for developing the prospect of moral regeneration after the war. Both the estrangement between Martin and Christine and their reconciliation are interlinked with their respective relationship to domestic objects.[18] Martin's bourgeois villa, filled with antiques, is presented ironically as pitch-perfectly cultivated and thus at odds with the realities of the war. This "exceedingly sophisticated home" and the elitist attitude that comes with it are strongly associated with the problems of an "old life." Yet the director of the film informs his colleagues that as a student Martin had built "wonderful modern furniture."

Film without a Title stands out among the early postwar films in the way it explicitly discusses the problem of narration and filmmaking after the war.[19] The film's solution to revert to the supposedly "real" love story heavily relies on the moral authority of "simple but honest furniture" and the impeccable way of life linked to it. Martin turns to this option as an alternative to the cultural dichotomy between the city and the countryside. His choice of simple but honest furniture brings to the fore the basic credo of a discourse on domestic aesthetics that had been popularized during the previous forty years and turns it into a supposedly ahistorical and apolitical solution for the postwar challenge of narrating German history and envisioning a morally redeemed German future. With this approach, *Film without a Title* fits squarely in a wider cultural tendency of the early postwar period.

In 1947 thirty-seven members of the reconstituted Werkbund asserted that the "visible collapse" of Germany's "breakdown" was also an "expression of a mental ruin." From "the bottom of all things" they introduced their mission in the context of reconstruction, summarized in five demands, the last of which reformulated the Werkbund's central dogma: "For residential and public buildings, for furniture and appliances we seek the simple and the valid instead of . . . miserable emergency design."[20] Just as *Film without a Title* did, the newly reconstituted Werkbund connected a moralized notion of simple forms with the necessary moral reconstruction after the war, notwithstanding the organization's deep entanglement with Nazi aesthetic policies.

Referring to modern design as a source of moral redemption became possible between 1945 and 1953 because a story about the Werkbund, the Bauhaus, modern design, and Nazism established itself in which the influence of modern design ideas had been sharply interrupted during the Nazi regime. The resulting narrative created a powerful fiction on the basis of a nebulous language and rhetorical maneuvers that systematically distorted the historical record. National newspapers and high-brow cultural magazines nearly unanimously proclaimed the Werkbund and its aesthetic program as an essential ingredient for reconstructing Germany. It was challenging, however, to connect this view to a coherent long-term story. The many contradictory or opaque statements about the continuity or discontinuity of modern design's previous importance and popularity in Germany eventually created a collectively accepted myth, a new historical "truth."

Reading through this body of literature was a disorienting experience. As I became aware that these texts, one by one, constructed a reality of the Nazi past at odds with today's academic knowledge, it was difficult to stay immune to the manipulative spell of orchestrated implicit assumptions. After all, they echoed my own unreflected intuitions, which I had inherited from my cultural upbringing. This postwar discourse's specific combination of denial and moral high ground created a haze that went on to have a long-lasting influence on the broadly accepted meanings of postwar modernism. At one point, in order to be able to find my way through the haze, I resorted to the physical act of writing down a note on paper with a different truth that said: "Modern design is not necessarily connected to democracy."

An article in the left-leaning *Frankfurter Hefte* declared in 1946 that the historical moment was "the hour of the Werkbund," whose principles of "simple, useful, functional, and genuine" objects were "confirmed and deepened by the war's process of demystification, but as early as 1907 it was preached and realized by the 'Werkbund.'"[21] The author added that "nobody" would still adhere to "the decorative and monumental style" because "the war" had "swept all that away." Such statements left the role of the Third Reich in the sphere of ambiguity. Walter Dirks stated in 1947 that the Werkbund idea of a "simple and truthful form" was "generally accepted" by the "educated" and even the youth.[22] According to a Bavarian daily, the war had "violently paved the way for endeavors to create a new living culture [*Wohnkultur*]" because the lack of living space compelled people with "dictatorial force" to find new solutions. In 1949, by contrast, "the shop windows of furniture stores mirror the *rejection of the immediate past* and the reconnection with an earlier style epoch."[23] The promotion of the "new living culture" ended up in a historical fog in which its "immediate past" could refer equally to before, during, and after the war.

In 1949 the first Werkbund exhibition after the war took place in Cologne. In the catalog, politicians and designers formulated their ideas about the importance of the Werkbund's principles for the future of Germany and used different strategies to obfuscate the influence of these principles during the Third Reich. Cologne's municipal director, Willi Suth, listed several former Werkbund exhibitions from before 1933 but kept silent about the Werkbund's major contributions to Nazi exhibitions.[24] The architect Rudolf Schwarz even stated that the Werkbund had been "barred from its work for the last twelve years." Evoking a politically foggy past, Schwarz spoke of how "recently apartments, which had shrunk beneath humane proportions, were misrepresented as 'people's apartments' and that the term *Volk* was misused to offer inferior things . . . to the big masses for a low price." But what does the word "recently" point to? The Nazi years, the war years, or the immediate postwar years of scarcity? Schwarz continued that, in contrast to this murky past, the Werkbund put the human being at the center, and that this human was "something definitive, that stands above the times, just like the *Volk* lives through the times and remains true to itself."[25]

The designer Jupp Ernst summarized the Werkbund's recent history regretfully: "Especially in the years between 1920 and 1930, architects and designers did a good job. That is why the current situation is all the more painful, because we were already once about to overcome the damage."[26] As a positive example he named Wilhelm Wagenfeld's designs for the glass factory in Lusatia. Wagenfeld's designs, however, continued to be mass-produced during the Third Reich and were repeatedly showcased in major Nazi exhibitions.[27] Ernst then spoke of a past in which everyone close to the Werkbund had been "removed" by the Nazis. The main purpose of the 1949 exhibition was therefore to connect German design back to the 1920s, "when the world still talked with respect of a 'German style.'"[28] The 1949 catalog even associated the big enemy of the Werkbund's good form, the "bad taste" of overly decorated objects, with the Third Reich, thereby contradicting the historical fact that the Nazis had constantly fought the very same "bad taste."

In the following years, similar conventions of speech on modern *Wohnkultur* (living culture) and the Werkbund legacy can be found in many different publications, generating a fuzzy discourse and referencing a nebulous historical chronology. The *Frankfurter Allgemeine Zeitung* in particular dedicated many pages to the topic of modern design. In 1951 an article claimed that the demands of the Bauhaus had evolved into "a silent practice that today every craftsman exercises." In spite of this sweeping success, there had supposedly been a "caesura" in the past whose character and moment, however, remain vague while its outcome was clear: it "led to military catastrophe and to the ruination of our cities."[29]

In August 1951 a columnist observed that a growing bourgeois attachment to domestic furnishings had developed and that people were "stuck again" in "a peacetime of a bygone age." The journalist narrated the Nazi past as a story about a deformed relationship to domestic materiality that everyone shared, glossing over not only the Nazi programs of home and work aesthetics but also the legacy of Aryanization: "First the non-Aryans saved their furniture, then the Aryans did the same, eventually ('we won't surrender') those masters who determined who was who." In this view, both Aryanization and the Allied bombings had played a similar historical role in exposing how a problematic relation to material objects dominated German culture during Nazism, with the main moral problem being the "hideousness of the rescued trash." For this author, the bombings might have "come in order to redeem us from this interior decoration." Such sobering of taste could have brought a brighter future, since "we would have pleased all of the Atlantic world with it, and we would have won a moral battle. Instead, people resort to a waned past that was so empty, so hollowed out that the whole noise of dictatorship found its place in it."[30] By mere association the bad taste of bourgeois representation virtually absorbs the whole moral burden of the Nazi past ("noise of dictatorship"), whereas subscribing to the right taste of simple forms promises a true redemption of the lost war and an ethically purified form of global influence.

In 1951 an author for *Die Gegenwart* was surprised that he had found no "disturbances" of the modern in an exhibition of decorative arts. This gave him "hope, also beyond the limits of decorative arts, into the domain of political despicableness, because we believe that the artists who were desperately outraged in the face of the luxuriating founders' years [*Gründerjahre*] had been quite demoralized." But when and because of what had these artists been demoralized? "At that time, they started attacking the spirit of flourish," the author added, "and they achieved something."[31] The obscurity of these formulations—At what time? Who are "they"?—creates the impression that modern design stood in opposition to National Socialism, at least if one assumes that the "domain of political despicableness" was supposed to mean the Third Reich. Behind the surface of this discourse hovers a strong identification of these well-educated middle-class writers with the promises embodied in the principles of modern design. What had happened to this identification during the Third Reich was clearly unspeakable. Telling the story in a way that fit in the postwar West German framework became an exercise in remembering selectively and in establishing contorted chains of association.

In Edith Nowak's eyes, writing in 1953, the "new style" had become an element of her and her generation's self-conception: "Once upon a time, we young people, captured by the new style, believed someone could live as he liked and not as he must. . . . Then the year 1933 arrived, and we had other worries. Not much has remained, neither of the furniture nor of the dreams." The year 1933 marks a diversion of this dream to express oneself through the new style without saying what this meant and how it happened. In the postwar present Nowak dreamed of absent "airy pieces of furniture" that had been "companions of a good struggle, which we have lost shamefully."[32] In the following paragraph the historical times flow into each other and create a confusing muddle:

> We felt like the spearheads of a good cause. Light and air into our lives, clear lines inside and outside, rather too much hygiene than too little, spiritually and physically, than dust and the burdens of a thousand-year-old tradition whose nobility we loved but whose embarrassing ready-made late form we ironized. No, we didn't take them seriously, these fossils, until they rolled over us with the weight of mountains, with blood and soil, with Beiderwand and bunting and all the glory of a heroic age.[33]

The principles of the new forms, "light and air," are associated with both a material and a spiritual form of hygiene and self-purification. The antagonist of this self-conception is introduced as the "burden of a thousand-year-old tradition," conjuring up the "thousand years" of the Third Reich. The terms "nobility" and "ready-made," however, instead belong to the mass-produced versions of a bourgeois representative style that the Nazis themselves abhorred. Yet the next sentence does not distinguish anymore between the kitsch of pseudoaristocratic representation and the bucolic styles associated with Nazi "blood and soil" heroism. All of it is mixed together as hopelessly antiquated "fossils" of the past that stand in clear opposition to the "old dreams" of a self and a world realized through "clear lines."

These often incoherent attempts at historically positioning the aesthetic ideal of unadorned forms contributed to a narrative that rigorously disavowed any enmeshment of the German modern design tradition with the Third Reich. In 1951 Theodor Heuss admitted that "naturally, not everything which was built, painted, or otherwise constructed after 1933 deserves the stamp of the bad purely because of this date," adding that a "political order" could not "extinguish" an already schooled "inner capacity to form." For a clearer demarcation, however, Heuss referred to Nazi architecture and to Nazi ideas about "degenerate" art, thus moving away from the topic of design.[34] Two years later, journalist Helene Rahms even stated that modern design itself was hit by the taboo of being "degenerate" during the Third Reich. Paradoxically, she also declared that the Nazi "living culture [*Wohnkultur*] of purity" actually "fed on the prohibited Bauhaus in its purist efforts."[35]

Laying claim to Werkbund principles of simple and functional industrial forms for the shaping of the young Federal Republic was part of the most pressing cultural challenge of that era: working out which German traditions could and should be saved from the "cultural rubble" left behind by National Socialism. In the broader realm of architecture and industrial design, the weight of the Nazi past was put on the monumental style of representative buildings, traditional rural forms, and, implicitly, even an often targeted aesthetic enemy of the Nazis: the historicist and decorative style of bourgeois architecture and interiors. Because they were opposed to a bad taste that was now associated with National Socialism itself, Werkbund and Bauhaus aesthetics appeared as inherently anti-Fascist. By erasing the historical reality of how ideas about good and simple forms had become part of Nazi culture, this postwar discourse both sidestepped and obscured the necessity to reinterpret these forms' cultural meanings.

Germany's Good Form and Its Other

In order to better understand the ingredients of political thinking that were at stake in the postwar discourse on modern design it is necessary to revisit the intellectual origins of the good form. The historiography of German modern design, especially of the German Werkbund, has for a long time been caught up in dichotomies of "reactionary" versus "progressive" that make it difficult to capture the way in which Werkbund ideas were linked to a certain vision of the nation.[36] Joan Campbell, in her classic study from 1978, certainly interpreted the Werkbund as a whole as a progressive movement. But she also pointed to its "deep-rooted nationalism of the pre-1914 years," which "continued to reveal itself during the Weimar years." In Campbell's eyes the Werkbund of the late Weimar Republic was "ideologically much closer to the 'German socialism' espoused by the Nazis than to any form of Marxism."[37] Other studies have shown that prominent Werkbund members actively supported the imperial project of a German *Weltpolitik* (world policy) and that connections between aesthetic ideals and racial notions were not unusual in the early Werkbund period.[38]

Many voices in the turn-of-the-century discourse on aesthetics and *Wohnkultur* articulated the aim of shaping national culture as "an organic and aesthetic whole" by transforming public and private spaces according to the new ideas about good form.[39] Building on a widespread call for discipline, unity, and harmony in German culture, the simplicity of form in everyday material culture should both reflect and realize the elevation of a self that was conceived as part of a national collectivity. These principles, as Mark Jarzombek has argued, were the cornerstone of a discourse that made form "the foundation on which rested the historical and military legitimacy of the German nation."[40] Modern design proponents largely operated within the era's deep-seated beliefs in the spiritual permanence, wholeness, and superiority of the German people. The supremacy and purity of the good German form was also meant to help conquer world markets and legitimate global dominance.[41] Hermann Muthesius, a cofounder of the Werkbund, proclaimed the triumph of "German form" as the coming of a new "global form."[42]

It is the merit of Jarzombek's analysis that it stresses the flip side of these new beliefs about aesthetics, namely their "confrontational stance vis-à-vis all opponents of harmony and order."[43] As Katherine Pence has put it, German modernism "aggressively" forged "links between private households and the national community."[44] Emphasizing these aspects does not make this cultural movement a *Sonderweg* phenomenon, an example of German history's supposedly special path that necessarily led to Nazism. Instead, it points to the potential of exclusion engrained in this as well as in other European countries' aesthetic reform projects similarly influenced by essentialist ideas of the nation at the apex of European imperialism.[45] After many internal differences on questions of style, a softened interpretation of the pragmatic functionalism of the 1920s art movement New Objectivity (Neue Sachlichkeit) had eventually prevailed in Werkbund circles by the early 1930s.[46] Both the softened Neue Sachlichkeit and connected beliefs about aesthetics and the nation went on to shape Nazi policies and propaganda during the Third Reich. As a consequence, the excluded Other, the ugly flip side of the good form that embodied the organic whole of the German people, also gradually became the Other of the Third Reich's racialized culture.

The discourse on modern design as it developed between 1936 and 1940 in the monthly magazine *Innen-Dekoration* (founded in 1890) provides a glimpse of how Werkbund ideas morphed into a National Socialist discourse.[47] It also illustrates how the aesthetic and moral enemy of the good form as embodiment of the nation gradually evolved into the aesthetic, moral, *and* racial enemy of the Third Reich. According to Hermann Gretsch, who by 1936 was head of the nazified Werkbund, Germany's architectural culture could only advance if people "subscribe again to a unified worldview and quietly accept the social order."[48] For Gretsch, Werkbund ideas were part of a long development that necessarily led to "the only possible form of a state consciousness with a clear ethnic [*völkisch*] outline." In 1940 Wilhelm Michel claimed that the concept of "modern living culture [*Wohnkultur*]" had always aimed at "the new social unanimity of the people."[49]

The ethical characteristic of the good form, its inherent quality of putting the human being at its center, later became a standard element of postwar discourses on modern design that supposedly assured its essential difference from Nazism.[50] This humanist quality, however, played an equally important role during the

Third Reich when it was systematically narrowed to humanity's national and racial manifestation. "Humanness" apprehended in this manner could develop best in spaces that were designed along the lines of the good form. Redesigning the home into "a clear, a decent world" entailed the "inner agreement of the spirit between this spatial design with what the German worker represents today as a human being" and aimed at transforming the "personal existence" of every German into a representation of "the people as a whole."[51] The objects of the home had to conform to a certain aesthetic standard in order to instill a new self-understanding and merge the individual identity of every German with the collective identity of the German people. This concept of material embodiment belonged to a vision of the world in which—parallel to the Nazi ideas on technology—nature, material objects, and the spirit of the people were intrinsically interconnected. In this view, Hitler's grandiose building policy directly filled up a collective "we" with a "bigger awareness of life and self."[52]

The good form as it was proclaimed by *Innen-Dekoration* gradually embodied a thoroughly nazified idea of the German people, a development strengthened further by the magazine's many reports on Nazi initiatives to promote "new German living culture." The excluded ugly side of the totalizing good form came to the surface more often once the Nazi regime increased its expansionism. On the occasion of the exhibition *Deutsches Wohnen* (German living) in the summer of 1939 in Leipzig, Hermann Gretsch explained that the "aspiration to a healthy, natural living culture" was "synonymous with the fight against dishonest representation." Objects that one acquired to own for a long time should not, he added, "have the spirit of the racially foreign addiction to sensation."[53] Attempts to educate Germans' taste in interior decoration not only affected the sphere of high-brow publications such as *Innen-Dekoration* but also were part of much more widespread efforts, among them frequent exhibitions organized by Nazi institutions.[54]

"The fight against the ugly and artificial continues" was the comment of the German Labor Front's main organ, *Arbeitertum*, in June 1939 on new quality labels created to help German consumers identify the right kind of interior decoration. The text underlined the interrelation between the design of Germans' private spaces and the national space of the new empire: "The spatial culture of the German people will one day achieve a level that is in accordance with the national greatness of Germany."[55] In this way "the fight against the ugly" became an inherent part of Germany's expansionism, and the language in *Innen-Dekoration* reflected this connection. In 1940 an article on an exhibition by the German Labor Front's Imperial Bureau of Homesteads rhetorically linked the "fight against falsity," started by artists and manufacturers half a century ago,

3.2 The German section at the triennial design exhibition in Milan. *Innen-Dekoration*, no. 7, 1940, cover. Reproduced from Staatsbibliothek Berlin.

to the ongoing war by claiming: "Today we see this cultural upheaval achieve its final victory."[56]

On the occasion of the triennial design exhibition in Milan in 1940 *Innen-Dekoration* made a claim to German aesthetic leadership in the new Europe under German domination. The cover of the issue showed a photograph from the German section, which had been curated by Hermann Gretsch. The visual focus lay on two simple but large black vases standing next to a hanging tapestry that depicts the Nazi Party eagle (fig. 3.2).[57] This arrangement of objects in space underneath the word "Germania" already expressed aesthetically what Gretsch put into words in his contribution. While German troops occupied Germany's neighboring countries and German settlers "Germanized" the new territories in the East, Gretsch defined Germany's modern design solutions for small households as a signpost for the nation's endeavor to reshape Europe under its command.[58] In the same issue, Wilhelm Michel connected the ideal of beauty with the "higher human form against everything that is beneath it," specifying that a "European, when he talks about a higher human form, inevitably means the white race."[59]

At the beginning of the war, the term *Wohnkultur* had been racially charged to such an extent that it could be used to legitimize the conquest of new *Lebensraum* (living space) in the East. An *Arbeitertum* article from July 1940 described the efforts of the Imperial Bureau of Homesteads to create new settlements for Germans in Poland by elaborating on the absence of proper housing in a country filled with "products of Polish primitivity."[60] In the summer of 1942, a daily newspaper focused on the poor standards of Russian furnishings and home decoration. Providing detailed descriptions of the inside of several Russian homes, the author lamented the "tasteless leveling" and concluded: "The obtuseness of these people is unimaginable. Their dwellings and living culture belie description."[61] Finally, the concept of *Wohnkultur*—which encompassed both the ideal of simplicity in form and the ideal of cleanliness—was also activated in the persecution of Jews. Right after the German invasion of Warsaw, one newspaper report complained about the "low living culture [*Wohnkultur*]" in the ghetto, which "cannot be measured with western European standards."[62] In the context of the destruction of the ghetto in Litzmannstadt (Polish name: Łódź), a German commissary for the economy announced in September 1942 that Jewish apartments could only be regarded as "carriers of infectious diseases" because of the "low living culture [*Wohnkultur*] of these people."[63]

Shortly before the German capitulation in March 1945, a curious report appeared in the formerly Austrian newspaper *Neue Warte am Inn* that conveys how strongly German self-understanding and pride were based on the nation's modern living culture. Mirroring the previously mentioned description of Russian homes in German-occupied territory, the article quotes from the letter of an American soldier who described his impressions of a German apartment. He claimed that he had been able to "form an image of what kind of people they are. The furnishings that I found are modern and tasteful. The apartment has all the comforts and sanitary facilities. In this respect, the Germans are way ahead of us and the English."[64] The newspaper praised him for acknowledging his enemy's superiority in the field of *Wohnkultur* while characterizing the American himself as a cultural "robot." The article expressed the hope that more soldiers would become aware of their false impression of Germany. Some years later, American appreciation of German modern interior design would indeed come to play an important role in the renewed recognition of postwar (West) German culture both in the eyes of the West and in the eyes of Germans themselves.

The Good Form Goes West

It is impossible to assess the effects of being surrounded by Nazi language and visual culture for twelve years, regardless of an individual's own conscious political opinions before and after 1933. How did Fascist culture shape seemingly self-evident everyday perceptions?[65] And what happened to these effects after 1945? As they did in many other cases during the Nazi years, state institutions successfully appropriated the good form and other Werkbund ideas that included elements compatible with the radicalized Nazi ideas of nation and race, thereby securing "greater government support in the Third Reich than they had commanded in the Weimar years."[66]

Most of the postwar advocates of the good form had lived through the Nazi years in Germany and had probably read magazines such as *Innen-Dekoration*. Passively or actively, they had taken part in a culture that invested an impressive amount of energy conflating the nationalist Werkbund tradition with Nazi ideas about nation, military expansionism, and racial purification. The seemingly irrational rhetorical maneuvers that shaped how postwar writers tried to dissociate the good form from National Socialism therefore reveal a peculiar logic. If one acknowledges that the good form had been deeply inscribed in the culture of the Third Reich and that openly continuing Nazi policies was taboo, the only option was denial and a language that concealed that denial.

Under Allied press control, *Innen-Dekoration* continued publishing with a new title: *Architektur und Wohnform*. Its editor was now Alexander Koch junior, son of the former editor, who had died in early 1939.[67] In the foreword to the first postwar issue, published in 1946, Hans Eckstein asserted that the modern design and architecture movement in Germany "experienced a violent disruption in 1933." In his view, architecture and design under Nazism consisted solely of "classicist monumental buildings," "historicist homeland [*Heimat*] style," and "mass kitsch." To underline Alexander Koch senior's role in Germany's tradition of "conscious modernity," Eckstein quoted from the former editor's foreword to the forty-eighth volume of the magazine, in which Koch saw the work of *Innen-Dekoration* "flow into a today that is animated by new strengths."[68] Eckstein did not mention the year in which the foreword was written: 1937.[69] In the foreword to the 1939 volume, Koch had praised the Third Reich's plans for residential construction and living spaces by underlining the essential role of "form" for the Nazi project: "This is how, piece by piece, the great achievement in form is put together, which the Third Reich has chosen as its task: the task of a total molding of the German people."[70]

In this and the following numbers of *Architektur und Wohnform*, many articles reiterated the invented past of modern design's absence during Nazism, while others presented furniture designs that were virtually identical to those in the Nazi furniture collections the magazine had reported on before 1945 (fig. 3.3 in comparison to fig. 3.1).[71] A similar rewriting of the Werkbund's and modern design's recent history took place in the magazine *Baukunst und Werkform*, founded in 1946. In its first issue, the editorial combined praise for the Werkbund ideas with the reiterated lie that its work "was killed" in 1933. The good form was presented as essential for solving the deep crisis of Germany's breakdown because the issue was "not about taste" but about a moral expression of "neatness and honesty."[72]

Within the rigid moral dichotomy of the discourse on modern design both before and after 1945, the place ascribed to the Nazi regime changed radically in the postwar transition. By contradicting or denying a huge area of historical reality, National Socialism was situated outside the frame of the modern and thereby became the new Other of modern design. The good form's Other was thus paradoxically identified with Nazism precisely by sticking to the same dualist doctrine that had previously underpinned Nazism's own exclusionary aesthetics. Once this shift had established itself, the dehistoricized purity and superior morality of the good form could help give shape to the Federal Republic's new version of moral and aesthetic superiority as a member of the postwar West, sealing the good form's new mythical function. *Architektur und Wohnform* saw the possibility of such an international repositioning as early as 1946, when it claimed that other countries had continued to develop what had been "violently disrupted" in Germany.[73] The magazine's second postwar issue, published in 1948, focused on modern designers and architects in Sweden and the United States,

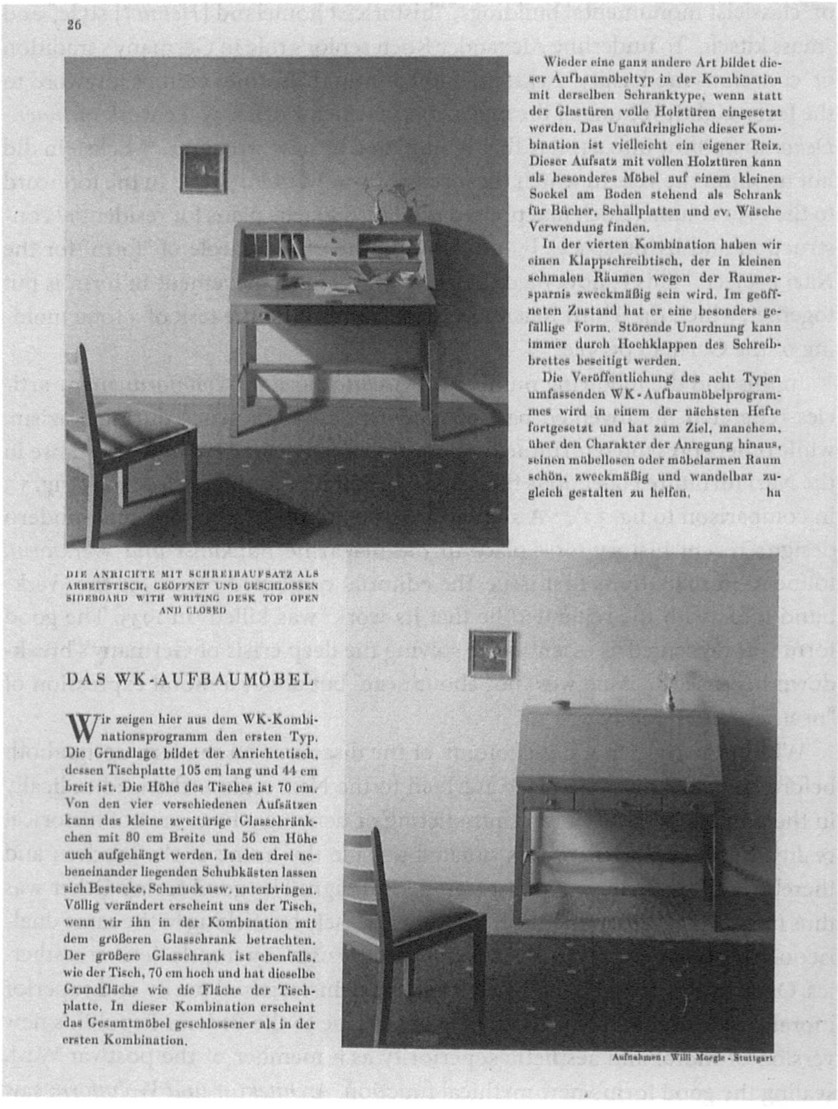

26

Wieder eine ganz andere Art bildet dieser Aufbaumöbeltyp in der Kombination mit derselben Schranktype, wenn statt der Glastüren volle Holztüren eingesetzt werden. Das Unaufdringliche dieser Kombination ist vielleicht ein eigener Reiz. Dieser Aufsatz mit vollen Holztüren kann als besonderes Möbel auf einem kleinen Sockel am Boden stehend als Schrank für Bücher, Schallplatten und ev. Wäsche Verwendung finden.

In der vierten Kombination haben wir einen Klappschreibtisch, der in kleinen schmalen Räumen wegen der Raumersparnis zweckmäßig sein wird. Im geöffneten Zustand hat er eine besonders gefällige Form. Störende Unordnung kann immer durch Hochklappen des Schreibbrettes beseitigt werden.

Die Veröffentlichung des acht Typen umfassenden WK-Aufbaumöbelprogrammes wird in einem der nächsten Hefte fortgesetzt und hat zum Ziel, manchem, über den Charakter der Anregung hinaus, seinen möbellosen oder möbelarmen Raum schön, zweckmäßig und wandelbar zugleich gestalten zu helfen. ha

DIE ANRICHTE MIT SCHREIBAUFSATZ ALS ARBEITSTISCH, GEÖFFNET UND GESCHLOSSEN
SIDEBOARD WITH WRITING DESK TOP OPEN AND CLOSED

DAS WK-AUFBAUMÖBEL

Wir zeigen hier aus dem WK-Kombinationsprogramm den ersten Typ. Die Grundlage bildet der Anrichtetisch, dessen Tischplatte 105 cm lang und 44 cm breit ist. Die Höhe des Tisches ist 70 cm. Von den vier verschiedenen Aufsätzen kann das kleine zweitürige Glasschränkchen mit 80 cm Breite und 56 cm Höhe auch aufgehängt werden. In den drei nebeneinander liegenden Schubkästen lassen sich Bestecke, Schmuck usw. unterbringen. Völlig verändert erscheint uns der Tisch, wenn wir ihn in der Kombination mit dem größeren Glasschrank betrachten. Der größere Glasschrank ist ebenfalls, wie der Tisch, 70 cm hoch und hat dieselbe Grundfläche wie die Fläche der Tischplatte. In dieser Kombination erscheint das Gesamtmöbel geschlossener als in der ersten Kombination.

Aufnahmen: Willi Moegle - Stuttgart

3.3 Furniture collection "WK-Aufbaumöbel," *Architektur und Wohnform*, no. 1, 1946. Photographer: Willi Moegle. Reproduced from Staatsbibliothek Berlin.

and in 1949 the magazine reported on the Werkbund exhibition's foreign section with examples from the United States, Sweden, Switzerland, the UK, and France.[74] An article on the exhibition called for German professionals to make use of the "credit" that the Werkbund and Bauhaus enjoyed abroad.[75]

By 1952 it was an accepted "truth" in Germany that the Werkbund had been banned during the Third Reich because of its "historic merits for the development of and support for artistically unobjectionable designs."[76] Simultaneously, "America" and the idea of a postwar "West" became an important part of modern design's new historical narrative.[77] By 1954 the radical dissociation of modern design from Nazism was certainly entrenched enough to proclaim its association with the recently established postwar political framework of the West, a move in which the special image of the Bauhaus as a beacon of liberal internationalism played an important role.[78] In the first issue of the magazine *magnum*, the Swiss designer Max Bill, director of the newly founded Ulm Institute of Design, succinctly summarized the connection between modern design and the self-definition of the young Federal Republic: "A young republic with faith in the future had seen the rise of the Bauhaus. . . . A reactionary, short-sighted autocracy crushed it as one of its first contributions to the pile of rubble into which it turned Europe. . . . After twelve years of oppression and destruction, during which there were only some islands in Europe and the United States that cherished Bauhaus ideas, the interest in the Bauhaus has now grown considerably."[79]

This new political framing of modern design arrived in two popular women's magazines, *Constanze* and *Brigitte*, in 1953. To be sure, between 1949 and 1953 modern design was already widespread in both magazines, neither of which mentioned any interruption of design development due to the previous political regime.[80] *Constanze* asked readers, for instance, to remove the decoration from inherited turn-of-the-century furniture and praised plain white porcelain as being "modern, contemporary, and therefore time appropriate."[81] *Brigitte*'s predecessor, *Das Blatt der Hausfrau*, presented the "beauty of the living room" conforming to such standards as an essential part of the housewife's task, which was "to help preserve and even create cultural values on a higher level."[82] In 1953, in spite of this continuously self-evident presence of the modern, both magazines started to argue emphatically for a general *change* in decoration styles toward "modern" forms. *Brigitte* suddenly began to make a sharp distinction between the "cold pomp" (kalte Pracht) of earlier times and the modern design of contemporary furnishing.[83] In February 1953 *Constanze* even declared an upcoming "revolution" and claimed that "new forms" were on the rise that only recently had been "bashfully" hidden in furniture shops. Emphasizing that the movement behind these forms had its roots in Germany, *Constanze* deplored that in the present "we lag behind. The reason: 1933 broke off what had just begun." The early years of the Federal Republic had allegedly witnessed the "renaissance" of an old bourgeois taste. This alleged comeback, however, had been entirely absent from the magazine's reporting until that moment. The now imminent "revolution" had been "prepared for more than a century" by "architects, engineers, and entrepreneurs around the world" who were "working together" to make it happen. With clear unadorned lines for tables and chairs, Germany, the magazine argued, was finally catching up again with the international standards once invented by German architects and designers.[84]

The same modern forms that had been present in these magazines all along were thus suddenly reintroduced as new and even revolutionary. In various publications, modern design was now linked to the existence of a broader Western and international development.[85] A contrast with the Nazi past was, often implicitly, built into this discourse.[86] These conspicuous changes were arguably an effect not only of the various efforts of early postwar West German writers to dissociate modern design from its Nazi entanglement but also of American efforts to establish modern design's Western political framing through exhibitions sponsored by the Marshall Plan across Europe, including in West Germany.[87] Only two month before *Constanze* published its article on the revolution in the living room, the magazine had reported on an exhibition in Berlin's Marshall-Haus featuring a fully furnished house (fig. 3.4). In this "ideal place to live," the dining and living rooms were provided with "simple, modern furniture from twelve different countries."[88] The magazine quoted the show's political message at some length: "Here you see a house that has been built by all free nations, a house that demonstrates the possibilities the Atlantic community can have for every one of us. . . . You can find in this house everything that comes out of modern European serial production every day. In such houses you will live healthier, more beautiful, and more practical lives."

As Greg Castillo has shown, this exhibition, entitled *Wir bauen ein besseres Leben* (We're Building a Better Life), was the last and most successful of a series of four exhibitions on the modern home in Germany organized by the US State Department under the umbrella of the Marshall Plan and aimed at promoting enhanced productivity and free trade as the best solution for Europe's problems. In 1951 the third of these exhibitions was the first to emphasize modern design. It focused on American household objects and was realized in cooperation with the Museum of Modern Art in New York. MoMA's industrial design curator, Edgar Kaufmann Jr., saw "American industrial design" as "the culmination of pioneering German efforts such as . . . the work of the German Werkbund and the legacy of Bauhaus design."[89] This message fell on receptive ears among

Hier wohnt man ideal!

Das Haus, in dem Ideals wohnen, hat keinen Keller und keinen Boden. Niemand vermißt das. Es hat keine Heizung, und die Zimmer sind trotzdem mollig. Es hat kein Dach, und es regnet doch nicht hinein. Dafür ist es auch ein ideales, ein Idealhaus. Die vierköpfige Familie fühlt sich in ihren Räumen sehr wohl. Der einzige Haken ist, daß sie dabei von Tausenden, von Hunderttausenden neugieriger Leute beobachtet wird. Sie kommen, um ein Haus zu sehen, das zwölf Nationen einrichteten. Privat sind Ideals gar keine Familie. Vater Günther und Mutter Adila tragen nur im Idealhaus Eheringe. Es sind stellungslose Schauspieler, die sich mit dem idealen Familie-Spiel je zwanzig Mark am Tag verdienen wollen. „Tochter" Bärbel und der „Sohn" Michael bekommen täglich zehn Mark. Nach der Ausstellung im Berliner Marshallhaus geht es zunächst nach Stuttgart und dann nach Hannover.

Ideals Haus ist einstöckig und besteht aus Küche, elektrischem Waschraum, Speise-, Wohn-, Schlaf- und Badezimmer. Hinter dem Haus gibt's ein Gärtchen, vorne einen Kinderspielplatz. Am liebsten spielen Bärbel und Micha dort mit Schaumgummitieren, die man beliebig umformen kann. Spazieren wir aber erstmal durchs Haus.

In der Küche sind die Schränke — selbstverständlich — eingebaut. Hier ist alles so eingerichtet, daß man jede Arbeit nur mit wenigen Handgriffen schaffen kann. Ein elektrischer Herd, der sich auf bestimmte Temperaturen einstellen läßt, schaltet sich automatisch aus, sobald die Suppe kocht, der Kuchen gebacken und das Fleisch gegrillt ist. Zum Abwaschbecken gehört gleich eine Geschirrspül- und Trockenanlage. Andere mechanische Küchengeräte: Teigmischer, elektrischer Messerputzapparat, Elektro-Kaffeemühle und -maschine und so weiter. In der Waschküche stehen ein Wäsche- und ein Trockenapparat. Diese Küche ist für den Hausherrn gleichzeitig eine vollmechanische Werkstatt. Im Kinderzimmer sind schaumgummigepolsterte Betten aus Raumersparnis übereinandergebaut. Zum schwarzgekachelten Bad mit eingebauter Badewanne gehört eine abgetrennte Sonderbrause. Im Speise- und Wohnzimmer stehen schlichte, moderne Möbel aus zwölf Herren Ländern. Über dem Idealhaus gibt ein Mann mit Mikrofon aus einem Turm den Ausstellungs-Besuchern (für dreißig Mark am Tag) folgende Erklärungen vom „besseren Leben im Idealhaus" ab: „Hier sehen Sie ein Haus, an dem alle freien Völker mitgearbeitet haben, ein Haus, das beweist, welche Möglichkeiten die atlantische Völkergemeinschaft für jeden von uns haben kann, wenn wir unsere technischen, wirtschaftlichen und industriellen Kräfte zusammentun. Hier sehen Sie die Wünsche vieler in einem Haus vereint. Sie finden in diesem Haus alles, was die moderne europäische Industrie täglich in Serienproduktion herstellt. In solchen Häusern wird man gesünder, schöner und praktischer leben. Dies Haus ist kein Traumhaus — es kann morgen schon für jeden von uns die übliche Wohnung sein. Alle Vorbedingungen sind gegeben: Energiequellen, Rohstoffe und Maschinen, Intelligenz und Erfindergeist. Es liegt an uns, ob sich ein freier Warenaustausch entwickelt. Wir müssen die Wirtschaftseinheit Europas wollen. Es liegt nur an uns!" Soweit der Mann aus dem „Krähennest". Sein und unser guter Wille scheitert zunächst einmal an der Ausstellungsleitung, die Kauflustigen erklären muß: „Diese Dinge sind nur in dem Land billig, aus dem sie stammen. In Deutschland gibt es die ausländischen Einrichtungsgegenstände nur zu einem kleinen Teil zu kaufen." Aus dieser Sicht müssen Sie sich leider auch die Spalte rechts anschauen.

Eine Schiebetür, die gleichzeitig Schiefertafel ist, macht der Familie Ideal den größten Spaß. Ideals bewohnen zu viert ein internationales „Idealhaus", das jetzt in Deutschland ausgestellt wird. Wie gesund, schön und praktisch man in diesem Haus lebt, erfahren Sie hier auf diesen zwei Seiten.

So verlockend die Hähne und Kacheln auch blitzen — ein Bad im idealen Badezimmer ist für Frau Ideal verboten. Was sollten die Besucher denken, die von morgens bis abends alles mit ansehen können, was Ideals so in ihren offenen vier Wänden tun. So begnügt Frau Ideal sich mit einem Trockenbad.

Eine abwaschbare Nylonwand trennt Ideals Eßzimmer von der Diele. Das Schlafzimmer schützt eine schalldämpfende Ziehharmonika aus Leder vor Lärm aus dem Wohnzimmer. Wenn die Familie Ideal Mittag ißt, schaut ihr immer eine Menge Leute von oben auf die Köpfe und in die Töpfe. Aber das macht ihr nichts aus. In ihren eigenen Häusern wohnen und essen Ideals nicht so ideal wie hier. Und dort fehlen ihnen auch die schönen Dinge, die sie Ihnen rechts so stolz vorführen und auf die wir noch lange warten müssen, weil es in der Welt leider viele Grenzen gibt.

Fotos: Cürlis

3.4 "This is the ideal place to live." An article on a Marshall Plan exhibition in Berlin published in *Constanze*, December 1952. Photographer: Cürlis. Reproduced from Staatsbibliothek Berlin.

German professionals, who quickly presented the importance of modern design and architecture for postwar "Western civilization" as the story of a German cultural endeavor to create "an epochal style" that had been taken on by the United States through the influence of émigrés such as Walter Gropius.[90]

We're Building a Better Life, the fourth exhibition, presented an even more internationalized Western version of the modern home, with commodities that were "manufactured in a Marshall Plan member nation," above all in Germany, France, and Italy. A board declared: "Thanks to technology, rising productivity, economic cooperation and free enterprise, these objects are available to *our western civilization.*"[91] In this hugely successful exhibition, which drew more than half a million visitors, the idea of "Western countries" was interlinked with a recognizably modern aesthetics of everyday life.[92] An official press release stated: "Just as these items from the various countries combine to form a *homogenous whole*, so the nations themselves can combine to form a *homogenous community.*"[93]

This new framework of the homogeneously modern shape of the postwar West under American leadership absorbed a German legacy of modern forms that, less than a decade earlier, had been proclaimed to realize the essence of a homogeneous national or racial community. With the exhibition, a new and decisively postwar context for modern design was introduced to the public under the guidance and with the official blessing of the major occupation power and new leader of the West, the United States. In *Baukunst und Werkform*, architect Alfons Leitl rejoiced at this campaign and interpreted the Marshall Plan exhibition's *political* project of "defending Western culture" as a return to the dream of "old Werkbund fighters." In Leitl's perspective, the whole project became a German endeavor to defend *Kultur* against the danger of being invaded by superficial *Zivilisation* and by "the atrocities" of the "international furnishing industry."[94]

Leitl was not the only one pleased about the possibility of continuing an old Werkbund dream in the framework of the postwar West. The question is, What kind of dream are we talking about? When, in the 1949 catalog for the Werkbund exhibition, the human being at the center of modern aesthetic principles was defined as "something definitive" standing "above time, just like the people [*Volk*]" and when it was contrasted with "a bad class of human being," namely, "a human being without taste," the project of realizing the nation's wholeness through modern design seemed still alive. When, in the same catalog, Jupp Ernst proclaimed modern design as the remedy that could prevent Germany from becoming a "half-colonial raw material supplier," the logic derived from a belief that Germany's superior aesthetics had legitimated its claim to dominate—or colonize—culturally inferior peoples.[95]

In his 1952 introduction to the book *Die schöne Wohnung* (The beautiful dwelling), architect Guido Harbers pointed to countries like Sweden, Switzerland, Austria, and the United States that, next to Germany, also cultivated good principles of design. Harbers added that a "uniform society" that would adopt the attitude behind such principles was "still missing." In 1952 such an imagined uniform society would be amalgamated with the larger western Atlantic context. Harbers, a former Nazi Party member who had been Munich's officer for residential construction during the Third Reich, also referred to the Ramersdorf settlement in Munich as a model. He did not mention, however, that he himself had been responsible for Ramersdorf or that it was presented in 1934 as a "model settlement" of the National Socialist regime.[96]

The successful advice book *Unser Heim* (Our home), by Heinrich and Marga Lützeler (first published in 1939, with new editions published in 1940, 1942, 1950, and 1953), illustrates how the fusion of the modern design discourse with National Socialist culture was superficially replaced after the war by an emphasis on postwar renewal in an international context.[97] In 1940 *Unser Heim* professed a vitalist philosophy of the home in which "a cheery, upward-moving life" had to "emanate from the rooms."[98] Such a *Heimkultur* presupposed "a personality that . . . stands in the community." In 1940 the Lützelers explicitly expressed their thankfulness that this kind of *Heimkultur* was on the rise in Germany "like nowhere else." A number of Nazi initiatives illustrated this observation, including "the purification of the profession of architects" (meaning the exclusion of Jews). The authors especially praised the "designs and exhibitions" of the Imperial Bureau of Homesteads and referred to the Volkswagen as a model for developing affordable products. While the chapters show interiors accompanied by texts without explicit political content, the book's last sentence expressed the wish that the home of its readers would become the "high altar of our folklore [*Volkstum*]."[99]

In the 1950 edition this sentence had vanished, and a new preface deplored the dire living conditions of "millions of people in today's Europe." In the area of "living and working," the Lützelers now mentioned foreign countries like Switzerland as having seen progress that "we barely know yet." The sentence in which the 1940 edition spoke about the positive developments in the authors' National Socialist present is only slightly adapted in the 1950 version, where it expresses the authors' gratefulness that "even today, in the midst of chaos," there were many successful efforts to "revive home culture [*Heimkultur*] again." The period of the Third Reich has now disappeared, while the same expressions that had praised Nazi efforts in 1940 have reappeared, praising postwar efforts. The former reference to the Volkswagen was replaced by a general reference to "the low-cost car," as if mentioning it by name would have exposed the silenced political history of a timeless modern.[100] The rest of the introduction has stayed the same, repeating the hope for renewal just as it was expressed in 1940. In both editions, the next chapter starts with the seemingly universal truth that "people and times with good instincts naturally embrace the good form."

The Modern Home in Limbo

If the Marshall Plan propaganda efforts made it possible to transfer older ideas about modern aesthetics as the manifestation of an inherently homogeneous and superior (German, Aryan, or white) culture to the new framework of the West, the question remains if and how those ideas continued to be relevant in the coming years. After all, the most popular modes of advocating modern design focused on its rational, pragmatic, and occasionally even playful side. Explicit references to "German" culture, relatively rare since the war, all but disappeared from popular discourse and were gradually replaced by references to an "international" Western or European style (see chapter 4). Simultaneously, modern design was promoted by political authorities as the symbol of a democratic and rational Western modernity.

Between 1953 and 1958 a number of state-sponsored events and developments established the political meaning of modern design for how the Federal Republic represented itself to its Western partners. In 1953 the West German parliament founded the German Design Council to help invigorate German design in order to support economic export and growth. In the same year, the West German government and the High Commission for Occupied Germany jointly funded the Ulm Institute of Design as the successor to the Bauhaus school. In 1957 the Interbau, an international architecture exhibition sponsored by the German government, took place in West Berlin. It presented Berlin's Hansaviertel as a newly constructed modern urban space, including model interior designs. Finally, the German Design Council was responsible for the West German pavilion at Expo 58 in Brussels. Under the motto "Living in Germany," functional and simple modern furniture and other domestic objects of the exhibition were, following the press release, supposed to "give birth to a new conception of life."[101]

One could easily assume that, at least after 1953, the good form with all its problematic German legacy had been denationalized, deracialized, and given a completely new meaning. The cultural reality of the 1950s, however, seems more complicated. In a society whose very existence as a sovereign state rested on its self-definition against the Third Reich, the search for explicit references to Nazism only carries historical interpretation so far. In order to disentangle the various political meanings that modern design offered to postwar West Germans, we need to look closely at the web of messages that were available in the public sphere. What kind of dreams and fantasies were connected with those messages? What were their unspoken assumptions, and how did they relate to the past?

In 1952 and 1953 both *Brigitte* and *Constanze* promoted the WKS company. WK Sozialwerk Möbel was the successor of the alliance of German workshops (Deutsche Werkstätten) for art in the home, founded in 1912. This alliance had sold its furniture under the label WK-Möbel during the 1920s and promoted it under the nationalist slogan "German WK furniture in the German home" in 1935.[102] In 1952 it proudly advertised its "forty-year" anniversary of "decent home décor [*Wohnkultur*]."[103] The alliance had cooperated with the Nazi Imperial Bureau of Homesteads to produce the latter's program of simple and affordable furniture for German (settler) homes. *Innen-Dekoration* frequently reported on these WK programs, as well as on the closely related Deutsche Werkstätten (see fig. 3.1).[104] In 1937 an article referred to Goebbels's plea for a "comfortable and modern home" for every member of the racial community and presented the Deutsche Werkstätten as the quintessential furniture producer for a truly German home culture, or *Heimkultur*: "When the concept of home culture is so well understood in Germany, when so many racial comrades [*Volksgenossen*] see it as desirable, and when home culture has become an attainable goal, this is in part thanks to the sacrificial and pioneering work of the Deutsche Werkstätten."[105] The Deutsche Werkstätten Hellerau continued this programmatic merger by publishing advertisements in which it assigned itself "the role of a trailblazer for a new German *Wohnkultur*." In 1939 the company even declared itself as "an important bearer of the general cultural movement in Germany."[106]

In 1953 *Constanze* announced that a certain Frau Henkel was the lucky winner of a WKS-Möbel prize competition. Frau Henkel explained that it "has always been my biggest wish to furnish my home in this style." She "always had to think about dwelling and furnishing" because she had been "bombed out twice during the war."[107] The reference to the bombing reminded the readers of the war deprivations and the fact that new furnishings for the home marked an important material milestone in overcoming these deprivations. This also meant, however, that Frau Henkel's heightened concern with the style of home furnishing began at a moment in which modern home aesthetics had been incorporated into the propagated vision of the Third Reich's racial community.

There is no way to grasp or prove, for that matter, an unequivocal cultural connection between Frau Henkel's enthusiasm for this particular style and the promotion of it as part of Nazi culture until 1945 or of the relevance of such a connection for the readers of *Constanze*. If concrete material objects can silently embody contradictory relationships to the past, then the aesthetic shape of newly acquired objects surely cannot be assumed to carry an unambiguous meaning. The way in which such objects can become banal symbols of how the social itself is understood is paved with the inarticulate, the vague, the latent, and the whole messiness of ordinary life. Such objects always remain banal objects. They did so even while they were absorbed in various ways during the Third Reich into a discourse in which the right objects were overflowing with the metaphysical essence of an Aryan people.[108]

The cultural movement that led to the founding of the Werkbund had embraced precisely this capacity of modern material objects to *embody* meaning instead of *symbolizing* it. The absence of symbolic decorations became the very essence of what was called the "good form," "modern," or "timeless." This absence was deemed crucial for recognizing material objects in their aesthetic purity and "clarity" as powerful embodiments of the organic and superior nation before 1933, of the radically racialized nation after 1933, and, eventually, of the social and political order posited as Western after 1945. The ideological emptiness of unadorned forms was the very aspect through which they acquired ideological meaning. As a result of this paradoxical constellation, these objects and forms carried with them a political limbo that marked much of the postwar period's culture and how it built a national *and* transnational make-believe space. Modern objects were not self-explanatory political symbols. They embodied political meaning in an obscure and at times disorienting way.

In her book about the popular attraction of German Fascism, the psychoanalyst Gudrun Brockhaus, born in 1947, describes how she was struck by "a very inconspicuous" object when visiting an exhibition in Munich's House of Art on art and furnishing in the Nazi era. The wooden paneling of a heater that had been in Hitler's apartment in Munich captured her attention.[109] Brockhaus noticed the paneling because it resembled, "down to the smallest detail," the one in the living room of her childhood home. In hindsight she was struck most, however, by her own "angry surprise," which made her accept only reluctantly the obvious kinship in taste between her parents and Hitler. Her parents, who had been Nazi supporters, had married in 1939 and had subsequently furnished their house. After the war, they explained their choice of style to their children by referring to concepts such as "simplicity, expediency, and genuineness." They deemed the baroque period furniture of their own parents as not only aesthetically but also morally inferior. With its superfluous decorations, it was judged as "vain, complacent, redundant."

Listening to her parents during the 1950s, Brockhaus could not discern that their moral judgment of aesthetic choices stemmed from a time in which such verdicts derived their meaning from the Nazi context. She was surprised to see this familiar object from her childhood in an exhibition on the Nazi era because she had never thought about such material continuities or about the mental continuities potentially looming beneath them. We can now add that there could be another reason for her surprise, namely, the fact that the "simplicity" of domestic objects had been pronounced again and again after the war as the very thing that placed these objects on the right side of Western history. This postwar discourse had aimed precisely at confusing the link that Brockhaus had such trouble reestablishing several decades later.

Before 1954, when both the message about modern design's anti-Nazi character and its framing as a Western style had not yet established itself firmly, critical voices occasionally expressed some measure of discomfort about a dogmatic promotion of modern design, while larger parts of the population rejected it. From 1954 onward the Allensbach Institute for Public Opinion Research regularly asked West Germans about their taste in interior decoration, letting them choose between drawings that sketched out models of four different living room interiors (fig. 3.5). By the end of the decade Germans were roughly split in half between a penchant for various modern interiors and one for bulky and decorated furniture. In 1955 a mere 8 to 11 percent opted for what was called a "modern" style, which resembled the 1952 Marshall Plan exhibition. This number rose to 23 percent in 1962. A second model interior, Werkstätten-Möbel, consisted of sedate interiors with simple wooden furniture resembling those promoted during the 1930s by the Werkbund as well as by many Nazi institutions. *Constanze* and *Brigitte* often promoted this style, mixing it with pieces closer to Allensbach's "modern" category. In 1955 30 percent preferred this "Werkstätten" style, rising to 38 percent in 1962.[110] Curved, bulky pieces of furniture and heavy armchairs labeled "cold pomp" (later "Chippendale") received the largest percentages in the middle of the decade (60 percent in 1954, 56 percent in 1955, falling to 38 percent in 1960). The turn-of-the-century style called "Grandmother" or "Makartstil," referring to rooms overstuffed with nineteenth-century furniture and ornate draperies, was the least popular style, continuously chosen by only 2 to 4 percent.[111] The younger the respondents and the higher their salary and level of education, the more likely it was that they opted for the "modern" or the "Werkstätten" style. In 1959 the bulky "Chippendale" style was still by far the most popular among people earning the lowest salaries (61 percent).[112]

„Kalte Pracht", ausgewählt von..........47%

Werkstättenstil, ausgewählt von....31%

Moderne Auffassung der Innenarchitektur, ausgewählt von ... 17%

„Großmütterchens gute Stube", ausgewählt von 2%

3.5 Living room interior styles. Allensbach Institute for Public Opinion Research press release, March 1959.

Before 1954 journalists sometimes hinted at the tension between the large claims of modern design advocates and the principle of free consumer choice. There was never any criticism, however, of the good form's assumed moral authority. In September 1951 *Der Spiegel* published its first article on modern interior design, focusing on the mismatch between designers' ideals and a majority of consumers who opted for bulky, curved, and adorned pieces of furniture.[113] Retailers and designers called this style "deceitful pomp" and had no sympathy for what they saw as its underlying intentions: "The furniture is supposed to 'show off,' be big, and suggest with a few bashful flourishes the remnants of former wealth." These moral allegations about the "wrong" taste had been repeated over and over again for many decades, including during the Third Reich, and had obviously become an uncontested truth for most of the educated classes.

There was only one topic that triggered diverging opinions among experts. While the Werkbund and some housing consortiums began to promote the good form through centers that advised citizens on how to furnish and decorate their apartments, many furniture dealers thought such centers tried to manipulate customers into choosing the modern style and thus interfered with free consumer choice in an improper way.[114] In their efforts to educate German tenants, some housing programs had even started to rent out prefurnished apartments, inciting the criticism of furniture dealers, who believed this meant "committing an act of violence against the average customer of 1951."[115] Accordingly, journalist Marlies Flesch-Thebesius criticized a new housing project with prefurnished apartments in the *Frankfurter Allgemeine* by defending the fundamental freedom to have bad taste.[116]

Two years later, in the spring of 1953, a federation of charitable housing associations called Gewobag prefurnished all sixty-eight apartments in one of their new settlements for German refugees.[117] *Brigitte* published a long opinion piece that seemed to react to critical comments on the topic. Journalist Lilo Aureden defended Gewobag by referring to modern furnishing's superiority because of its break with a vaguely defined "past." Many people, Aureden wrote, "stick to the past and live with it, and everybody who risks breaking the traditional chains is confronted with the most scathing criticism. What used to be misunderstood and be carped about has nevertheless taken hold within a generation. Why? Because every real creator . . . recognizes the mission of his time and, in spite of all the know-it-alls, finds affirmation in the development of the future."[118] The passage combines a metaphysical argument about good design (representing the "mission of his time") with claims that it was confronted with "scathing criticism," thereby turning the reality of the period's hegemonic discourse upside down. Aureden assured her readers that the choice for the future Gewobag dwellers was "rich" and dismissed anyone who did not like these interiors as having a "personal spleen."

The following December, Barbara Reichek-Hopf criticized the same initiative in *Die Zeit* with a series of odd remarks: "We have tried to find out more about it. The success gives cause for reflection. . . . Somewhere something is not quite right." She also mentioned "attacks" by "organizations and authorities" complaining that the furniture trade "would not fulfill its task in a 'progressive' and 'modern' way." A number of formulations were put in quotation marks without identifying who had said them. Gewobag had started "a socialist experiment" of fully furnished apartments in order to (and here Reichek-Hopf quotes again) "form the false pursuit of bygone times, with gentle force, in the sense of the new community life." This twisted formulation exposes a perceived sense of entitlement to shape people's convictions by "forcing" the right kind of furniture on them. The author's main criticism is expressed with some urgency: "A good objective is pursued by means that don't seem harmless. . . . More problematically, standardized apartments are coupled with the propaganda of furnishings that are standardized down to the last detail . . . and that the 'ignorant' customer is supposed to design his private living space in line with the wishes of the experts."[119]

Reichek-Hopf was worried about the way the organized trade and the state authorities used their power to influence the private sphere of German citizens, whose own tastes and perceptions were disparaged. That she associated her unease with the enemy of "socialism" fit, of course, in a Cold War paradigm. One wonders, however, if her criticism might also have been informed by a consciousness about the fact that such practices not only were "socialist" but also continued a *National* Socialist practice of forming a "new community life," given the importance of standardized "good form" interiors for Nazi policies. The German Labor Front had aimed at providing German households with "ideological notions in the form of usable cultural assets" through the production of household goods "according to uniform, politically determined directives."[120] To point to continuities with such policies, however, was apparently unpublishable or maybe even unspeakable. It is impossible to know if they also had become unthinkable.[121]

From 1953 onward, modern design was given political meaning as the symbol of a West shaped by an internationalized German aesthetic tradition. It was also linked to the hope of turning German society into a harmonious, rational, egalitarian, future-oriented, and morally immaculate community. The emphatically "modern" of this postwar discourse often confused any sense of historical time. In 1955 *Brigitte* launched a series written by Eva Noack-Mosse that presented the careers of influential German designers. These professional life stories contradicted the supposedly sharp contrast between modern design and National Socialism when the artists were said to have had successful careers *until* the war, as was the case with Wilhelm Wagenfeld's role as art director of the "Lusitanian glass plant." In line with the Western framework of modern design, the presentation of Wagenfeld's postwar career culminated in the huge success of his silverware design in the United States.[122]

Hermann Gretsch, the former director of the nazified Werkbund who had died in 1950, was also included in the series. The dominant theme of his professional biography in *Brigitte* was the Werkbund idea of a "timeless" aesthetic. The article concludes with the astonished (and astonishing) observation: "Some of the dinnerware that Gretsch designed and that we see everywhere nowadays and that appeals to us again and again is already more than twenty years old. One of its most essential qualities, apart from its modern, timeless shape, is that it does not need much space. It is as if Gretsch had anticipated our current lack of space."[123] The proclaimed aesthetic "timelessness" of modern porcelain design becomes a trait that ensures an unproblematic continuity, implicitly bridging the gap between political regimes. In this sphere outside of history, modern design floats in the air like an angel of time over and above all crimes and destruction. The journalist Eva Noack-Mosse was born in a Jewish family in 1908 and had experienced ostracism and violence from the Nazi regime firsthand, which culminated in her deportation to Theresienstadt in 1945.[124] This information is relevant insofar as it underlines that the continuities and contradictions of the discourse on modern design exceed the realm of straightforward political convictions or conscious remembrance of the Nazi past. The myth creating character of the discourse systematically undermined the very possibility of forming such a consciousness or articulating it openly.

Art historian Michael Lingohr has systematically traced Gretsch's most famous porcelain design, "model 1382," for Arzberg from its successful introduction in 1930 through the National Socialist period, when it was frequently shown in many exhibitions and catalogs and recommended in advice literature, as well as in the official Nazi guidebook for household objects. Gretsch's influential position helped to enhance the official promotion of this specific coffee service, including its use in international exhibitions.[125] It seems odd that the common argument for modern pieces of furniture, namely, that they are relatively small, became so important in Noack-Mosse's article on Hermann Gretsch's dinnerware. After all, even overly decorated plates don't tend to be larger than unadorned ones.

Gretsch was responsible for the German exhibition at the triennial in Milan in April 1940. On this occasion he presented some of his vases in a way that underlined the German claim to geographic space (see fig. 3.2).[126] At the same time, he promoted the Imperial Bureau of Homesteads' programs of simple furniture for small settler houses. The small domestic and the large geographic space went harmoniously together in the context of a self-proclaimed egalitarian and expansionist Nazi culture. Against this background the sentence "It is as if Gretsch had anticipated our current lack of space" sounds like an ironic reference to the results of this policy: a housing shortage in Germany due to the bombings and the reduction of Germany's geographic size due to its loss of the war. The formulation might also reflect a subliminal knowledge that the love affair of West German elites with modern design had a double edge, that these objects' timelessness consisted in their capacity to be simultaneously connected to two Germanys and two historical times that were supposed to be each other's political and cultural opposites. When *magnum* reported on the tenth triennial design exhibition in Milan in 1954, the magazine chose the title "Models of Optimism" yet commented that it was "an optimism that could be of yesteryear."[127]

A Dream of Timeless Homogeneity

In order for an element of culture to work as a myth and transform "history into nature," its concrete prehistory and historical genesis must have become undiscernible.[128] Such a myth can create a timeless, hermetical social world without any proper entry points for direct criticism. When modern design had been successfully dehistoricized and disassociated from its own prehistory, the path was cleared to use it to create a mythical dreamworld of social homogeneity and harmony suitable for the "economic miracle" and its increasingly commercialized public sphere. The period between 1953 and 1958 is characterized by constant efforts to promote modern design and to further naturalize its dehistoricized aesthetics. These efforts explicitly denied the legitimacy and even at times the actual existence of deviating tastes. In 1957 the *Frankfurter Allgemeine* proclaimed that the modern had already prevailed and that only those who could not (yet) afford to buy modern furniture would still stick to their "Chippendale."[129]

The huge success of these efforts in tandem with various state initiatives can be measured by the absence of voices that would publicly articulate a deviating taste in interior design even though more than 50 percent of West Germans preferred furnishings that looked very different from any version of the hegemonic design ideal. Some publications found implicit ways to convey their different take on the matter. The illustrated magazine *Quick*, more attuned to popular and working-class sensibilities, conspicuously refrained from advocating modern design and recoiled completely from joining in the widespread practice of bashing outdated styles. It very rarely even reported on these topics, although it frequently published approving articles on modern architecture such as the United Nations building in New York and new theaters, opera houses, and churches in West Germany.[130] When *Quick* did report on innovations in furniture production it focused on technical aspects, usually without mentioning the question of style.[131] In 1957, when *Quick* and *Der Stern* published photo reports on the international architecture exhibition Interbau in Berlin, they focused on architecture and left out the aspect of interior design, which was, however, discussed at length in newspapers.[132]

In contrast to this general absence, *Quick* raised the issue of modern interior design regularly between 1953 and 1955 in the form of cartoons that made fun of the hype and highlighted people's lack of enthusiasm about it. These cartoons ridiculed contemporary interiors that belonged to Allensbach's "modern" category with a conspicuous presence of organic forms and a kidney table in nearly every picture, indicating the symbolic status this version of the modern had acquired by then.[133] In February 1953 one cartoon showed a sales assistant in a modern furniture store who is caught by his colleague retreating into a cozy back room stuffed with turn-of-the-century pieces in order to "relax."[134] Some cartoons shed light on design aficionados' inability to tolerate anything in their home that would disturb the harmony and homogeneity of its aesthetics. In one of them, a woman breaks down in tears because her husband, dressed in traditional southern German clothing, drinks his beer out of a bulky beer stein at odds with her living room's style. On her knees she cries out desperately: "Otto . . . I beg you, at least use a glass!"[135] Some of these cartoons imply that men were more skeptical of the new forms than women, an idea probably evoked by how magazines like *Constanze* and *Brigitte* as well as advertising campaigns propagated the modern home. The Allensbach polls, however, do not show a significant gender gap in this area.

The contemporary association of modern design with liberal democracy was not lost on the *Quick* cartoonists either. In 1954 one of them depicted a scene set in a modern living room, in which a father had just hit his son with a belt. The son, still rubbing his buttock, exclaims: "This I tell you. Your outdated educational method doesn't fit in this modern ambience" (fig. 3.6).[136] Given that *Quick* had never proclaimed the superiority of modern interior design, the cartoon was probably seen as ridiculing the very idea that an interior could be "democratic." To all appearances, such cartoons were the only way in which

3.6 "Your outdated educational method doesn't fit in this modern ambience." Cartoon, *Quick*, September 1954. Original with color. Cartoonist: Leo von Malachowski. Reproduced from Staatsbibliothek Berlin.

the huge moral, political, and cultural pretensions connected to modern design were criticized. While it must have represented a feeling of discontent that was shared much more broadly, such criticism was nevertheless a marginal phenomenon in the public sphere.

After 1953 writers in popular lifestyle magazines embarked on a massive campaign to educate their readers about the benefits of good modern household objects by referring to their inherently "good" quality and by insinuating that embracing those objects was equivalent to a practical, rational, and therefore morally "good" life. This, of course, continued to a large extent the very discourse that had developed at the beginning of the twentieth century and was also disseminated during the Third Reich. Consumers were not told anymore that decorating their apartments in the right manner was a crucial way to realize their self as part of an organic and culturally and racially superior nation. They were still told, however, that decorating their apartments in the right manner was a crucial way to realize their self and to belong to an implicitly national and at times transnational "we." "How Modern Are We Actually?" was the title of the most programmatic article on the topic published in *Brigitte*. The first-person plural appeared in endless repetition throughout the text to chart what the magazine identified as "our" "moderately modern" taste.[137]

Between 1953 and 1955 the readers of *Constanze*, which promoted modern design even more rigorously than *Brigitte*, came across formulations over and over again that assumed that they all agreed on the fundamental principles of how their homes should look:

> "the new forms of *our* furniture and everyday objects"
> "the modern furniture for *our* small apartments"
> "a house in which *we* can breathe again"
> "*we* live differently from our parents and grandparents"
> "the furnishings of *our* time"
> "adequate for *our* attitude toward life"
> "matching *our* lifestyle"[138]

This suggestive way of writing made it difficult for readers to find a subject position outside of this aesthetic and moral paradigm of domestic modernity, especially once the expanding commercial advertising began to join the chorus. An ad for upholstery foam shows a woman in front of a kidney table interior with the slogan "My home is my world," suggesting the self-evident equivalence of "home" with a modern interior (fig. 3.7).[139] Other advertisers still acknowledged their customers' different tastes and used both modern and traditional pieces of furniture for their featured interiors.[140] In the course of the 1950s, however, the representation of modern interiors started to spread more widely in ad campaigns for a broad range of products such as curtains, carpets, mattresses, fabrics, and vacuum cleaners. In the second half of the decade,

3.7 "My home is my world." Upholstery foam advertisement, *Constanze*, June 1955. Reproduced from Staatsbibliothek Berlin.

modern interiors began to show up in ads for washing machines, televisions, silk stockings, typewriters, detergents, sanitary pads, condensed milk, and instant coffee.[141]

The German hi-fi producer Braun arguably went further than any other company in explicitly emphasizing modern design's great triumph in West German society as a whole (fig. 3.8). In the fall of 1955, the company published an advertisement in *Constanze* that specifically promoted modern design radio and TV sets. The full-page ad announced: "Already every third woman desires a bright and modern apartment."[142] Next to photos demonstrating how the Braun devices fit perfectly inside very modern interiors the ad quoted from an Allensbach survey claiming that "44 percent of all women under thirty, 54 percent of all female employees, and 56 percent of all women with a high school diploma [an *Abitur*] want to live in a way that conforms to our time." By listing increasing percentages and combining them with a suggestive formulation, the text creates the impression of an inevitable development of women's taste toward an equally inevitable modern aesthetics. The two photos, however, show interiors that closely resemble what Allensbach called "modern," whereas this "modern" category was, in reality, chosen by only 8 percent of all respondents in May 1955 and by only 7 percent of female respondents in July 1954.[143] One could arrive at the claim that more than 30 percent of respondents preferred modern interiors only if the much more popular "Werkstätten" style, with its closer proximity to the forms heavily promoted by the Nazis, would be included in Braun's "bright and modern" category.

By mentioning only women, the Braun advertisement directly addressed female readers as those responsible for the aesthetics of the home, thereby conforming to a broader tendency in advertisements of the time to focus on female consumers.[144] The ad also linked modern design to female emancipation by naming "female employees" and women with the highest German secondary school degree as being especially open to the modern, playing into the highly debated topic of women's equality at a time that was also shaped by the conservative family policies of the governing Christian conservative party. *Constanze* regularly promoted women's emancipation on its pages and often presented successful working women and even female entrepreneurs. This was especially true during the first half of the decade, before the growing focus on home, consumption, and lifestyle superseded the theme of gender equality after 1955.[145] The percentage of married working women grew steadily from 34 percent in 1950 to 45 percent in 1960. Simultaneously, women's traditional role as responsible guardians of the domestic sphere continued, while their newly defined role as rationally consuming housewives was tied closely to the self-definition of the

3.8 "Already every third woman." Braun radio and TV set advertisement, *Constanze*, September 1955. Reproduced from Staatsbibliothek Berlin.

Federal Republic as a social market economy.[146] *Constanze* endlessly repeated that women needed to choose a modern style of interior decoration in order to furnish the smaller apartments of the postwar era in a rational and space-saving way.[147] The rational household that women consumers were deemed responsible for in the 1950s was supposed to realize an aesthetic norm that not only was seen as practical but also carried with it ideals of social and national harmony and homogeneity. Women's "cultural function" of producing a postwar "consumer order" was thus conceived as including their responsibility to (re)produce the home as a constitutive element of a national make-believe space.[148]

In 1954 Musterring, a cooperation between German furniture dealers and furniture producers founded in 1938, launched what became the biggest advertising campaign for furniture in the early Federal Republic.[149] This campaign is typical of how the modern home was popularized as the only feasible aesthetic model for Germans' apartments. The ideal of the practical household featured prominently when *Constanze* reported that Musterring's designers were focused on producing furniture constructed for "our small apartments" and "our clever budget plan" and that an apartment "freed from ornamentation" could "be easily managed" and "kept in order." The "clear and beautiful forms" specifically promised to help to turn "your home truly into your world."[150] The long-running campaign of the following years would contribute much to establish modern furnishings without ornaments as the appropriate style for every German's "home." In the first year of the campaign, the ads often underlined that the choice they offered was "astonishingly varied and rich," with something for "every taste."[151] This was a remarkable declaration, as the program excluded any furniture with ornaments, such as copies of traditional styles (so-called *Stilmöbel*), or the bulky and curved pieces of furniture that were popular with the lower social strata.

Most Musterring advertisements combined photographs of model interiors with drawings of their supposed inhabitants. The texts emphasized a contrast between a stressful or menacing outside world and a secure and cozy inner world of the appropriately furnished apartment as the place of one's true life and identity. An initial relative diversity of male and female roles disappeared quickly to be replaced by the housewife and male breadwinner model. In this manner, the campaign became a strong advocate for women as the caretakers of the domestic sphere, both its material order and its aesthetic shape. The contrast between outer and inner world thereby acquired a gendered meaning. In a typical example from 1955 (fig. 3.9), the ad photo shows a kidney table interior and the drawing of a housewife who welcomes her husband at the door. The

3.9 "She never has to wait for him." Musterring furniture advertisement, *Quick*, February 1955. Reproduced from Staatsbibliothek Berlin.

text reads, "She never has to wait for him" because he "likes so much coming home, . . . where they are comfortable and happy in order to gain new strength for the following day."[152] In such ads the couple was the primary individual consumer unit as well as a "living community" cultivating a meaningful relationship with their furniture: "We live with it day and night, and it outwardly bears testament to what we really are."[153]

A standard text of the campaign explained how "good" furnishing determined the way the people of this community related to themselves: "How much money we spend for useless things we believe make us 'bigger' in the eyes of people! But what are we worth to ourselves—much or only little?"[154] Buying things in order to show off one's elevated social status was deemed morally dubious, a kind of criticism that was part of the Werkbund ideology and also shaped the discourse on the Volkswagen. Since many publications of the previous four years, building on the previous forty years, had made clear what kind of aesthetic embodied this moral weakness, Musterring did not have to mention it. Instead, Musterring presented the home and its right furnishing as the sphere where the "worth" of the individual human being was realized. Modern design's aesthetic Other thus disappeared from view and with it the idea that the modern home stood in opposition to a past. As a result, aesthetic homogeneity emerged as the self-evident and timeless shape of the German couple's and family's "home."

In 1956 the campaign subtly began to acknowledge possible tensions in the lives of traditional couples. New ads presented the right aesthetic order of the home as the prime solution to these problems.[155] One advertisement acknowledged the possibility of conflicts in the headline: "After seven years—and still no marriage crisis." The secret formula for this harmony was a husband who sometimes brought his wife breakfast in bed and a home the couple had designed "personally." "The things of their apartment" were living embodiments of their relationship and as such "not dead and unexpressive to them. They belong to them, to their atmosphere of love."[156] The brand continued to propagate its ideal of the modern home and its implicit promise of cultural homogeneity as the ultimate remedy for the various social harmony challenges West Germany faced. Among those challenges was an emerging youth culture that embraced American popular music such as jazz and rock and roll and thereby produced one of the biggest moral panics of the time, with racial and gendered connotations that included fears about boys' masculinity being endangered by "negro songs."[157]

Musterring reacted in October 1956 by using the English proverb "My home is my castle" (English in the original ad) to present its ideal home to a younger generation. In the text young customers talk about the "necessity to find our way back to our home" and "to build our own world . . . just like our parents did." They already knew that "the noisy pleasures of the day" could not "free their inner selves from the engine of rushing time." They needed a home to "insulate" them "against what hounds and pushes us."[158] In February 1957 an advertisement showed a roughly rastered photograph of four African American jazz musicians hovering above the ad text and above two smaller photographs of interiors in the "Werkstätten" style: a teenager's room and a dining table with a corner seating unit (fig. 3.10).[159] Whereas a similar layout was used regularly, the photos normally featured people on the street who were themselves imagined as the inhabitants of the ideal home.[160] This was not the case with the jazz musicians. The four Black men's upper bodies, photographed from below while they play their instruments in a dynamic way, appeared as if they could physically intrude into and thereby threaten the sphere of the home that was above all associated with German women.

In spite of its conciliatory headline ("Joy has many faces"), the text emphasized the menacing and exotic foreignness of the unnamed jazz: "In the days of our youth we encounter [joy] often in the twilight of amusements outside the home, in the hubbub of the rhythms and trumpet blasts, in the experience of wild dance leaps. But after the hours of exuberance even the young person wants to return to the shelter of a cozy home arranged by Mother's hands. Let us prepare this return for the young person." The ad interpreted young people embracing foreign and even African American music as an understandable aberrance that would soon be overcome. Most importantly, it positioned the

3.10 "Joy has many faces." Musterring furniture advertisement, *Constanze*, February 1957. Reproduced from Staatsbibliothek Berlin.

home and its aesthetics squarely in opposition to this deviation into the exotic and thereby brought to the surface its implicitly racial character.[161]

Different strands in the discourse and popular culture of the early Federal Republic worked together to bring about a meaning of modern design as a prime marker of a nationally and internationally homogenized space. In conjunction with this, modern forms also became a medium that homogenized historical time. While intensified by the presentism of commercial advertising, this tendency did not begin in this manner. The early postwar discourse on the Werkbund established a narrative that detached the good modern form from its deep impregnation by Nazi culture and associated modern design's Other with the Third Reich itself. According to film historian Bernhard Groß, a great number of early postwar movies also used the negative image of turn-of-the-century interiors and bourgeois attachments to antiques in order to identify Germany's dynamic future citizens with the opposite of this aesthetic, namely, a modern organization of relatively empty space.[162] Like *Film without a Title*, these films used an influential pattern of the Third Reich's own discourse on the good form to produce a collective image of physically regenerated and morally redeemed postwar Germans.

The 1954 film *Eine Frau von heute* (*A Woman of Today*) exemplifies a next phase, in which the past itself disappears from sight and is replaced by the mythical present of the economic miracle.[163] In this film the modern home forms a setting that eventually helps the couple to solve their marriage crisis. The past is relevant only because it triggers an estrangement between the wife and her husband due to their different war experiences and the woman's accompanying emancipation. The couple's home is a practical and modern attic apartment typical of the postwar period and the advice pages in lifestyle magazines. It forms the space in which the marital conflict both arises and resolves, serving as the unspoken basis of shared aesthetic beliefs. With its emphasis on female autonomy, *A Woman of Today* demonstrates the modern home's potential association with egalitarian gender relations during the early 1950s. This association, however, is developed in connection with dreams of homogeneity whose political legacy is concealed behind the disorienting surface of supposed timelessness.

In line with this, the Volkswagen appears in significant scenes as an icon of Germany's transformed geographic expansion (fig. 3.11). This politically charged presence of aesthetic modernity could build on the postwar discourse in which West Germans were invited to embrace a modern home that stood in opposition to *a* past. This rejected past, however, did not clearly overlap with Nazi culture. The idea of the postwar modern resided in a murky historical sphere

3.11 Two screenshots from *Eine Frau von heute* (*A Woman of Today*, 1954). Reproduced from Fama F.A. Mainz Film.

that was called "timeless." In this sphere pre-1945 dreams of cultural homogeneity could merge with the versions proclaimed in the context of the Marshall Plan. As a result, a powerful myth established itself of a modern aesthetic order that represented a harmonious German world outside of history. This harmonious German world lent itself to both updated dreams of global expansion and new forms of exclusion.

4

Expanding Objects

At Home in Globalizing Germany

An Unhomely Home

In 1957 Ruth Leuwerik, one of the major movie stars of the young Federal Republic of Germany, played Franziska, the female part in a romantic film released under the title *Franziska*.[1] The color film, directed by Wolfgang Liebeneiner, tells the story of Franziska and Stefan, who fall in love and then struggle to build a life together while Stefan travels off to the crisis regions of the world as a newsreel reporter. After having tastefully redecorated Stefan's old house, Franziska reacts to her husband's adventurous approach to life by developing her own career. She creates modern costume jewelry and sells her products in "Munich," "Chicago," and "Baltimore." When Franziska cannot endure Stefan's constant absence any longer she asks for a divorce. After Stefan's workmate dies suddenly, Stefan finally understands that he must settle down, and he swiftly transforms from a photojournalist to a fashion photographer for the women's magazine *Constanze*. This change enables the happy reconciliation of the couple.

At a moment when the economic miracle was in full sway in West Germany, *Franziska* gave everyday objects a central role in defining the two main characters, their challenges, and their relationship to the world inside and outside the nation's borders. This narrative function of home aesthetics encapsulates much of the ideas spread widely in popular and highbrow publications of the time. The chaotic mixture of global souvenirs and antiquated furniture in Stefan's overstuffed old house embodies his moral deficiency. Franziska, on the other hand, creates a morally and aesthetically proper place in postwar West Germany. She forges the path that Stefan eventually follows so that both characters end up solving their conflict by becoming successful citizens of West Germany's globalizing consumer's republic.[2]

Franziska's optimistic ending, however, has something peculiarly unconvincing about it. The scenery changes surprisingly from the couple's redecorated home in southern Germany to a new and nearly empty apartment in a northern German metropole. Why does this happy ending take place in a setting that is unfurnished and *unhomely*, while the whole story has been about the difficulty of creating and sustaining a *home*? "In the stirrings of the unhomely, another world becomes visible," writes Homi Bhabha.[3] The postcolonial novels that Bhabha discusses focus on the "unhomely" in order to bring an unspeakable and painful past to presence. In contrast to this, *Franziska* constructs a world geared toward West Germany's bright future as a model country of the West struggling with seemingly ahistorical conflicts between men and women. Was the unhomely feeling that befell me when I first watched this movie merely produced by a defect in the internal logic of the narrative? Eventually, I stumbled across a clue from cinema history that set in motion the scholarly process that has resulted in this book. What disturbed the message of postwar homeliness in *Franziska* turned out to be a signpost to "unrepresented pasts that haunt the historical present" hidden underneath the film's flashy staging of postwar West German consumerism.[4]

The 1957 *Franziska* is a remake. The original film, entitled *Auf Wiedersehen, Franziska!* (*Goodbye, Franziska!*) and directed by Helmut Käutner, premiered in April 1941, two months before the Third Reich invaded the Soviet Union. *Goodbye, Franziska!* was a huge cinematic success in Nazi Germany.[5] Most of the film's story, including the significance of everyday objects, reappears in its remake.[6] There are two exceptions. First, in the original film Franziska ends her professional activities after marrying Michael (called Stefan in the remake). Second, Michael only discovers the true importance of his home when he must leave it to take part in Germany's invasion of Poland in the diegetic time of 1939. As Franziska convinces him that his departure is finally for the right cause, Michael understands the deeper meanings of his home and his homeland as well as his duty with respect to both, and he once again says good-bye.

Goodbye, Franziska! from 1941 connects the morality and aesthetics of the home to visions of an aggressively expanding German Empire. It also exposes the dangers of immersing oneself in exotic cultures. Its emphasis on female endurance and sacrifice was a recurrent theme of wartime cinematic Nazi propaganda.[7] Taken together with its release date shortly before the invasion of the Soviet Union and four months after Hitler had announced a social housing project for Germany's postwar future, the film's success arguably gave it a significant role in the regime's endeavor to gain Germans' support for the second phase of its aggressive war campaign.[8] The 1957 remake substitutes the original's prospect of a bright future through conquering new "living space" in the East with the peaceful promise of a moralized aesthetic consumerism and of West Germany's export boom. The 1957 *Franziska*, however, presented this different postwar message by revisiting, reproducing, and adapting a story that was imbued with Nazi culture, including the way it defined and organized the relationship between domestic and global space.

Reading *Franziska* in relation to the wartime *Goodbye, Franziska!* throws a different light on the postwar promotion of modern home aesthetics and on West German consumers' imagined relation to the world at large. In 1941 the Nazi version of colonial conquest and its connection to the good German home was presented as the necessary alternative to the life of adventures that alienated the male character from his home, his nation, and his *Volk*. In 1957 this outcome was replaced by the consumerist dream of a well-organized, harmonious, and homogeneous world. The manner in which this postwar dream was related to the world at large, however, still contained many echoes of the original movie. The world outside the West, with its alluring, disorienting, and pernicious exotic character, was to be controlled, domesticated, and integrated into a home designed along the lines of moralized aesthetic principles that had been popularized for many decades as realizing the essence of a superior national life. In 1957, however, this home was also defined by how it was embedded in a newly conceived transnational network of commodity circulation in the West.

Goodbye, Franziska! uses established colonial fantasies of white men's adventures and reworks them into a nazified vision of empire. In doing so, the film illustrates the importance of the colonial paradigm for twentieth-century German history. Both the global imagination of the two *Franziska* movies and the imagination of the Volkswagen as a miraculous object conquering global and exoticized geographic space point to postwar West Germany as a postcolonial society shaped by the unruly presence of a double colonialist past. A growing body of historical scholarship has revealed the manifold entanglements between Germany's earlier colonial presence outside of Europe and the Nazi version of a colonial project on European ground.[9] At the same time, postwar West German history is intimately tied to the development of a postwar West that was itself deeply shaped by colonialism. As the idea of the "West" emerged at the beginning of the twentieth century it was closely intertwined with European imperialism.[10] West Germany's political imaginary, therefore, cannot be understood separately from colonialism and imperialism as a European legacy.

The Federal Republic's resurrection as a model country of the postwar West happened when Europe's "own postcoloniality with respect to the Nazi empire was instituted." The process of formally ending the imperial regimes of the other

European countries, however, took much longer and produced a long-lasting "postcolonial condition."[11] Postcolonial scholars insist that, as Stuart Hall has put it, "in the case of the colonial and the post-colonial, what we are dealing with is not two successive regimes but the simultaneous presence of a *regime and its after-effects*."[12] The previous chapters have tried to grasp how the simultaneous presence and aftereffects of the Nazi regime pervaded the experience of the rubble moment and subsequently shaped West German political imaginaries of modern consumer objects. For the Volkswagen as well as for modern design, the transatlantic West provided an important framework that enabled older fantasies to glide through the proclaimed 1945 zero hour into postwar West German culture.

The Cold War and the 1945 divide have dominated scholarly interpretations and collective memory to such an extent that the ramifications of imperialism and colonialism for the postwar histories of Western societies are still far from being fully understood. This is particularly true regarding consumer culture and the postwar modern. Few scholars have begun to study the relationship between the political dimensions of postwar consumer cultures and the previous imperialist, colonialist, and Fascist politicization of the commercial sphere.[13] Equally, the context of decolonization has scarcely played any role in histories of postwar consumer culture.[14] Using the two *Franziska* movies as a framing device, this chapter aims to understand how the imaginary world of consumer objects helped to create a collective vision of the West German "home," in its domestic, national, and ethnocultural sense, in relation to the larger world outside the national borders. By following objects and representations that served as signifiers of societies different from and similar to what was seen as the West German norm, my reading focuses on the function of this "outside" world in a reconstructed "inside" culture. I interpret this complex postwar presence of the outside in manifestations of sameness and otherness in relation to relevant phenomena in Germany's and Europe's colonial pasts and—not yet—postcolonial present.

The chapter, therefore, must try to comprehend the intricate, contradictory, and still ongoing and fragile shift from a world self-evidently structured by systems of racialized categories and their premise of white superiority to a world in which such thinking became less acceptable. After Germany's war defeat, the Nazi regime and its specific ideas of racial supremacy officially landed on the wrong side of history, prompting the introduction of the concept of "racism."[15] Given the absence of discussions in the West German public sphere about the content and manifestations of racist ideas, the end of "racism" as a cultural framework was rather assumed than broadly enforced.[16] A similar silence also marked the way in which other West European countries and the United States turned to antiracism as a norm so that "the language of European colonialism only slowly became outmoded and 'passé.'"[17] Cultural displays of the colonial paradigm could thus continue in the context of a dominant discourse that only reluctantly began to acknowledge the dawning end of the colonial era.

Aspects of postwar European history that are claimed from today's perspective as one's (or "our") own have often been interpreted as necessarily anticolonial and antiracist, preventing the complexity of the postwar transition to come into view. The founding of the European Economic Community (EEC), for instance, was strongly influenced by ideas that were circulating since the 1920s in France and Germany about creating a European African region, "Eurafrica," to provide Europe with cheap access to African raw materials. The EEC was only one manifestation of West Germany's integration into a transatlantic West that was formed in the context both of an accelerating Cold War and of European countries' efforts to "reclaim empire."[18] In 1955 the Federal Republic had acquired nearly full sovereignty and became a member of NATO, a step accompanied by a passionate public debate about German rearmament. Just like the EEC, the NATO alliance included countries with overseas colonies; its defense article also encompassed French Algeria.[19]

Parallel to these institutional developments, the Western world outside West Germany's borders was increasingly present in the exploding realm of consumer culture. This was accompanied by cultural tensions that came to the surface with force in the year before the movie *Franziska* was released in theaters. German youth's intensified interest in jazz, rock and roll, and American films like *The Wild One* triggered a moral panic among the older generation that was heavily informed by racial patterns of perception.[20] The Musterring furniture ad that positioned Black jazz musicians as the Others that threatened the harmonious sphere of the culturally homogeneous modern German home (fig. 3.10) must be read in this context.

The year 1957 also saw the culmination of the Steinstrasse affair, which was widely covered in the press. The inhabitants of Kaiserslautern mobilized against mostly Jewish bar owners and exclusively Black American GIs who frequented these bars and allegedly had improper sexual contact with German women. Deeply racist structures of perception were universally accepted as normal by both Germans and white Americans. At the same time, an emerging antiracist moral code prevented the mayor from closing off the Steinstrasse to Black soldiers, arguing that this would violate the German Basic Law. Maria Höhn concluded that the tendency of many Germans "to identify only *black* GIs" with the problems of the occupation "suggests that Germans envisioned their alliance with America foremost as an alliance between two white nations."[21]

In 1956 Helmut Käutner, director and scriptwriter of *Goodbye, Franziska!*, probably reacted to his own perception of shifting moral codes when he crossed out words like "nigger song" and "nigger waiter" from the film's original script and replaced them with "jazz song" and "black waiter" as he produced what he called a "reconstructed version" of the script.[22] By 1956 Käutner had become one of the most acclaimed film directors of the Federal Republic. After the war, the Allied Control Council had banned *Goodbye, Franziska!* from the screen as too politically tainted. In 1951 the Self-Regulatory Body of the Movie Industry licensed a censored version of *Goodbye, Franziska!* for West German cinemas.[23] In one censored scene, Franziska's father and a friend in Wehrmacht uniform follow the progress of the German army into Poland on a map while the radio announces that the Wehrmacht has arrived near Warsaw and that the air force has destroyed the station in Bialystok (see fig. 4.24, image in the middle). One censored part begins with Franziska's father's comment "It is like a miracle!" and his advice not to become "arrogant" when his friend worries about coming "too late" to the front. This reminded viewers in 1941 of 1939's Blitzkrieg campaign in Poland, a military success that was repeated in 1940 in a number of other countries, including France. When the film premiered at the end of April 1941, Yugoslavia and Greece had just been overpowered by the Wehrmacht in a similarly quick manner. Only a few months later, the German army conquered Bialystok once again as part of its attack on the Soviet Union.

In 1941 reviewers grasped the political significance of the film. *Filmwelt* magazine underlined that the "serious and deep reconciliation" between Franziska and Michael happened "at the threshold to the big war."[24] The Nazi organ *Völkischer Beobachter* praised the realistic character of Michael's conscription for a propaganda unit in which "his work will receive a deeper meaning for the first time."[25] According to the Nazi magazine *NS Frauen-Warte*, the "restless man recognizes just in time that his life up to then could not give him anything lasting," while it described the ending as his call to "the front of the fight for Greater Germany's freedom."[26]

When *Goodbye, Franziska!* was shown again in some West German cinemas in 1954, the reviews give the impression that this version did not contain references to the war or Michael's need to leave Franziska again.[27] By contrast, the extensive public reception of the 1957 remake, well documented in the archive of its production company, Artur Brauner's CCC Filmkunst, was very much about the film's relationship with the original and included many references to the latter's ending. The original's enmeshment in Nazi propaganda was often referred to in a self-evident manner. It was rare that a review did *not* mention the original.[28] Even the majority of neutral or positive reviews of the remake regularly compared the new film with the universally cherished original. Twice, the new ending was appreciated as a morally improved turn of the plot. Yet this ending was also criticized as implausible, while a substantial number of reviewers expressed a preference for the original movie in comparison with the remake.

Käutner's *Goodbye, Franziska!* still resonated strongly in the minds of many journalists who seemed to assume that their (old enough) readers had also been able to identify with the story sixteen years earlier. No journalist indicated that the war-embracing ending of the original had diminished this identification in 1941, even though in 1957 the remake's new ending seemed "the only possible" way to update the story. Not once did a writer raise concerns about producing a remake of a film that was so deeply shaped by Nazi propaganda. For the reviewers, the memory of 1941's *Goodbye, Franziska!* was connected to a past feeling of recognizing oneself in the domestic and national home staged on-screen. If they uttered any sense of unhomeliness, it was because the postwar *Franziska* failed to deliver that feeling once again. Where *Goodbye, Franziska!* was praised, authentic enthusiasm surfaced. Where *Franziska* was complimented, the praise was moderate or appeared motivated by reason more than affect, which is especially evident in comments on the new "redeeming" ending.

According to Sarah Ahmed, unconscious feelings often appear as if they were residing in objects "as an effect of a certain history, a history that may operate by concealing its own traces."[29] The case of *Goodbye, Franziska!* and its remake can tell us something about the power of films to amalgamate personal feelings with ideology, resulting in the subjective experience of an emotional truth whose origin in propagandistic manipulation is blocked from view. The conspicuous role of the home's aesthetic and its relationship to foreign worlds are crucial aspects of how these two films produced, or failed to produce, their emotional truths. Domestic materiality contributes in an unobtrusive way to this meaningful cinematic experience. How this home appears on-screen must therefore be read in the context of how the home's relation to the world was shaped by political frameworks before, during, and after the Third Reich. After 1945 the cultural relationship between the home and the world was constructed on the basis of emotional truths whose histories were both present and concealed.

At Home in the World, 1941/1957

The release of *Franziska* in 1957 coincided with an increasing emphasis on internationalism in the discourse on the modern home. In 1957 the international architecture exhibition Interbau took place in Berlin, feeding the public image of West Germany as a part of an international West defined by modern architecture and design. While the exhibition was ongoing, some reviewers of the *Franziska* movie saw the film's interior decoration as relevant for the story's placement in the context of the economic miracle. Mostly, however, the cinematic role of modern interior design was assessed negatively by film reviewers, reflecting a general inclination to place film and interior design in different cultural registers.[30] One reviewer lamented that the film corresponded "substantially" with the inside of the magazine *Constanze*.[31] Accordingly, postwar reviewers deplored that the commercial side of modern domestic ideals in *Franziska* deprived the story of the deeper emotional truth associated with the original.[32]

Indeed, *Franziska* fit in well with the moment's emphasis on interior design as an expression of internationalism. In the summer of 1957 the big national periodicals reported on the Interbau's international model interiors, and *Brigitte* invited readers to imagine their own home as being furnished by modern household objects from various Western countries.[33] A new rubric called "The *Brigitte* room" described the imagined inhabitants of a room, depicted by models in the photographs. In June 1957 the *Brigitte* room photo and article presented an international lifestyle associated with equally international furnishings: "The table is set—the guests will soon arrive. . . . The hostess (right) is not keen on the traditional look. She prefers an ambience of international standing. Her girlfriends in Rio, New York, and Sydney have chosen similar styles for their homes. The furniture and other pieces shown here were created by Finnish, American, Italian, French, and German designers" (fig. 4.1).[34] Interrelating interior design and character, the text ascribed a Western cosmopolitan outlook on life to a "cheerful" and "sociable" "working young lady" with a "sense of objectivity." In July the rubric introduced two sisters who had assembled much of their furniture from "the North," "the black continent," and Japan.[35] Modern design internationalism emphasized how the *similarity* of the modern style in Western countries reflected "the extensive commonalities that exist today in the attitude toward building and living."[36] In *Franziska* this internationalism was therefore only implicitly present through a set design that resembled the internationalized interiors of lifestyle magazines.

Additionally, the film presented the idea of Western internationalism through Franziska's export of her costume jewelry and through the presence of air travel. The casting of Carlos Thompson for the role of Stefan also came with a specific kind of cosmopolitan flair. Born in Argentina, Thompson had previously played in US adventure stories in a colonial setting before working for the first time in a German production in 1956.[37] His unconventional profile as an actor and novelist between South America, the United States, and Europe provided an attractive story that some magazines picked up on. Embodying the world of

4.1 The international style in "the *Brigitte* room." *Brigitte*, June 1957. Original in color. Reproduced from Staatsbibliothek Berlin.

international glamour, Thompson was regularly introduced by reviewers as "the Argentinian" or "the South American," but these same reviewers also criticized him for his "forced dark and foreign accent" or his "broken German."[38] Some authors found it hard to accept Thompson in the role of a *Volksdeutscher* (ethnic German living outside of Germany or Austria), as his character refers to himself when mentioning his background as a refugee from the East. The official press kit of the film distribution company presented the actor as an "Argentinian with Nordic rather than Spanish features."[39] The transnational character of Thompson's star persona could thus feed into the role of Stefan by opening up to a cosmopolitan world while still holding on to notions about ethnic Germans exporting German, or Nordic, culture abroad.[40] The creation of a sustainable home in *Franziska* thereby involved not only a consumerist redefinition of adventurous masculinity but also the integration of an actor with an ambiguous ethnic background into the screen version of a modern German home.

This integration itself, however, evoked anxieties about race mixing. When Stefan receives a telegram informing him of the birth of his son he is drowning in alcohol and debauchery, surrounded by lascivious Latino-typed women in a bar where Black and white customers mingle (fig. 4.2). When he comes home to Franziska and his redecorated house, he asks Franziska's father for permission to marry his daughter (fig. 4.3). These two scenes stage a sharp opposition

4.2 Two screenshots from *Franziska* (1957): Latin American bar scene. Original in color. Reproduced from CCC Filmkunst.

4.3 Two screenshots from *Franziska* (1957): Stefan's house redecorated. Original in color. Reproduced from CCC Filmkunst.

between a threateningly chaotic and exotic world in which the boundaries between cultures and races dissolve in a sexually loaded atmosphere and a well-ordered German world that conforms to the aesthetic standards of good modern taste and to bourgeois moral standards of family life. In the sedentary "white" life to which Stefan returns, the remaining "black" elements are safely contained in the form of African masks on the walls of a family home's interior that is reminiscent of the internationalized home promoted in lifestyle magazines.

Stefan's workmate, conspicuously named "Blacky White," embodies the threat of dissolving racial distinctions. In the 1941 version, Michael equally risks being sucked into cultural alienation, which here too is embodied by Michael's colleague Buck Standing (the corresponding character to Blacky White).[41] In the African desert with native Black people in the background, Michael asks Buck where he is "at home," and Buck explains his lack of a home and a home country due to his international upbringing. Michael answers the same question in turn simply with "in Germany." Robert C. Reimer has foregrounded the importance of this moment for the film's reinforcement of "negative and positive stereotypes by juxtaposing foreign and domestic scenes."[42] Echoing antisemitic stereotypes of the wandering Jew, Buck embodies the dangers of a life without a national cause, dangerously luring Michael away from his German home. That Buck experiences his own death at the front during the Second Sino-Japanese War as senseless is the logical outcome of his rootlessness. The following sequence of newspaper headlines announces the successes of the Wehrmacht in Poland and prepares Michael's conversion to a life rooted in the value of his home. In the 1957 remake, the two dialogues that positioned Buck as the embodiment of dangerous rootlessness have disappeared. Yet Blacky's death still triggers Stefan's conversion, and the contrast between the German home and the alienating foreign world remains central.

In both movies this contrast reappears in the main characters' relationship to domestic material culture. The male character's alienation from his roots is captured by his old house, with its chaotic mixture of old furniture and exotic souvenirs that matches his vagabond lifestyle. In the postwar *Franziska*, the overstuffed interior is staged as the essence of the turn-of-the-century "Tante Frieda" style, dominated by red velvet, fringes, bulky buffets, old furniture, and decorative objects called "lumber from all continents" by Stefan. In a pan-shot view of the living room, a row of African masks dominates the final frame (fig. 4.4). In contrast to Stefan, Franziska recognizes the aesthetic value of some of these pieces. In 1941 Michael's unstable life is embodied similarly by his provisional home's messy mixture of old-fashioned and antique furnishings, Christian sculptures,

4.4 Screenshot from *Franziska* (1957): Stefan's old house. Original in color. Reproduced from CCC Filmkunst.

and exotic art objects. The living room is dominated by a huge pole-like sculpture that the screenplay identifies as "an idol figure from the South Seas" (fig. 4.5).[43] The scene exposes both the unruly material presence of the non-European world in Michael's house and his lack of relationship to these objects as a masculine character flaw that stands between him and Franziska.

When the two meet again in Berlin, where Franziska has started an independent life, both films construct a contrast between the eclectic interior of Michael's/Stefan's house and Franziska's "well-arranged and practical" apartment as an embodiment of her character. In the postwar *Franziska*, the apartment's improvised and cozy mixture of old and new items reflects Germans' dim postwar economic situation (fig. 4.6).[44] In the 1941 version, the modernity of the space is more in line with a sober form of New Objectivity (fig. 4.7). A photo of this scene was chosen for the cover of a *Goodbye, Franziska!* novel that accompanied the film in 1941.[45] This book situated Franziska and Michael's love explicitly inside a new Germany shaped by an ideologically charged aesthetics. In Berlin Michael discovers "the communal life's new design principles" and feels "the stirrings of a new and effective order," while Franziska observes

4.5 Screenshot from *Goodbye, Franziska!* (1941): Michael's old house. Reproduced from Terra-Filmkunst.

how workmen remove the opposite building's "fake" decorations, which represent a "misconceived bourgeois pride" in contrast to her own apartment's "honesty."[46]

In the 1941 film, Michael's house reappears redecorated by Franziska. With its white walls, it seems less cluttered and more spacious. Instead of exotic objects we see armchairs newly upholstered with fashionable paisley patterns. Although this is not a modern interior in the strict sense, its well-ordered spatial arrangement and clear stylistic order certainly evoke Werkbund principles. The incorporation of some exotic objects ascribes to them a clearly defined place within the proper aesthetic of a German home (fig. 4.8). Michael's conversion to the value of family life in this home evokes the Third Reich's dominant ideas about the meaning of home aesthetics. The movie thus strengthens its ideological message by skillfully using the silent world of objects (see chapter 3).[47] When Franziska redecorates their home she integrates it into a new national whole in the making. As Michael is called to serve the cause of a Greater Germany, he finally understands that his desire "to conquer worlds at any cost" merely "makes sense" in its connection to the Germanized "home" and thereby to the National Socialist project.[48]

4.6 Two screenshots from *Franziska* (1957): Franziska's Berlin apartment. Original in color. Reproduced from CCC Filmkunst.

4.7 Two screenshots from *Goodbye, Franziska!* (1941): Franziska's Berlin apartment. Reproduced from Terra-Filmkunst.

In the form of a love story, the film spelled out widespread ideas about modern domestic interiors' relationship to an expanding national totality understood in terms of Nazism. Such ideas, however, were also related to a broader context of European colonialism. An article published in 1938 in *Innen-Dekoration* stressed the importance of a "national style" as the "life expression of a national community," adding that "race" was "another community that extends beyond the nations." The article conjured up the dangers faced by colonial administrators who adapted too much to a vagabond life: "European officials, even missionaries, who serve in the colonies have to come back to Europe from time to time . . . in order to find their way back into the European human form, which they gradually lose in the countries of dark-skinned people."[49] The racial Other represents the absence of a civilized "life expression" and evokes an existential danger of alienation that Europeans and Germans face if they mingle too intensely with non-European cultures. A similar danger was of central importance to the wartime *Goodbye, Franziska!* and continued to structure 1957's *Franziska*.

In the postwar discourse on the modern home, the explicit evocation of race disappeared, but the dichotomy between the moralized good form and dubious deviations from it remained paramount. As the development of this postwar discourse was intertwined with the emerging concept of the West, its internationalism necessarily reflected the European and white exclusivity of this "West." For the 1957 Interbau exhibition, architects from different countries built model social housing units in West Berlin. A large majority of architects and interior designers came from the northern parts of Europe (especially Germany and Scandinavia), while a small number came from France and Italy. Brazil was represented by Oscar Niemeyer and the United States by Walter Gropius.[50] A book published by the Berlin Werkbund documented the interior designs of the new Interbau buildings and claimed that the project was marked by "a global harmony" and by an organic relationship between the domestic space and "the human being of today."[51] The stylistic homogeneity of the model interiors appeared like the dreamscape of an ideal social world without any deviation. What did not harmonize with these spaces was seen as a dangerous moral catastrophe.[52]

In 1953, when the Marshall Plan exhibition We're Building a Better Life had successfully introduced the idea of a recognizably modern aesthetic of the home in western Europe and the United States, the magazine *magnum* was founded to provide a forum on the modern character of the present. The editorial of the first issue presented the aesthetic form of everyday objects as pivotal for its vision of society as an organic whole composed of both matter and spirit. An emphatic "we" excluded everybody who did not embrace modern aesthetics

4.8 Two screenshots from *Goodbye, Franziska!* (1941): Michael's house redecorated. Reproduced from Terra-Filmkunst.

and its "new historic type of human," calling anybody a "misfit" who "evades this development."[53] This aesthetic modern was established as a characteristic of the postwar Western "Hemisphere" and was cast in stark contrast both to the Nazi past and to the Communist regimes of the present. The images presented modern design and architecture from the United States, Germany, Austria, Switzerland, Sweden, Denmark, Italy, and, more rarely, France and England. The juxtaposition of images informed readers about the fact that they were looking at an aesthetically homogeneous West.[54]

The proclaimed international character of modern design and architecture was used to reformulate on a supranational level older assumptions about the relationship between the aesthetics of everyday objects and the undisturbed social "harmony" and homogeneity previously ascribed to the German nation. The internationalism of this fantasy had its own structure, with German, Scandinavian, and some Swiss designers dominating the scene. In 1958 Theodor Heuss, the first president of the Federal Republic and former Werkbund secretary, applauded the "epochal" quality of the Interbau but questioned the assumption that this aesthetic had to be embraced by everyone. He also presented the Interbau's achievement as the product of architects with German and northern European ethnic roots: "If someone likes the site as a whole, if he rejects it, if he judges the building of the Finn, of the Brazilian (who is called Niemeyer), of the 'American' who was chased away to the United States (namely, Gropius) . . . in this or in that manner is altogether irrelevant."[55]

In 1955 Alexander Koch, son of the former *Innen-Dekoration* editor, published a richly illustrated volume on international modern architecture and interior design that featured model houses and interiors built by architects from all over the world. The houses stood in Germany, Italy, Holland, the United States, Japan, Switzerland, and South Africa. According to the volume, the South African house could just as well be found in Germany, because "the ideas about modern dwelling and living are obviously shared by the progressive people in the whole world," adding that "this thought produces much hope and somehow, in the subconscious, the belief in a true-to-life organic further development of our human community."[56] Including South Africa in this way in 1955 made it obvious that the international "human community" of the globalized modern home proclaimed in this book was supposed to be white.[57]

From 1948 onward, South Africa was governed by the white supremacist National Party, which had introduced a system of racial segregation called apartheid. In this context, German illustrated magazines often expressed a "feeling of solidarity with white Africans."[58] More Left-leaning magazines like *Der Spiegel* and the *Frankfurter Hefte* emphasized the international criticism of the apartheid regime and its similarities with Nazi Fascism. But even those publications did not unambivalently promote a critical stance toward South Africa's racial system.[59] In December 1954 *Der Spiegel's* cover story on South Africa relativized the problematic aspects of the Afrikaner government by pointing out that "racial segregation is self-evident for every Englishman on the black continent."[60]

The casual appearance of South Africa in Koch's book indicates the subliminal importance of whiteness for West German ideas on international modern living. Dianne Harris has interpreted the promotion and practice of modern homes in the growing suburbs of the United States in the context of a structural racial segregation that continued in new forms in the postwar period. The construction of "little white houses" (the title of her book) created a spatial and aesthetic separation from the specter of both Blackness and the poverty and dirtiness associated with it.[61] The imaginary of the modern home in the United States thus implicitly comprised the assumption of whiteness and the exclusion of a racial Other. Unsurprisingly, the racial politics of postwar US consumer culture were not addressed in the Marshall Plan exhibitions' presentation of the modern home. Although Black GIs had become part of West German everyday life, they were absent from images and stories promoting the American home abroad. That being Western implied being white was accepted as self-evident. *Goodbye, Franziska!* could be transposed into postwar West Germany because the opposition between the home as the apex of Western civilization and the menacing specter of unclear racial boundaries continued to shape not only the Federal Republic's but also other Western countries' political imaginaries. While the Nazi past of the modern home was disavowed, the legacy of a shared European culture of imperialism was woven into the consumerist dreamworld of the postwar modern.

Cozy German Cosmopolitanism?

This entanglement of postwar modern domesticity with the legacy of imperialism contradicts the dominant interpretation of the modern home as expressing a cosmopolitanism that countered western European countries' nationalist rivalry. In this view, design internationalism decisively contributed to distance West Germany from its National Socialist past.[62] Assuming the moral integrity of all forms of cosmopolitanism and their self-evident opposition to the Third Reich, however, stands in the way of understanding design internationalism's complex meanings in postwar West Germany. The idea of the modern home as a key site for cultural internationalization was early on promoted in West German highbrow publications. Popular lifestyle magazines picked up on the trend in 1953, reworking a widespread skepticism about American influences in particular.[63] In December 1952 *Constanze* reported on the Marshall Plan exhibition We're Building a Better Life. Afterward, the magazine began to beat the drum for modern interior design and to positively refer to the United States.[64]

When articles on modern interior design abounded in these magazines, positive references to other Western countries also increased.[65] America was initially mentioned as responsible for reintroducing modern design to Germany. References to the United States became rare, however, as the decade advanced, while countries such as France and Italy generally appeared only seldomly. At the same time, Scandinavia, "known for the highest state of *Wohnkultur*," emerged as *the* dominant foreign model.[66] With their use of wood and their mixture of antique and modern furniture, "cozy" Scandinavian interiors represented, as one writer enthused, "an architectural concept that gains influence in the whole world."[67] At the end of the decade a positive image of the "typical interior style of the Nordic countries" was well established.[68] "Are Germans still ready," asked the *Frankfurter Allgemeine Zeitung* in 1960, to regard Scandinavian furniture as "the pinnacle of *Wohnkultur*?"[69]

What were the underlying meanings of this intense enthusiasm for a cozy Scandinavian cosmopolitanism, and how did those meanings relate to the past? In 1950 the journalist Margarete Richter claimed that these countries had "neither experienced nor lost the war" and could therefore "do what we can't, namely, be themselves in everything." Insinuating that the influence of modern design had been interrupted during the Nazi years, the author went on to laud the "new ways of living" in Finland and Sweden as a "real expression of our present being."[70] In 1957 the *Frankfurter Allgemeine Zeitung* recognized a "German touch" in a Danish design exhibition that exposed how in "Nordic countries, traditions were continued for which the groundwork was laid in Germany before World War I."[71] The impression of a basic commonality between Germany and the Scandinavian countries also pervaded a 1954 *Brigitte* report on Sweden. The author was enthralled by Swedish everyday life because of its aesthetically homogenized consumer culture and because it exemplified a wider geographic reach of both the German language and the German Volkswagen.[72] In 1959 a *Constanze* article about the Swedish project of a *Volksvilla* for the average Swedish family featured the ground plan of a house that included a Volkswagen.[73] Clearly, there was a sense that a special cultural relationship between Scandinavia and Germany was expressed in Scandinavian design of everyday objects.

Given the absence of studies on modern design's international orientation during the Third Reich, the reporting in the magazine *Innen-Dekoration* must serve as an indicator of the ideas circulating during the Nazi years. While the magazine had written about England and the United States regularly since 1900, the two countries disappeared from its pages after 1936. France was never mentioned often and became even less important after 1938.[74] This did not mean, however, that *Innen-Dekoration* only reported on German design. The idea of "a common European language" in the area of living culture, formulated in the 1920s, remained important and was adapted to the political framework of Nazism.[75] In 1938 an article highlighted the "modern home" as the place that captures the dominance of "reason and will," which have "bred" Europeans "to become the master race."[76] With examples from different European countries, the magazine illustrated how the culture of the home and its decoration embodied a shared cultural supremacy.[77] Both commonalities and national specificities shaped the way these countries realized good design principles. Between 1939 and 1942 the magazine often referred to Italy, Sweden, and Finland as models for an international cultural movement led by Germany.

Italy was not only the first European country to establish a Fascist regime but also an ally and partner of Nazi Germany. *Innen-Dekoration*'s review of the 1936 triennial design exhibition in Milan praised the ideological commonality between Italy and Germany for positively influencing Italian developments in interior design.[78] In June 1940 the magazine commented on the architect Gio Ponti's ideas as "clearly written from a Fascist standpoint" that recognized "the *Volkstum* (racial folklore) as a . . . leading factor of the first order."[79] In this discourse, both Germany and Italy were exemplary among "civilized nations" for the way in which modern design principles of an "ordering will" had established themselves as an "exercise of power." This politically loaded understanding of modern design operated explicitly "across national boundaries."[80]

Long before the advent of Nazism, Sweden and other Scandinavian countries had a reputation in Germany of being at the forefront of the modern tendencies in interior design.[81] After 1933 this reputation was more often linked to specific ethnic roots and "the character of people and country."[82] Scandinavian design's combination of New Objectivity principles with older national arts and crafts traditions corresponded particularly well with how the Nazis tried to harmonize urban functionalism and rural coziness.[83] But the Nordic countries also figured as close cousins of a Germany that cherished the idea of a superior Nordic race.[84] Nazi Germany hoped that Sweden, a neutral country that cooperated closely with the Third Reich, would help to create a New Europe under German leadership.[85] In line with this, *Innen-Dekoration* photographs of Swedish interiors were accompanied in May 1942 by the claim that recent aesthetic innovations would "forever remain significant as an important achievement in the forging of a new Europe" (fig. 4.9).[86]

124 INNEN-DEKORATION

IN ALTEN SCHLÖSSERN sieht man die kostbaren Möbelstücke, wie sie sich aus den letzten drei Jahrhunderten dort vielfach angesammelt haben, und sie stimmen das Gemüt zu reinster Bewunderung. Diese Truhen, diese Kabinettschränke, diese Tische und Himmelbetten sind von menschlicher Kunst zu Gebilden erhoben, in denen sich eine Vielheit von Form- und Materialwerten zu hoher, gleichsam seliger Schönheit verklärt. Nicht Stücke, sondern Ganzheiten stellen sie dar. Schnitzerei und Intarsie, figürliche Darstellung und üppiges Zierwerk, Holzton und Goldglanz breiten sich vielstimmig aus und fügen sich doch zu einer klaren Einheit, die wie im Bewußtsein ihrer edlen Individualität blumenhaft still ist, reich wie eine Welt, glänzend im eignen Wert.

Aber es hängt an diesem höchstgezüchteten Hausrat etwas, das wie sein Schatten zu ihm gehört. Das ist der soziale Kastenunterschied, die Kluft zwischen einer höfischen Kultur, die solche bis ins letzte verfeinerten Gebilde dem Fürsten, dem Begüterten be-

PROFESSOR CARL MALMSTEN–STOCKHOLM »ESSPLATZ« KIEFERNHOLZ ENTFARBT UND MATTIERT »RYA«-TEPPICH (NACH ALTER SCHWEDISCHER WEBTECHNIK): ROST UND HELLGRAU

4.9 Swedish interior, *Innen-Dekoration*, no. 5, 1942. Reproduced from Staatsbibliothek Berlin.

Like other professional publications after 1945, the successor of *Innen-Dekoration*, *Architektur und Wohnform*, was among the early trailblazers of a Western internationalism in which the United States, the Scandinavian countries, England, and Switzerland most often appeared. The magazine's first two articles on Scandinavian design echoed the Nazi years, when "artistic cleanliness" was described as being the "mirror image of Nordic nature" and was said to be "mentally influenced" by "landscape, atmosphere, race, popular belief, and history."[87] If there was a consensus during the 1950s that the Scandinavian style embodied a particularly high form of international *Wohnkultur*, this perception had certainly not originated in the postwar period. While it had existed before 1933, it gained a stronger influence and a more distinct political meaning during the Third Reich, when the idea of a superior Nordic race had reached its apex.[88]

A fable for Nordic culture was certainly not the only feature of the West German internationalization of the modern home. In many ways, the 1952 Marshall Plan exhibit gradually turned into a widespread cultural reality. It became increasingly common to report on new international tendencies in the production of modern household objects focusing not only on Scandinavian but also on other western European countries, the United States, and occasionally Japan.[89] Lifestyle magazines as well as political periodicals paid attention to designers from different countries who often worked in the United States, thereby constructing the modern home's interior as a Western international endeavor.[90] The French American designer Raymond Loewy and the Knoll International company received particularly strong attention. In 1960 *Der Spiegel* dedicated a cover story to Florence Knoll and her company, located in Pennsylvania, which furnished an extraordinary number of public buildings in Germany and was known for its international staff of designers.[91] When *Brigitte* published a long article on the Ulm Institute of Design in 1956, the magazine described the international provenance of the school's students as a cosmopolitan utopia.[92]

Highlighting the international success of German designers was also an important aspect of the ongoing internationalization of the modern home. *Brigitte*'s 1955 series on designers consisted of nine portraits of German professionals. Skillfully mediating between the foreign and domestic, they were admired for finding aesthetic solutions to conquer the world market, with export to the United States as the ultimate sign of success.[93] That four of the nine portraits were about women reflected how strongly the *Zeitgeist* valued female designers as important experts for the rapidly emerging postwar consumer society, an aspect that also resonated in fictional Franziska's successful career as a creator of modern jewelry. Moreover, after 1953 German consumers were frequently invited to imagine their own home as being furnished by modern household objects stemming from a wide array of Western countries.[94] This invitation to open up one's living room to transnational modern consumerism constituted a postwar innovation that seems incompatible with the importance National Socialist culture had attached to a German(ized) private interior as a crucial aspect of Germans' identities.

Japan was the first non-Western country to become part of this internationalized ideal of the modern home.[95] Under the label "Japanese modern," Japanese design had successfully been placed in international exhibitions. At the 1955 Swedish Werkbund exhibition in Helsingborg, Japanese design appeared in a self-evident manner between the contributions of Germany, Britain, Switzerland, and France.[96] Starting in 1957, Japanese-style lamps regularly showed up in *Brigitte*, sometimes even in "Nordic-style" interiors, occasionally accompanied by baskets and so-called Japan mats that were used as wall decorations.[97] The perception that Japanese material culture seamlessly blended into the Western modern had already begun earlier in the decade. In 1951 *Life* magazine published a report on Japan that praised traditional Japanese houses for their "impact on the West's modern architecture" and specified that "Japan's furniture and home decorations are strikingly familiar to Americans accustomed to modern furnishings."[98] The main ideas of this article reappeared in June 1956 in *Brigitte* under the title "Japanese Becomes Modern." According to Eva Noack, features of traditional Japanese houses were consistent with core tenets of modern interior design, thereby representing a rapprochement of Western and "ancient East Asian culture."[99]

The notion that traditional Japanese interiors and art contributed to a shared Western culture could build on a longer European tradition. Japan's intense modernization in the second half of the nineteenth century, orchestrated by the government "in order to present itself as an empire in its own right," had produced a unique cultural relationship with Europe. Westerners wanting to record Orientalism's culmination in the Far East ended up "claiming the Japanese as Europeans."[100] In the 1920s many European modernists began to notice traditional Japanese culture at the same time that modern arts and crafts developed in Japan.[101] After World War II the United States used some of these existing perceptions to integrate the former Fascist war enemy Japan into the imaginary of the West, a project similarly important in a Cold War context as the integration of West Germany.[102]

Germany had its own history of cultural rapprochement with Japan. After World War I Japan had been "consistently portrayed by the press as a westernized great power" that successfully appropriated German or Western knowledge. The *Völkischer Beobachter* saw Japan as the racially superior "Asian colonial power" analogous to Germany's position in Europe.[103] The ideal of a "spiritual community" between the two countries became official Nazi policy and propaganda.[104] In line with the focus on ancient traditions in Japan's own "national aestheticizing project," Nazi Germany paid little attention to Japanese forms of modernity.[105] Although *Innen-Dekoration* regularly appreciated Japanese interior design during the 1920s, it neglected the country during the Third Reich. *die neue linie*, by contrast, published a special issue about Japan in January 1937. *die neue linie* was an avant-garde lifestyle magazine influenced by Bauhaus aesthetics. After 1933 it combined its trademark modernist layout with "conformist contents."[106] Special issues of the magazine on Italy and Japan were used by the Third Reich to promote the cultural relationship with these countries.[107] The 1937 Japan issue's article on interior decoration emphasized a contrast between modern European and traditional Japanese design but conceded that both styles lent themselves to existing in great aesthetic harmony within the same home (fig. 4.10).[108]

Japanese-style lampions also appear in Franziska's attic apartment in 1941's *Goodbye, Franziska!* (fig. 4.7). Those viewers who noticed the inconspicuously placed objects could have seen them as an expression of Franziska's expert

4.10 Japanese interior, *die neue linie*, no. 5, January 1937. Reproduced from Bayerische Staatsbibliothek.

knowledge of how to give non-European elements their proper place within her modern German home. As Japanese-style artifacts had already entered modern design culture in the 1920s, the lamps might not have registered as foreign. The postwar *Franziska* movie more prominently reflects the period's ideas of the convergence between Japanese interiors and the modern home. The attic apartment scene visibly and repeatedly shows two modern white lamps in Japanese style and a Japan mat as a wall decoration (fig. 4.6), corresponding with the emphasis on these lamps in *Brigitte*.

Interpreted in relation to the Nazi past and a broader European cultural context, both the dominance of Scandinavia and the inclusion of Japan carry complex and ambivalent meanings. The extraordinary popularity of Scandinavia could implicitly build on older notions about a special commonality between these countries as representatives of the Nordic race and its superior living culture. Whereas Japan's integration into the modern Western home broadened the scope of postwar internationalism, it had also been preceded by Nazi policies that underlined similarities between the two cultures as well as by the general tendency in Europe since the end of the nineteenth century to "claim the Japanese as Europeans."

By embracing Scandinavia and Japan, the postwar discourse inscribed cultural traces of racial supremacy and imperialism into the cosmopolitanism of West Germany's modern home. This modern home could be "cozy" because it generated a cultural sense of being "at home" that crossed the 1945 rupture. If we use the term "cosmopolitan" to describe the internationalization of the modern home in West Germany, then it should not be defined as inclusive. Studying the meanings of consumer internationalism from a critical angle requires acknowledging cosmopolitanism's longer intellectual history as a project of peace that was conceived "from one particular location: that of Europe, of the most civilized nations."[109] In order to avoid reproducing this pattern, it is necessary to apply what Walter Mignolo has termed "border thinking" and focus on those positioned at or outside cosmopolitanism's borders.

The Modern Home Exotic

Beyond Japan, the internationalization of modern design extended only in a limited way to other Eastern countries, illustrated by Asian students at the Ulm Institute of Design or by the fact that the Chinese-born painter Chow Chung-Cheng developed porcelain design for the West German Rosenthal company.[110] The "Orient" in general, however, occupied a very different position. How Orientalist patterns of thought emerged in the postwar discourse on modern design can be illustrated by an article on Iranian interiors published in October 1953 in *Die Zeit*, thus shortly after the neocolonialist coup by British and American secret services against Iranian prime minister Mohammad Mosaddegh. Precisely when there was an increased promotion of modern design after the Marshall Plan exhibition, journalist Kyra Stromberg declared that "the Oriental" had allowed Iran's traditional culture to degenerate through the influx of mass-produced European objects.[111] Young Iranians' apartments were filled with a tasteless mixture of "Chippendale" furniture, rugs with patterns adapted to "European taste," "steel tube chairs and tables," and "radios" and "record players." Iranians had no appreciation for the beauty of their traditional furnishings, "precious metalwork," or the real Oriental "rugs of life" and used radios without knowing "European music." All of this proved that "you can't catch up on a foreign tradition" and thereby cemented what had already been the premise of the analysis, namely, the superiority of Western culture.

This superiority is very much in line with Edward Said's analysis of the nexus between knowledge and power that produced Orientalism as a "Western style for dominating, restructuring, and having authority over the Orient."[112] The article in *Die Zeit* is pervaded by a naturalized way of thinking in which only the West (represented by Germany) possesses the expertise that makes it possible to judge the value of "tradition" in non-Western cultures. Iranians' own reform efforts in the arts and crafts were reduced to resembling a "less extensive and effective" version of "our Werkbunds." Between the lines of this reflection hovers a regret that the modernization of Iran and, by extension, "the Orient" blurred formerly self-evident differences between the East and the West.

The central role in Stromberg's account of the Oriental rug as representing both Oriental difference and Western knowledge about Eastern traditions must be understood against the backdrop of this object's long history in Europe. In 1962 a German art historian declared that "the Oriental rug has grown together with our *Wohnkultur*."[113] The Oriental rug, a part of European court culture since the Renaissance, was discovered anew as an exotic status symbol for bourgeois interiors during high colonialism; it quickly became the most widespread Oriental household object in Europe. The carpets with appropriated or copied Oriental patterns were eventually mass-produced by European companies in the Middle East and later by factories in Europe.[114] Adapted European copies of Oriental rugs were subsequently integrated into modern interiors. It is thus not surprising that Oriental rugs also appeared in German modern design literature during the Third Reich.[115] Some commentators felt the need to justify this presence by emphasizing that the German color design made sure the rug would "not have the air of an exotic foreign object." In general, however, the compatibility of the effectively Europeanized Oriental rug with modern interiors seemed well accepted.[116]

During the earlier postwar period, Oriental rugs had a marginal presence in West German publications that promoted modern interior design.[117] Sometimes they were even used to represent stereotypically outdated interiors.[118] In 1953 *Brigitte* explained that it was not necessary to "buy carpets with Oriental patterns" because "we don't need a carpet as an essential part of our interior design, like the Oriental does. We only need a functional floor covering."[119] From the middle of the decade onward, however, Oriental rugs appeared more often. The Oriental rug even became compatible with the period's ideas about modern internationalism.[120] The rug's aesthetic function was explained by the "happy combination of the straight lines of our times with the playful patterns of Oriental artists."[121] Commercial advertisings for carpets, which had previously focused on modern patterns, now presented different carpet styles together with different interior designs.[122] All in all, the Oriental carpet was present above all as a German quality product that expertly appropriated a foreign influence. In 1958 *Brigitte* highlighted that a German carpet proudly named "Expo 58" had received "much attention" at the world's fair in Brussels for its combination of a "sternness of the modern style with the vibrant diversity of traditional Oriental patterns."[123]

As a part of this shift, representations of Oriental carpets symbolized an exotic that could play into subliminal desires that otherwise were excluded from the ideal of rational consumption. One article asked consumers in 1956 to "Stay on the carpet!;" in the original German the expression is equivalent of the idiom "keep your feet on the ground." Several drawings presented modernist interiors that included big rugs with abstract motifs, all produced by German carpet companies. The eye-catcher, however, was a photograph of a woman on a flying Oriental carpet; the caption stated that "a carpet" took consumers "to the land of dreams about beautiful living."[124] In a similar vein, a full-page ad for Schaeffler carpets featured a happy couple sitting on a flying Oriental carpet above a bleak-looking urban center (the city of Hamburg). The text praises the "Schaeffler Persian rug" as the "foundation of sophisticated *Wohnkultur*."[125] The image evokes a dreamlike position of dominating space made possible by expertly appropriating Oriental culture and its "authentic patterns." The colorful carpet scene calls to mind the phantasmagoria of a safe and aesthetically perfect home against the backdrop of gray and stressful city life. The solution the ad offers for the tension between outside and inside feeds on the Oriental as a vague exotic signifier.[126]

The flip side of this Orientalist "land of dreams" supporting postwar consumer fantasies was the figure of the Oriental Other. Different advertisements referred to the Oriental's lack of civilization in order to promote a postwar consumer identity. A 1954 ad for a vacuum cleaner evoked an East-West contrast with a drawing of a woman in a niqab using a vacuum cleaner in the desert, thus placing her far away from both European domesticity and authentic Oriental interiors (fig. 4.11).[127] The text stated that a vacuum cleaner "doesn't help in the desert" but was, instead, very useful to "housewives." The joke capitalized on the acceptance of Orientalist stereotypes in order to produce the comfortable notion that owning a vacuum cleaner would be a sign of one's own cultural superiority with respect to the East.[128]

Echoing how the article in *Die Zeit* had defined electronic devices as foreign to Oriental culture, BBC electronics company advertised its refrigerators in 1955 with the headline "Enviable!" and the drawing of a well-fed pasha who savored the attention of three harem women cooling him with a palm branch. The text praised the device as facilitating the housewife's work by stating that "even today, it is not that difficult to enjoy some of the pasha's comforts."[129] Ironically projecting a male erotic desire onto an exotic setting, the ad both summons an Orientalist fantasy and presents it as ridiculous, thereby inviting German husbands and wives to feel superior for owning (or identifying with) a home with state-of-the-art household technology. Conjuring the stereotype of the harem as "shorthand for Eastern slavery and female oppression," the ad presented the postwar modern home as the East's opposite and Western housewives as progressive and liberated.[130]

Such imagery worked in relation to a larger context of Orientalist exoticism in postwar West German popular culture, from German *Schlager* (popular songs) to feature films.[131] Escapist Hollywood movies of the 1950s, shown in West German cinemas, imagined the Arab world as a place filled with barbarous men and harem women.[132] With *The Indian Tomb* (1921) and *The Tiger of Eschnapur* (1937) Weimar and Nazi era audiences experienced a German variant of cinematic Orientalism. After the war the German director Fritz Lang returned from Hollywood and produced remakes of both films that built on an established tradition of visually excessive erotic harem fantasies. The main character of *The Indian Tomb* is an architect, and the original 1922 novel illustrates the opposition between Eastern and Western culture by juxtaposing the architect's room in India—furnished in a perfectly rational and practical manner—with the irrational behavior of the maharaja.[133] That such Orientalist dichotomies between East and West influenced German notions about the modern home as early as the 1920s explains the ease with which Middle Eastern people could be

4.11 "It doesn't help in the desert," AEG vacuum cleaner advertisement, *Simplicissimus*, November 1954. Cartoonist: Berg. Reproduced from Staatsbibliothek Berlin.

presented in the 1950s as having neither a sense of taste nor any knowledge of their own traditions and as being incapable of properly using mass-produced Western household objects.[134]

Even though the "Oriental" and the "African" activated different sets of associations, both were identified with inferior cultures in a way that made it possible to position postwar consumer ideals against and above them. An advertisement that contained both versions of exoticism was published in March 1958 by Besmer carpets (fig. 4.12).[135] The full-page ad shows five adults on and around a modern yellow sofa and a modern wooden table at the rear end of a large Oriental rug. Holding a printed brochure in his hand, the man of the house smiles and points with his index finger to an African mask with a gesture that speaks of both his expert knowledge and his owner's pride. Through the physical relationship between the modern consumers and the African objects, the scene radiates a sense of cultural mastery and ownership. Whereas the carpet is called a "masterpiece" and represents the European appropriation of a foreign cultural influence into the idealized sphere of the modern home, the mask is staged as an exotic foreign object that is subjugated to a superior regime of knowledge and power.

In the 1957 *Franziska* film African masks occupy a special place in Stefan and Franziska's redecorated home in Passau. They hover visibly in the scene when Franziska's father lectures Stefan before accepting him as his son-in-law (fig. 4.3). They are also present when Franziska accuses Stefan of treating her like one of his "pleasing curiosities." One can therefore read their presence not only as similar to the Besmer ad—a sign of Franziska's aesthetic expertise—but also as a visual reminder of the looming danger that Stefan might relapse into a world of cultural and racial ambiguity, alienating him from his home. *Franziska*'s release coincided with an increased attention to antiques and non-European art objects in the lifestyle magazines. In 1956 *Constanze* invited readers to "play explorer," unravel exotic objects' "secrets," and establish an "inner relation" with them. The article presented a whole wall filled with non-European masks whose original function it explained as "fending off demons."[136] African masks and other "primitive" artworks were nevertheless a rare sight in postwar representations of modern interiors.[137] An "African negro sculpture" appeared in only one 1958 *Brigitte* room as revealing "the artistic interest" of the female inhabitant, a connoisseur of French art.[138]

Although Germany had lost its short-lived overseas empire after World War I, the global visions inscribed in the country's 1950s consumer culture have to be understood as part of the broader European context of colonialism and decolonization. "Colonial fantasies" had been influential before a German colonial

4.12 Besmer carpet advertisement, *Constanze*, March 1958. Original in color. Reproduced from Staatsbibliothek Berlin.

empire was created and continued to be so during the Weimar Republic, the Nazi years, and the postwar period.[139] While the European process of decolonization was ongoing, "primitive" artworks and the "Oriental" surfaced in the late 1950s as exotic in the sense of "the space of an Other, outside or beyond the confines of a 'civilization,'" and thus invited West German readers to assume a superior knowledge position as Westerners.[140] The "imagined community" of transnational consumption in postwar West Germany was thereby conceived inside a colonial cultural paradigm.

Some colonial era assumptions about Africans, however, began to destabilize at least slightly in the course of the decade. In 1951 *Constanze* would still combine a moralized ideal of the modern home and racist tropes to legitimize anti-American resentment. In June a photo showed the actors Stewart Granger and Jean Simmons in the living room of their Hollywood home, equipped with traditionally styled furniture, oil paintings, and a row of white bookshelves. The title "Cold Pomp in Hollywood" already contained the article's central message.[141] With mocking disdain, *Constanze* attacked the actors' "sober home" as a collection of "tasteless" decorations, fake antique furniture, and pseudointellectualism. Four months later, the magazine reported that some readers had complained that it was unfair to criticize the two actors for a "purely private" matter. In defense, *Constanze* compared the public display of the Grangers' private life with the exhibition of "cannibals in the human zoo of a big circus company": "Everybody is allowed to think and say whatever he likes about the habits of such cannibals. . . . Neither Stewart Granger nor his wife are cannibals. It would be slanderous and offensive to call them ones. Nevertheless, they cannot . . . expect admiration for their courage in making cinema propaganda with their furniture. Because there could be people who perceive such display of the private as, say, 'cannibalistic.'"[142]

It was certainly unusual to place two famous Hollywood actors' taste so emphatically outside the normative (German) home and its "good form."[143] In its reaction to the critical readers, however, the magazine drew an even deeper line of demarcation. By comparing the actors with cannibals as the prototypical racial Others, *Constanze* claimed the right to objectify the two actors in the same way as human zoos had objectified non-European people as exotic specimens to be looked at and judged. Such human zoos were extremely popular in Europe around 1900 and appeared in Germany for the last time between 1936 and 1940, when the German Africa Show toured the Reich and propagated a recovery of the German colonies.[144] The "cannibal" comparison linked the actors' exhibition of their supposedly tasteless home to those outside the sphere of civilization and thereby used the implicit racial Othering inscribed into the ideal of the good form.

In March 1956 *Constanze* announced that "the 'savages' don't live so uncomfortably after all." In four photographs the article presented exhibits from an ethnic museum with a smiling young woman attempting to sit on or eat from "household utensils" from Cameroon, the Congo, and the Amazonas that were all characterized as "amazingly simple, functional, and even beautifully crafted. They fit in exactly with their environment and with the people who use them, something that cannot be said about some of the modern furniture in our homes."[145] Ironically, including African artworks in this way in the area of modern living effectively underlined their otherness. The awkward ambiguity of the piece, however, produced at least some distance from naturalized notions of "savage" people. Eight months later, *Constanze* declared self-reflexively that the recent independence of African states had to change "our image of the negroes" who had started to "study astrophysics," while "in our thoughts we still decorate these people with glass pearls and colorful cotton flags."[146]

In 1960 a *magnum* photo essay on the "awakening peoples" wove the antagonism between modern design and bourgeois historicism into a Cold War contrast by invoking the idea that Africans lacked a properly modern taste. The African peoples had awakened to "Karl Marx," "the refrigerator," "historicism," and "porcelain kitsch."[147] The porcelain statue in the hand of a man from the Ivory Coast is explained to be a gift from East Germans. Describing the independence of African people as awakening them to both "cleanliness" and historicist "kitsch" certainly still reproduced the notion of their innate lack of civilization. Placed in a special issue on the topic of taboos, the article nevertheless illustrates that the perception of Africans as exotic outsiders to civilization had started to wobble. The people in these photographs were not labeled "cannibals" or "savages." While the article still placed Africans outside of the modern home as a symbol of Western civilization, it represented them above all as entering the wrong, that is, Communist, version of modernity.

The Economic Miracle's Colonial Fantasies

The *Franziska* movie updated the original movie's Nazi fantasies of supremacy and global domination and adjusted them to the postwar framework of Western consumer modernity and transnational trade relations. There is an argument to be made that this adjustment represented a wider cultural phenomenon that was at its peak when *Franziska* was released in 1957. Between the moment when *Goodbye, Franziska!* hit German screens in 1941 and the distribution of its remake in 1957 the Third Reich's violent expansionist drive, fueled by a racist ideology, reached its destructive apex and spiraled down to total war defeat. Within the next thirteen years, the war-riven international outcast under foreign occupation turned into an economically booming and internationally recognized republic. Simultaneously, West Germans' collective self-image transformed from an occupied and worn-down people to a reemerging Western power experiencing an economic miracle. In the context of the imperial and colonial paradigm's postwar transition, the myth of the economic miracle appears in yet another light. If we broaden the view from the focus on the modern home to how the postwar transformation of West German society as a national home was imagined in popular culture, the colonial fantasies that shaped this transformation come into full view.

After 1948 the production, consumption, and export of commodities became heavily charged symbols of this unlikely national renewal, making the sphere of consumer culture a compelling terrain in which to trace the accompanying affective economies and their relationship to a European colonizing culture before decolonization began to destabilize the latter.[148] Prior to exploring such symbolizations in the realm of West German advertising, it is important to dwell on how, in the early period of transition, "colonization" worked as a framework of perception. The occupation ended symbolically with the currency reform of 1948 and the founding of the Federal Republic in 1949. Toward the end of this period occasional comments, situated both at the margins and at the center of public discourse, deplored contemporary societal conditions by comparing occupied Germany to colonized peoples.[149] The disquiet about West German society experiencing reversed colonial roles found expression above all in the form of humor. In the Carnival season of 1948–49, a song became enormously popular that described West Germans as the "natives of Trizonesia," a reference to the merged American, British, and French occupations zones, called the Trizone. Lamenting how a "small bunch of diplomats . . . create zones and change states," the song likens occupied West Germany to other world regions previously "discovered" by Europeans. German "Trizonesians" are described as having "humor," "culture," and spirit, and they claim their new identity in an ironic and defiant manner:

We are the natives of Trizonesia.
We have maidens with a fervently wild nature.
We are no cannibals, it is true,
but we kiss all the better.
We are the natives of Trizonesia.[150]

"I am not a cannibal" is a German idiom that refutes concerns about one's character, and thus the idiom's use reminded Germans that their character was being questioned. Cannibalism was a common stereotype for African peoples' supposed primitive character and kept popping up in jokes and cartoons of the era.[151] Singing along in a foxtrot march rhythm, Germans could thus canalize their frustration about being at the mercy of the occupation powers by ironically appropriating the identity of colonized people and simultaneously rejecting it. The joke worked because comparing Germany with primitive people was, of course, absurd inside a European colonial paradigm. The chorus was also loaded in a gendered way when it illustrated the savage status of the Trizonesians with the "fervently wild nature" of German women. Such lines reflect contemporary anxieties about sexual encounters between German women and Black occupation soldiers.

While openly racist arguments gradually disappeared from political discourse, German officials kept turning to a language of morality that "rhetorically excluded" these German women "from the white German nation."[152] When sexual relations across the color line produced mixed-race offspring, these children embodied the danger of diminishing racial boundaries as well as the moral degeneration of their mothers.[153] In June 1949 the satirical magazine *Der Simpl* published a cartoon on its cover showing a nearly naked and overweight African man with thick lips, a bowler hat, and a large ring in his ear (fig. 4.13). A young, slender, and neatly dressed white woman stands in front of him holding the hand of a small Black girl in a white dress. In the background, a half-naked Black woman is working in front of two simple huts. The caption "housemaids urgently needed in foreign countries" is followed by the Black man's question in broken German, "Oh, you already work here before?" ("*Oh, du schon bei uns gearbeitet?*").[154]

The situation alludes to the children of German women and Black GIs, many of whom were the same age as the girl in the cartoon. Image and text insinuate that these German mothers could be forced by their difficult circumstances to apply for a job as a housemaid in an African country. At the same time, the cartoon makes fun of such a scenario. The huts, the man's nakedness, and his futile attempt to appear as the head of a bourgeois household defy any comparison with a proper German house. The image highlights the improbability of the situation through a stereotypical rendering of the African man that conforms to a motif that had been firmly established in the visual culture of Germany since around 1900.[155] It is thus by invoking the colonial paradigm and its visual culture that the cartoon both articulates and ridicules Germans' resentful difficulty recognizing themselves in their precarious postwar home. Laughter

4.13 “Housemaids urgently needed in foreign countries,” *Der Simpl*, June 1949, cover. Original with color. Cartoonist: Kriesel. Reproduced from Staatsbibliothek Berlin.

about the African man posing as a white bourgeois is superimposed on laughter about those German fears. The Black stereotype conjures up the affective assurance that as white people the Germans, the social and the moral underdogs of Europe, could nonetheless never fall as low as the Africans.[156]

Although these kinds of representations were presumably less present in the 1950s than around 1900, both popular and highbrow periodicals still regularly reflected a racist worldview.[157] Denigrating images of the primitive Black Other continued to be common sights in the popular visual culture of advertisements and cartoons.[158] Moreover, their appearance was often directly or indirectly linked to a West Germany striving for international recognition. In 1951 *Quick* published a cartoon in which a white man presents a Black man who is dressed only in a grass skirt as a "great discovery for the Olympics." A chain of five rings hangs from the Black man's nose. After Germany had been banned from the 1948 Olympics but was accepted again for the upcoming games in 1952, the cartoon delivered the ridiculous image of a Black body carrying the Olympic symbol by chance due to his primitive habits of self-decoration, an image that mocked the very idea that Africans could compete as equals in the games.[159]

An ad from 1950 for SABA radios (fig. 4.14) described living without a radio as living "primitively and obtusely" "like the negroes."[160] A white woman in the foreground underlines the cultural and racial contrast to the Black people in the background (thick lips, earrings, scanty dress). In a previous ad, published a month earlier, SABA had illustrated its product's "global prestigiousness" with two of its European customers introduced as "Monsieur Duval in Paris" and "Mister Shaw in Bombay."[161] The two ads together demonstrate the relevance of the colonial paradigm for reimagining West Germany as an economically successful nation. Featuring a British white man as a customer in Bombay matched the subsequent effort to distance German consumers from the specter of primitive Blackness and placed them inside a modern Western civilization whose racial boundaries were defined by its whiteness. The expansion of German products into the world through export was a crucial aspect of this way to reenter the West.

A 1954 cartoon ad for the fountain pen brand Pelikan (German for "pelican") showed two white men on a safari trip.[162] They encounter an African man, stereotyped in the usual manner with big lips and wide eyes, who sits naked in front of his hut. As they ask him if there are pelicans in the region the man smilingly shows a Pelikan fountain pen and says in broken German: "Oh yes, Pelikan, verry many!" The accompanying text underlines the success of the pen with

4.14 "Like the negroes," SABA radio advertisement, *Constanze*, March 1950. Reproduced from Staatsbibliothek Berlin.

"millions" of customers in ninety countries. Such ads appear to be the counterpart to earlier anxieties about being "colonized," but by making jokes about Africans as inconceivable customers, they also established the postwar transnational community of Western consumers as white.

In 1955 Germany became a sovereign state; it was also the year in which the production of the millionth Volkswagen was celebrated. In the same year, the magazine *Quick* published two items on the opening of a new German hosiery factory in South Africa.[163] This interest in the topic might have been due to the fact that silk stockings had become a widespread symbol of Western consumption in 1950s Cold War culture.[164] In November a full page of cartoons linked the opening of the factory to the legacy of German colonialism.[165] One cartoon shows two Germans with pith helmets driving a van decorated with the black, white, and red flag of the former German Empire, with the slogan "German stockings above everything" and with the model of a female leg. The line "Germany, Germany above everything" from the first verse of the German national anthem had been adopted for German imperialism at the end of the nineteenth century and was also used by the National Socialists. The song once again became the national anthem of the Federal Republic in 1952, yet only the third and not the first verse was sung on official occasions.[166] The cartoons highlight the strangeness of modern stockings for the stereotypical indigenous "negroes" based on the color difference between the stockings and the Africans' black skin. A sales agent lambasts astonished Black women for "walking around with naked legs," and Black women employ the stockings as alternative material for their grass skirts and hair decoration. In a blatant manner, this humor relied on well-established stereotypes about Black people to celebrate Germany's efforts for global expansion through export. The jokes make fun *only* of the fantasy that Germans could try to sell their export product to primitive Africans.

Two weeks later, *Quick* published a photo report on the opening of the German hosiery factory in South Africa (fig. 4.15).[167] A photograph showed a white model displaying her German stockings while dancing a "negro dance" in front of a group of Black people in tribal regalia identified as Basutos. The article delivered concrete information about how the racial divide characterized work in the German factory. While the Black people in their tribal regalia obviously did not qualify as consumers, in the other two photographs Black people appeared as "marveling" visitors strictly separated from whites due to the apartheid system and as (female) Black workers under the command of a white German foreman, who is quoted as being "very satisfied with his Basuto ladies."

In the 1950s *Quick*, like other popular illustrated magazines, reported on the African continent from the perspective of European powers. Articles were saturated with expressions of Cold War anti-Communism and a modicum of German colonial nostalgia. Rosemarie Lester has noted, moreover, that these magazines regularly showed a "sympathetic interest" in the South African state as the last bulwark against "world communism," which was accompanied by an approval of the apartheid structure and a "feeling of solidarity" with the Afrikaner population.[168] *Quick*'s treatment of the German hosiery factory in South Africa fits squarely into this analysis and could build on a rich cultural repertoire from European colonialism. As Anne McClintock has shown, representing astonished Black people in awe of modern Western commodities whose use value they cannot fully understand was a common trope in British nineteenth-century narratives of conquest. European commodities fulfilled the function of a fetish object embodying the promise of civilization brought to the Africans by European explorers, while these objects, at the same time, epitomized the impossibility of turning native Africans into civilized Europeans.[169] After 1945 these deep-seated tropes were used to reposition West Germany among the white nations that dominated the world. The *Quick* article on the hosiery factory highlighted the importance of this event for reboosting Germany's reputation abroad: even those South African newspapers that had "not printed a nice line about Germany" since the war now "praised and applauded" the German company's "courageous start."[170]

The economic miracle of mass production, mass consumption, and rising export was thus repeatedly linked to colonial fantasies of supremacy based on images of inferior and primitive Africans. This constellation also left its traces in West German films. A successful 1952 feature film told the story of a mixed-race girl named Toxi who appears at the door of a German family. Heide Fehrenbach has described *Toxi* as "a banner moment in the cultural expression of postwar racial liberalism" but one that remained skeptical about the very possibility of integration.[171] This exceptional attempt to promote antiracist awareness also displayed the tensions between postwar consumer culture and the presence of Black children. In an iconic scene, Toxi wanders as an outsider among the symbols of West German economic recovery, most notably, silk stockings. In the 1957 film *Franziska*, the title character emerges as a topical heroine for the West German economic miracle because she can sell her jewelry to consumers in a larger transatlantic world, a world, however, that implicitly excludes Black people. In one scene Franziska works on her modern jewelry while her son plays on the floor at her side. When she asks him, "Bertie, what are you making there?" he answers, "Nose rings for the negroes."[172]

Da staunen die Schwarzen. Sie passen genau auf, wie vor ihren Augen Masche für Masche deutsche Perlonstrümpfe entstehen. Die größte Strumpffabrik Deutschlands hat jetzt in Südafrika feierlich ein Zweigwerk eingeweiht. Eines der kühnsten Wirtschaftsunternehmen der Nachkriegszeit ist damit gestartet worden, denn der südafrikanische Markt gilt als ein Zentrum der Weltkonkurrenz. Und gerade dort, in dem kleinen Ort Parys bei Johannesburg, ist diese erste deutsche Strumpffabrik im Ausland eröffnet worden. Genau wie das deutsche Hauptwerk, hat auch der südafrikanische „Ableger" einen gläsernen Besuchergang. Im Lande der „Apartheid", der scharfen Rassentrennung, dürfen jedoch die neugierigen Schwarzen niemals zusammen mit Weißen die Fabrik besichtigen.

In Südafrika: Deutsche Strumpf-Premiere

Von deutschen Fachkräften angelernt, entwickeln die schwarzen Arbeiterinnen schnell große Geschicklichkeit im Bedienen der komplizierten Maschinen. Max Metzger aus Auerbach im Erzgebirge ist mit seinen Basuto-Damen sehr zufrieden. Mit flinken Händen streifen sie die Strümpfe auf die „Plastifiziermaschine", die den hauchdünnen Geweben Form gibt. Die Schwarzen sind auf ihre „Fabrik-Uniform", grüne Kittel und weinrote Baskenmützen, besonders stolz. Zweihundert Menschen arbeiten in der neuen Fabrik. Mehr als die Hälfte davon sind Schwarze. Bald aber werden nur noch die Schlüsselpositionen von Deutschen eingenommen werden. Das „Lehrpersonal" geht dann gleich an eine neue Aufgabe: in einem kleinen Ort bei New York wird das zweite Auslandswerk gebaut.

Quick 64

Auch Emilio Schuberths Starmannequins kamen zur Einweihung:

Schwarzweißer Freudentanz

Margit, der temperamentvolle Mannequin des italienischen Modekönigs Schuberth, wurde vom Rhythmus der in ihrem Stammesschmuck tanzenden Basutos mitgerissen und tanzte solo einen Negertanz. Auf einer großen Modenschau zeigten Margit und ihre Kolleginnen am Abend die schönsten Modelle ihres Meisters — und Strümpfe aus der neuen deutschen Fabrik in Parys (rechts). Dort läuft inzwischen die Produktion auf vollen Touren. Rund 100 000 Dutzend Paar Strümpfe sollen jährlich hergestellt werden. Regierung und Presse Südafrikas haben dem mutigen Start des jungen deutschen Unternehmens höchstes Lob und viel Beifall gezollt. Selbst Zeitungen, die seit dem letzten Weltkrieg nicht eine gute Zeile über Deutschland veröffentlicht haben, brachten große Berichte und wünschten dem neuen deutschen Werk unter afrikanischer Sonne besten Erfolg.

65 Quick

4.15 "In South Africa: German hosiery premiere," *Quick*, December 1955. Reproduced from Staatsbibliothek Berlin.

Redeeming Globalization

When the German company Henkel started to advertise again in the 1950s for its famous washing powder brand, Persil, it produced a short animated film entitled *Die weiße Weste* (The white vest).[173] The cartoon is set in a fictional polar region whose originally white animals were soiled black by the earth when the sun melted the snow. When the region was covered in snow again, however, the penguins stayed black. On a ship docked at the edge of the ice, a sailor has just washed many white shirts with Persil, and the penguins ask him to make them "that white again, too." After the man has washed the penguin's chest white, more and more penguins appear demanding "Persil, Persil." Declaring there was "only enough Persil for white vests," the sailor cleans all the penguins, who cheerfully sing, "Our white vests we owe to Persil. It is the best for us. Persil stays Persil." As the penguins march proudly with their white breasts held high, each holding up a packet of Persil, they continue singing: "Hein from the navy only washes with Persil, even us penguins. Persil stays Persil."[174]

For anyone who is acquainted with postwar West German history, it is difficult not to identify a strong moral and political subtext in this film. After all, *weiße Weste* is a German expression for someone's morally impeccable past. What is more, *Persilschein* had entered the German vocabulary during the Allied denazification campaign as the word for the letters many Germans wrote vouching for someone's alleged anti-Nazi attitude during the Third Reich.[175] As the penguins march like soldiers singing about their "white vests," thanks to Persil, the comparison with West Germans' postwar desire to dispense with the moral stain stamped on their national reputation seems obvious. Remarkably, the film also uses this fictional cartoon to envision the well-known German washing powder reaching places as far away as the polar region.

Persil's whitewashing of the penguins is suggestive of a deep-seated cultural trope that had been common in European soap advertising since high colonialism: the imagination that soap could wash parts of Black people's bodies white. In the second half of the nineteenth century, soap became a symbolic commodity for the British colonial civilizing mission. Advertisements implied that African colonial subjects were to be civilized through soap but simultaneously remained barred from ever achieving a European level of civilization. Africans were forever marked by the stain of backwardness ingrained in the unredeemable blackness of their skin.[176] After 1905 German soap advertising took on this theme and established soap as "a requisite product for whiteness."[177] In Nazi Germany, which concentrated its main colonial ambitions on the East, the morally loaded categories of filth versus cleanliness structured the regime's dehumanization of

Jews and other ostracized ethnic groups.[178] Accompanying West Germany's economic miracle, *Die weiße Weste* playfully invited Germans to see themselves as bringing the civilization of cleanliness to the world and simultaneously as the soiled penguins who are finally liberated from the stains of postwar occupation and misery thanks to the wonders of Persil.

The Persil ad exemplifies in a unique way how the two themes of global outreach and moral redemption were interconnected in the imaginary universe of postwar West German advertising. Since the late nineteenth century, mass advertising shaped popular imaginations of Germany's role in the wider world and provided the German Empire with a "consumer identity marked by race and global power."[179] Studies on advertising in Weimar Germany have generally not focused on this aspect, yet examples such as Sarotti chocolate and—from the early 1930s onward—Afri-Cola suggest that the connection between colonial fantasies and advertising certainly did not disappear.[180] During the Third Reich, that connection was continued and reappropriated on a large scale. The Nazi regime differentiated the role of state propaganda and advertising while giving the latter nonetheless an important political role. Recent studies have underlined that much advertising during the Nazi years contained ideological messages that consistently supported the regime and merged "commerce and race." Big brands continued to be present even during the war through their cooperation with Nazi efforts to inform consumers about available products and to keep their support during wartime deprivations.[181]

Advertising in postwar West Germany has been said to activate and channel private consumer desires after the hardships of war and occupation. It has also been interpreted as contributing to a West German consumer identity that accompanied the establishment of a social market economy and was strongly influenced by conservative family and gender ideals.[182] Imperial or racial connotations have not played an important role in most of these interpretations. While racial stereotypes were used in some postwar ads as a negative foil for West German export successes, many more ads reimagined West German industry and, by extension, the whole of West Germany as a global player in the postwar world. This eruption of global self-assurance in the commercial sphere was arguably helped along by the way in which early postwar ads employed advertising's reductive language to let the "stain" of the recent past vanish from sight.

When advertising increased again after the currency reform, ads often assured customers that a commodity was offered "with peacetime quality" meaning that the quality compromises of the war were over. Stating that a product was available "today as in the past" bridged the historical gap of war and postwar privations somewhat less explicitly.[183] Many commodities were indeed reintroduced by establishing their long historical continuity. Pelikan fountain pen stated in January 1948 that it had proved its quality "since 1889." Other early ads mentioned the year in which the company was founded, usually during the German Empire. Some used nebulous expressions such as "across all times" and "time goes by, but quality persists" and thereby positioned the brand on a sanitized historical timeline.[184] Maggi, the well-known producer of stock cubes and ready meals, simply stated in an ad from May 1948: "For the last 50 years, the name Maggi has assured the first-class quality of our products."[185]

Even more widespread was the strategy of pointing to a product's already existing global success. Between 1948 and the end of the 1950s, West German advertising pages were full of expressions such as "world brand" (*Weltmarke*), "world reputation" (*Weltruf*), "world importance" (*Weltgeltung*), "world success" (*Welterfolg*), "world-famous" (*weltberühmt*) and "world-proven" (*weltbewährt*). Commodities were "known in the whole world," were "used in the world," were "delivered to the whole world," had a "global success," enjoyed the "trust of the world," went "around the world," or even "conquered the world."[186] Such claims accompanied the reintroduction of many brands even before West Germany's export boom took off. Between September and November 1948 the eau de cologne brand 4711 published three big ads on the theme of a high-quality "world brand." The first ad simply stated in big letters: "The world brand through quality." Under the headline "a worldwide success," the second ad elaborated that the commodity's "greatness," "reputation," and "global importance" were based on the "rock-solid foundation" of its high quality. A subsequent ad hazily looked back in time by stating that 4711 had "grown into the favor of the world" by cultivating a "sense of responsibility" that had "preserved exemplary purity" (fig. 4.22).[187]

Even though the word "German" never appears in the 4711 campaign and only occasionally surfaced in others, such ads made it possible for readers to associate the circulating key words with Germany itself. It was well-known that the export of German products was "an existential question for Germany."[188] Accordingly, the first exhibitions of German industrial production at home and abroad attracted a lot of attention in the media. The poster of the 1947 export exhibition in Hannover was relatively sober, with a grayish-blue globe that exposed the contours of Europe set against a background of gray clouds.[189] The poster for the 1948 Hannover exhibition looked more self-assured, showing a globe encircled by a myriad of national flags from different countries (fig. 4.16).[190] The contours of Europe appear in the center of the globe, while North America, parts of South America, Africa, and most of Asia are also visible. Germany's location is marked with a red dot. When West Germany was still a nonstate entity without

4.16 Poster for the Hannover export exhibition, 1948. Original in color. Reproduced by permission from bpk / Deutsches Historisches Museum / Indra Desnica.

a national flag, this iconography put the country at the center of postwar global trade relations.

This use of a globe for the export exhibition posters was echoed by German advertisers (figs. 4.17 and 4.18). As early as October 1947, German Shell resorted to the image of a globe in combination with the adjectives "world-experienced" and "world-famous." Many other companies soon followed suit. Advertisements for such different products as motor oil, razor blades, brooms, steel tube furniture, cars, insecticide, corselettes, cigarette lighters, and many more employed an image of the earth.[191] Mostly, the ads also provided information on the location of the production site, making sure readers knew an ad was about a German commodity. Although a proper quantitative assessment is beyond the reach of this study, the material I have assembled suggests that such globalization advertisements took off in 1948, slightly ebbed around 1952–53, and emerged again from 1954 onward. Frigidaire refrigerators, Mouson soap, Kuba music equipment, Güterman sewing silk, Rollei cameras, Neo-Silvikrin hair restorer, and Gold-Zack ribbons all deployed the globe theme.[192] Sometimes the globe only silently associated the product with its worldwide presence; sometimes the text further emphasized the connection. Some ads explicitly paraded their commodity's export success as representing the German economy as a whole. A 1948 ad for a fountain pen placed the name, National, in front of a globe and combined a slogan about the brand with one about German export (fig. 4.18). In 1949 an ad for the hair tonic Trilysin positioned the tonic bottle in front of a globe, explaining that "Trilysin helps not only your hair but also through its export the reconstruction and the return of better times."[193]

How should we interpret the extraordinary ubiquity of the globe and of global references in postwar West German advertising? One intended effect of global references was, of course, to convince potential customers of a given commodity's good quality: if a product is appreciated by customers around the world, it must be good. The globe as a visual prop had the added value that it made the commodity in comparison seem larger than in real life and could thus generate attention.[194] This does not explain, however, why so many advertisers opted for the same strategy. As the 4711 campaign illustrates, the quality message could be infused with a second, more latent one, which was not only about the global recognition of the product but also about the recognition of Germany as a whole. When the sparkling wine brand Kupferberg advertised in 1949 that "letters from India, Australia, and other overseas countries" proved that Kupferberg brands "still enjoyed their good reputation," this could certainly assure readers of the wine's quality. But it could also assure them of the ongoing global success of a German product, a message emphasized by the logo of the business branch

4.17 "A car that goes into the world," Borgward car advertisement, *Constanze*, May 1949. Reproduced from Staatsbibliothek Berlin.

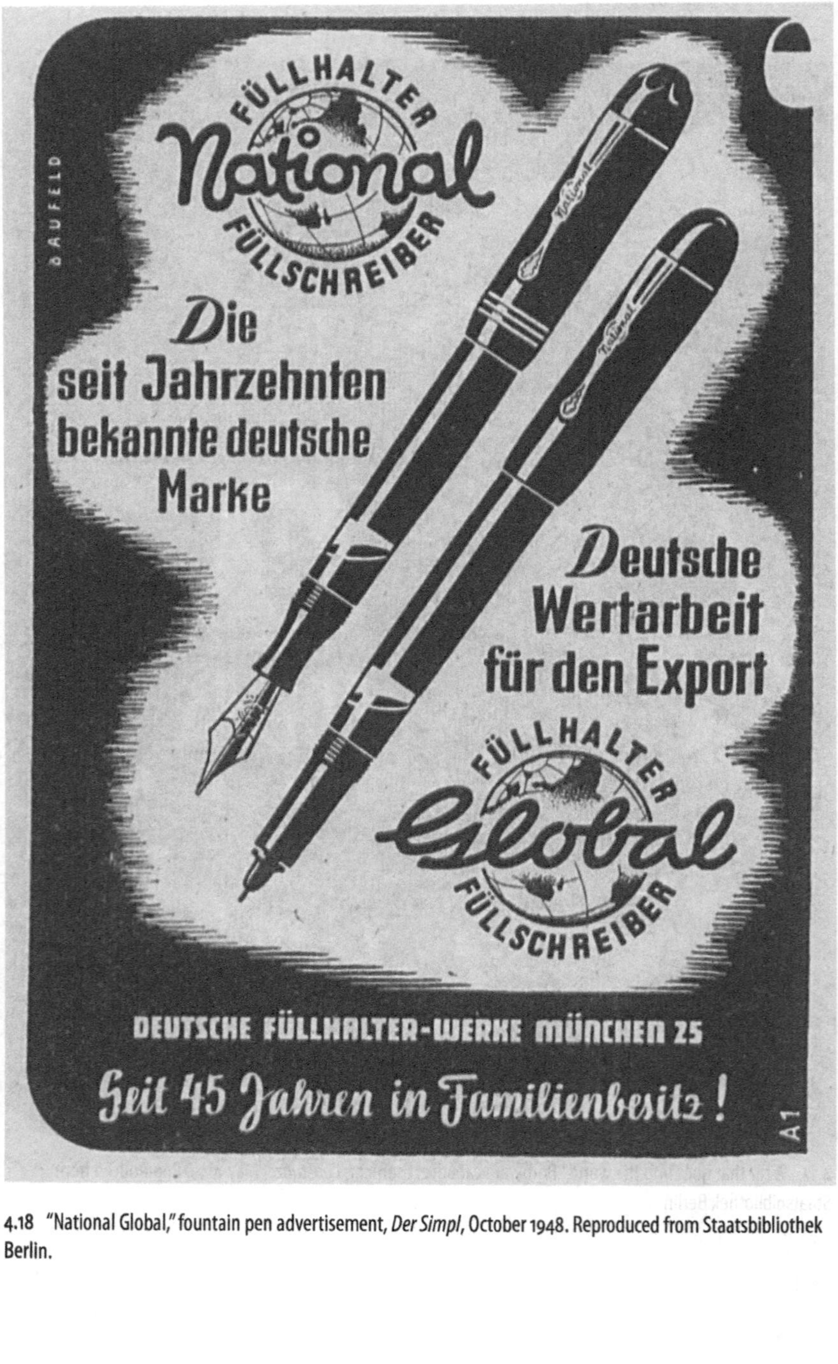

4.18 "National Global," fountain pen advertisement, *Der Simpl*, October 1948. Reproduced from Staatsbibliothek Berlin.

"German sparkling wine."[195] The image, moreover, identified "overseas" customers who praised Kupferberg (and implicitly Germany) as white Europeans: a white man sits at a table in a tropical setting writing a letter while a dark-skinned man stands to the side as if awaiting instructions (fig. 4.19). At the beginning of the 1950s, conjuring global success had become a standard trope that was obviously assumed to be generally pleasing to West German customers. An ad for a cigarette lighter placed a globe above a text on the product's technical characteristics. On top of the globe, an anthropomorphized drawing of the cigarette lighter with arms and running legs illustrated the tagline "the new Tausendzünder conquers the world!"[196]

Even though there is no systematic study of global references in German advertising, it seems clear that advertising with a globe and with a self-denomination as a "world business" or a "world brand" first arose in the context of German

4.19 "Letters from India and Australia," Kupferberg Gold sparkling wine advertisement, *Der Simpl*, February 1949. Reproduced from Staatsbibliothek Berlin.

imperialism around 1900. Angelika Epple has shown how the use of the globe in advertising for Stollwerck chocolate, combined with the German symbol of the eagle, loaded the commodity with "imperialist and nationalist connotations."[197] This language also occurred in advertisements during the Nazi period.[198] The brandy Asbach Uralt placed the product on top of a globe with the slogan "in Germany and overseas," and Rosenthal used the tagline "world brand of porcelain." Deinhardt sparkling wine illustrated a text about its large share in the "export of German sparkling wine" with a globe showing people raising their wineglasses on different continents.[199] These ads reflect that the German economy gained strength in the second half of the 1930s—a phenomenon for which the Nazis took full credit and for which they coined the term "the German miracle." The ads also illustrate the availability of the global export trope for messages of self-confidence that could be associated with the nation.

After the Third Reich started its aggressive campaign of geographic expansion, some ads resorted to strategies that fit in well with the idea of an expanding German geography.[200] In October 1938, six months after the incorporation of Austria into the Reich and only a few days after the Sudeten German territories of Czechoslovakia were conceded to Germany, the coats brand Eres used a map of Europe to praise the availability of its merchandise in "all big European capitals."[201] Two weeks after the invasion of Poland, Mercedes-Benz, the automobile used by Hitler and other Nazi officials, placed a full-page ad in the Nazi periodical *Arbeitertum* with a Mercedes limousine beneath the Mercedes star. In addition, two sides of a globe appeared next to each other, forming a world map (fig. 4.20).[202] After the Wehrmacht had successfully invaded Poland, Denmark, the Netherlands, Belgium, Luxemburg, Norway, and France, an ad for the sparkling wine brand Söhnlein emphasized in November 1940 that the brand had helped "German sparkling wine—*made in Germany*" to "conquer its undeniably due place in the whole world." In December 1940 a second ad reminisced about the brand's "first big international success" at the 1867 world's fair in Paris. Under the headline "Baptism of Fire in the Land of Champagne," it placed a Champagne bottle depicted as a firing cannon in front of a view of Paris and the Eiffel Tower. Six months after the Wehrmacht had marched into Paris, this combination of image and tagline created a less than subtle reference to the invasion of France and thereby linked the global success of the brand to Germany's military expansion.[203]

In February 1941 German Ford triumphantly declared that its automobiles "were involved" in the German army's conquering of Poland, Norway, Holland, Belgium, and France and would go on helping with the "peacetime construction of Greater Germany."[204] When in early 1942, as Germans fought in the Soviet

4.20 Mercedes-Benz advertisement, *Arbeitertum*, September 1939.

Union, the Balkans, and North Africa, the company praised the success of its cars under "tropical conditions," the connection to the war was self-evident.[205] Although the quantity of advertisements diminished after 1942 because it was prohibited to advertise goods that were scarce, many manufacturers continued to place ads using expressions like "world brand," "world-famous," and "world reputation."[206] Some companies promised consumers the swift return of their product after the war. The brand of a dry fuel product, Esbit, published an ad in which the product itself was pictured as a soldier sitting in front of his tent and writing to those customers who had to do without him/it. The text explains that his absence at home was due to his presence "with the soldiers in East, West, far and near, and with Rommel in Africa."[207]

In the foreign propaganda magazine *Signal* the abundance of advertisements using global tropes is especially conspicuous. *Signal* was developed at the end of 1939 by advertising specialists and war psychologists working for the German Wehrmacht. It informed its readers about the German war with high-quality photo reports while promoting a greater European economic area under German leadership. Printed from 1940 until March 1945 in many different languages, the magazine appeared in more than fourteen European countries and reached 2.4 million copies in June 1942, making it the second-highest-sold illustrated magazine in all of Europe.[208] While the number of commercial ads decreased in the German press during the course of the war, advertisements for German brands were placed in high quantity in *Signal*, indicating that German exports continued at a relatively high level during the war.[209] From 1941 onward many of these ads began to use an image of the globe, and expressions such as "in the whole world," "world brand," "world name," "world reputation," and "world-famous" proliferated.

Sometimes a brand's wartime campaign in *Signal* was similar to its subsequent advertising in postwar West Germany. In *Signal*, a series of 4711 cologne ads focused on its global presence. In March 1942 a 4711 bottle was placed prominently on top of a big globe that was surrounded by the slogan "the world brand through quality" (fig. 4.21).[210] When 4711 reintroduced itself after 1948 as a "world brand" (fig. 4.22), it thus took up a theme it had recently disseminated through *Signal* in a war-torn Europe under German domination. Mercedes-Benz, too, continued to publish already established motifs after the war with ads whose visual language centered on the star in combination with the globe.[211] In 1944 especially, many ads in *Signal* explicitly merged their brand with Germany itself. The producer of office supplies Geha promoted a new Europe with higher consumption and free trade as Germany's war aim, exclaiming: "What prospects for the time after victory!" In September 1944 Goldpfeil, the "world brand for leather goods," praised the "German capacity" to continuously produce "tasteful purses of 'prewar' quality." After the war, the brand went back to the established slogan, "world brand for leather goods."[212]

Signal was available only in occupied countries and allies of Nazi Germany. It also had an edition in German that reached 413,000 copies in 1943 and was very popular among Wehrmacht soldiers, SS members, and other Germans stationed in occupied territories.[213] It is impossible to know how many of the ads described above were also published in periodicals within Germany. Advertisements that we encounter in *Signal*, particularly in the last year of the war, were geared toward alluring Europeans outside Germany with a message centered on consumption and the promises of a strong postwar European economy dominated by Germany and its industry. This was an industry whose ongoing "capacity" was, not to forget, based to a large extent on forced labor by foreigners and racial Others.[214]

4.21 "The world brand through quality." Advertisement for 4711 cologne, *Signal*, March 1942. Reproduced from Universiteitsbibliotheek Amsterdam.

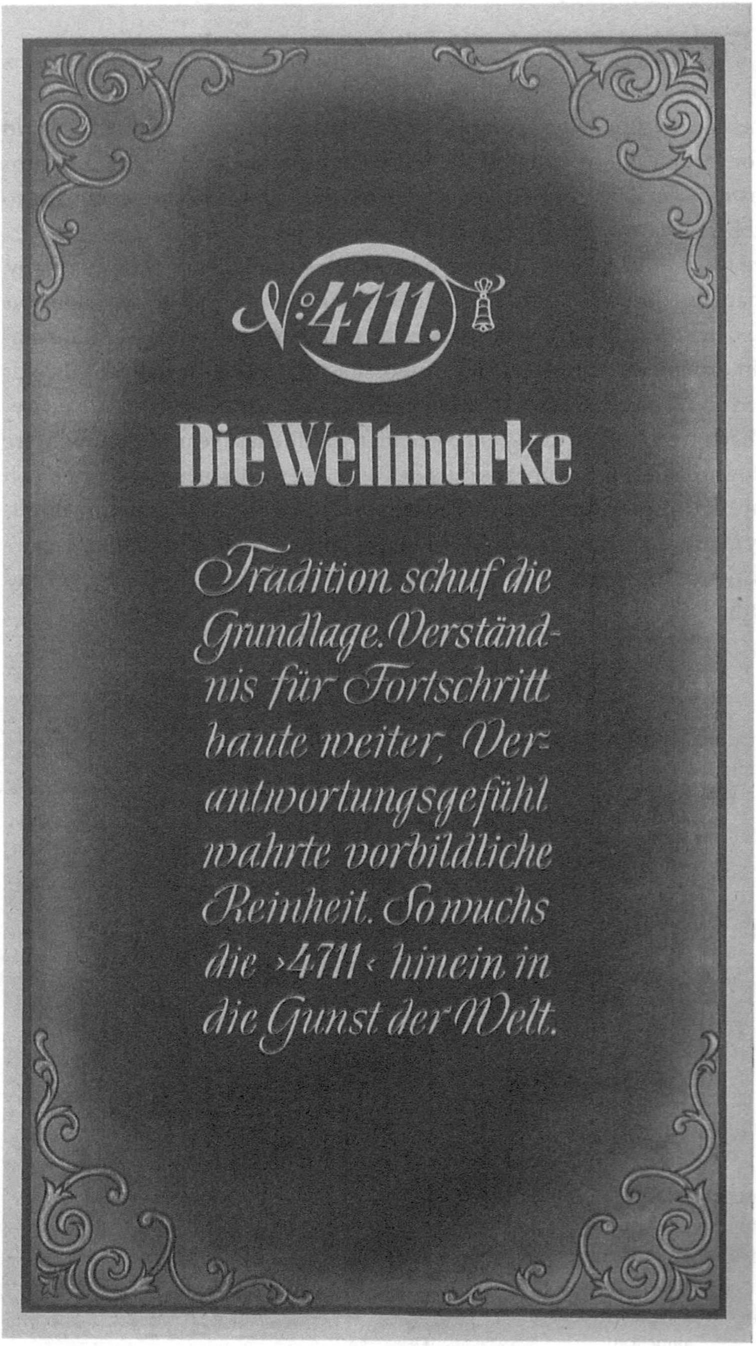

4.22 "The world brand." Advertisement for 4711 cologne, *Constanze*, November 1948. Reproduced from Staatsbibliothek Berlin.

After the war, once the Marshall Plan was under way with its message of productivity, economic cooperation, and free trade, ad campaigns for many West German commodities relied on a globalization imagery that had been practiced in the context of the war within Germany but even more so in the pages of *Signal*, read by many Germans abroad. The personal continuities in the sphere of German advertising may be one reason for this phenomenon.[215] More importantly for our context, the global orientation in many postwar advertisements implicitly tied in with Nazi consumer promises for a postvictory world spread through advertisements and many other propaganda channels. In this sense, the case of the Volkswagen (chapter 2) can be seen as paradigmatic for the creation of a national consumer imaginary after 1948. The Federal Republic as a state restrained from any grandiosity in the way it presented itself both nationally and internationally. West Germans, for all we know, were indeed skeptical of being manipulated again by state propaganda. The sphere of commercial advertising, however, seemed to have been exempt from such skepticism. Advertising invited West Germans on a massive scale to identify again with a national home that expanded "into the world" through the global reach and recognition of German commodities. In such postwar ads, production, consumption, export, and national self-image intertwined, and the collective self-respect of a resurgent West Germany was conflated with the supposed regained international prestige of its products. By visually reconnecting to earlier German fantasies of global conquest, this consumer imagery delivered a redemptive message that superseded the sense of collective humiliation of the immediate postwar years.

Linking German commodities to the country's imperialist ambitions was certainly not a new phenomenon. This association exploded in the German Empire, did not entirely disappear after the end of World War I, and was taken on again by the Third Reich in the context of a new form of aggressive imperialist expansion. What does this trope's revival in the postwar period tell us about the make-believe space that emerged at the very moment when West Germany reconstituted itself as a quasi-national entity? To all appearances, West German merchandise, with its long cultural "service" in the imperialist imagination, had the capacity to magically transform *the* German into a global player "without blemish" (fig. 4.23). Once the "great miracle" of the currency reform had opened up a make-believe space in which German commodities could make Germans' tarnished vests white again, the path was clear to praise a mouthwash product "from Berlin" for its "triumphant march through Western Europe," to illustrate the quantity of Grundig's hi-fi production with a line reaching "from the North Cape to the Bosporus," and to exemplify the worldwide success of the painkiller Togal with a photograph of two Bedouins in the desert, sitting in front of a camel while

4.23 "The razor blade without blemish," Bonsa razor blade advertisement, *Neue Illustrierte*, January 1948. Reproduced from Staatsbibliothek Berlin.

admiring the product in their hands.[216] Such advertising strategies were clearly deemed effective tools for enchanting potential West German customers in 1957.

If, as Uta Poiger has observed, colonialist and imperialist imagery emerged again in German advertising during the 1970s and 1980s, it was arguably not only because of the persistence of German colonial myths in general but also because such motifs had been reintroduced at the birth of the Federal Republic to imagine the country's redemption through commercial globalization.[217] This chapter has traced how, during West Germany's emerging economic miracle, a sense of being at home in the world was created through the capacity of the country's symbolically charged commodities to let both recent and older German dreams of global influence and racial supremacy hide inside and thereby become a constitutive part of their redemptive function. This redemptive function was thus steeped deeply in the political framework of the postwar era's not yet postcolonial West. Through countless semiotic acts of association and dissociation, the mythical present of West Germany's redeeming objects became a founding cultural figuration. As a result, this mythical present made a new home for structures of feeling that had survived the 1945 break without ever being denormalized.

It is only from today's perspective, with its different structures of feeling, however, that the West German dreams that perpetuated both a German and a shared European legacy of imperialism may appear as "hidden." This became manifest when I experienced a form of "unhomeliness" with respect to the 1957 movie *Franzika* before encountering its 1941 original. In *Goodbye, Franziska!* maps and globes are conspicuously placed inside Franziska's father's house, thereby anticipating the moment when Michael is called to connect his German home with Germany's expansionist war. One of these maps is then used by Franziska's father to follow the progress of the Wehrmacht in Poland (fig. 4.24). Shortly afterward, Michael comes back, receives his conscription order, and listens to Franziska as she tells him why he has to leave her again and go to war. In Liebeneiner's remake, the wider world to be conquered through export appears in the form of papers listing the mail orders for Franziska's jewelry alongside piles of packed merchandise, upon which Stefan stumbles in astonishment when he comes home after his friend Blacky has died. The scene in which Franziska works on her jewelry and her son claims to make "nose rings for the negroes" positions Franziska's artisanal contribution to the export-oriented West Germany in contrast to an imagined primitive Africa. Whereas in 1941 Michael had to transform his penchant for global adventure into serving an expansionist army, Stefan is suddenly seen again as the photo editor for the magazine *Constanze* in front of a world map giving advice to his correspondents for their trip to Asia, while Franziska is the one who is astonished (fig. 4.25).

4.24 Three screenshots from *Goodbye, Franziska!* (1941): globe and maps, a map of the war, the final good-bye. Reproduced from Terra-Filmkunst.

4.25 Three screenshots from *Franziska* (1957): packages ready for export, a world map in the editorial office, inside the empty home. Original in color. Reproduced from CCC Filmkunst.

This turn of the plot swiftly provides Stefan, surrounded by the modern interior of his office and by photographs of Franziska with her jewelry, with a new consumption-oriented global competence before the film ends with the couple's lighthearted dialogue in a not yet homely domesticity. Did this change redeem the story from its aggressively expansionist finale in 1941? Most of the reviewers, nostalgic as they were about the original, did not care. Perhaps the new morally redeeming make-believe space that recycled fantasies of cultural homogeneity and geographic expansion wrapped in implicit racial hierarchies was so naturalized by 1957 that both films ended up in the same timeless and fundamentally mythical present of the modern German home.

EPILOGUE

Postwar Mythologies and Their Ghosts

The most successful West German movie of 1960 was called *Das Spukschloss im Spessart* (*The Haunted Castle*). It was a so-called "grusical" that combined the genres of comedy, musical, and horror with a fantasy plot set in the present.[1] At the beginning of the film, construction workers dig up a shrieking skeleton from beneath a section of the Autobahn in Germany, thereby provoking a bunch of ghosts to rise from the ground and take control of the machines. Later in the film, four of these spooks from the Spessart castle's ancient past march cheerfully through the modernist cityscape of the Federal Republic's capital, Bonn. As they sing "Let's see if there aren't any ghosts in Bonn" they interfere with the economic and material order by, among other things, making military uniforms disappear from a shop window. When a judge angrily declares, "There are no ghosts in the Federal Republic," he bangs his fist on the table, causing a part of the official decoration to crumble into pieces and thereby laying bare a swastika. In a subsequent scene, several Volkswagens pass along a city street as the words "Let's see if there aren't any ghosts in Bonn" are broadcast from speakers on the roof of a Volkswagen van.

This musical sequence turns the emphatic denial of the existence of "ghosts" in the Federal Republic into a major joke. The episode's liberating silliness conveys in its own way some of what I have tried to unravel in the preceding chapters with different tools. Even today, its anarchic staging can make me laugh about the uncomfortable observation that the cultural effects of twelve years of Nazi rule, its unprecedented level of mass propaganda, and its subsequent downfall have been so pervasive, so layered and twisted by taboos, that we can only grasp it in the notion of "ghosts." On the preceding pages I have dug up and chased a specific set of these ghosts, namely, those that promised postwar West

Germany a redemption from a haunting past. Modern design, the Volkswagen, and other products of Germany's export economy conflated past promises of material affluence undergirded by violent conquest and racial purification with the phantasmagorias of a postwar present embodied in a world of mass production that was imagined as devoid of a burdensome past or any traces of violence. By creating a myth about the absence of ghosts, redeeming objects produced a cultural world that was in fact populated by them.

Popular humor was one way to express an awareness of such ghosts. Experimental artistic expression was another. In Ottomar Domnick's unique movie *Jonas* (1957), the sleek surfaces of postwar material modernity disturb any clear sense of how past and present interrelate. Jonas, an Everyman protagonist, gets lost between the facades of Stuttgart's inner city in "a world nailed up with signs," as Hans Magnus Enzensberger's peculiar voice-over text to the film formulates it. The voices that accompany Jonas oscillate between a moral thought police, news headlines, and advertising slogans in which consumption and unfathomable guilt become one entangled whole.[2] The protagonist's experience of haunting is exacerbated by an inscrutable storyline in which Jonas does what an advertisement tells him to do and buys a hat, then loses the hat, then replaces it by picking up one that does not belong to him but that has initials stitched into it that conjure guilt-ridden memories of a war experience that remains nebulous. An innocent act of banal consumption becomes the trigger for the moral burden of past deeds to invade the protagonist's present.

It would be apt to describe the process of writing the chapters of this book as a journey into West Germany's world of commodities "nailed up with signs." Films like Domnick's *Jonas* and books like *Das Haus der Kindheit* (The house of childhood, 1956) by Marie Luise Kaschnitz and the later novel *How German Is It?* (1979) by the American author and Austrian immigrant Walter Abish that I picked up along the way encouraged me to pursue what initially seemed like loose threads, unusual and often confusing trouvailles, that I was unsure would ever lead to something coherent or readable.[3] At the provisional end of this journey, I still perceive a kindred spirit between my work and these artists' efforts to depict a world that had become indecipherable while its shiny surfaces radiated unspeakable echoes of something indigestible. The present that they struggled with is not yet history; the myth of redeeming objects, as well as the larger myth of the postwar modern encompassing it, still shapes our present, even if by now the cracks in its soothing cocoon might be closer than ever to reaching a critical mass. While I was assembling my own findings, piecing together and rearranging the material of every chapter as if working on a big jigsaw puzzle, others were also doing the work of breaking open the surface of postwar modernity's myths, especially in the field of art history. A case in point are the interrelated recent debates on the Bauhaus, the German expressionist Emil Nolde, and the documenta art exhibition.

The Bauhaus was praised on the occasion of the school's ninetieth anniversary in 2009 for its "identificatory meaning" for the "self-conception of a nation" that was a "better Germany."[4] Its one hundredth anniversary in 2019 saw similar appraisals but also gave rise to much more critical comments informed by the scholarship of the past decades. A notable article in *Die Zeit* dissected the Bauhaus "myth." It pointed to the pervasive spiritual dreams of purity and superiority and an "aesthetic fundamentalism" that prominent Bauhaus members attempted to put to work for the Third Reich. Hanno Rauterberg summarized that the "Bauhaus dream" to "move the world of things into timelessness" met "the needs of the postwar years—and still does so in some ways today."[5]

Emil Nolde has been celebrated since the 1950s as the quintessential anti-Nazi artist, a modern German painter who was banned by the Nazis as "degenerate." The full opening of his personal archive has led to a radical reinterpretation in the form of a much-discussed exhibition in 2019 that exposed his great ambition, pursued until 1945, to become the first National Socialist artist. The exhibition also addressed how what is now known as "the Nolde myth" established itself after the war.[6] In 2021 the German Historical Museum in Berlin opened an exhibition on the documenta, the quinquennial show of contemporary art in Kassel launched in 1955 with considerable support by the German government and the ambition to establish West Germany as an important center of modern art in the West. A section of the 2021 documenta exhibition was dedicated to the director of the first three documenta shows, art historian Werner Haftmann, and how his past as a Nazi Party member influenced the way he promoted abstract and expressionist art after 1945: he displayed artists formerly banned as degenerate while simultaneously excluding German Jewish artists.[7] Haftmann also played a crucial role in creating the image of Emil Nolde as an ideal embodiment of the expressionist painter as a "natural anti-Fascist."

In her analysis of the cultural meanings behind early documenta's artistic programs, art historian Nanne Buurman emphasizes the discursive affinities between Haftmann's catalog introductions and notions of Nordic or Germanic expressionism. Buurman concludes that "Haftmann's assertion of 'abstraction as a world language' . . . in the context of *documenta II* (1959), could be understood as a declaration of the universal victory of the German spirit fourteen years after the end of the 'Third Reich.'"[8] She also describes her intellectual undertaking as a form of "ghost busting" that requires consciousness of the long-term effects of the discourse she studies. documenta's claim on modern art as a "world language" also echoed after the war in the Venice Biennale art exhibition, which was similarly characterized by a conspicuous absence of Jewish artists, as a recent article by Frances Tanzer exposes. Using the Biennale as a vehicle, post-Fascist western European countries like West Germany, Austria, and Italy reinvented modernist art and artists as representatives both of a cosmopolitan and democratic heritage and of a "European identity without Jews," a cultural maneuver for which they also had to blot out modernism's continuing significance during the Fascist era.[9]

There is a commonality between these very recent findings about the language surrounding the documenta and the Venice Biennale and my own findings about both high-brow and popular discourses surrounding modern design interiors and the Volkswagen in West Germany. One of these commonalities is the importance of the Western international context for both reusing some of modernism's political meanings during the era of Fascism and, in doing so, whitewashing national culture in the double sense of the word: making the stain of the Fascist past disappear while embracing an idea of the West shaped by latent notions of racial homogeneity and superiority. While the latter manifested itself in the form of excluding Jewish artists from these high-profile postwar events in the field of contemporary art, I have argued that the exclusion of Africans, Black Americans, and Oriental Others from the political imaginaries of the modern home and of German export commodities was an equally significant aspect of these realms' political meaning. The logic of redemption inscribed into the objects and aesthetics of postwar West German modernity worked and resonated inside the cultural context of a transatlantic West whose identity had evolved from a deeply established and ongoing colonial paradigm. Because it was ongoing, it could not produce ghosts in the same way as National Socialism did. There was no satire about the ghosts of colonialism. It is only from today's perspective, in the midst of an intensified reckoning with Europe's colonial past and its "debris," that we may encounter this postwar heritage as ghostly.

In *The Haunted Castle* the uniforms and the swastika, a "stranded object" that silently exposes the former Nazis who continued to serve as judges in German courts, were manifest ghosts of the past; the Volkswagen, however, remained an opaquely coded signifier of a timeless world of commodities. Today, we are able to recognize the image of Volkswagen cars spreading from the globe into outer space as uncannily reminiscent of the Nazi past. Yet an image connecting the German Volkswagen with geographic expansion also adorned a *Time* magazine cover in 1954 with the headline "Germany: The Fabulous Recovery": the VW logo was situated in the middle of West Germany as the sun, while the rows of VWs radiated outward as sunrays.[10] The postwar dream for which

Volkswagen became symbolic was certainly crucial for the identity of the Federal Republic, but it also extended far beyond Germany.

Shortly after New Yorkers demonstrated in front of the German trade fair in New York in 1949 carrying placards with the slogan "Today the Volkswagen—tomorrow the death wagon," Christopher Columbus appeared in front of a globe on a poster that advertised the third postwar export exhibition in Hannover, West Germany (fig. E.1). On the poster Columbus is surrounded by what looks like a cloud or stormy water, and his figure dominates the view on the globe behind him in such a way that it seems to define the latter's very meaning. Sixty years earlier, in Paris, another Columbus figure was painted on a cloud. In that case, the cloud hovers above a train that is heading toward America. The huge fresco painting to which this scene belongs decorates the upper walls inside the circular hall of the Bourse de Commerce (Commodities Exchange) in Paris. It was first presented to the public at the 1889 Exposition Universelle. The fresco's succession of images unfolds the story of how European commerce conquered the world in a benign way. As the mythical beginning of that story, Columbus resides both inside and outside of it, like a god, or maybe like a ghost.

From the eighteenth century onward, European colonialists acted on the notion of a promised land of global hegemony based on a mythology of time in relation to global space in which European civilization was always positioned as the apex of all human development. By situating itself at the endpoint of time, "Europe" defined what History was and thereby stood both inside and outside of it, both time-bound and timeless. From this position it was possible to transform what was threatening to appear as the moral stain of colonial violence into an ethical act of creating a future for the colonized. European colonialism was thus based on a make-believe time that organized a global make-believe space and that was applied, as Priya Satia has shown for the British Empire, to restore the image of a morally impeccable and "civilized" collective self especially in moments of crisis, when too much disconcerting evidence to the contrary leaked to the surface of public discourse.[11]

Referring to Columbus in 1949 to reestablish West Germany's redeemed self-image could build on this story's cultural *longue durée* as well as on how the concerted efforts of the US-led Marshall Plan information campaign refurbished the same story at precisely that historic moment.[12] The United States, Britain, France, and other Western countries cooperated for the Marshall Plan information campaign to proclaim postwar Europe's "recovery" by telling and retelling a tale in which hard work, technology, and the exchange of commodities had miraculously generated welfare for all in the past and would only have to be jump-started again to deliver once more. This "liberal tale of origins" emptied

E.1 Poster for the Hannover export exhibition and the Hannover technical export exhibition. Artist: Axelle. 1949. Original in color. Reproduced by permission from bpk / Kunstbibliothek, SMB / Knud Petersen.

Atlantic history of "conquest and slavery, of imperial wars and national competition, of racism and authoritarianism." In Sheryl Kroen's thoughtful reading of the campaign, "the eighteenth century idea of *doux commerce* was re-invented and re-imagined as the antidote and cure for the horrors perpetrated in the heart of civilized Europe in the twentieth century."[13] Her interpretation suggests the experience of a different kind of 1945 "zero hour," namely, a Western and a European one in which the shock of the Nazi war and its crimes also shook the self-image that an imperialist Europe had created of itself over two centuries.

Aimé Césaire was probably the first to observe this effect. In 1950, when the Marshall Plan information campaign was well under way, Césaire published his *Discours sur le colonialisme* (*Discourse on Colonialism*). By that time, the Martinican poet had been an elected member of the French parliament for five years, a period in which European powers attempted to recover their weakened empires through warfare. The Netherlands used what the country recently officially acknowledged as "extreme violence" against Indonesian forces after the Dutch colony had declared its independence in August 1945.[14] Between 1945 and 1949 France violently suppressed anticolonial revolts in Algeria and Madagascar and began a war against the Vietnamese national liberation movement. In 1950 Césaire reflected on the relationship of these events to the violence of occupation and warfare that Europeans themselves had endured from Nazi Germany. For "Western civilization," he stated provocatively, the experience of Nazism on European grounds had been a "choc en retour."[15]

The violence that "returned back" to Europe in the form of the Nazi Empire was a revenant that brought with it a "shock" of recognition. Against their will, Césaire stated, Europeans recognized an aspect of themselves in the horrors of the Nazi Empire, an aspect that their own frameworks of perception had rendered invisible before, yet they simultaneously hid this realization from themselves. In order to make visible to his readers what was artfully hidden from view after 1945, Césaire caused this interior "demon" to appear in the text itself. He presented a quote by Hitler on the necessity of turning the "country of a foreign race" into a "country of serfs" only to subsequently reveal to the reader that this was actually a quote by the French philosopher and "humanist" Ernest Renan writing in 1871 on the natural role of the superior "European race" to rule as "masters and soldiers" over "the inferior races."[16]

Césaire ingeniously demonstrated that the words had different meanings once they became associated with Hitler. Evoking "Hitler" in this way had the power to turn colonialism itself into a scary ghost. It could transform the colonial past and present into something indigestible, something that therefore had to be made invisible again. It had to be transferred to a category so thoroughly dissociated from the metropolitan past and present that it could not be integrated again, producing the cultural effect of aphasia. The French government's censorship measures during the Algerian War were one expression of this urgency, which left its mark on a whole era of French cultural production coerced into finding indirect forms of addressing the crisis.[17] It is in this context that the image of Hitler in a Peugeot becomes a coded comment in Jean-Luc Godard's New Wave film *Le petit soldat* (*The Little Soldier*), produced in 1960.[18] *Jonas* was a West German cinematic attempt to grapple with how the smooth surfaces of postwar modernity and the banality of consumerism had set the indigestible aspects of the Nazi past apart in a way that was beyond understanding. *The Little Soldier* in turn was ripe with a latent and inexpressible awareness that consumer modernity, the Vichy and Nazi pasts, and the present colonial warfare were all closely interconnected.

The film tells a story set in May 1958 in Geneva at the moment when the European settlers, or Pieds-Noirs, reacted to the Algerian war of liberation by seizing power from the sitting government in Algiers, thereby causing the political crisis in France that led to the founding of the Fifth Republic. The plot follows Bruno, who is part of a French right-wing antiterrorist organization that assassinates supporters of Algerian liberation. This organization orders Bruno to kill a Swiss radio journalist who reports from a critical angle about the Algerian War. When Bruno first refuses, then only reluctantly attempts to kill the journalist, we see him sitting in a Peugeot 403, from 1955, while hiding behind the cover of a magazine. The cover of *L'Express*, in reality stemming from the production year 1960, shows the title "twenty years after" next to a full-page photo of Adolf Hitler. For a moment, Bruno's pistol emerges right next to the image of Hitler, a shot that visually fuses the reluctant postwar French agent for the cause of colonialism with the personification of the Nazi past. Just as Césaire had done, the shot stages the violence of colonialism by evoking Nazism. One might say that it also captures the logic of a cultural operation that hides that same violence behind the symbolic shield of a Nazism that stands for an ultimate and therefore forever ex-territorialized evil.

The Little Soldier speaks to us from the margins of history. The film was banned by the French government and only released in 1963 in a censored version.[19] It conveys the disorienting effect of the Algerian War on French self-understanding as well as the uncanny presence of the Vichy and Nazi past in an opaque and unreadable world of colonial and anticolonial violence that blends with modern consumerism, seemingly unrelated yet cinematically connected. American and French automobiles, modern apartment buildings, and modern interiors dominate much of the scenery. Bruno's voice tells the viewer that the French antiterrorist organization for which he worked was financed by a "deputy" who "had had his moment of glory with Vichy." He meets Veronica. They have an enigmatic conversation in her impeccably modern and sparsely furnished apartment. Bruno tells her that his father was shot at the liberation because "he was a friend of Drieu La Rochelle," a famous Vichy collaborator.[20] In another scene, members of an Algerian group torture Bruno in the bathroom of their modern apartment; afterward, he receives electroshocks through a small device in their living room. A scene in which French agents torture Veronica, who is on the side of the Algerians, was cut out of the original film by the censorship of the French government.

Without mentioning *The Little Soldier*, Kristin Ross argued in 1995 that France's exploding mass consumption of the late 1950s and early 1960s, its notion of modernity, and its culture of cleanliness were entangled with the violence of the Algerian War and the dawning end of the French Empire.[21] France "cleaned house" as the French introduced shiny new commodities into their homes, while the French army used some of these commodities for systematic torture, a practice that was described by one French soldier as an act of "cleaning the country." Both realms relied on a "modernism" that brought with it a sense of "immobile time" while systematically defining those outside of its norms as lagging behind. This, together with the massive censorship, made it possible to cut the Algerian War out of the French experience in the metropole and "relegate it to another temporality."[22] Ross's groundbreaking interpretation counteracts colonial aphasia by reading together what the discourse of the time had vigorously set apart. The cartoon of a French paratrooper who uses the laundry soap "Pax" to torture a prisoner serves as an important heuristic bridge between the two worlds. Ross's observations make evident that the postwar modern and the postwar colonial must be thought together if we want to understand how this era has shaped our present. In her story, too, the objects of postwar modernity conjured a timelessness that was meant to clean the moral stain of an indigestible violence from collective consciousness precisely by enacting a cultural logic that was interwoven with that same kind of violence both in the Algerian War and, I would add, in Nazism, Vichy France, and the colonialism of the French and other European empires.

In a Pears soap advertisement from the turn of the century with the title "Birth of Civilization," a Black man on a beach looks at a bar of soap in his hand that came from a shipwreck visible in the background. Anne McClintock summarizes the ad's meaning: "Civilization is born, the image implies, at the moment of first contact with the Western commodity."[23] Like a palimpsest, this mythical visualization of "first contact" was superimposed on the reality of very different violent contacts in the colonization of Africa that were legitimized by the very same notion of "civilization." The whitewashing of moral stains was not only a constitutive part of this civilization's mythical time but also entrenched in the mythical function of commodity capitalism long before 1945. How did the postwar consumer modernity of a self-consciously transnational "Western civilization" update this specific cultural legacy to create a new sense of a stainless and timeless and thus a redeemed present in response to Nazism's "choc en retour"? What role did the foundational success story of the German economic miracle, created out of the "debris" of a shipwrecked Nazism, play in this much larger cultural transition? How, finally, did this postwar transition of the political imaginary result in structures of feeling shared within the postwar West that still influence and limit our thinking today? Working on such questions will entail more uncomfortable encounters with the archive and more conscious efforts to recognize the ghosts of the past and hear how they speak to us in the present.

NOTES

Introduction

1. As Michel-Rolph Trouillot wisely remarked, "Professional historians alone do not set the narrative framework into which their stories fit. Most often, someone else has already entered the scene and set the cycle of silences" (*Silencing the Past: Power and the Production of History* [Boston: Beacon Press, 1995], 26).

2. Robert G. Moeller, "The 'Remasculinization' of Germany in the 1950s: Introduction," *Signs* 24, no. 1 (1998): 101–6, quote 103. See also Moeller, *Protecting Motherhood: Women and the Family in the Politics of Postwar West Germany* (Berkeley: University of California Press, 1992); Malte Thiessen, "Erinneringen an die 'Volksgemeinschaft': Integration und Exklusion im kommunalen und kommunikativen Gedächtnis," in *"Volksgemeinschaft": Mythos, wirkumgsmächtige soziale Verheißung oder soziale Realität im "Dritten Reich,"* ed. Detlef Schmiechen-Ackermann (Paderborn: Schöningh, 2021), 319–34. For a recent overview of literature on postwar Germany, see Karen Hagemann, Konrad H. Jarausch, and Tobias Hof, "Introduction: Burdens and Beginnings: Rebuilding East and West Germany after Nazism," *Central European History* 53, no. 2 (2020): 275–93.

3. Jeffrey K. Olick, *In the House of the Hangman: The Agonies of German Defeat, 1943–1949* (Chicago: University of Chicago Press, 2005); Till van Rahden, *Demokratie: Eine gefährdete Lebensform* (Frankfurt am Main: Campus, 2019); Nina Verheyen, *Diskussionslust: Eine Kulturgeschichte des "besseren Arguments" in Westdeutschland* (Göttingen: Vandenhoeck & Ruprecht, 2010); Heide Fehrenbach, *Cinema in Democratizing Germany: Reconstructing National Identity after Hitler* (Chapel Hill: University of North Carolina Press, 1995); Dagmar Herzog, *Sex after Fascism: Memory and Morality in Twentieth-Century Germany* (Princeton, NJ: Princeton University Press, 2005).

4. Norbert Frei, *Vergangenheitspolitik: Die Anfänge der Bundesrepublik Deutschland und die NS-Vergangenheit* (Munich: C. H. Beck, 1996); René Wolf, "'Mass Deception without Deceivers'? The Holocaust on East and West German Radio in the 1960s," *Journal of Contemporary History* 41, no. 4 (2006): 741–55; Judith Keilbach and Irmgard Zündorf,

eds., *Eichmann: Die deutsch-deutsche Berichterstattung über den Eichmann-Prozess*, DVD and booklet (Fridolfing: absolut Medien, 2021); Robert G. Moeller, *War Stories: The Search for a Usable Past in the Federal Republic of Germany* (Berkeley: University of California Press, 2001).

5. Richard Bessel, *Germany 1945: From War to Peace* (London: Simon & Schuster, 2009), 389–90. For a summary of the debates on the "zero hour," see Pertti Ahonen, "Germany and the Aftermath of the Second World War," *Journal of Modern History* 89, no. 2 (2017): 355–87.

6. Sheryl Kroen, "Robinson Charley: The Ideological Underpinnings of Atlantic History," in *Biography and the Black Atlantic*, ed. Lisa A. Lindsay and John Wood Sweed (Philadelphia: University of Pennsylvania Press, 2014), 66–89. See also David W. Ellwood, "The Propaganda of the Marshall Plan in Italy in a Cold War Context," *Intelligence and National Security* 18, no. 2 (2003): 225–36.

7. Axel Schildt, *Ankunft im Westen: Ein Essay zur Erfolgsgeschichte der Bundesrepublik* (Frankfurt am Main: Fischer, 1999); Axel Schildt and Arnold Sywottek, eds., *Modernisierung im Wiederaufbau: Die westdeutsche Gesellschaft der 50er Jahre* (Bonn: Dietz, 1998); Kaspar Maase, *BRAVO Amerika: Erkundungen zur Jugendkultur in der Bundesrepublik der fünfziger Jahre* (Hamburg: Junius, 1992); Erica Carter, *How German Is She? Postwar West German Reconstruction and the Consuming Woman* (Ann Arbor: University of Michigan Press, 1997); Uta G. Poiger, *Jazz, Rock and Rebels: Cold War Politics and American Culture in a Divided Germany* (Berkeley: University of California Press, 2000); David F. Crew, ed., *Consuming Germany in the Cold War* (Oxford: Berg, 2003). For a critique of the "liberalization" narrative with respect to postwar semantics of individuality, see Moritz Föllmer, *Individuality and Modernity in Berlin: Self and Society from Weimar to the Wall* (Cambridge: Cambridge University Press, 2013), esp. 181–211.

8. Only a few scholars of the Nazi period have pointed to this largely unexplored field of the relationship between the political meanings of mass consumption under Nazism and during the early Federal Republic. See Hans Dieter Schäfer, *Das gespaltene Bewusstsein: Vom Dritten Reich bis zu den langen fünfziger Jahren*, rev. ed. (Göttingen: Wallstein, 2009), esp. 9–87; Wolfgang König, *Volkswagen, Volksempfänger, Volksgemeinschaft, "Volksprodukte" im Dritten Reich: Vom Scheitern einer nationalsozialistischen Konsumgesellschaft* (Paderborn: Schöningh, 2004), 262; Pamela Swett, *Selling under the Swastika: Advertising and Commercial Culture in Nazi Germany* (Stanford, CA: Stanford University Press, 2014), 252–60.

9. Alon Confino and Rudy Koshar, "Régimes of Consumer Culture: New Narratives in Twentieth-Century Germany," *German History* 19, no. 2 (2001): 135–61, 150–51. See also Confino, "Traveling as a Culture of Remembrance: Traces of National Socialism in West Germany, 1945–1960," *History and Memory* 12, no. 2 (2000): 92–121.

10. On the concept of "social memory," see Harald Welzer, *Das soziale Gedächtnis: Geschichte, Erinnerung, Tradierung* (Hamburg: Hamburger Editionen, 2001), 9–21.

11. Rudy Koshar, *Germany's Transient Pasts: Preservation and National Memory in the Twentieth Century* (Chapel Hill: University of North Carolina Press, 1998); Koshar, *From Monuments to Traces: Artifacts of German Memory, 1870–1990* (Berkeley: University of

California Press, 2000); Atina Grossmann, "Family Files: Emotions and Stories of (Non-) restitution," *German Historical Institute London Bulletin* 34, no. 1 (2012): 59–78; Neil Gregor, *Haunted City: Nuremberg and the Nazi Past* (New Haven, CT: Yale University Press, 2009); Gudrun Brockhaus, "Die Lederhose—ein verkanntes Emblem der 50er," in *Von Dingen und Menschen: Funktion und Bedeutung materieller Kultur*, ed. Hans A. Hartmann and Rolf Haubl (Wiesbaden: Westdeutscher Verlag, 2000), 37–60; Susanne Vees-Gulani, "From Frankfurt's Goethehaus to Dresden's Frauenkirche: Architecture, German Identity, and Historical Memory after 1945," *Germanic Review* 80, no. 2 (2005): 143–63; Bernhard Rieger, "Was Roland a Nazi? Victims, Perpetrators, and Silences during the Restoration of Civic Identity in Postwar Bremen," *History and Memory* 19, no. 2 (2007): 75–111.

12. Karl Marx, "Der Fetischcharakter der Ware und sein Geheimnis," in *Das Kapital: Kritik der politischen Ökonomie*, vol. 1, bk. 1 (Berlin: Dietz Verlag, 1962), 85–98. Walter Benjamin took on this formulation to interpret the "dreamworld" of nineteenth-century commodity culture. See Susan Buck-Morss, "Benjamin's *Passagen-Werk*: Redeeming Mass Culture for the Revolution," *New German Critique*, no. 29 (Spring–Summer 1983): 211–40.

13. Quoted in Buck-Morss, "Benjamin's *Passagen-Werk*," 231–32.

14. Michael Becker, Dirk Braunstein, and Fabian Link, "Postnazistisches Sprechen: Einführung in Peter von Haselbergs Beitrag zum Gruppenexperiment," in *Schuldgefühle: Postnazistische Mentalitäten in der frühen Bundesrepublik; Eine Studie aus dem Gruppenexperiment am Institut für Sozialforschung*, by Peter von Haselberg, ed. Michael Becker, Dirk Braunstein, and Fabian Link (Frankfurt am Main: Campus Verlag, 2020), 11–32, here 21–22.

15. Raymond Williams, *The Long Revolution* (Harmondsworth: Pelican Books, 1965), 65–66.

16. Williams, *The Long Revolution*, 63.

17. Becker, Braunstein, and Link, "Postnazistisches Sprechen," 21.

18. George Steiner, "The Hollow Miracle," in *Language and Silence: Essays on Language, Literature, and the Inhuman* (New York: Athenaeum, 1986), 95–109, quotes 95, 96, 108.

19. Hannah Arendt, "The Aftermath of the Nazi Rule: Report from Germany," *Commentary* 10, no. 4 (October 1950): 342–53, here 345.

20. Schäfer, *Das gespaltene Bewusstsein*, 10, and chap. 2.

21. Monica Black, *A Demon-Haunted Land: Witches, Wonder Doctors, and the Ghosts of the Past in Post-WWI Germany* (New York: Metropolitan Books, 2020).

22. On the waves of suicides at the war's end, see Christian Goeschel, *Suicide in Nazi Germany* (Oxford: Oxford University Press, 2015), 149–66.

23. Saul Friedländer used the term "redemptive anti-Semitism" in his *The Years of Extermination: Nazi Germany and the Jews, 1939–1945* (New York: HarperCollins, 2007), xviii.

24. Anna M. Parkinson, *An Emotional State: The Politics of Emotion in Postwar West German Culture* (Ann Arbor: University of Michigan Press, 2015), quote 148.

25. "Niemand sieht es ihm an . . . ," *Neue Illustrierte*, no. 20, May 19, 1949, 4.

26. Roland Barthes, *Mythologies*, selected and trans. Annette Levers (London: Vintage Books, 2009), 154, 163, 169–70. On the unarticulated presence of the recent genocidal

past in Barthes's analysis, see Esther Rashkin, *Unspeakable Secrets and the Psychoanalysis of Culture* (Albany: State University of New York Press, 2008), esp. 2–11.

27. "Hitlers Geisterauto," *Neue Illustrierte*, no. 16, August 6, 1948, 3. On an exhibition in France of another one of Hitler's former cars, see "Hitlers Wagen bringt Devisen," *Neue Illustrierte*, no. 12, June 13, 1947, 11. The German word *Führersitz* was a play on words on *Fahrersitz*, the driver's seat.

28. Paul Betts, *Ruin and Renewal: Civilising Europe after the Second World War* (London: Profile Books, 2020), esp. chap. 5.

29. Stuart Hall, *Familiar Stranger: A Life between Two Islands* (Durham, NC: Duke University Press, 2017), 250.

30. Susan Buck-Morss has brilliantly worked through a comparable similarity in her *Dreamworld and Catastrophe: The Passing of Mass Utopia in East and West* (Cambridge, MA: MIT Press, 2000).

31. The article "Theses on Theory and History," which landed on my screen in 2018, was a very welcome intellectual boost for the completion of this book. See Ethan Kleinberg, Joan Scott, and Gary Wilder, "Theses on Theory and History," *History of the Present* 10, no. 1 (2020): 157–65 (originally published online in May 2018).

32. Catherine Hall, "Thinking Reflexively: Opening 'Blind Eyes,'" *Past & Present* 234, no. 1 (February 2017): 254–63. Along with countless conversations, some books have contributed more than others to change what my eyes were able to see in the postwar cultural archives. Kristin Ross's *Fast Cars, Clean Bodies: Decolonization and the Reordering of French Culture* (Cambridge, MA: MIT Press, 1995) showed me how postwar consumer culture echoed events that it simultaneously worked to make invisible; Paul Betts's *The Authority of Everyday Objects: A Cultural History of West German Industrial Design* (Berkeley: University of California Press, 2004) first taught me the historical importance of how everyday aesthetics and political imaginary were linked in West Germany and that the Nazi past had to be taken into account in this constellation; Johannes von Moltke's *No Place Like Home: Locations of Heimat in German Cinema* (Berkeley: University of California Press, 2005) revealed to me the centrality of films to understand the relationship between Nazi and postwar modernity; in *Das gespaltene Bewusstsein* Hans Dieter Schäfer wrote about the first "economic miracle" and its postwar legacy in a way that confirmed my intuitions and emboldened my thinking; Patrick Thaddeus Jackson's *Civilizing the Enemy: German Reconstruction and the Invention of the West* (Ann Arbor: University of Michigan Press, 2006) brought the importance of the framework of the West to my consciousness; Stuart Hall's *Familiar Stranger* helped me to integrate the colonial context in my thinking about the postwar period.

33. The same challenge also pervades Roland Barthes's *Mythologies*, which are, after all, about his own time.

Chapter 1. Stranded Objects

1. On ordinary Germans' attitudes toward the war and the regime, see Nicholas Stargardt, *The German War: A Nation under Arms, 1939–1945* (London: Vintage, 2015); and

Peter Fritzsche, *Life and Death in the Third Reich* (Cambridge, MA: Belknap Press of Harvard University Press, 2008).

2. I browsed through the collection of private photo albums archived by the Stadtmuseum München. In addition, Bernd Stiegler, professor of modern German literature at the University of Konstanz, generously allowed me to study the private photo albums that are part of his personal collection of photographs. On private photo albums, see Timm Starl, "Die Bildwelt der Knipser: Eine empirische Untersuchung zur privaten Fotografie," *Fotogeschichte: Beiträge zur Geschichte und Ästhetik der Fotografie* 14, no. 52 (1994): 59–68; Cord Pagenstecher, "Private Fotoalben als historische Quelle," *Zeithistorische Forschungen / Studies in Contemporary History* 6, no. 3 (2009): 449–63.

3. The following photos are in the collection of private photo albums, Stadtmuseum München: local Nazi Party meeting and the official Nazi commemoration event, K 208/3; visit to the German pavilion at the world's fair in Paris in 1937, K 210/3; streets decorated with Nazi flags, K 233/1 and K 233/3; woman posing in a street decorated with Nazi flags, K 234/26; "vacation 1938," K 237/21; Nazi monuments and man with Nazi Party pin, K 429. "Unsere schönen Reichsautobahnen" and a Nuremberg party rally are from the private collection of historical photographs and photo albums, Bernd Stiegler, Konstanz.

4. Claude Lefort, "The Question of Democracy," in *Democracy and Political Theory* (Minneapolis: University of Minnesota Press, 1988), 9–20; Lefort, *The Political Forms of Modern Society: Bureaucracy, Democracy, Totalitarianism* (Cambridge, MA: MIT Press, 1986).

5. Yael Navaro-Yashin, *The Make-Believe Space: Affective Geography in a Postwar Polity* (Durham, NC: Duke University Press, 2012). Leora Auslander's work stands out as the most important analysis of the interrelation between material culture and the political in modern European history. See *Taste and Power: Furnishing Modern France* (Berkeley: University of California Press, 1996) and *Cultural Revolutions: The Politics of Everyday Life in Britain, North America and France* (Oxford: Berg, 2009).

6. Gosewijn van Beek, "On Materiality," *Etnofoor* 9, no. 1 (1996): 5–24.

7. Victor Klemperer, *LTI: Notizbuch eines Philologen* (1947; repr., Stuttgart: Reclam, 2010), 21–22.

8. Hans Ulrich Gumbrecht, *After 1945: Latency as Origin of the Present* (Stanford, CA: Stanford University Press, 2013), 201, 162. The German version specified that this world from "before the war" was "*nach wie vor unbestritten und sogar unverdächtig*" (still uncontested and even unsuspicious) (Gumbrecht, *Nach 1945: Latenz als Ursprung der Gegenwart*, trans. Frank Born [Frankfurt am Main: Suhrkamp, 2012], 244).

9. Gumbrecht, *Nach 1945*, 329–31, 344.

10. Among many others, see Brandon Taylor and Wilfried van der Will, eds., *The Nazification of Art: Art, Design, Music, Architecture and Film in the Third Reich* (Winchester: Winchester Press, 1990); Gudrun Brockhaus, *Schauder und Idylle: Faschismus als Erlebnisangebot* (Munich: Antje Kunstmann, 1997); Frank Bajohr, *"Aryanisation" in Hamburg: The Economic Exclusion of Jews and the Confiscation of Their Property in Nazi Germany* (New York: Berghahn Books, 2002); Shelley Baranowski, *Strength through Joy: Consumerism and Mass Tourism in the Third Reich* (Cambridge: Cambridge University

Press, 2004); Joshua Hagen, "The Most German of Towns: Creating an Ideal Nazi Community in Rothenburg ob der Tauber," *Annals of the Association of American Geographers* 94, no. 1 (2004): 207–27; Elizabeth Harvey, *Women and the Nazi East: Agents and Witnesses of Germanization* (New Haven, CT: Yale University Press, 2003); Paul Steege, *Black Market, Cold War: Everyday Life in Berlin, 1946–1949* (Cambridge: Cambridge University Press, 2008); Carolyn Birdsall, *Nazi Soundscapes: Sound, Technology and Urban Space in Germany, 1933–1945* (Amsterdam: Amsterdam University Press, 2012); Claus-Christian W. Szejnmann and Maiken Umbach, eds., *Heimat, Region and Empire: Spatial Identities under National Socialism* (Houndmills: Palgrave Macmillan, 2012); Alon Confino, *A World without Jews: The Nazi Imagination from Persecution to Genocide* (New Haven, CT: Yale University Press, 2014); Teresa Walch, "With an Iron Broom: Cleansing Berlin's Bülowplatz of 'Judeo-Bolshevism,'" *German History* 40, no. 1 (2022): 61–87.

11. Marie Luise Kaschnitz, *Von Menschen und Dingen: Zwölf Essays mit einem Nachwort von Karl Krolow* (Frankfurt am Main: Insel Verlag, 1995), 56.

12. Lynn Rapaport, *Jews in Germany after the Holocaust: Memory, Identity, and Jewish-German Relations* (Cambridge: Cambridge University Press, 1997), 27–28.

13. Original edition, Marie Luise Kaschnitz, *Von Menschen und Dingen*, Schriften der Wandlung 2 (Heidelberg: Lambert Schneider, 1946).

14. Kaschnitz, *Von Menschen und Dingen* (1995), 25, 27, 51.

15. Kaschnitz, *Von Menschen und Dingen* (1995), 105–6. In a similar vein, an inhabitant of Tutzing commented in April 1945 that "it would match with the monstrosity of the dying system if the Autobahnen would only have been built in order to eventually be destroyed" (Walter Kempowski, *Das Echolot: Abgesang '45; Ein kollektives Tagebuch* [Munich: Albrecht Knaus Verlag, 2005], 249).

16. Alexander Mitscherlich and Margarete Mitscherlich, *Die Unfähigkeit zu trauern: Grundlagen kollektiven Verhaltens* (Munich: Piper, 1967).

17. Eric Santner, *Stranded Objects: Mourning, Memory, and Film in Postwar Germany* (Ithaca, NY: Cornell University Press, 1990).

18. Santner, *Stranded Objects*, 25–26, 45. See also Donald Woods Winnicott, *Playing and Reality* (London: Routledge, 2005), 20–27.

19. The ghostly aspect of West Germany's "economic miracle" will be discussed in more detail in chapter 2.

20. Teresa Walch, "Degenerate Spaces: The Coordination of Space in Nazi Germany" (PhD diss., University of San Diego, 2018).

21. See, for instance, Erich Kästner, *Das Blaue Buch: Kriegstagebuch und Roman-Notizen*, ed. Ulrich von Bülow and Silke Becker, 2nd ed. (Marbach: Deutsche Schillergesellschaft, 2007), 95–96; and Dolf Sternberger, "Tagebuch, Reise in Deutschland—Sommer 1945," *Die Wandlung* 1, no. 1, November 30, 1945: 7–17, 13.

22. Dorothea Klein, "Rückblick auf fünf inhaltsreiche Lebensjahre," *Frankfurter Hefte*, no. 9 (December 1946): 843–59, here 854–55.

23. Bessel, *Germany 1945*, 320–59.

24. Götz Aly, *Hitler's Beneficiaries: Plunder, Racial War, and the Nazi Welfare State* (New York: Metropolitan Books, 2008); Tim Schanetzky, *"Kanonen statt Butter": Wirtschaft*

und Konsum im Dritten Reich. Die Deutschen und der Nationalsozialismus (Munich: C. H. Beck, 2015).

25. Saul K. Padover, *Experiment in Germany: The Story of an American Intelligence Officer* (New York: Duell, Sloan and Pearce, [1946]), 50.

26. Julius Posener, *In Deutschland: 1945 bis 1946* (Berlin: Siedler Verlag, 2001), 18.

27. Paulheinz Wantzen, *Das Leben im Krieg 1939–1946: Ein Tagebuch* (Homberg: Verlag Das Dokument, 2000), 1445–46. For another example, see Padover, *Experiment in Germany*, 70.

28. Bessel, *Germany 1945*, 321; Wantzen, *Das Leben im Krieg*, 1445; Kempowski, *Das Echolot*, 114–15 (Russian soldiers in Danzig), 208–10 (Russian soldiers in Berlin), 268 (British soldiers in Bremen), 298–99 (Russians and Germans in Berlin).

29. Kästner, *Das Blaue Buch*, 18.

30. Kästner, *Das Blaue Buch*, 60.

31. Kästner, *Das Blaue Buch*, 90, 137, 138, 143.

32. Erich Kästner, *Notabene 1945: Ein Tagebuch von Erich Kästner* (Zurich: Atrium Verlag, 1961), 153.

33. Kempowski, *Das Echolot*, 299. On the rape of German women in Berlin, including its experience, contemporary perception, and historical interpretation, see Atina Grossmann, "A Question of Silence: The Rape of German Women by Occupation Soldiers," *October* 72 (Spring 1995): 43–63.

34. Barbara Bronnen, ed., *Geschichten vom Überleben: Frauentagebücher aus der NS-Zeit* (Munich: C. H. Beck, 1998), 221.

35. Kästner, *Das Blaue Buch*, 68.

36. Karl Zimmermann, "Nach einer Reise in Westdeutschland," *Die Gegenwart* 1, no. 10/11, May 24, 1946, 28–31, quote 31.

37. "Unser Leben: Drei Seiten Bilder aus deutschen Städten," *Neue Illustrierte*, no. 3, October 4, 1946, 7.

38. "Die Welt, in der wir leben," *Neue Illustrierte*, no. 22, October 31, 1947, 8–9.

39. "Bei Ortsgruppenleiters," *Der Simpl*, no. 11 (September 1946): 127.

40. Hans Mäder, "Kriegsgeschehen und Erleben in Wort und Bild 1940–1947," photo album, collection of private photo albums, Stadtmuseum München. The album is accompanied by a note from Hans Mäder's son stating that it was put together around 1965. Its quality and aesthetics, however, suggest a somewhat earlier date. The album did not have an archival number when I consulted it.

41. In the album there is no hint of criticism of the German war endeavor. On the influence of the concept of Heimat on how Germans commemorated the bombings and destruction, see Jörg Arnold, *The Allied Air War and Urban Memory: The Legacy of Strategic Bombing in Germany* (New York: Cambridge University Press, 2016).

42. On the "bewilderment at the improbability of the post-war imagery," see Stefan-Ludwig Hoffmann, "Gazing at Ruins: German Defeat as Visual Experience," *Journal of Modern European History* 9, no. 3 (2011): 328–50.

43. See Posener, *In Deutschland*, 12.

44. Kästner, *Das Blaue Buch*, 88–89; Kästner, *Notabene*, 18–19. On the role of women in the Nazi occupation of Poland, see Harvey, *Women and the Nazi East*.

45. Dolf Sternberger, "Tagebuch, Reise in Deutschland—Sommer 1945: Fortsetzung," *Die Wandlung* 1, no. 2, January 24, 1946, 99–112, here 102–3.

46. Many more examples can be found in the Portal to Texas History, for instance, "Photograph of Soldiers and Nazi Flag," creator unknown, 1941–45 (https://texashistory.unt.edu/ark:/67531/metapth616970/) and "A Group of Soldiers Standing behind a German National Flag," creator unknown, 1945 (https://texashistory.unt.edu/ark:/67531/metapth690832/).

47. Kathleen J. Nawyn, "'Striking at the Roots of German Militarism': Efforts to Demilitarize German Society and Culture in American-Occupied Württemberg-Baden, 1945–1949" (PhD diss., University of North Carolina at Chapel Hill, 2008), esp. 316, 336, 339, 351–53, 397–98, 403, 409. See also Nawyn, "'Ausrottung des "kämpferischen Geistes!"': Zur Beseitigung militaristischer Denkmäler im amerikanisch besetzten Württemberg-Baden, 1945–1947," in *Banal Militarism: Zur Veralltäglichung des Militärischen im Zivilen*, ed. Tanja Thomas and Fabian Virchow (Bielefeld: transcript, 2006), 129–48.

48. Kästner, *Das Blaue Buch*, 152–53.

49. Kästner, *Das Blaue Buch*, 108; Kästner, *Notabene*, 70.

50. Kästner, *Das Blaue Buch*, 129.

51. Kästner, *Notabene*, 127. In Württemberg-Baden the red fabric was used for clothing or later on for the new flag of the FDR. See Nawyn, "'Striking at the Roots,'" 339.

52. Kästner, *Notabene*, 144.

53. Quoted in Nawyn, "'Striking at the Roots,'" 171n181.

54. Nawyn, "'Striking at the Roots,'" 108.

55. "Hohe Preise für Heldentum," *Neue Illustrierte*, no. 12, June 11, 1948, 2.

56. In March 1945 the Iron Cross was presented to teenagers who fought in the Volkssturm, a ritual that was included in the newsreel. See Michael Hughes, *The Anarchy of Nazi Memorabilia: From Things of Tyranny to Troubled Treasure* (New York: Routledge, 2022), 91.

57. Nawyn, "'Striking at the Roots,'" 317–19.

58. "Das Geheimnis der alten Mamsell," *Der Simpl*, no. 20 (October 1947): 246. If one looks closely, one can detect a small swastika on a badge or an item in the old lady's drawer. For another example, see *Der Simpl*, no. 3 (February 1948): 35.

59. Heinz Hartwig, "Kurzsichtigkeit," *Der Simpl*, no. 17 (September 1947): 210.

60. Hartwig, "Kurzsichtigkeit," 210.

61. Hartwig, "Kurzsichtigkeit," 210.

62. *Deutschland im Jahre Null / Germania Anno Zero*, Germany and Italy, 1948, directed by Roberto Rossellini, Tevere Film.

63. Karl Zimmermann, "Bericht aus Düsseldorf," *Die Gegenwart*, no. 8/9, April 24, 1946, 22–24.

64. "Sie rief die Jugend," *Neue Illustrierte*, no. 5, March 7, 1947, 8. Even today the German public struggles with the question of how to deal with NS sites such as the Olympic Stadium. See Claire Copley, "'Stones Do Not Speak for Themselves': Disentangling Berlin's

Palimpsest," *Fascism* 8, no. 2 (2019): 219–49. The discussion continued in 2020: Peter Strieder, "Weg mit diesen Skulpturen," *Die Zeit*, no. 21, May 14, 2020, 43; Hans Kollhoff, "Lasst die Skulpturen stehen!," *Die Zeit*, no. 22, May 20, 2020, 54.

65. Arnd Krüger, "Germany: The Propaganda Machine," in *The Nazi Olympics: Sport, Politics, and Appeasement in the 1930s*, ed. Arnd Krüger and William Murray (Urbana: University of Illinois Press, 2003), 17–43. See also the Olympic Games issue of the magazine *die neue linie* no. 12 (August 1936): 13–35.

66. "Münchener Bilderbogen April 1947," *Neue Illustrierte*, no. 8, April 18, 1947, 12–13. On the suggestion to use the Ehrentempel as a chapel, see *Der Simpl*, no. 1 (January 1947): 5. On denazification in Munich, see Gavriel D. Rosenberg, *Munich and Memory: Architecture, Monuments, and the Legacy of the Third Reich* (Berkeley: University of California Press, 2000), 76–106.

67. The *Süddeutsche Zeitung* noted during the winter of 1946–47 that the "savings bank for the capital of the movement" still had its advertisements in some of Munich's cable cars. Quoted in Nina Krieg, "'Solang' der alte Peter . . . : Die vermeintliche Wiedergeburt Alt-Münchens nach 1945," in *Geschichte der Stadt München*, ed. Richard Bauer (Munich: C. H. Beck, 1992), 394–412, here 400. My thanks go to Ulrike Haerendel for pointing me to this quote.

68. Jennifer V. Evans, *Life among the Ruins: Cityscape and Sexuality in Cold War Berlin* (Basingstoke: Palgrave Macmillan, 2011).

69. Evans, *Life among the Ruins*, 37.

70. "Friedlicher Beton," *Neue Illustrierte*, no. 9, May 2, 1947, 14.

71. Anthony D. Kauders, "Juden als Gabe, oder: Eine andere Geschichte der westdeutschen Demokratie," in *Demokratie im Schatten der Gewalt: Geschichten des Privaten im deutschen Nachkrieg*, ed. Daniel Fulda et al. (Göttingen: Wallstein Verlag, 2010), 152–73.

72. "Raten Sie mal wo das ist: Ein Hotel im stillen Winkel?," *Constanze*, no. 9, 2nd number in July, 1948: 11.

73. In general, even the Jewish sites that were not destroyed during Nazism were often cleared away after the war. See Michael Meng, *Shattered Spaces: Encountering Jewish Ruins in Postwar Germany and Poland* (Cambridge, MA: Harvard University Press, 2011), 60–110.

74. "Raten Sie."

75. Zimmermann, "Bericht aus Düsseldorf," 23.

76. Zimmermann, "Bericht aus Düsseldorf," 23.

77. Arne Lieb, "Als Hitler 1938 nach Düsseldorf kam," *RP-Online*, November 9, 2013, https://rp-online.de/nrw/staedte/duesseldorf/als-hitler-1938-nach-duesseldorf-kam_aid-9407419.

78. Zimmermann, "Bericht aus Düsseldorf," 23.

79. Zimmermann, "Bericht aus Düsseldorf," 24.

80. Albert Leo Schlageter had been sentenced to death in 1923 by the French military occupation of the Rhine-Ruhr area. On the Schlageter propaganda and monument in Düsseldorf, see Birdsall, *Nazi Soundscapes*, chap. 1. On the exhibition *Schaffendes Volk*, see Stefanie Schäfers, *Vom Werkbund zum Vierjahresplan: Die Ausstellung "Schaffendes Volk" in Düsseldorf 1937* (Düsseldorf: Droste Verlag, 2001).

81. Josef Dünninger, "Auf der Suche nach dem Lebensgesetz einer zerstörten Stadt," *Frankfurter Hefte* 1, no. 5 (August 1946): 49–53, quotes 50.

82. Dünninger, "Auf der Suche."

83. Koshar, *Germany's Transient Pasts*, 165–97; Rudy Koshar, "Altar, State and City: Historic Preservation and Urban Meaning in Nazi Germany," *History and Memory* 3, no. 1 (1991): 30–59; Hagen, "The Most German of Towns."

84. Lotte Paepcke, *Unter einem fremden Stern* (Frankfurt am Main: Verlag der Frankfurter Hefte, 1952), 16, 122. On the Jewish experience of space, see Guy Miron, "'Lately, Almost Constantly, Everything Seems Small to Me': The Lived Space of German Jews under the Nazi Regime," *Jewish Social Studies* 20, no. 1 (2013): 121–49.

85. See, for example, Arianna Giachi, "Trier: Bericht und Bildnis," *Die Wandlung*, no. 46/47, November 30, 1947, 25–27.

86. Wilhelm Hausenstein, "München—gestern, heute und morgen," *Die Wandlung*, no. 7, October 1947, 596–617, quote 601.

87. Hausenstein, "München," 602.

88. Hausenstein, "München," 602, emphasis added.

89. Robert Minder, "Hausenstein, Wilhelm," *Neue Deutsche Biographie* 8 (1969): 113–15, http://www.deutsche-biographie.de/ pnd118547003.html.

90. Hausenstein, "München." 615.

91. Sternberger, "Tagebuch, Reise in Deutschland—Sommer 1945," *Die Wandlung* no. 1, November 30, 1945, 11.

92. Dolf Sternberger, "Tagebuch—im April, das Frankfurter Goethehaus," *Die Wandlung*, no. 3 (April 1947): 191–201.

93. Vees-Gulani, "From Frankfurt's Goethehaus."

94. Walter Dirks, "Mut zum Abschied: Zur Wiederherstellung des Frankfurter Goethehauses," *Frankfurter Hefte*, no. 8 (August 1947): 819–28, here esp. 825–26.

95. Sternberger, "Tagebuch—im April, das Frankfurter Goethehaus," 193–94.

96. Sternberger, "Tagebuch—im April, das Frankfurter Goethehaus," 193–94.

97. Sternberger, "Tagebuch—im April, das Frankfurter Goethehaus," 194.

98. A similar absence occurs in Ernst Benkard's text on Frankfurt, which takes great pains to evoke the memory of the Jewish parts of the city, including the "red synagogue." Yet while he gives the bombing of the Goethehaus a prominent place, he fails to even mention the destruction of Frankfurt's synagogue. See Ernst Benkard, "Genius Loci," *Die Gegenwart* 1, no. 2/3, January 24, 1946, 16–19.

99. Atina Grossmann, *Jews, Germans, and Allies: Close Encounters in Occupied Germany* (Princeton, NJ: Princeton University Press, 2007).

100. Confino, *A World without Jews*.

101. Bajohr, *"Aryanisation" in Hamburg*; Angelika Baumann and Andreas Heusler, eds., *München "arisiert": Entrechtung und Enteignung der Juden in der NS-Zeit* (Munich: C. H. Beck, 2004).

102. Claus-Christian W. Szeijnmann, "'A Sense of *Heimat* Opened Up during the War': German Soldiers and *Heimat* Abroad," in Szejnmann and Umbach, *Heimat, Region and Empire*, 112–47.

103. See Atina Grossmann, "Family Files: Emotions and Stories of (Non-)restitution," *German Historical Institute London Bulletin*, 34, no. 1 (2012): 59–78.

104. Franziska Becker, *Gewalt und Gedächtnis: Erinnerungen an die nationalsozialistische Verfolgung einer jüdischen Landgemeinde* (Göttingen: V. Schmerse, 1994).

105. The American occupation zone announced a law of restitution in November 1947. See Michael Brenner, *After the Holocaust: Rebuilding Jewish Life in Postwar Germany* (Princeton, NJ: Princeton University Press, 1997), 61.

106. Quoted in Frank Bajohr, "'Arisierung' und Restitution: Eine Einschätzung," in *"Arisierung" und Restitution: Die Rückerstattung jüdischen Eigentums in Deutschland und Österreich nach 1945 und 1989*, ed. Constantin Goschler and Jürgen Lillteicher (Göttingen: Wallstein, 2002), 39–59, 50.

107. Padover, *Experiment in Germany*, 71. The quote is also cited by Bajohr, "'Arisierung' und Restitution."

108. Cited in Olick, *In the House*, 283.

109. Clemens Münster, "Wiedersehen mit Bildern," *Frankfurter Hefte*, no. 2 (May 1946): 93–95, here 93. On art under National Socialism, see Jonathan Petropoulos, "The Art World in Nazi Germany: Choices, Rationalization, and Justice," in *The Arts in Nazi Germany: Continuity, Conformity, Chance*, ed. Jonathan Huener and Francis R. Nicosia (New York: Berghahn Books, 2006), 135–63.

110. Angelika Bammer describes how her parents went to see the collection of Renaissance and Baroque art in the Zwinger museum in Dresden in the last months of 1941. See *Born After: Reckoning with the German Past* (New York: Bloomsbury Academic, 2019), 122–23.

111. In 1939 around seven hundred artworks were auctioned off in Cologne. The auctions were advertised in a way that made their provenance clear. See Schanetzky, *"Kanonen statt Butter,"* 173.

112. K. H. Böcher, "Das Gewissen," *Der Simpl*, no. 1 (January 1947): 4.

113. "Schweigen ist—verfluchtes Gold," *Der Simpl*, no. 13 (August 1947): 161.

114. Two months later *Der Simpl* published a moving poem in which a mother explains to her child the yellow star. See "Kind und Stern," *Der Simpl*, no. 15 (September 1947): 178.

115. F. W. Kloeck, "Postwurfsendung," *Der Simpl*, no. 9 (April 1949): 99. See Constantin Goschler, "Die Politik der Rückerstattung in Westdeutschland," in Goschler and Lillteicher, *"Arisierung" und Restitution*, 99–125; Tobias Winstel, "Verordnete 'Ehrenpflicht': Wiedergutmachung für jüdische NS-Opfer," in Baumann and Heusler, *München "arisiert,"* 218–36.

116. Goschler, "Die Politik der Rückerstattung," 110–11.

117. A beautiful reflection on materiality on-screen is Lesley Stern, "Paths That Wind through the Thicket of Things," *Critical Inquiry* 28, no. 1 (2001): 317–54. The term "tangible events" is taken from Beek, "On Materiality." An earlier version of this paragraph's analysis with a stronger focus on gender was published as Natalie Scholz, "Gender and the Morality of Things in Postwar Germany," *Clio. Women, Gender, History*, no. 40 (2014): 89–113.

118. *Die Mörder sind unter uns*, Germany, 1946, directed by Wolfgang Staudte, Deutsche Film AG, East Berlin; *Zwischen gestern und morgen*, Germany, 1947, directed by Harald Braun, Neue Deutsche Filmgesellschaft, Munich.

119. Even the exact date is specified: March 22, 1938.

120. On the exclusion of Jews from hotels and public baths under National Socialism, see Frank Bajohr, *Unser Hotel ist judenfrei: Bäderantisemitismus im 19. und 20. Jahrhundert* (Frankfurt am Main: Fischer Taschenbuchverlag, 2003), 116–41; Marion A. Kaplan, *Between Dignity and Despair: Jewish Life in Nazi Germany* (Oxford: Oxford University Press, 1998), 45; Peter Hanke, *Zur Geschichte der Juden in München zwischen 1933 und 1945* (Munich: Stadtarchiv, 1967), 139.

121. In 1948 Dolf Sternberger acknowledged the importance of the object of the necklace for the storyline of the film. See "Zweimal im Kino," *Die Wandlung*, March 10, 1948, 99–105, here 99. Another review conspicuously focused on an inconspicuous object: an armchair in the hotel lobby that had been "rescued" from the rubble of the real hotel. See Erika Fries, "Zwischen Gestern und Morgen," *Filmpost-Magazin*, no. 1 (1948): 34–35. Contemporary scholars of *In Between Yesterday and Tomorrow* have spotlighted the perception of the rubble, the flashbacks of the bombings, and the mnemonic aspects of the hotel and cityscape. While authors have noticed that the film's storyline is activated by a specific object, they have not considered the implications of this object's materiality. See Jaimey Fisher, "Bombing Memories in Braun's *Zwischen Gestern und Morgen* (1947): Flashbacks to the Recent Past in the German Rubble-Film," in *Bombs Away! Representing the Air War over Europe and Japan*, ed. Wilfried Wilms and William Rasch (Amsterdam: Rodopi, 2009), 329–43; Bernhard Groß, "Wahrnehmen—Observieren—'Checken': Geschichtlichkeit als ästhetische Erfahrung in *Zwischen Gestern und Morgen*," in *Demokratisierung der Wahrnehmung? Das westeuropäische Nachkriegskino*, ed. Hermann Kappelhoff, Bernhard Groß, and Daniel Illger (Berlin: Vorwerk 8, 2010), 115–34.

122. The Dutch angle, first introduced by German expressionist directors, is a visual and symbolic device that is employed several times throughout the movie.

123. Wallner's close relation to the optician Mondschein, who himself is implicitly identified as Jewish, may be seen as the strongest indication of her Jewishness. Her bright skin and blond hair must have counteracted this association for the contemporary viewer used to Nazi racial stereotypes. Ulrike Weckel points to the fact that in the original script, Wallner is identified as a (possible) Communist. See "*Die Mörder sind unter uns* oder: Vom Verschwinden der Opfer," *WerkstattGeschichte* 25 (2000): 105–15, 108. The ambivalence about this question, however, keeps the possibility of her Jewishness open. The problem of dispossession can apply either way, as Communists were also stripped of basic civil and property rights. See Hanke, *Zur Geschichte der Juden*, 290.

124. Erica Carter and Anke Pinkert have highlighted how, in this film, the figure of the innocent woman who suppresses her own past helps to reconstruct the male character's tarnished masculinity. Erica Carter, "Sweeping Up the Past: Gender and History in the Postwar German Rubble Film," in *Heroines without Heroes: Reconstructing Female National Identities in European Cinema, 1945–1951*, ed. Ulrike Sieglohr (London: Cassell, 2000),

91–110; and Anke Pinkert, "Can Melodrama Cure? War Trauma and Crisis of Masculinity in Early DEFA Film," *Seminar: A Journal of Germanic Studies* 44, no. 1 (2008): 118–36.

125. Pointed out also by Anke Pinkert, *Film and Memory in East Germany* (Bloomington: Indiana University Press, 2008), 40.

126. I agree with Pinkert's assessment that "although the film avoids addressing the mass annihilation of the Jews, the issue is nevertheless *the* fundamental, albeit not fully articulated, not quite remembered, not quite forgotten, knowledge of the film" (*Film and Memory*, 35).

127. Kaplan, *Between Dignity and Despair*, 157–60. The first mass deportations of Jews from the territory of the German Reich took place in February 1940. From January 1940 onward Jews were forbidden to buy shoes, leather, or cloth. From August onward they were not allowed to possess any property. See Klaus W. Tofahrn, *Chronologie des Dritten Reiches: Ereignisse Personen, Begriffe* (Darmstadt: Wissenschaftliche Buchgesellschaft, 2003), 74, 77.

128. What follows is Mertens's attempt to kill Brückner, Wallner preventing this act, and Mertens's declamatory statement about the "obligation to accuse" the guilty, accompanied by images of crosses marking soldiers' graves. This nonviolent ending was imposed by the Soviet occupier. See Robert R. Shandley, *Rubble Films: German Cinema in the Shadow of the Third Reich* (Philadelphia: Temple University Press 2001), 42.

129. André Habib, "Runies, décombres, chantiers, archives: L'évolution d'une figure dans le cinéma en Allemagne (1946–1993)," *Cinhémas: Revue d'études cinématographiques* 18, no. 1 (2007): 29–52; Groß, "Wahrnehmen"; Jaimey Fisher, "Wandering in/to the Rubble-Film: Filmic Flânerie and the Exploded Panorama after 1945," *German Quarterly* 78, no. 4 (2005): 461–80. Shandley calls the rubble landscape in *The Murderers Are among Us* a "lawless wasteland" (*Rubble Films*, 32).

130. Frank Stern, *The Whitewashing of the Yellow Badge: Antisemitism and Philosemitism in Postwar Germany*, trans. William Templer (Oxford: Pergamon Press, 1992), 6–7. See also Stern, "Antagonistic Memories: The Post-war Survival and Alienation of Jews and Germans," in *Memory and Totalitarianism*, ed. Luisa Passerini (1992; repr., New Brunswick, NJ: Transaction Publishers 2009), 21–43, here 28.

131. On this aesthetic principle of melodrama, see Hermann Kappelhoff, *Matrix der Gefühle: Das Kino, das Melodrama und das Theater der Empfindsamkeit* (Berlin: Vorwerk 8, 2004).

132. See Leonie Treber, *Mythos Trümmerfrauen: Von der Trümmerbeseitigung in der Kriegs- und Nachkriegszeit und der Entstehung eines deutschen Erinnerungsortes* (Essen: Klartext Verlag, 2014); Elizabeth Heineman, "Gender, Sexuality, and Coming to Terms with the Nazi Past," *Central European History* 38, no. 1 (2005): 41–74; and Heineman's influential article "The Hour of the Woman: Memories of Germany's 'Crisis Years' and West German National Identity," *American Historical Review* 101, no. 2 (1996): 354–95; Annette Brauerhoch, *"Fräuleins" und GIs: Geschichte und Filmgeschichte* (Frankfurt am Main: Stroemfeld Verlag, 2006); Frank Biess, "Survivors of Totalitarianism: Returning POWs and the Reconstruction of Masculine Citizenship in West Germany, 1945–1955," in *The Miracle Years: A Cultural History of West Germany, 1949–1968*, ed. Hanna Schissler (Princeton, NJ: Princeton University Press, 2001), 57–82.

133. *In jenen Tagen*, (West) Germany, 1946–47, directed by Helmut Käutner, Camera-Filmproduktion G.m.b.H. Hamburg.

134. Sabine Mueller, "Narration, Rubble Film, and Narratability: Helmut Käutner's *In jenen Tagen*," *Modern Language Review* 107, no. 4 (2012): 1168–90, quote 1177; see also Wolfgang Becker and Norbert Schöll, *In jenen Tagen: Wie der deutsche Nachkriegsfilm die Vergangenheit bewältigte* (Opladen: Leske und Budrich, 1995), 22, 52; "Ein Auto fährt durch zwölf Jahre: Menschen in unmenschlicher Zeit," *Der Spiegel*, no. 24, June 14, 1947, 12.

135. Mueller, "Narration," 1178.

136. E. Bingel-Erlenmeyer, "Ein Auto als Film Star," *Das Auto*, no. 5–6 (May/June 1947): unpaginated.

137. Shandley, *Rubble Films*, 23, 61–64; Mueller, "Narration"; Christiane Fritsche, *Vergangenheitsbewältigung im Fernsehen: Westdeutsche Filme über den Nationalsozialismus in den 1950er und 1960er Jahren* (Munich: Martin Meidenbauer Verlag, 2003), 29–50; Gerhard Bliersbach, *Nachkriegskino: Eine Psychohistorie des westdeutschen Nachkriegsfilms 1946–1963* (Gießen: Psychosozial-Verlag, 2014), 52–56. For film reviews, see Erika Müller, "*In jenen Tagen*: Zur Uraufführung des Käutner Films in Hamburg," *Die Zeit*, June 26, 1947; "Das erlösende Wort," *Die Gegenwart*, no. 17 (March 1948), printed in *Käutner*, ed. Wolfgang Jacobsen and Hans Helmut Prinzler (Berlin: Edition Filme, 1992), 197–200; Wolfdietrich Schnurre, "Erfindungsgabe und Improvisationstalent," *Der neue Film*, no. 4, July 7, 1947, printed in Jacobsen and Prinzler, *Käutner*, 201–3.

138. See Paul Dobryden, "Good Germans, Humane Automobiles: Redeeming Technological Modernity—*In Those Days*," *Film & History* 40, no. 1 (2010): 7–24.

139. *In Those Days* is the first feature film to represent the violence of Kristallnacht. See Lawrence Baron, "Kristallnacht on Film: From Reportage to Reenactments, 1938–1948," in "The Space Between: Literature and Culture 1914–1945," special issue, *International Cinema and the Space Between: The Long Decade of the 1930s* 16 (2020), https://scalar.usc.edu/works/the-space-between-literature-and-culture-1914-1945/vol16_2020_baron.

140. This is the only moment when several Volkswagens appear briefly on-screen, parked at the side of the street in a way that was anachronistic with respect to the diegetic time.

141. "Was ist ein Omnibus-Film?," *Neue Illustrierte*, no. 8, April 18, 1947, 6–7.

Chapter 2. Miraculous Objects

1. I use the name "Volkswagen" for the Volkswagen Beetle. The car was known as *the* Volkswagen in Germany until the launching of the follow-up model, the Golf, in 1974. A shorter version of this chapter's argument was published as Natalie Scholz, "Ghosts and Miracles: The Volkswagen as Imperial Debris in Postwar West Germany," *Comparative Studies in Society and History* 62, no. 3 (2020): 487–519.

2. Avery Gordon, *Ghostly Matters: Haunting and the Sociological Imagination* (Minneapolis: University of Minnesota Press, 2008), 7, 24–25.

3. I am referring here to scholars such as Robert Darnton, Natalie Z. Davis, Carlo Ginzburg, and Lynn Hunt.

4. Robert Darnton, *The Great Cat Massacre and Other Episodes in French Cultural History* (New York: Basic Books, 1984), 75–104.

5. Clifford Geertz, "History and Anthropology," *New Literary History* 21, no. 2 (Winter 1990): 321–35. This might be one reason why early modern and medieval historians have embraced a certain strand in anthropology more enthusiastically than scholars studying later periods.

6. Darnton, *The Great Cat Massacre*, 78.

7. For an inspiring exception, see Till van Rahden, "Clumsy Democrats: Moral Passions in the Federal Republic," *German History* 29, no. 3 (2011): 485–504, esp. 496.

8. Ann L. Stoler, "Colonial Aphasia: Race and Disabled Histories in France," *Public Culture* 23, no. 1 (2011): 121–56; Stoler, ed., *Imperial Debris: On Ruins and Ruination* (Durham, NC: Duke University Press, 2013).

9. Wolfgang König, *Volkswagen, Volksempfänger, Volksgemeinschaft, "Volksprodukte" im Dritten Reich: Vom Scheitern einer nationalsozialistischen Konsumgesellschaft* (Paderborn: Schöningh, 2004), 151–91; Gregor M. Rinn, "Das Automobil als nationales Identifikationssymbol: Zur politischen Bedeutung des Kraftfahrzeugs in Modernitätskonzeptionen des 'Dritten Reichs' und der Bundesrepublik" (PhD diss., Humboldt University Berlin, 2008), 29–105. The classic social and economic history of the Volkswagen during the Third Reich is Hans Mommsen and Manfred Grieger, *Das Volkswagenwerk und seine Arbeiter im Dritten Reich* (Düsseldorf: ECON, 1996).

10. Bernhard Rieger, *The People's Car: A Global History of the Volkswagen Beetle* (Cambridge, MA: Harvard University Press, 2013), 126.

11. König, *Volkswagen, Volksempfänger, Volksgemeinschaft*, 262; Schäfer, *Das gespaltene Bewusstsein*, 9–87; Confino, "Traveling"; Swett, *Selling under the Swastika*, 264–65.

12. Historical research on the cultural and semiotic aspects of West Germany's popular miracle tropes is scarce. On the "miracle" in connection with consumer exhibitions, see Jonathan S. Wiesen, "Miracles for Sale: Consumer Displays and Advertising in Postwar West Germany," in *Consuming Germany in the Cold War*, ed. David F. Crew (Oxford: Berg, 2003), 151–78. On miracles in the twentieth century with a focus on Germany, see Alexander Geppert and Till Kössler, eds., *Wunder: Poetik und Politik des Staunens im 20. Jahrhundert* (Berlin: Suhrkamp, 2011).

13. Hanna Schissler, "Writing about 1950s West Germany," in Schissler, *The Miracle Years*, 3–15, 11.

14. George Tabori, *Theaterstücke* 2, trans. from English by Ursula Grützmacher-Tabori (Munich: Hanser, 1994).

15. See Tabori, *Theaterstücke* 2, 59, 68, 77.

16. Alan Dundes and Thomas Hauschild, "Auschwitz Jokes," *Western Folklore* 42, no. 4 (1983): 249–60, 250.

17. Alan Dundes and Thomas Hauschild, "Kennt der Witz kein Tabu? Zynische Erzählformen als Versuch der Bewältigung nationalsozialistischer Vergangenheit," *Zeitschrift für Volkskunde* 83, no. 1 (1987): 21–31, here 21 and 22.

18. Rod A. Martin, *The Psychology of Humor: An Integrative Approach* (Burlington, MA: Elsevier Academic Press, 2007), 34. See also Giselinde Kuipers, "The Sociology of

Humor," in *The Primer of Humor Research*, ed. Victor Raskin (Berlin: Walter de Gruyter, 2008), 361–98.

19. Confino, *A World without Jews.*

20. Rieger, *The People's Car*; Bernhard Rieger, "The 'Good German' Goes Global: The Volkswagen Beetle as an Icon in the Federal Republic," *History Workshop Journal* 68, no. 1 (2009): 3–26; Erhard Schütz, "Der Volkswagen," in *Deutsche Erinnerungsorte: Eine Auswahl*, ed. Étienne François and Hagen Schulze (Munich: C. H. Beck, 2005), 351–68; Hans Walter Hütter, *VW Käfer . . . und läuft und läuft und läuft* (Bonn: Stiftung Haus der Geschichte der Bundesrepublik Deutschland, 2005).

21. A notable exception is the dissertation by Gregor M. Rinn, "Das Automobil als nationales Identifikationssymbol." Rinn exposes two continuities between the Third Reich and the early Federal Republic: the theme of a consumer society based on a racialized people's community and the virtue of usefulness attached to the conception of a German automobile, embodied first and foremost by the Volkswagen.

22. Michael T. Taussig, *Defacement: Public Secrecy and the Labor of the Negative* (Stanford, CA: Stanford University Press, 1999), 5.

23. Leora Auslander, "Beyond Words," *American Historical Review* 110, no. 4 (2006): 1015–45; Siân Jones, "Negotiating Authentic Objects and Authentic Selves: Beyond the Deconstruction of Authenticity," *Journal of Material Culture* 15, no. 2 (2010): 181–203; Karen V. Fernandez and John L. Lastovicka, "Making Magic: Fetishes in Contemporary Consumption," *Journal of Consumer Research* 38, no. 2 (2011): 278–99; Tilman Habermas, *Geliebte Objekte: Symbole und Instrumente der Identitätsbildung* (Frankfurt am Main: Suhrkamp, 1999).

24. Daniel Miller, *The Comfort of Things* (Cambridge: Polity Press, 2008), 163.

25. See Stoler, *Imperial Debris*. On various structural similarities between Germany's colonial and National Socialist empires, see Pascal Grosse, "What Does German Colonialism Have to Do with National Socialism? A Conceptual Framework," in *Germany's Colonial Pasts*, ed. Eric Ames, Marcia Klotz, and Lora Wildenthal (Lincoln: University of Nebraska Press, 2005), 115–34.

26. Volkswagen advertisement published in *magnum*, no. 32 (October 1960): 61. The catchword "critical generation" in quotation marks is reminiscent of the famous sociological study on young West Germans by Helmut Schelsky, which had been published three years earlier. Helmut Schelsky, *Die skeptische Generation: Eine Soziologie der deutschen Jugend* (Cologne: Diederichs, 1957). "Chrome-sparkling" was a term used to describe bulky American cars, the very opposite of what the Volkswagen stood for. The ad therefore also evokes a contrast between the VW and American car culture, which itself had already been an essential element of the Nazi campaign. See Rinn, "Das Automobil," esp. 77–79.

27. "Kraft durch Freude" was part of the German Labor Front. See Baranowski, *Strength through Joy.*

28. *Deutschland-Berichte der Sozialdemokratischen Partei Deutschlands (Sopade) 1934–1940*, vol. 6, 1939 (Frankfurt am Main: Zweitausenteinds, 1980), 480–90, 488.

29. "Ist der VW veraltet? Ein Spiegel-Gespräch mit Generaldirektor des Volkswagenwerks, Professor Dr.-Ing. Heinz Nordhoff," *Der Spiegel*, no. 40, September 30, 1959, 40–58.

30. The headline of the same number's cover (no. 40, 1959) was "Noch eine Million vom gleichen Typ?" (Another Million of the Same Type.)

31. This resembles the "strange accidents" that can be associated with instances of defacement. See Taussig, *Defacement*, 3.

32. "Ist der VW veraltet?," 47.

33. Spoerl, born in 1917, worked as an engineer until 1945 and published humorist novels and stories after the war; "Spoerl, Alexander," in *Munzinger Online/Personen, Internationales Biographisches Archiv*, http://www.munzinger.de/document/00000006988 (accessed 17 November 2019).

34. A. Spoerl, "Ist der VW veraltet?," *Der Stern*, no. 43, October 26, 1957, 54–61, quotations 56.

35. Spoerl, "Ist der VW veraltet?," 56 and 57.

36. Spoerl, "Ist der VW veraltet?," 57.

37. D. Korp, "Alter oder neuer Volkswagen: Kluge Reden am falschen Kamin," *Das Auto: Motor und Sport*, no. 1 (1959): 9–11. See also "Unser Test: Volkswagen 1958," *Das Auto: Motor und Sport*, no. 21 (1957): 13.

38. Rieger, *People's Car*, 212–16, 227–28; see also Dirk Schlinkert, "Von der Reklame zum Marketing," in *50 Jahre Volkswagenwerbung* (Hamburg: Gruner und Jahr, 2002), 8–17.

39. "Volkswagenwerk: In König Nordhoffs Reich," *Der Spiegel*, no. 33, August 10, 1955, 16–26, here 17 and 21.

40. "Volkswagenwerk," 24.

41. Jan Molitor, "Neue Wege zur Nazisuche," *Die Zeit*, no. 5, January 29, 1953, 2.

42. See the HICOG survey report no. 167 (January 12, 1953), in *Public Opinion in Semisovereign Germany: The HICOG Surveys, 1949–1955*, ed. Anna J. Merritt and Richard L. Merritt (Urbana: University of Illinois Press, 1980), 197–99. A survey by the Allensbach Institute conducted a year later with the same set of questions had nearly the same result. See Elisabeth Noelle and Erich Peter Neumann, eds., *Jahrbuch der öffentlichen Meinung 1947–1955*, 2nd ed. (Allensbach: Verlag für Demoskopie, 1956), 276–77.

43. Quoted in Parkinson, *An Emotional State*, 152–53.

44. "Der VW setzt sich durch," Volkswagen advertisement published in *Quick*, no. 2, January 13, 1952, 22–23.

45. Spoerl, "Ist der VW veraltet?," 54.

46. Franz Ulrich Glass, "Tankwart Herbert meint . . . ," *Gute Fahrt*, no. 1 (1950): 15.

47. *Volkswagen-Geschichten*, West Germany, 1950, directed by Herbert Kruchen, Melodia-Film Produktion Werner Grünbauer Hamburg.

48. This happened in 1950, before the rising number of deadly car accidents in the early 1950s provoked a public discussion. See Dietmar Klenke, "Die deutsche Katastrophe und das Automobil: Zur 'Heils'geschichte eines nationalen Kultobjekts in den Jahren des Wiederaufstiegs," in *Moderne Zeiten: Technik und Zeitgeist im 19. und 20. Jahrhundert*, ed. Michael Salewski and Ilona Stölken-Fitschen (Stuttgart: Steiner, 1994), 157–73.

49. "Unproduktive Botschaft: In Bildung inbegriffen," *Der Spiegel*, no. 25, June 19, 1948, 16–17.

50. "Unproduktive Botschaft," 17.

51. Paul Kluke, "Hitler und das Volkswagenprojekt," *Vierteljahreshefte für Zeitgeschichte* 8, no. 4 (1960): 341–83, here 341.

52. C. O. Windecker, "MR-Reisetest VOLKSWAGEN: Vinzenz auf dem besten Wege," *Motor-Rundschau*, no. 22, November 25, 1949, 563–64, 563.

53. Bernhard Rieger, "Schulden der Vergangenheit? Der Mammutprozess der Volkswagensparer, 1949–1961," in *Mit dem Wandel leben: Neuorientierung und Tradition in der Bundesrepublik der 1950er und 1960er Jahre*, ed. Friedrich Kießling and Bernhard Rieger (Cologne: Böhlau, 2011), 185–208.

54. "Porsche von Fallersleben: Geschichte eines Automobils," *Der Spiegel*, no. 20, May 18, 1950, 21–27, 24.

55. "Unser KdF-Wagen," *Arbeitertum*, no. 10 (August 1940): unpaginated. In December 1940 a long article emphasized the importance of the KdF-Wagen for Danzig and West Prussia to catch up quickly with the state of cultural development in the Third Reich after they had suffered under Polish rule. The author took pains to underline the huge interest for the car in this region, which had been newly reintegrated into the Reich as a result of the war. "Der KdF-Wagen erobert Danzig," *Arbeitertum*, no. 18 (December 1940): 6–7.

56. "KdF-Wagen auf den Wegen des Sieges," *Arbeitertum*, no. 28 (May 1941): unpaginated.

57. "Die Front bestätigt es: Der Volkswagen hat alle Erwartungen übertroffen," *Arbeitertum*, first March number (1942): 6–7.

58. For examples of similar descriptions in German automobile magazines, see Rinn, "Das Automobil," 104–5.

59. "Kreuz und quer durchs Mittelmeer," *Der Stern*, no. 26, July 1, 1951, 5.

60. "Keine Angst bei Notlandung," *Quick*, no. 2, January 3, 1952, 5. See also "Rommel's Men in Africa Again," *Sydney Morning Herald*, October 7, 1951, 12. Hermann Schultze-Dewitz apparently returned to Africa regularly in the same outfit. In 1954 *Der Spiegel* mentioned that the members of the entourage of the British queen were shocked when they saw his "uniform-like khaki suit and peaked cap." ("Personalien: Hermann Schultze-Dewitz," *Der Spiegel*, no. 20, May 12, 1954, 24).

61. Confino, "Traveling," esp. 107–11.

62. *"Kleiner Wagen . . . große Liebe": Ein Film für Autofreunde*, West Germany, 1949, directed by Ulrich Kayser, UKA Film-Produktion.

63. Heinz Todtmann and Alfred Tritschler, *Kleiner Wagen auf großer Fahrt* (Offenburg: Verlag Dr. Franz Burda, 1949), 186.

64. The Norwegian harbor city Narvik was occupied by the German Wehrmacht in the spring of 1940.

65. "Sieben Jahre 'Kraft durch Freude': Auch im Kriege kein Stillstand—große Zukunftspläne," *Arbeitertum*, no. 18 (December 1940): 2–3.

66. On the Nazi vision of a "new order" in Europe, see Elizabeth Harvey, "International Networks and Cross-Border Cooperation: National Socialist Women and the Vision of a

'New Order' in Europe," *Politics, Religion & Ideology* 13, no. 2 (2012): 141–58; and Mark Mazower, *Hitler's Empire: Nazi Rule in Occupied Europe* (London: Allen Lane, 2008). See also Paul Corbach, "Soziales Europa von Morgen," *Arbeitertum*, no. 2 (February 1942): 4.

67. Michael Kriegeskorte, *Automobilwerbung in Deutschland 1948–1968* (Cologne: Dumont, 1994), 120.

68. They were shown in commercial cinemas, at car dealers, and at big automobile exhibitions, attracting a spectatorship of several hundred thousand, in other words, an audience comparable in size to that of the most successful German feature films of the time. Günter Riederer, *Auto-Kino: Unternehmensfilme von Volkswagen in den Wirtschaftswunderjahren* (Wolfsburg: Volkswagen Aktiengesellschaft, 2011), 12–34.

69. Riederer, *Auto-Kino*, 33, see also 13, 22, 50. *Kulturfilme* were documentaries or educational films on different topics shown in cinemas before the main feature film. Under National Socialism Joseph Goebbel's propaganda ministry largely controlled the production of these films.

70. Riederer, *Auto-Kino*, 143.

71. Barry Fulks, "Walter Ruttmann, the Avant-Garde Film, and Nazi Modernism," *Film & History* 14, no. 2 (1984): 26–46, here 4.

72. *Aus eigener Kraft*, West Germany, 1953–54, directed by Franz Schroedter, Franz Schroedter–Studio KG for the Volkswagen factory.

73. Jeffrey Herf, *Reactionary Modernism: Technology, Culture, and Politics in Weimar and the Third Reich* (Cambridge: Cambridge University Press, 1984), 641. Herf refers here especially to the views of Fritz Todt, founder of the Nazi engineering organization Todt.

74. Quoted in Herf, *Reactionary Modernism*, 642. See the speeches of Goebbels and Hitler published in *Kräfte sammeln, Kräfte lenken, Kräfte sparen: Drei Reden zur Internationalen Automobil- und Motorrad-Ausstellung Berlin 1939*, Reichsverband der Automobilindustrie e.V. (Berlin, June 1939).

75. Heinz-B. Heller, "'Stählerne Romantik' und Avantgarde: Beobachtungen und Anmerkungen zu Ruttmanns Industriefilmen," in *Triumph der Bilder: Kultur- und Dokumentarfilme vor 1945 im internationalen Vergleich*, ed. Peter Zimmermann (Konstanz: Konstanz UVK, 2003), 105–18, quote 109. See also Michael Cowan, *Walter Ruttmann and the Cinema of Multiplicity: Avant-Garde—Advertising—Modernity* (Amsterdam: Amsterdam University Press, 2014), 133–72.

76. Markus Lupa, *Das Werk der Briten: Volkswagenwerk und Besatzungsmacht 1945–1949*, 3rd ed. (Wolfsburg: Volkswagen-AG, Unternehmensarchiv, 2005), 7.

77. Jan Otakar Fischer has stressed the "special propaganda value of the Volkswagen complex" and described its facade as "a mask and a manifesto at once" ("Memento Machinae: Engineering the Past in Wolfsburg," in *Beyond Berlin: Twelve German Cities Confront the Nazi Past*, ed. Gavriel D. Rosenfeld and Paul B. Jaskot [Ann Arbor: University of Michigan Press, 2007], 89–115).

78. *Aus eigener Kraft* premiered on March 30, 1954, in cinemas in Berlin, Hamburg, Munich, and Frankfurt am Main. Cabinet ministers and members of parliament attended a special premiere in Bonn. The film found its audience of more than six hundred thousand people through various channels, among them matinees organized by contract

dealers and two big tours of special screenings around the country. It also won a prize for its excellent color photography at the documentary film festival in Venice and was officially assessed as "worthy" (*wertvoll*) by the West German Office of Film Evaluation. The film failed to acquire the category "exceptionally worthy." Six years after its release, the Volkswagen company showed no interest in extending the film's official categorization as "worthy." Riederer, *Auto-Kino*, 17, 35–36, 42, 44, 53.

79. See Hermann Kappelhoff, "Kriegerische Mobilisierung: Die mediale Organisation des Gemeinsinns," *Navigationen: Zeitschrift für Medien- und Kulturwissenschaften* 9, no. 1 (2009): 151–65.

80. *Sinfonie eines Autos*, West Germany, 1949, directed by Ulrich Kayser and Werner Liesfeld, UKA Film-Produktion Freiburg.

81. Wolf Dieter Lützen, "Jubiläen, Jubiläen: Die Volkswagen-Annoncen der Jahre 1951 bis 1964," in *Das deutsche Auto: Volkswagenwerbung und Volkskultur*, ed. Knut Hickethier, Wolf Dieter Lützen, and Karin Reiss (Gießen: Anabas-Verlag, 1974), 64–88, here 64–70. There is no in-depth study of the whole variety of early Volkswagen advertising.

82. "Werk und Wagen der grosse Erfolg!" printed in Riederer, *Auto-Kino*, 73. The author does not specify in which journal or magazine the advertisement was published.

83. "Volkswagenwerk," 16–17.

84. *Die Welt huldigt dem Volkswagen*, West Germany, 1955, produced by Walter Knoop.

85. There was even a juridical side to this symbolic overlap. The factory was "legally without owner," since the dissolved German Labor Front still stood in the trade register as its owner. See "Volkswagenwerk," 17. On the Federal Republic's restraint in matters of self-representation, see Johannes Paulmann, "Representation without Emulation: German Cultural Diplomacy in Search of Integration and Self-Assurance during the Adenauer Era," *German Politics and Society* 25, no. 2 (2007): 168–200.

86. Horst Mönnich, *Die Autostadt: Roman* (Frankfurt am Main: Deutscher Jugendbuchverlag, 1951), 57, emphasis in the original.

87. Horst Mönnich, *Geboren Neunzehn-Hundert-Achtzehn: Von einem Ende zum Anderen* (Munich: Franz Schneekluth Verlag, 1993), 53.

88. Mönnich became a member of the famous literary Gruppe 47.

89. Manfred Grieger, "Eine Meistererzählung vom Volkswagen und der dazugehörigen Stadt: Der Roman *Die Autostadt* von Horst Mönnich aus dem Jahr 1951," in *Die Wolfsburg-Saga*, ed. Christoph Stölzl (Stuttgart: Konrad Theiss Verlag, 2008), 144–47.

90. Quoted in Grieger, "Eine Meistererzählung," 145.

91. Mönnich, *Die Autostadt*, 14, 8, 21, 51, 51–52.

92. Claude Lefort, *Essais sur le politique, XIXe–XXe siècles* (Paris: Seuil, 1986), 29.

93. Mönnich, *Die Autostadt*, 13–15.

94. In Lower Saxony, to which Wolfsburg belongs, refugees and expellees from the East formed 26.4 percent of the population in 1949. Klaus J. Bade and Jochen Oltmer, "Einwanderungsland Niedersachsen: Zuwanderung und Integration seit dem Zweiten Weltkrieg," in *Zuwanderung und Integration in Niedersachsen seit dem Zweiten Weltkrieg*, ed. Klaus J. Bade and Jochen Oltmer (Osnabrück: Universitäts-Verlag Rasch, 2002), 11–36, here 14.

95. The character Maria Reuter has been identified as coming from Transylvania. The family of the character Willy Maertens has been described as living in "the East." Father and son Buttgereit are simply labeled as *heimatlos* (homeless). See Mönnich, *Die Autostadt*, 58–62, 80, 63.

96. Ulfert Herlyn et al., *Faszination Wolfsburg, 1938–2012* (Wiesbaden: Verlag für Sozialwissenschaften, 2012), 142–43.

97. Mönnich, *Die Autostadt*, 300 (quote), 81. On the presentation of the city of the Kdf-Wagen as a classless social utopia during the Third Reich, see Mommsen and Grieger, *Das Volkswagenwerk*, 188–89.

98. Mönnich, *Die Autostadt*, 88–89.

99. Mönnich, *Die Autostadt*, 89.

100. Mönnich, *Die Autostadt*, 16–19.

101. The ambivalence of transition is also captured in a scene in which the soldiers, father and son Franz and Stefan Buttgereit, come back from the war and turn to the factory and city. Ragged people come out of the factory and say, "We build cars for the Tommies. Cars of the magnificent führer" (Mönnich, *Die Autostadt*, 66–67).

102. Mönnich, *Die Autostadt*, 193.

103. Mönnich, *Die Autostadt*, 232, 252.

104. For the Volkswagen being described as a "miracle," see Mönnich, *Die Autostadt*, 56, 275, 277.

105. Mönnich, *Die Autostadt*, 187.

106. Mönnich, *Die Autostadt*, 188–90.

107. Mönnich, *Die Autostadt*, 190–91.

108. Mönnich, *Die Autostadt*, 192.

109. In the first part of the novel, a girl is introduced who moves around signs for the location of Volkswagen dealers on the "ordnance map" (*Generalstabskarte*) of the factory. Mönnich, *Die Autostadt*, 82.

110. Mönnich, *Die Autostadt*, 237. In 1945 about half of the sixteen thousand inhabitants were forced laborers. See Herlyn et al., *Faszination Wolfsburg*, 22, 142. On the plight of forced laborers and concentration camp inmates working for the Volkswagen factory during the war, see Mommsen and Grieger, *Das Volkswagenwerk*, 496–598, 713–39, 766–99.

111. For the expression "German miracle," see "Unser Ziel heißt die vollendete Sicherheit unseres Volkes und ein Deutschland der Größe," *Jeversches Wochenblatt*, no. 278, November 29, 1937, 1; and "Glückliche Weihnacht im Schicksalsjahr 1938," *Der Führer: Das Hauptorgan der NSDAP Gau Baden*, no. 356, December 27, 1938, 2. The term "economic miracle" appears, for instance, in "Ein Rückblick: 1938: Jahr der großdeutschen Erfüllung," *Völkischer Beobachter*, Vienna edition, January 1, 1939, 11; Ministerialdirektor Durst, German Labor Ministry, "Der soziale Wohnungsbau," *Völkischer Beobachter*, Vienna edition, January 30, 1941, 13; "Führen, nicht verwalten!," *Völkischer Beobachter*, Vienna edition, August 1, 1944, 6. *The Times* of London also spoke of the "German 'miracle'" in 1937: "German Claim to Colonies," *The Times* (London), October 4, 1937, 14. This use of the term was not forgotten after the war. See Gerd Bucerius, "Hintergründe eines

Wirtschaftswunders: Ein Beitrag zum Fall Schacht," *Die Zeit*, no. 14, April 3, 1947, 2. See also Schäfer, *Das gespaltene Bewußtsein*, 10; Mark Spoerer, "Demontage eines Mythos? Zu der Kontroverse über das nationalsozialistische 'Wirtschaftswunder,'" *Geschichte und Gesellschaft* 31, no. 3 (2005): 415–38, 415.

112. "Das deutsche Wirtschaftswunder: Unsere Korrespondenten berichten, was das Ausland dazu sagt," *Frankfurter Allgemeine Zeitung*, March 29, 1952, 7; "Es gibt kein Deutsches Wunder," *Der Spiegel*, no. 37, September 9, 1953, cover, 11–17; Jens Daniel, "Das Zwinkern mit dem Wunder," *Der Spiegel*, no. 47, November 17, 1954, 5. Chancellor Adenauer used the expression in March 1952 while addressing the Germans in a radio speech. See "Adenauer fordert Mut zur Entscheidung," *Frankfurter Allgemeine Zeitung*, March 8, 1952, 1.

113. Falko Schneider, "Unfassbares Produzieren: Zur politischen Epistemologie des Wunderbegriffs im 20. Jahrhundert," in Geppert and Kössler, *Wunder*, 305–31, 323.

114. Fritzsche, *Life and Death*, 268.

115. See Bessel, *Germany 1945*, 7, quoting Fritz Stern's essay "Verlorene Heimat," published in *Verspielte Größe: Essays zur deutschen Geschichte im 20. Jahrhundert* (Munich: C. H. Beck, 1996), 63. See also van Rahden, "Clumsy Democrats"; Olick, *In the House*; Werner Sollors, *The Temptation of Despair: Tales of the 1940s* (Cambridge, MA: Belknap Press of Harvard University Press, 2014); Florian Huber, *Kind, versprich mir, dass du dich erschießt: Der Untergang der kleinen Leute 1945* (Berlin: Berlin Verlag, 2015); Black, *A Demon-Haunted Land*.

116. Ulrike Weckel, *Beschämende Bilder: Deutsche Reaktionen auf alliierte Dokumentarfilme über befreite Konzentrationslager* (Stuttgart: Steiner, 2012); Weckel, "Disappointed Hopes for Spontaneous Mass Conversion: German Responses to Allied Atrocity Film Screenings 1945–46," *Bulletin of the GHI* 51 (Fall 2012): 39–53; Sollors, *The Temptation of Dispair*, 85–150; Olick, *In the House*.

117. In his autobiographical novel *Der Alpdruck*, published first in 1947, Hans Fallada gives a rare insight into the urgency behind this affective constellation. Hans Fallada, *Der Alpdruck* (Berlin: Aufbau, 2015), 35–40.

118. The focus on objects thus allows for an integration of the symbolic and the affective, that is, bodily dimensions in the evolution of identities. When it comes to objects, affects, and the workings of self-consciousness, Winnicott's ideas about "transitional objects" are still the most important reference. See *Playing and Reality*, 1–34.

119. "Keine Liefermöglichkeit für den Volkswagen," *Das Auto*, no. 10 (1947): 18.

120. "Steine statt Brot: Ein Amt zweifelt an sich selber," *Der Spiegel*, no. 14, April 3, 1947, 1–2. See also "Können Demonstrationen helfen?," *Neue Illustrierte*, no. 18, April 18, 1947, 3.

121. "Ruhr Hunger March. Workers' Protest. British Army Cars Overturned," *The Times* (London), March 29, 1947, 4. On the connection between Germans' resentment and the occupation forces' monopoly on automobiles, see "Der Mann im Auto," *Das Auto*, no. 8 (1947): 25.

122. "Strömt herbei . . . ? Messebesucher haben es leicht," *Der Spiegel*, no. 31, August 1, 1947, 15.

123. "Melken mit der Hand: Und was sagt die Kuh dazu?," *Der Spiegel*, no. 36, September 6, 1947, 3.

124. Jan Molitor, "'People's Car' auf neuen Wegen: Jubiläumsbesuch im Volkswagenwerk zu Wolfsburg," *Die Zeit*, no. 5, January 29, 1948, 2.

125. Rieger, *The People's Car*, 113.

126. "Neues Leben in Rotterdam" and "Unseren kleinen Volkswagen," *Quick*, no. 14, October 17, 1948, 6–7; "A Nice Little Car," *Quick*, no. 16, October 31, 1948; "Millionen-Geschäft in New York," *Quick*, no. 20, May 15, 1949, 4–5. See also Herbert Engst, "New York übertraf alle Erwartungen," *Die Zeit*, no. 17, April 28, 1949, https://www.zeit.de/1949/17/new-york-uebertraf-erwartungen.

127. "Deutschland stellt aus," *Neue Illustrierte*, no. 19, May 12, 1949, 6–7. See also "German Exhibits Draw Picket Line," *New York Times*, April 10, 1949, 14. The satirical magazine *Der Simpl* commented: "Apropos: Volks-Wagen. He was the sensation of the German Industries Fair in New York. The von Fallersleben! (Deutschland über alles)" (no. 10 [May 1949]: 111).

128. "Wir machen uns auf den Weg: Frischer Wind von Ortega," *Der Spiegel*, no. 36, September 1, 1949, 25–26.

129. "Porsche von Fallersleben: Geschichte eines Automobils," *Der Spiegel*, no. 18, May 4, 1950, 21–26, here 21.

130. "Porsche von Fallersleben," 24.

131. "Porsche von Fallersleben," 24–25.

132. *Life*, May 16, 1949, 38–43.

133. First quote from David Ellwood, *Rebuilding Europe: Western Europe, America and Postwar Reconstruction* (Harlow, Essex: Longman House, 1992), 16; second quote from Sheryl Kroen, "Liberal Tales of Origin at the Berlin Industries Fair," manuscript. Thanks to the author for giving me access to this manuscript.

134. *Gateway to Germany*, publication on behalf of the German Federal Ministry of the Marshall Plan (Bonn: Verlag fur Publizistik of MBH Bonn, 1952), quoted in Kroen, "Liberal Tales."

135. See the Marshall Plan film *Air of Freedom*, West Germany, 1951, produced by HICOG Film Section for ECA Germany.

136. Kroen, "Liberal Tales." See also Kroen, "Robinson Charley"; Brian Angus McKenzie, *Remaking France: Americanization, Public Diplomacy, and the Marshall Plan* (New York: Berghahn Books, 2005); Ellwood, "The Propaganda"; Greg Castillo, "Domesticating the Cold War: Household Consumption as Propaganda in Marshall Plan Germany," *Journal of Contemporary History* 40, no. 2 (2005): 261–88.

137. See, for example, "Wolfgang Weber machte einen Besuch am D-Mark-Strand," *Neue Illustrierte*, no. 19, September 2, 1948, 8–9.

138. "Ein drittel Volkswagen: Wenige Marken beherrschen den deutschen Markt," *Frankfurter Allgemeine Zeitung*, September 7, 1957, 7; Rieger, *The People's Car*, 150. Volkswagens also served as police cars and as cars for the members of the new West German parliament. See "Der Bundestag soll erweitert werden," *Frankfurter Allgemeine Zeitung*, January 20, 1951, 3.

139. This observation is based on the collection of private photo albums, Stadtmuseum München. Photos with the Volkswagen can be found in the following albums: K 424 (1955), K 208/11 (1955), K 436 (1955), K 232/4 (1957), K 208/5 (1956 and 1957), K 234/29 (1957 and 1958), K 234/31 (1957), K 233/1 (1950s, without a year), and K 125 (without a year). To these examples I can add my mother's photo album of the 1950s.

140. See the feature films *Die Landärztin*, West Germany, 1958, directed by Paul May, KG Divina Film, Munich; *Natürlich die Autofahrer*, West Germany, 1959, directed by Erich Engels, Deutsche Film Hansa, Hamburg. With a similar atmosphere, see also Erich Kuby's two youth novels about a boy in Wolfsburg: *Alarm im Werk: Der Junge mit dem Volkswagen* (Munich: F. Schneider, 1955) and *Thomas und sein Volkswagen* (Munich: F. Schneider, 1956).

141. "Personalien: Lale Andersen," *Der Spiegel*, no. 51, December 16, 1953, 32. For another example, see "Eine VW-'Panne,'" *Die Zeit*, no. 9, February 28, 1952, https://www.zeit.de/1952/09/eine-vw-panne.

142. For the Volkswagen as a positive trait of a movie production company, see "Massenfilm: Hundert stöhnen 'uff,'" *Der Spiegel*, no. 51, December 20, 1950, 38–39; for a physician, see "Prügel-Strafe: Machen Sie was," *Der Spiegel*, no. 40, September 30, 1953, 12–14, here 12; for a factory owner, "Industrie: Strümpfe; Der Hans fängt wieder an," *Der Spiegel*, no. 10, March 3, 1954, 29–33, here 33; for a principal stockholder, "Großaktionär Krages: Das Gardemaß der Ruhr," *Der Spiegel*, no. 6, February 8, 1956, 18–26, 18; for a general, "Personalien: Frank Novotny," *Der Spiegel*, no. 21, May 21, 1958, 64; and for the attorney general, Walter Henkels, "Mit 1 PS fing es an: Sollen Abgeordnete ein Auto fahren?," *Frankfurter Allgemeine Zeitung*, March 21, 1953, 3 (*Bilder und Zeiten*); Robert Strobel, "Thomas Dehler," *Die Zeit*, no. 41, October 9, 1952, https://www.zeit.de/1952/41/thomas-dehler; "Thomas Dehler: Das ist nicht Vati" (cover story), *Der Spiegel*, no. 34, August 19, 1953, 9–15, here 9.

143. "Dr. Nordhoffs Rede," *Das Auto: Motor und Sport*, no. 2 (1954): 23–24. See also "Eine 'Spiegel'-Seite für Heinz Nordhoff: Passion fürs Auto," *Der Spiegel*, no. 45, November 6, 1948, 19. Rinn, "Das Automobil," 72–79, 94–105.

144. Rinn, "Das Automobil."

145. *Wir Wunderkinder*, West Germany, 1958, directed by Kurt Hoffmann, Filmaufbau Göttingen.

146. Ann L. Stoler, "Introduction: 'The Rot Remains'; From Ruins to Ruination," in Stoler, *Imperial Debris*, 1–35, 5.

147. Stoler, "Introduction," 5 and 8.

148. On December 3, 1938, Himmler passed a decree prohibiting German Jews from driving. In May 1938 Hitler laid the foundation stone for the Volkswagen plant. In February 1939 the Volkswagen was presented to the German public at the International Automobile Exhibition in Berlin. See Tofahrn, *Chronologie*, 60, 65.

149. In this sense it continued Nazi humor as a "communicative contract between non-Jews" to "act out exclusion and inclusion." Martina Kessel, "Race and Humor in Nazi Germany," in *Beyond the Racial State: Rethinking Nazi Germany*, ed. Devon O. Pendas,

Mark Roseman, and Richard F. Wetzell (Cambridge: Cambridge University Press, 2017), 380–401, here 380.

150. See Michael Geyer, "Die eingebildete Heimkehr: Im Schatten der Niederlage," in *Demokratie im Schatten der Gewalt: Geschichten des Privaten im deutschen Nachkrieg*, ed. Daniel Fulda et al. (Göttingen: Wallstein, 2010), 72–96.

151. Ann L. Stoler, "Intimidations of Empire: Predicaments of the Tactile and Unseen," in *Haunted by Empire: Geographies of Intimacy in North American History*, ed. Ann L. Stoler (Durham, NC: Duke University Press, 2006), 1–22.

Chapter 3. Timeless Objects

1. Karl Pawek, "Wirklichkeit ist mehr als ein Mythos," *magnum*, no. 35 (April 1961): 64, 90–91, here 64, emphasis added. Pawek founded the right-wing Austrian cultural magazine *die pause* in 1935 and transformed it into a periodical with propagandist content during the Third Reich. In 1954 he became a cofounder of and frequent contributor to the magazine *magnum*, a self-proclaimed standard bearer of the postwar modern. See Margarethe Szeless, *Die Kulturzeitschrift "magnum": Photographische Befunde der Moderne* (Marburg: Jonas Verlag, 2007), 9; Timm Starl, "Die Kehrseite der Geschichte. Karl Pawek: Priesterzögling, Zeitschriftengründer, NSDAP-Anwärter, Kriegsverbrecher, Psychopath, Ausstellungsmacher, Kulturpreisträger," *Fotogeschichte* 23, no. 87 (2003): 65–69. An article containing the central arguments of this chapter was published as Natalie Scholz, "'A Final Solution for Humanity'? Modern Design and the Ambivalences of Redemption in Post-war West Germany," *Cultural History* 12, no. 1 (April 2023): 74–97.

2. Penny Sparke, "'A Home for Everybody?' Design, Ideology and the Culture of the Home in Italy, 1945–1972," in *Modernism in Design*, ed. Paul Greenhalgh (London: Reaktion Books, 1990), 185–203; Fredie Floré and Mil de Kooning, "The Representation of Modern Domisticity in the Belgian Section of the Brussels World's Fair of 1958," *Journal of Design History* 16, no. 4 (2003): 319–40; Jonathan Woodham, "Design and Everyday Life at the *Britain Can Make It* Exhibition, 1946: 'Stripes, Spots, White Wood and Homespun versus Chintzy Armchairs and Iron Bedsteads with Brass Knobs,'" *Journal of Architecture* 9 (Winter 2004): 463–76; Greg Barnhisel, "*Perspectives USA* and the Cultural Cold War," *Modernism/Modernity* 14, no. 4 (2007): 729–54; Katherine Pence and Paul Betts, eds., *Socialist Modern: East German Everyday Culture and Politics* (Ann Arbor: University of Michigan Press, 2008); David Crowley and Jane Pavitt, eds., *Cold War Modern: Design 1945–1970* (London: Victoria and Albert Museum, 2008); Eli Rubin, "The Form of Socialism without Ornament: Consumption, Ideology, and the Fall and Rise of Modernist Design in the German Democratic Republic," *Journal of Design History* 19, no. 2 (2006): 155–68; Greg Castillo, *Cold War on the Home Front: The Soft Power of Midcentury Design* (Minneapolis: University of Minnesota Press, 2010).

3. Natalie Scholz and Milena Veenis, "Cold War Modernism and Postwar German Homes: An East-West Comparison," in *Divided Dreamworlds? The Cultural Cold War in East and West*, ed. Peter Romijn, Giles Scott-Smith, and Joes Segal (Amsterdam: Amsterdam University Press, 2012), 155–80; Winfried Nerdinger, ed., *Bauhaus-Moderne im Nationalsozialismus: Zwischen Anbiederung und Verfolgung* (Munich: Prestel-Verlag,

1993); Schäfers, *Vom Werkbund zum Vierjahresplan*; Kathleen James-Chakraborty, ed., *Bauhaus-Culture: From Weimar to the Cold War* (Minneapolis: University of Minnesota Press, 2006); Kathleen James-Chakraborty, "Beyond Cold War Interpretations: Shaping a New Bauhaus Heritage," *New German Critique* 39 (2012): 11–24; Patrick Rössler, "Vielfalt in der Gleichschaltung—die 'domestizierte Moderne' am Kiosk: Eine Lifestyle-Illustrierte zwischen Bauhaus-Avantgarde und NS-Propaganda; 'die neue Linie' 1929–1943," *Jahrbuch für Kommunikationsgeschichte* 9 (2007): 150–95; Michael Tymkiw, *Nazi Exhibition Design and Modernism* (Minneapolis: University of Minnesota Press, 2018).

4. Joan Campbell, *The German Werkbund: The Politics of Reform in the Applied Arts* (Princeton, NJ: Princeton University Press, 1978), 243–87; Sabine Weißler, ed., *Design in Deutschland 1933–45: Ästhetik und Organisation des Deutschen Werkbundes im "Dritten Reich"* (Gießen: Anabas-Verlag, 1990); Betts, *The Authority*, 23–72; Sabine Zentek, *Designer im Dritten Reich: Gute Formen sind eine Frage der richtigen Haltung* (Dortmund: Lelesken-Verlag, 2009); Michel Lingohr, "Die letzte ideologische Bastion? Der nationalsozialistische Angriff auf den Haushalt," in *Entnazifizierte Zone? Zum Umgang mit der Zeit des Nationalsozialismus in ostdeuschen Stadt- und Regionalmuseen*, ed. Museum Association of the State Brandenburg (Bielefeld: transcript, 2015), 93–110.

5. Ellie Tschauner, "Zum Sieg der Guten Form: WK-Verband und Reichsheimstättenamt als Wegbereiter," *Innen-Dekoration*, no. 5 (1940): 152–53.

6. Original German quote in Campbell, *The German Werkbund*, 260n48.

7. Theodor Heuss, "Der Werkbund vor neuen Aufgaben," *Vossische Zeitung*, June 10, 1933, 6.

8. Campbell, *The German Werkbund*, 275–76; Sabine Weißler, "Worum es geht," in Weißler, *Design in Deutschland*, 8–9; Dieter Högermann, "Gretsch, Hermann," in Allgemeines Künstlerlexikon—Internationale Künstlerdatenbank—Online (Munich: K. G. Sauer, 2009 and later updates), https://www.degruyter.com/database/akl/html. On Gretsch's influence under National Socialism, see Lingohr, "Die letzte ideologische Bastion?"; and Xenia Riemann, "Die 'Gute Form' und ihr Inhalt: Über die Kontinuität des sachlichen deutschen Designs zwischen 1930 und 1960," *kritische berichte* 34, no. 1 (2006): 52–62.

9. This also corresponds with the concept of a "banal nationalism" that manifests itself silently in everyday objects. Nancy Reagin has productively interpreted German cultures of domesticity in that context. See *Sweeping the German Nation: Domesticity and National Identity in Germany, 1870–1945* (Cambridge: Cambridge University Press, 2007); Michael Billig, *Banal Nationalism* (London: Sage Publications, 1995).

10. Betts, *The Authority*, citations on 2, 3, 7, 11, 50.

11. See also Christopher Oestereich, *"Gute Form" im Wiederaufbau: Zur Geschichte der Produktgestaltung in Westdeutschland nach 1945* (Berlin: Lukas Verlag, 2000); Paulmann, "Representation"; Castillo, *Cold War*; Deborah Barnstone, "Nomina Sunt Omina—Capital City Bonn: Inventing an Image for the Federal Republic of Germany," *Journal of Design History* 27, no. 2 (2014): 148–66.

12. Gerd Selle, *Geschichte des Design in Deutschland* (Frankfurt am Main: Campus Verlag, 1984), 238–40, 244.

13. On how to study denial in history, see Catherine Hall and Daniel Pick, "Thinking about Denial," *History Workshop Journal* 84, no. 1 (2017): 1–23.

14. Pawek, "Wirklichkeit," 64.

15. On how Bauhaus acquired its sacrosanct status in the early 1950s, see Paul Betts, "The Bauhaus as Cold-War Legend: West German Modernism Revisited," *German Politics and Society* 14, no. 2 (1996): 75–100.

16. *Film ohne Titel*, Germany, 1948, directed by Rudolf Jugert, Camera Filmproduktion Hamburg.

17. Moltke, *No Place Like Home*, 78.

18. In this way the film shares some characteristics with *Goodbye, Franziska!* (1941) and *Franziska* (1957), both of which are discussed in chapter 4.

19. See also Hester Baer, *Dismantling the Dream Factory: Gender, German Cinema, and the Postwar Quest for a New Film Language* (New York: Berghahn Books, 2009), 49–72; Shandley, *Rubble Films*, 152–60.

20. "Ein Aufruf des Deutschen Werkbundes," *Die Gegenwart*, no. 7/8 (March 1947): 24.

21. "Die Stunde des Werkbundes," *Frankfurter Hefte*, no. 2 (May 1946): 88–90.

22. Walter Dirks, "Mut zum Abschied: Zur Wiederherstellung des Frankfurter Goethehauses," *Frankfurter Hefte*, no. 8 (August 1947): 819–28, here 820–21.

23. "Was kostet die Einrichtung einer Zweieinhalb-Zimmer-Wohnung?," *Mittelbayerische Zeitung*, no. 121, October 19, 1949, 6–7, emphasis added.

24. Deutscher Werkbund, ed., *Werkbund-Ausstellung Neues Wohnen: Deutsche Architektur seit 1945, Köln 1949, 14. Mai bis 3. Juli* (Cologne: Lang, 1949), 11. See also the foreword by Erik Nölting in the same catalog (15). On the role of the Werkbund in an important exhibition during the Third Reich, see Schäfers, *Vom Werkbund*.

25. Foreword by Rudolf Schwarz in Deutscher Werkbund, *Werkbund-Ausstellung Neues Wohnen*, 17–19. In 1952 Rudolf Schwarz published a polemical article that attacked the rigid functionalism of the Bauhaus and Gropius and associated it with Nazi aesthetics, unleashing a heated debate that ultimately helped to establish the Bauhaus's sacred symbolic status in West Germany for decades to come. See Betts, "The Bauhaus"; and Winfried Nerdinger, *Walter Gropius: Architekt der Moderne 1884–1969* (Munich: C. H. Beck, 2019), 332–35.

26. Jupp Ernst, "Die Form aus der Maschine," in Deutscher Werkbund, *Werkbund-Ausstellung Neues Wohnen*, 23–25, 24.

27. Zentek, *Designer im Dritten Reich*, 291–316; Magdalena Droste, "Bauhaus-Designer zwischen Handwerk und Moderne," in Nerdinger, *Bauhaus Moderne*, 85–101; John Heskett, "Art and Design in Nazi Germany," *History Workshop* 6, no. 1 (October 1978): 139–53, 146; Riemann, "Die 'Gute Form,'" 55; and Markus Eisen, "Wilhelm Wagenfeld und Hermann Gretsch," in *100 Jahre Deutscher Werkbund 1907–2007*, ed. Winfried Nerdinger, exhibition catalog (Munich: Prestel, 2007), 206–7.

28. Ernst, "Die Form," 25, English in the original.

29. R.B., "Die Wahrheit der Architektur: Von der Leipziger Bauausstellung zur Constructa, Hannover," *Frankfurter Allgemeine Zeitung*, February 17, 1951, 15.

30. Harold Theile, "137 Wohngeräte wünschen Einheirat," *Frankfurter Allgemeine Zeitung*, August 9, 1951, 3.

31. K., "Abschied vom Makartsträußchen: *Das Haus des deutschen Kunsthandwerks*," *Die Gegenwart*, no. 18 (September 1951): 13–14. The term "founders' years" commonly refers to the years of economic boom right after the unification of Germany in 1871.

32. Edith Nowak, "Von alten Träumen und von neuen Möbeln," *Frankfurter Allgemeine Zeitung*, March 14, 1953, Bilder und Zeiten, 6.

33. Nowak, "Von alten Träumen," 6. Beiderwand is a double-woven cloth that was often used for traditional rural costumes during the nineteenth century.

34. Theodor Heuss, *Was ist Qualität? Zur Geschichte und Aufgabe des Deutschen Werkbundes* (Tübingen: Rainer Wunderlich Verlag Hermann Leins, 1951), 63–66.

35. Helene Rahms, "Die Anmut der strengen Linie," *Frankfurter Allgemeine Zeitung*, July 4, 1953, Bilder und Zeiten, 6.

36. This point was made by Jennifer Jenkins, "The Werkbund Exhibition 'The New Age' of 1932," in *German Modernities from Wilhelm to Weimar*, ed. Geoff Eley, Jennifer Jenkins, and Tracie Matysik (London: Bloomsbury Academic, 2016), 283–300.

37. Campbell, *The German Werkbund*, 231, 234.

38. Sebastian Conrad, *Globalisation and the Nation in Imperial Germany* (Cambridge: Cambridge University Press, 2012), 353–56; Mark Jarzombek, "The 'Kunstgewerbe,' the 'Werkbund,' and the Aesthetics of Culture in the Wilhelmine Period," *Journal of the Society of Architectural Historians* 53, no. 1 (1994): 7–19, 13, 16, 18.

39. Jennifer Jenkins, "The Citizen at Home: *Wohnkultur* before World War I," in *Citizenship and National Identity in Twentieth-Century Germany*, ed. Geoff Eley and Jan Palmowski (Stanford, CA: Stanford University Press, 2008), 95–107, quote 104.

40. Jarzombek, "The 'Kunstgewerbe,'" 14–15, 11.

41. Wolfgang Hardtwig, "Kunst, liberaler Nationalismus und Weltpolitik: Der Deutsche Werkbund 1907 bis 1914," in *Nationalismus und Bürgerkultur in Deutschland 1500–1914*, ed. Wolfgang Hardtwig (Göttingen: Vandenhoeck & Ruprecht, 1994), 246–73, 257.

42. Muthesius is quoted in John Maciuika, *Before the Bauhaus: Architecture, Politics and the German State, 1890–1920* (Cambridge: Cambridge University Press, 2005), 283.

43. Jarzombek, "The 'Kunstgewerbe,'" 15.

44. Katherine Pence quoted in Jennifer L. Jenkins, "Introduction: Domesticity, Design and the Shaping of the Social," *German History* 25, no. 3 (2007): 465–89, here 471.

45. Elise Marie Moentmann, "The Search for French Identity in the Regions: National versus Local Visions of France in the 1930s," *French History* 17, no. 3 (2003): 307–27. See also Anthony King, "Imperialism, Colonialism and Architects of the Arts and Crafts Movement in Britain," in *Spaces of Global Cultures: Architecture, Urbanism, Identity* (London: Routledge, 2004), 161–86. On the complex connections between architectural modernism and colonialism in Germany, see Itohan Osayimwese, *Colonialism and Modern Architecture in Germany* (Pittsburgh, PA: University of Pittsburgh Press, 2017).

46. The good form could thereby develop into an "eternal form," projecting the modern tradition back into a preindustrial past. See Campbell, *The German Werkbund*, 218, 227–28.

47. On the early years of *Innen-Dekoration*, see Maren-Sophie Fünderich, *Wohnen im Kaiserreich: Einrichtungsstil und Möbeldesign im Kontext bürgerlicher Selbstrepräsentation* (Berlin: De Gruyter, 2019), esp. 261–64. The *Journal of the Royal Society of Arts* wrote in 1930 about the magazine that it "reflects faithfully one aspect of the present-day mentality of a typical progressive community" (*Journal of the Royal Society of Arts* 78, no. 4050 [July 1930]: 916).

48. Hermann Gretsch, "Kunst und Kunsthandwerk am Bau," *Innen-Dekoration*, no. 6 (1936): 371–74, here 372–73.

49. Wilhelm Michel, "Raumkunst im Lebensdienst," *Innen-Dekoration*, no. 2 (1940): 52–53, here 53.

50. Betts observes that "West Germany's design culture insisted on grounding design in humanist morality, since this was certainly one ideology that the Nazis disdainfully trampled underfoot" (*The Authority*, 12).

51. H.R., "Haus und Hausrat in der Siedlung," *Innen-Dekoration*, no. 6 (1937): 213–16, here 216; Wilhelm Michel, "Zweckform und Kunstform," *Innen-Dekoration*, no. 6 (1940): 166–68. See also "Die Wohnweise und ihre kulturelle Grundlage," *Innen-Dekoration*, no. 3 (1939): 79–81.

52. Wilhelm Michel, "Wir und die Dinge," *Innen-Dekoration*, no. 6 (1939): 135–36, here 135.

53. Hermann Gretsch, "Deutsches Wohnen," *Innen-Dekoration*, no. 7 (1939): 225–32, here 228, 232; "Ausstellung 'Deutsches Wohnen 1939,'" *Innen-Dekoration*, no. 7 (1939): 233–37.

54. On the "never ending stream of exhibitions" on arts and crafts as well as design during the Third Reich, see Hellmut Lehmann-Haupt, *Art under a Dictatorship* (New York: Oxford University Press, 1954), 131.

55. "Auf dem Weg zu einer neuen Wohnkultur: Stoffe mit dem Zeichen 'DAF Haus und Heim,'" *Arbeitertum*, no. 6, June 15, 1939, 6.

56. "Deutscher Hausrat," *Innen-Dekoration*, no. 5 (1940): 155–56, here 155.

57. The Nazi Party eagle faced to its left, while the otherwise similar state eagle faced to its right. Margarete Myers Feinstein points out that Nazi leaders claimed the Nazi eagle "looked to the east, where Germany's destiny lay" (*State Symbols: The Quest for Legitimacy in the Federal Republic of Germany and the German Democratic Republic, 1949–1959* [Boston: Brill, 2001], 39).

58. Hermann Gretsch, "Deutschland auf der VII. Triennale in Mailand," *Innen-Dekoration*, no. 7 (1940): 191–94, here 194. See also Harvey, *Women*.

59. Wilhelm Michel, "Gedanken über das Schöne," *Innen-Dekoration*, no. 7 (1940): 209–11, here 210–11.

60. Erich Adam, "*Neue Heimat* für viele tausend Deutsche: Das Heimstättenamt der DAF. hilft mit bei ihrer Gestaltung," *Arbeitertum*, no. 8 (July 1940): 4–5.

61. Hans Wolfram Hockl, "Eindrücke aus dem Sowjetparadies," *Südostdeutsche Tageszeitung*, August 14, 1942, 5. See also "Das Deutschtum im Osten," *Der Führer: Das Hauptorgan der NSDAP Gau Baden*, November 26, 1942, 4.

62. "Warschaus Steine erzählen," *Banater Deutsche Zeitung*, October 6, 1939, 4.

63. Quoted in Michaela Kipp, *"Grossreinemachen im Osten": Feindbilder in deutschen Feldpostbriefen im Zweiten Weltkrieg* (Frankfurt am Main: Campus Verlag, 2014), 374.

64. "Ein aufschlussreicher Brief," *Neue Warte am Inn*, March 28, 1945, 2. After the end of the war, German pride in the Allies' recognition of Germany's *Wohnkultur* would continue to articulate itself occasionally, for example, when the *Neue Illustrierte* reported about the "sentimental inclination" of American housewives to "adorn and embellish" their "'German home' with good German objects." See "In Frankfurt wird gehext: Das Wunder-Warenhaus, in dem es alles zu kaufen gibt," *Neue Illustrierte*, no. 2, January 24, 1947, 6–7; "Lebensstandard, hier und drüben," *Die Zeit*, no. 36, October 24, 1946, 7.

65. According to the internal Security Service of the SS, writing in March 1942, the population complained about the danger that the deteriorating quality of artifacts would produce "a confusion of taste that would disturb all the positive efforts by the state and the party to educate the people on the terrain of art" (Heinz Boberach, ed., *Meldungen aus dem Reich: Die geheimen Lageberichte des Sicherheitsdienstes der SS 1938–1945* [Herrsching: Pawlak Verlag, 1984], 9:3476–79, quote 3477–78). Many complaints made use of negative stereotypes such as "trashy goods," "dirty fellows," "bunglers," "rotten elements," and the "contaminated" field of art trade. Lehmann-Haupt concludes from the report that "the people in general accepted the [aesthetic] doctrines and expected to see them lived up to" (*Art under Dictatorship*, 128–29).

66. Campbell, *The German Werkbund*, 285.

67. See Max Fengler, "Alexander Koch," in Deutsche Biographie, accessed November 20, 2022, https://www.deutsche-biographie.de/ppn118967029.html.

68. Hans Eckstein, "Der Weg von 1890 bis heute: Der 'Innen-Dekoration' beim Neubeginn zum Geleit," *Architektur und Wohnform*, no. 1 (1946): 1–3, 3.

69. Alexander Koch, "Die Wohnform von Heute," *Innen-Dekoration*, 1937, editorial of the volume.

70. Alexander Koch, "Zum fünfzigsten Jahrestag," *Innen-Dekoration*, 1939, editorial of the volume.

71. See, for instance, Richard Döcker, "Das verlorene Niveau," *Architektur und Wohnform*, no. 2 (December 1949): 33; E. Schirmer, "Möbel der Neuen Gemeinschaft für Wohnkultur," *Architektur und Wohnform*, no. 2 (December 1949): 46–50.

72. "Anmerkungen zur Zeit," *Baukunst und Werkform*, no. 1 (1947): 3–7.

73. Eckstein, "Der Weg," 3.

74. Marieluise Henniger, "Schwedische Raumkunst," *Architektur und Wohnform*, no. 1/2 (1948): 22; Marieluise Henniger, "Charles Eames," *Architektur und Wohnform*, no. 1/2 (1948): 30; Wera Meyer-Waldeck, "Werkbund-Ausstellung 'Neues Wohnen' Köln 1949," *Architektur und Wohnform*, no. 6 (1949): 121–28.

75. Werner Witthaus, "Ein Bauhaus-Tapeten-Pavillon auf der dwb-Ausstellung in Köln," *Architektur und Wohnform*, no. 6 (1949): 129–32, here 130.

76. "'Werk und Zeit': Neues vom Deutschen Werkbund," *Frankfurter Allgemeine Zeitung*, April 26, 1952, 11.

77. Nowak, "Von alten Träumen."

78. Betts, "The Bauhaus"; Betts, *The Authority*, 139–77.

79. Max Bill, "Vom staatlichen Bauhaus in Weimar zur Hochschule für Gestaltung Ulm," *magnum*, no. 1 (1953): 59–60, here 60.

80. See, for example, "Unser winterlicher Freund," *Das Blatt der Hausfrau* (the precursor of *Brigitte*), no. 2 (1952): 8; "Mein Dachkämmerchen," *Das Blatt der Hausfrau*, no. 11 (1952): 7; "Aus eins mach zwei," *Das Blatt der Hausfrau*, no. 25 (1952): 4–5; "Wohin mit dem Baby?," *Constanze*, no. 2, 2nd number in January, 1951: 30–31; "Größere Fenster bitte!," *Constanze*, 3rd number in April, 1951: 41.

81. "Schnörkelmöbel sind kein Unglück—die Säge schafft's!," *Constanze*, no. 7, 3rd number in March 1954: 88–89; "Guter Rat für junge Ehefrauen: Kein Porzellan zerschlagen!," *Constanze*, no. 14, July 4, 1951, 41.

82. Edina Lettinger-Vogel, "Wer ist Hausfrau?," *Das Blatt der Hausfrau*, no. 18 (1951): 3. See also "Phantasie tapezieren," *Das Blatt der Hausfrau*, no. 6 (1952): 5.

83. For instance, see Schwarzer, "Himmel, wir haben geerbt!," *Brigitte*, no. 4 (1953): 4–5; "Sind Handarbeiten noch modern?," *Brigitte*, no. 23 (1953): 20; "Mut zum Bequemen," *Brigitte*, no. 24 (1953): 6–7; "Sind Esszimmer noch modern?," *Brigitte*, no. 1 (1954): 6–7; "Nicht nur eine Raumfrage: Bett oder Couch?," *Brigitte*, no. 20 (1953): 4–5.

84. "Warum denn so verschnörkelt?," *Constanze*, no. 3, 1st number in February 1953: 48–49. The article equates an artisanal, soil-bound (*bodenverbunden*) style with the Nazi years.

85. See Paula Andersen, "Schönheit der Technik als praktische Aufgabe: Die Stuttgarter Ausstellung 'Schönheit der Technik—die gute Industrieform,'" *Frankfurter Allgemeine Zeitung*, April 18, 1953, Bilder und Zeiten, 4; "Aus dem Passauer Kulturleben / Rokoko aus Leichtmetall," *Passauer Neue Presse*, January 19, 1952, 7; Herbert Hofmann, "Die transportable Wand: Neue Möbel populär gemacht," *Die Zeit*, no. 32, August 7, 1952, https://www.zeit.de/1952/32/die-transportable-wand; Helene Rahms, "Die Anmut der strengen Linie," *Frankfurter Allgemeine Zeitung*, July 4, 1953, Bilder und Zeiten, 6.

86. "Versuchen Sie es doch mal schräg," *Brigitte*, no. 11 (May 1954): 8–9.

87. See several articles by Gay McDonald: "Selling the American Dream: MoMA, Industrial Design and Post-war France," *Journal of Design History* 17, no. 4 (2004): 397–412; "The Modern American Home as Soft Power: Finland, MoMA and the 'American Home 1953,'" *Journal of Design History* 23, no. 3 (2010): 387–408; "The 'Advance' of American Postwar Design in Europe: MoMA and the Design for Use, USA Exhibition 1951–1953," *Design Issues* 24, no. 2 (2008): 15–27.

88. "Hier wohnt man ideal!," *Constanze*, no. 25, December 3, 1952, 72–73.

89. Quoted in Castillo, "Domesticating the Cold War," 271–72. On the positive reception of Bauhaus by the MoMA in 1938, see Gregor Langfeld, *German Art in New York: The Canonization of Modern Art 1904–1957*, trans. Steven Lindberg (Amsterdam: Amsterdam University Press, 2011), 111–16.

90. Godo Remszhardt, "Neues Bauen in den USA," *Baukunst und Werkform*, July 1951, 50–52, here 51.

91. Quoted in Castillo, *Cold War*, 67, emphasis added.

92. In comparison: the German Architecture and Applied Arts exhibitions in the House of German Art in Munich in 1938 and 1939 attracted 260,000 and 295,000 visitors,

respectively. See Despina Stratigakos, *Hitler at Home* (New Haven, CT: Yale University Press, 2017), 189.

93. Quoted in Greg Castillo, "East as True West: Redeeming Bourgeois Culture; From Socialist Realism to *Ostalgie*," in *Imagining the West in Eastern Europe and the Soviet Union*, ed. György Péteri (Pittsburgh, PA: University of Pittsburgh Press, 2010), 87–104, here 91, emphasis added.

94. Alfons Leitl, "Die Wohnkultur der westlichen Völker," *Baukunst und Werkform*, no. 12 (December 1952): 39–41.

95. Ernst, "Die Form," 25.

96. Guido Harbers, *Die schöne Wohnung*, 6th ed. (Munich: F. Bruckmann, 1952), 5. On Harbers and Ramersdorf, see Ulrike Haerendel, *Kommunale Wohnungspolitik im Dritten Reich: Siedlungsideologie, Kleinhausbau und "Wohnraumarisierung" am Beispiel Münchens* (Munich: R. Oldenbourg Verlag, 1999), 71–79, 251–64, 429–30.

97. Heinrich Lützeler and Marga Lützeler, *Unser Heim* (Bonn: Verlag der Buchgemeinde, 1939), with subsequent editions in 1940, 1942 (fifty thousand copies), 1950 (sixty thousand copies), and 1953.

98. Lützeler and Lützeler, *Unser Heim*, 2nd ed. (1940), 6.

99. Lützeler and Lützeler, *Unser Heim*, 2nd ed. (1940), 7, 268.

100. Heinrich Lützeler and Marga Lützeler, *Unser Heim*, 4th ed. (1950), 5–7.

101. Betts, *The Authority*, 139–211; Paulmann, "Representation"; Castillo, *Cold War*; Castillo, "Making a Spectacle;" Christopher Oestereich, "Umstrittene Selbstdarstellung: Der deutsche Beitrag zur Weltausstellung in Brüssel," *Vierteljahrshefte für Zeitgeschichte* 48, no. 1 (January 2000): 127–53. Quote in Jane Pavitt, "Design and the Democratic Ideal," in Crowley and Pavitt, *Cold War Modern*, 73–93, 85.

102. "Deutsche WK-Möbel im deutschen Heim." See ads in *die neue linie*, no. 9 (May 1935): 48, no. 10 (June 1935): 46, no. 11 (July 1935) 43. See also Hans Wichmann, *Deutsche Werkstätten und WK-Verband: Aufbruch zum neuen Wohnen* (Munich: Prestel, 1992).

103. "Die Möbel wachsen mit," *Das Blatt der Hausfrau*, no. 26 (1952): 4–5; and "WK Sozialwerk Möbel 40 Jahre" (advertisement), *Das Blatt der Hausfrau*, no. 26 (1952): 19.

104. Wilhelm Michel, "Möbel der deutschen Werkstätten," *Innen-Dekoration*, no. 6 (1936): 178–83; Ellie Tschauner, "Zimmer unter 500 Mark: 'WK'-Möbel. Mit dem Gütezeichen des Reichsheimstättenamtes," *Innen-Dekoration*, no. 2 (1939): 54–61; Tschauner, "Zum Sieg der Guten Form."

105. Käte Brandel-Elschner, "Neue Arbeiten der deutschen Werkstätten," *Innen-Dekoration*, no. 2 (1937): 87–91, here 91.

106. Advertisements "Deutsche Werkstätten A.G., Hellerau," *die neue linie*, no. 3 (November 1938): 54, and no. 5 (January 1939): 103.

107. "Ich bin so glücklich!," *Constanze*, no. 24, November 2, 1953, 28–29.

108. In an official Nazi publication about appropriately "beautiful" household items for the German home, this capacity for banality becomes apparent in the fact that explicit Nazi symbols only appeared very inconspicuously on three of the many photographs and drawings: a framed photo of Hitler on a drawer, a bust of Hitler on a bookcase, and a framed photo of Hitler on the wall of a living room. See Reichsheimstättenamt der

Deutschen Arbeitsfront (Imperial Bureau of Homesteads of the German Labor Front), *Schönheit des Wohnens: Ein Bildwerk über deutsche Wohnmöbel* (Freiburg im Breisgau: Karl Popp Verlag, [1941]), unpaginated. In 1948 a new edition was published stripped of the 1941 edition's three political prefaces and without these explicit Nazi symbols. See August Großkinsky, comp., *Schönheit des Wohnens*, 2nd ed. (Freiburg: Otto Kehrer, 1948).

109. Brockhaus, *Schauder und Idylle*, 32. On the interior of Hitler's homes and propaganda about them during the Third Reich, see Stratigakos, *Hitler at Home*.

110. "Wie schnell wandelt sich der Geschmack? Der Weg zur modernen Innenausstattung," press release of the opinion research institute Allensbach, March 23, 1959; Elisabeth Noelle and Erich Peter Neumann, *Jahrbuch der öffentlichen Meinung, 1947–1955* (Allensbach: Verlag für Demoskopie, 1955), 110–11; Elisabeth Noelle and Erich Peter Neumann, *Jahrbuch der öffentlichen Meinung, 1958–1964* (Allensbach: Verlag für Demoskopie, 1965), 176–77.

111. Hans Makart was a nineteenth-century painter, designer, and decorator. On Makart and the well-known interior of his atelier, see Klaus R. Scherpe, "Der Orient im Interieur," in *Mit Deutschland um die Welt: Eine Kulturgeschichte des Fremden in der Kolonialzeit*, ed. Alexander Honold and Klaus R. Scherpe (Stuttgart: Metzler, 2004), 329–37, 335–36.

112. "Wie schnell wandelt sich," 3.

113. "Weg von Tante Frieda—Möbel—Stil," *Der Spiegel*, no. 39, September 26, 1951, 32–33.

114. See Oestereich, *"Gute Form" im Wiederaufbau*, 340–57.

115. "Weg von Tante Frieda."

116. Marlies Flesch-Thebesius, "Die Architekten und die Löwenklauen: Zeitgemäßes zur Wohnkultur," *Frankfurter Allgemeine Zeitung*, February 10, 1951, 9.

117. Oestereich, *"Gute Form" im Wiederaufbau*, 347.

118. "Lilo Aureden sagt JA zum Thema: Neubauwohnungen—fertig möbliert," *Brigitte*, no. 10 (1953), unpaginated.

119. Barbara Reichek-Hopf, "Sozial—zeitgemäß—formschön," *Die Zeit*, no. 53, December 31, 1953, https://www.zeit.de/1953/53/sozial-zeitgemaess-formschoen.

120. *Schönheit des Wohnens: Ein Bildwerk* [1941], unpaginated.

121. *Der Spiegel*, for instance, reported that Wilhelm Wagenfeld had "purified" the Lusitanian glass plants in 1936 from turn-of-the-century kitsch. It is unclear, however, if the use of the verb "purify," (*säubern*) which could be associated with "racial purification," was a form of subliminal critique. "Industrie—Form: Lochstickerei in Porzellan," *Der Spiegel*, no. 30, July 22, 1953, 30–31, here 30.

122. Eva Noack-Mosse, "Sie formen unseren Lebensstil," *Brigitte*, no. 11 (May 1955): 10–11 (Ernest Igl), no. 14 (June 1955): 12 (Heinz Löffelhardt), no. 15 (July 1955): 10–11 (Wilhelm Wagenfeld), no. 16 (July 1955): 10–11 (Trude Petri-Raben). In Petri-Raben's case, the "life story" only starts after the war, when she moved to the United States with her husband, thereby emphasizing the international character of her work and avoiding any reference to the Nazi past, even though her porcelain design "Urbino" had become "an icon of Nazi home culture," according to Michael Lingohr. Lingohr also mentions that

Löffelhardt's designs had been integrated into the Nazi aesthetic programs. See "Die letzte ideologische Bastion?," 107, 110.

123. Eva Noack-Mosse, "Sie formen unseren Lebensstil," *Brigitte*, no. 17 (August 1955): 14–15.

124. Her memories were recently published. See Eva Noack-Mosse, *Last Days of Theresienstadt*, trans. Skye Doney and Biruté Ciplijauskaité (Madison: University of Wisconsin Press, 2018).

125. Lingohr, "Die letzte ideologische Bastion?," passim.

126. Heskett, "Art and Design," 146; Hermann Gretsch, "Deutschland auf der VII. Triennale in Mailand," *Innen-Dekoration*, no. 7 (1940): 190–94.

127. "Modelle de Optimismus," *magnum*, no. 4 (1954): 57–69, quotation 59. A confusing criticism of modern design that associates its dominance with monarchic reigns of the past also appears in "Modern ohne Dienstvorschrift," *magnum*, no. 15 (December 1957): 16.

128. Barthes, *Mythologies*, 128.

129. Helene Rahms, "'Gestaltung' und kein Ende: Anmerkungen zum internationalen Kongreß der Industrie-Entwerfer," *Frankfurter Allgemeine Zeitung*, October 4, 1957, 14.

130. *Quick* was one of the biggest illustrated magazines of the time and sold 678,661 copies in 1954. See Horst Holzer, "Selbstverständnis und Inhaltsstruktur aktueller Illustrierten dargestellt an den Zeitschriften *Quick*, *Revue* und *Stern*" (PhD diss., Munich, 1966), ii. Some *Quick* articles on modern architecture: "Das Eigenheim der Vereinten Nationen," *Quick*, no. 38, September 21, 1952, 4; "Moderne Großzügigkeit und Würde!," *Quick*, no. 43, October 26, 1952, 11; "Für deutsche Studenten in Paris," *Quick*, no. 45, November 8, 1953, 11; "Kirche aus dem Betonbaukasten," *Quick*, no. 2, January 10, 1954, 26–27; "Nehru baut seine Hauptstadt," *Quick*, no. 3, January 17, 1954, 32–33; "Aus Kassel," *Quick*, no. 23, June 6, 1954, 4; "In Köln: Deutschlands modernstes Opernhaus," *Quick*, no. 43, October 24, 1954, 3; "Konzert in Beton: Ein Neubau in Berlin," *Quick*, no. 28, July 9, 1955, 12; "Der Bundestag als Gast zu Haus—der Berliner Volksmund," *Quick*, no. 42, October 19, 1957, 11.

131. "Die billigste Wand: Der Schrank," *Quick*, no. 31, August 3, 1952, 10; "Weshalb nicht einfach, wenn es geht . . . ," *Quick*, no. 36, September 5, 1954, 12. Modern American interiors appear in "Das Haus mit den wandernden Wänden," *Quick*, no. 35, August 27, 1950, 1158; "Bei uns geht es rund!," *Quick*, no. 11, March 15, 1953, 47; "Tisch mit zwei Stockwerken . . . ," no. 37, September 12, 1954, 43; "Ohne Nagel und Schraube," *Quick*, no. 31, August 3, 1957, 8. The magazine only twice reported positively on examples of modern design, but exclusively in the context of modern art: "Die Bilder sind abstrakt, die Möbel sind's beinahe!" (an article on an exhibition of both modern art and modern design in Munich's Haus der Kunst), *Quick*, no. 30, July 27, 1952, 10; "Abstrakte Japankunst!," *Quick*, no. 3, January 18, 1953, 29.

132. "In Berlin: Interbau," *Quick*, no. 27, July 6, 1957, 8–9; "Die Luxuswohnung für jedermann," *Der Stern*, no. 15, April 23, 1957, 6–9.

133. Paul Betts, "The Nierentisch Nemesis: Organic Design as West German Pop Culture," *German History* 19, no. 2 (2001): 185–217.

134. "Moderne Möbel: Nicht erfunden aber getreulich nachgezeichnet von Peter Großkreuz," *Quick*, no. 7, February 15, 1953, 40. See also "Der Tisch mit der Glasplatte" (cartoon), *Quick*, no. 7, February 12, 1955, 43; "Wo verstecken wir bloß die Eier?" (cartoon), *Quick*, no. 15, April 9, 1955, 58; "Weißt du Johnny, am Lokal kann's nicht liegen" (cartoon), *Quick*, no. 24, June 11, 1955, 48.

135. "Otto . . . ich flehe dich an, nimm wenigstens ein Glas!" (cartoon), *Quick*, no. 30, July 25, 1954, 19. See also "Mein Kater Negus" (cartoon), *Quick*, no. 10, March 5, 1955, 56. Similar cartoons already existed during the Weimar Republic. See an example in *Allemagne / Années 920 / Nouvelle Objectivité / August Sander*, exhibition at the Centre Pompidou, Paris, May 11–September 5, 2022.

136. "Das sage ich dir: Deine veraltete Erziehungsmethode paßt keineswegs in das moderne Milieu . . ." (cartoon by Leo von Malachowski), *Quick*, no. 36, September 5, 1954, 52.

137. "Wie modern sind wir eigentlich?," *Brigitte*, no. 6 (March 1954): 4–6.

138. "Warum denn so verschnörkelt?," *Constanze*, no. 3, 1st number in February 1953: 48–49; "Blick nach innen," *Constanze*, no. 14, 1st number in July, 1953: 56–57; "Wunschhaus wurde Wirklichkeit," *Constanze*, no. 16, 3rd number in July, 1954: 90–91; "'Schöner Wohnen,' das neue Constanze Sonderheft," *Constanze*, no. 7, March 23, 1955, 112–13; "Ein Traum wird wahr: Wir richten uns neu ein!," *Constanze*, no. 11, May 18, 1955, 124–25; "Eine Frau zog in eine alte Villa, denn sie hatte—keine Angst vor unmodernen Wohnungen," *Constanze*, no. 26, December 14, 1955, 122–23. All emphasis added.

139. "Mein Heim ist meine Welt" (advertisement for Continental Schaum), *Constanze*, no. 13, June 15, 1955, 63. The same ad appeared also in *Quick*.

140. See "Fakir" (cleaning product advertisement), *Constanze*, no. 20, September 21, 1955, 100, and no. 24, November 15, 1955, 114.

141. Some examples: "Sie ist zufrieden" (Bemberg Marquisette curtains advertisement), *Constanze*, no. 7, March 23, 1955, 66; "Der Punkt auf dem I" (Wehra carpets advertisement), *Brigitte*, no. 5 (February 1958): 36; "Die gute alte Zeit hat ihre Tücken" (Dunlopillo mattresses advertisement), *Constanze*, no. 21, October 5, 1955, 88, and *Quick*, no. 30, July 23, 1955, 29; "Hier fühlt man sich wohl" (Zellwolle advertisement), *Brigitte*, no. 22 (October 1956): 45; "Moderne Wohnkultur" (Progress vacuum cleaner advertisement), *Brigitte*, no. 6 (1953): 7; "Bellinda" (stockings advertisement), *Constanze*, no. 8, April 6, 1955, 111; Triumph portable typewriter advertisement, *Constanze*, no. 2, January 21, 1959, 47; "Für fortschrittliche Hausfrauen—Rondo Waschautomat," *Constanze*, no. 10, May 2, 1956, 147; Telefunken television advertisement, *Constanze*, no. 24, November 26, 1958, 62; "Alles strahlt im Festtagsglanz—Pril" (detergent advertisement), *Constanze*, no. 26, December 12, 1956, 7; "Die neue Camelia" (sanitary towels advertisement), *Constanze*, no. 21, October 14, 1959, 35; "Libby's Kondensmilch" (condensed milk advertisement), *Constanze*, no. 24, November 25, 1959, 15; "Bei dir schmeckt der Kaffee immer am besten" (Nescafé advertisement), *Quick*, no. 50, December 14, 1957, 71.

142. "Bereits jede 3. Frau wünscht sich eine helle und moderne Wohnung" (Braun radio and TV set advertisement), *Constanze*, no. 20, September 21, 1955, 139. See also *Brigitte*, no. 21 (October 1955): 47.

143. Noelle and Neumann, *Jahrbuch der öffentlichen Meinung, 1947–1955*, 110–11; Elisabeth Noelle and Erich Peter Neumann, *Jahrbuch der öffentlichen Meinung, 1957* (Allensbach: Verlag für Demoskopie, 1957), 108–9.

144. Carter, *How German Is She?*, 158–70.

145. Laura Dekker has exposed this development in "Niet gelijk, wel gelijkwaardig?" (master's thesis, University of Amsterdam, 2017).

146. Carter, *How German Is She?*, 37 and 1–106.

147. The argument for modern furnishing to allow a rationalized form of housework was most convincing regarding the kitchen. From early 1952 *Constanze* promoted both the technically and the aesthetically modern in the kitchen as the epitome of a rational household, which included discarding the traditional kitchen buffet—"Away with the overly embellished buffet!"—as the epitome of the outdated household. "Raus mit dem Schnörkelbuffet," *Constanze*, no. 9, April 23, 1952, 56–57.

148. Carter, *How German Is She?*, 15.

149. The following analysis is based on Musterring advertisements that appeared in *Constanze*, *Quick*, and *Der Stern*.

150. "Wie wohnen diese jungen Damen?," *Constanze*, no. 7, 3rd number in March 1954; "Damit macht das Wohnen Spaß! Das große Wohn-Preisausschreiben" *Constanze*, no. 8, 1st number in April 1954: 19–23.

151. Musterring advertisements published in *Constanze* and *Quick* in 1954 and 1955.

152. "Nie braucht sie auf ihn zu warten . . ." (Musterring advertisement), *Quick*, no. 9, February 26, 1955, 28.

153. "Wie lange sind sie schon verheiratet?" (Musterring advertisement), *Constanze*, no. 8, April 4, 1956, 83.

154. "Der schönste Abend—der Feierabend" (Musterring advertisement), *Quick*, no. 37, September 14, 1957, 39. See also "40 Minuten Aufenthalt . . ." (Musterring advertisement), *Der Stern*, no. 9, March 2, 1957, 33.

155. See, for instance, "Alle Männer: Bitte mal herhören!" (Musterring advertisement), *Quick*, no. 14, April 7, 1956, 58.

156. "Nach 7 Jahren—und noch keine Ehekrise . . ." (Musterring advertisement), *Quick*, no. 20, May 19, 1956, 58. See also "Ein Tip für Ehefrauen . . ." (Musterring advertisement), *Quick*, no. 35, September 1, 1956, 44; "Familienleben mit verteilten Rollen . . ." (Musterring advertisement), *Constanze*, no. 16, August 6, 1958, 45.

157. Uta G. Poiger, "American Music, Cold War Liberalism, and German Identities," in *Transactions, Transgressions, Transformations: American Culture in Western Europe and Japan*, ed. Uta G. Poiger and Heide Fehrenbach (New York: Berghahn Books, 2000), 127–47; see also Poiger, *Jazz, Rock and Rebels*, chap. 2.

158. "My home is my castle . . ." (Musterring advertisement), *Constanze*, no. 21, October 31, 1956, 127.

159. "Die Freude hat viele Gesichter . . ." (Musterring advertisement), *Constanze*, no. 5, 2nd number in February, 1957: 81; see also a version of this ad with a different photograph of only one jazz musician in *Quick*, no. 46, November 16, 1957, 51.

160. See, for example, "Der schönste Abend—der Feierabend" (Musterring advertisement), *Quick*, no. 37, September 14, 1957, 39; "40 Minuten Aufenthalt . . ." (Musterring advertisement), *Der Stern*, no. 9, March 2, 1957, 33.

161. Chapter 4 of this book addresses in more detail the exclusion of racial or exotic Others with respect to redeeming objects.

162. Bernhard Groß, *Die Filme sind unter uns: Zur Geschichtlichkeit des frühen deutschen Nachkriegskinos; Trümmer-, Genre-, Dokumentarfilm* (Berlin: Vorwerk 8, 2015), 421–23.

163. *Eine Frau von heute*, West Germany, 1954, directed by Paul Verhoeven, Fama F.A. Mainz Film.

Chapter 4. Expanding Objects

1. Later, the film was also circulated under the title *Auf Wiedersehen, Franziska!*, West Germany, 1957, directed by Wolfgang Liebeneiner, CCC Filmkunst.

2. The term "consumer's republic" was introduced by Lizabeth Cohen, *A Consumer's Republic: The Politics of Mass Consumption in Postwar America* (New York: Knopf, 2003).

3. Homi Bhabha, "The World and the Home," *Social Text*, no. 31/32 (1992): 141–53, here 141.

4. Bhabha, "The World," 147.

5. *Auf Wiedersehen, Franziska!*, Germany, 1941, directed by Helmut Käutner, Terra-Filmkunst GmbH. According to the *Deutsche Tagespost* from 1957, the first *Franziska* film was "*the* success of the year 1941" ("Auf Wiedersehen, Franziska: Ruth Leuwerik auf Marianne Hoppes spuren ihr Partner Carlos Thompson," *Deutsche Tagespost*, June 14, 1957). See also "Eine Liebesgeschichte: 'Franziska,'" *Kasseler Zeitung*, October 12, 1957. All the reviews are archived in the file "Auf Wiedersehen, Franziska!," Presseecho, Artur Brauner Archive, Deutsches Filminstitut e.V., Frankfurt am Main. *Goodbye, Franziska!* still played in some cinemas of the Third Reich as late as January 1945. See "Nachrichten aus den Kreisgebieten," *Der Führer: Hauptorgan der NSDAP Gau Baden*, no. 17, January 20, 1945, 3.

6. Remakes made up 10 percent of West German cinema production during the 1950s, more than in any other period. Two-thirds of these postwar remakes' predecessor films were produced in the prewar Nazi era. See Stefanie Mathilde Frank, *Wiedersehen im Wirtschaftswunder: Remakes von Filmen aus der Zeit des Nationalsozialismus in der Bundesrepublik 1949–1963* (Göttingen: Vandenhoeck & Ruprecht, 2017).

7. Franzis Courtade and Pierre Cadars, *Geschichte des Films im Dritten Reich* (Munich: Carl Hanser Verlag, 1975), 213–14; and Manfred Hobsch, *Film im "Dritten Reich": Alle deutschen Spielfilme von 1933 bis 1945* (Berlin: Schwarzkopf & Schwarzkopf Verlag, 2010), 1:185.

8. On the social housing project, see Haerendel, *Kommunale Wohnungspolitik*, 408–12.

9. Volker Berghahn, "German Colonialism and Imperialism from Bismarck to Hitler," *German Studies Review* 40, no. 1 (2017): 147–62; and Uta Poiger, "Imperialism and Empire in Twentieth-Century Germany," *History & Memory* 17, no. 1/2 (2005): 117–43.

10. Alastair Bonnett, *The Idea of the West: Culture, Politics, and History* (Houndmills: Palgrave Macmillan, 2004), 14–39; Christopher L. Gogwilt, *The Invention of the West: Joseph Conrad and the Double-Mapping of Europe and Empire* (Stanford, CA: Stanford University Press, 1995), 220–42.

11. Robert J. C. Young, "The Postcolonial Condition," in *The Oxford Handbook of Postwar European History*, ed. Dan Stone (Oxford: Oxford University Press, 2012), 600–611, quotes 604. On how the intricacies of the long decolonization process marked the postwar period in Europe, see Elizabeth Buettner, *Europe after Empire: Decolonization, Society, and Culture* (Cambridge: Cambridge University Press, 2016).

12. Hall, *Familiar Stranger*, 24.

13. In 2005 Uta Poiger called for such a perspective on consumer culture with respect to German history. See Poiger, "Imperialism and Empire," esp. 118, 134–37. See also Cristina Lombardi-Diop, "Spotless Italy: Hygiene, Domesticity, and the Ubiquity of Whiteness in Fascist and Postwar Consumer Culture," *California Italian Studies* 2, no. 1 (2011), https://escholarship.org/uc/item/8vt6rovf.

14. An inspiring exception is Ross, *Fast Cars*.

15. See, for instance, Ruth Benedict, *Race: Science and Politics* (New York: Viking Press, 1945).

16. Wulf D. Hundt, *Wie die Deutschen weiss wurden: Kleine (Heimat)Geschichte des Rassismus* (Stuttgart: J. B. Metzler Verlag, 2017), 149–66.

17. Dienke Hondius, *Blackness in Western Europe: Racial Patterns of Paternalism and Exclusion* (London: Routledge, 2014), 267–71, quote 255.

18. Betts, *Ruin and Renewal*, 223–66.

19. Jason Verber, "The Conundrum of Colonialism in Postwar Germany" (PhD diss., University of Iowa, 2010), 37–38.

20. Poiger, *Jazz, Rock and Rebels*, 71–105.

21. Maria Höhn, *GIs and Fräuleins: The German-American Encounter in 1950s West Germany* (Chapel Hill: University of North Carolina Press, 2002), 198–222, here 222.

22. In Käutner's archive at the Berlin Academy of Arts, two scripts are filed as "reconstructed version of 1956." One of these two is in fact the original. See Käutner archive, Akademie der Künste, Berlin, "reconstructed version of 1956" under the signature Käutner 4 (the original) and Käutner 3 (the reworked version). In a letter to Artur Brauner, Käutner mentioned that he had a copy of "the new version of the script" at his disposal. Helmut Käutner to Artur Brauner, April 2, 1957, Artur Brauner Archive.

23. Hobsch, *Film im "Dritten Reich,"* 1:181. In an argument with Brauner's company about the rights to the script, Käutner claimed that "due to the war" he was forced to put in certain scenes, but that he intentionally cut them into the film in a way that would make them easy to remove later. He allegedly removed these scenes himself after the war for a version that "was shown for a short time in 1946" (Helmet Käutner Archive 2815, Akademie der Künste, Berlin). This contradicts the censorship by the Allies. The film was shown, however, in Austrian cinemas in 1946. See the database ANNO Historical Newspaper and Magazines, Austrian National Library.

24. "Auf Wiedersehen, Franziska!," *Filmwelt*, no. 21 (1941). See also Hansjürgen Wille, "Auf Wiedersehen, Franziska! Helmut Käutner's neuer Film mit Marianne Hoppe und Hans Söhnker," *Filmwelt*, no. 1 (1941). Both reviews are archived in the file Filmdokumentation 948, Akademie der Künste, Berlin.

25. Emi Ehm, "Auf Wiedersehen, Franziska!," *Völkischer Beobachter*, Vienna edition, May 17, 1941, 4.

26. Ingrid Binné, "Die monatliche Filmschau," *NS Frauen-Warte* 10, no. 1 (1941): 14.

27. Georg Herzberg, "Auf Wiedersehen, Franziska!," *Film-Echo*, July 10, 1954; and "Auf Wiedersehen, Franziska!," *Die Filmwoche*, July 24, 1954, Käutner Archive 43.

28. This stands in contrast to Frank's observation that from 1957 onward, the original or predecessor films of remakes were only rarely mentioned in reviews. See *Auf Wiedersehen*, 56.

29. Sarah Ahmed, "Affective Economies," *Social Text* 22, no. 2 (2004): 117–39, 119.

30. On the view of film as artwork, see Frank, *Auf Wiedersehen*, 58.

31. "Franziska," *Fränkisches Volksblatt*, October 25, 1957; "Auf Wiedersehen, Franziska!," Presseecho, Brauner Archive.

32. That *Goodbye, Franziska!* gave the aesthetic of the home an important place too was never mentioned in any of the reviews I studied, neither in 1941 nor afterward.

33. Sabina Lietzmann, "Wohnen im fließenden Raum: Impressionen von der Interbau in Berlin," *Frankfurter Allgemeine Zeitung*, July 25, 1957, 11–13; "Architektur. Interbau. Heiliger Otto," *Der Spiegel*, no. 48, July 31, 1957, 48–53.

34. "Das Brigitte-Zimmer," *Brigitte*, no. 13 (June 1957): 70–71.

35. "Das Brigitte-Zimmer," *Brigitte*, no. 15 (July 1957): 70–71. See also "Das Brigitte-Zimmer: Wir essen auf der Diele," *Brigitte*, no. 5 (February 1958): 62–63.

36. Deutscher Werkbund Berlin, ed., *Wohnen in unserer Zeit: Wohungsgestaltung der Interbau*, published on the occasion of Interbau Berlin 57 (Darmstadt: Verlag Das Beispiel, 1957), 2–3.

37. Thompson had appeared in *Fort Algiers* (United States, 1953), about a rebellion of tribal leaders in Northwest Africa, and in *Valley of the King* (United States, 1954), an archaeologist's adventure in Egypt. Both films were also released in West Germany. See www.imdb.com (accessed November 2022).

38. Bodo Kochanowski, "Schöner Mann aus Argentinien: Carlos Thompson erobert den deutschen Film," *Bella*, June 17, 1957; "Auf Wiedersehen, Ruth! 'Franziska' Leuwerik in einer starken Frauenrolle neben Carlos Thompson," *Star-Revue*, May 28, 1957; "Guter Reporter schlechter Ehemann," *Fränkische Landeszeitung*, June 15, 1957; "Franziska," *Rheinische Post*, September 7, 1957; "Franziska" (CCC/Gloria), *Film-Telegramm*, September 24, 1957; "Die Filmkritik: 'Franziska,'" *Taunusbote*, September 30, 1957. All articles are archived in the file "Auf Wiedersehen, Franziska!," Presseecho, Brauner Archive.

39. The category of "Volksdeutsche" was introduced by the Nazis to replace the former concept of "Auslandsdeutsche." "Carlos Thompson erobert den deutschen Film: Autor, Star und Produzent zugleich," Gloria Film Pressemappe Franziska, Brauner Archive. This perception of Thompson did not strongly influence the press coverage, yet it was mentioned in Kochanowski, "Schöner Mann aus Argentinien." The Berlin newspaper *Der Tag*

even transformed Thompson into an "Argentinian of German descent." See "Ein Mann und viele Pläne: Blick ins Atelier," *Der Tag*, May 12, 1957; "Auf Wiedersehen, Franziska!," Presseecho, Brauner Archive.

40. Bradley D. Naranch, "Inventing the *Auslandsdeutsche*: Emigration, Colonial Fantasy, and German National Identity, 1848–71," in *Germany's Colonial Pasts*, ed. Eric Ames, Marcia Klotz, and Lora Wildenthal (Lincoln: University of Nebraska Press, 2005), 21–40, here 27.

41. See the analysis by Robert C. Reimer, "Turning Inward: An Analysis of Helmut Käutner's *Auf Wiedersehen, Franziska, Romanze in Moll*, and *Unter den Brücken*," in *Cultural History through a National Socialist Lens: Essays on the Cinema of the Third Reich*, ed. Robert C. Reimer (Rochester, NY: Camden House, 2000), 214–39, here 215–21.

42. Reimer, "Turning Inward," 218. See the screenplay "Auf Wiedersehen, Franziska!," 163, Käutner Archive 4.

43. Screenplay "Auf Wiedersehen, Franziska!," 49, Käutner Archive 4.

44. Gisela Huve, "Zwei Welten," *Filmblätter*, May 10, 1957; "Auf Wiedersehen, Franziska!," Presseecho, Brauner Archive. This is the only article that includes Franziska's professional activity as a jewelry designer in an appreciative way.

45. Heinrich Heining, *Auf Wiedersehen, Franziska!* (Berlin: Ufa-Buchverlag G.m.b.H., n.d.).

46. Heining, *Auf Wiedersehen, Franziska!*, 94–95, 102, 104, 106, 107.

47. Nazi ideas on *Wohnkultur* were also disseminated in documentary films: *Aus gutem Holz*, Germany, 1938, Döring-Film; *Alltag in einer Siedlung*, Germany, 1942, Abteilung Film Propagandaamt der Deutschen Arbeitsfront; *Heimat und Boden*, Germany, 1942, Reichsheimstättenamt. Käutner included detailed descriptions of the sets in his screenplay. He had studied interior design in the 1920s and focused on it again during the Third Reich. Willibald Eser, *Helmut Käutner "Abblenden": Sein Leben, seine Filme* (Munich: Moewig, 1981), 8, 20.

48. Quote by Ehm, "Auf Wiedersehen, Franziska!"

49. Wilhelm Michel, "Vom 'Stil' und was damit zusammenhängt," *Innen-Dekoration*, no. 12 (1938): 404.

50. Twenty-two architects were German, two were Austrian, one was Swiss, four came from Scandinavian countries (Denmark, Sweden, Finland), one came from the Netherlands, two came from France, one came from Italy, Oscar Niemeyer came from Brazil, and Walter Gropius came from the United States. Among the interior designers, eighteen were German, eight were Swedish, one came from Finland, one came from Denmark, four came from Switzerland, and one team came from France. See Deutscher Werkbund Berlin, *Wohnen in unserer Zeit*, 81.

51. Deutscher Werkbund Berlin, *Wohnen in unserer Zeit*, 2–3.

52. Deutscher Werkbund Berlin, *Wohnen in unserer Zeit*, 6–9.

53. "Wieso modern," *magnum*, no. 1 (1953): 25–26.

54. A Germanic emphasis found its way into the captions by presenting Richard Neutra, an American citizen of Jewish Austrian descent, as "the Austrian architect in the USA" ("Wieso modern," 7).

55. Theodor Heuss, "Notizen und Exkurse zur Geschichte des Deutschen Werkbundes," in *50 Jahre Deutscher Werkbund*, ed. on behalf of the German Werkbund by the Landesgruppe Hessen (Berlin: Alfred Metzner Verlag, 1958), 19–26, 25.

56. Alexander Koch, *Praktisch Bauen + schön Wohnen = glücklich Leben* (Stuttgart: Alexander Koch, 1955), 46. Alexander Koch senior had passed away in 1939.

57. On the "ideal home" in the context of segregating South Africa, see Alta Steenkamp, "The Ideal Homes Competitions of the 1930's: Architectural Setting for a South African White Middle-Class," *Home Cultures* 16, no. 2 (2019): 95–108.

58. Rosemarie K. Lester, *"Trivialneger": Das Bild der Schwarzen in westdeutschen Illustrierten* (Stuttgart: Akademischer Verlag Hans-Dieter Heinz, 1982), 193.

59. Monika Albrecht, *"Europa ist nicht die Welt": (Post)Kolonialismus in Literatur und Geschichte der westdeutschen Nachkriegszeit* (Bielefeld: Aisthesis Verlag, 2008), 109–15. On the international criticism, see Verber, "The Conundrum," 194.

60. "Wer hat Angst vorm schwarzen Mann?," *Der Spiegel*, no. 49, December 1, 1954, 29–38, 33–34. It is astonishing that Albrecht overlooked this cover story and maintains that nothing like the "solidarity with the white Africans" is to be found in *Der Spiegel*'s reporting. See *"Europa ist nicht die Welt,"* 109–14.

61. Dianne Harris, *Little White Houses: How the Postwar Home Constructed Race in America* (Minneapolis: University of Minnesota Press, 2013). On racial segregation as part of the postwar move to the suburbs in the United States, see Cohen, *A Consumer's Republic*, 194–256.

62. Greg Castillo, "Marshall Plan Modernism in Divided Germany," in Crowley and Pavitt, *Cold War Modern*, 66–71, 67.

63. "Raus mit dem Schnörkelbuffet," *Constanze*, no. 9, April 23, 1952, 56–57; E. L.-V., "Die Wirtschaft im Dienste der Hausfrau," *Das Blatt der Hausfrau* (later *Brigitte*), no. 16 (1952): 18, 21; "Revolution der Sessel und Stühle: Sitzen Sie bitte bequem!," *Constanze*, no. 11, May 21, 1952, 56–57; "Blick nach innen," *Constanze*, no. 14, 1st number in July, 1953: 56–57; "Auf einen Nenner gebracht: Traum und Wirklichkeit," *Brigitte*, no. 16 (1953): 4–5; "Nicht nur eine Raumfrage: Bett oder Couch," *Brigitte*, no. 20 (1953): 4–5.

64. "Besser leben—aber wie? Ein Bummel durch eine Ausstellung, die 1000 Fragen offenließ," *Constanze*, no. 19, September 19, 1953, 74–75.

65. "In England kauft man heute: Hübsche Möbel—viel billiger," *Constanze*, no. 11, May 23, 1951, 38–39; "Nicht nur eine Raumfrage: Bett oder Couch," *Brigitte*, no. 20 (1953): 4–5; Eva Noack-Mosse, "Vier Länder—vier Stilarten: Deutschland, Schweden, Italien, Amerika," *Brigitte*, no. 4 (1954): 12–13; "Der Mann, der Geschmack verkauft," *Brigitte*, no. 6, March 1, 1954, 26–27; "Federgewichtler unter den Möbeln: Leicht, leichter—am leichtesten," *Brigitte*, no. 7, March 2, 1955, 14–15; "Hokuspokus in der Einbau-Wohnung," *Brigitte*, no. 10, May 1, 1955, 9; "Zwei Welten, eine Idee: Sonnenschein und Ferien," *Constanze*, no. 15, July 23, 1958, 10–11; "Der erste Blick in Constanzes neues Sonderheft: So ist das Wohnen eine Lust," *Constanze*, no. 22, October 29, 1958, 10–12; "Alt und neu in einem Raum," *Constanze*, no. 7, April 1, 1959, 54–59; "Glas aus Künstlerhand," *Constanze*, no. 10, May 13, 1959, 118–19; "Die Wohnung für Jedermanns," *Constanze*, no. 20, September 30, 1959, 111–17.

66. Helene Rahms, "Tapeten—ernst genommen," *Frankfurter Allgemeine Zeitung*, July 11, 1953, Bilder und Zeiten, 6.

67. "Wunschhaus wurde Wirklichkeit," *Constanze*, no. 16, 3rd number in July, 1954: 90–91. See also "Die Schönheit in der Ecke: Möbliere sparsam—auch im Schlafzimmer!," *Constanze*, no. 14, 1st number in July, 1954: 90–91; "Behaglich wohnen mit alten Möbeln: Stilgemisch mit persönlicher Note," *Brigitte*, no. 23 (October 1956): 42–43; "Müssen moderne Häuser kalt und nüchtern sein? Hier ein Gegenbeispiel: Modern und gemutlich," *Constanze*, no. 18, August 24, 1955, 86–87; "Ein Haus fürs Herz," *Constanze*, no. 8, April 4, 1956, 119; "Ein Haus fürs zweite Leben," *Constanze*, no. 14, June 29, 1955, 92–93.

68. "Das Brigitte-Zimmer: Wohnraum mit Erker," *Brigitte*, no. 19, September 8, 1959, 82–82; "Ein Raum mit Atmosphäre" (Fackelmöbel advertisment), *Constanze*, no. 17, August 19, 1959, 60; "Aus dem Land der Mitternachtssonne" (Fackelmöbel advertisement), *Constanze*, no. 14, July 8, 1959, 99. In 1957 the same brand had resorted to a rare form of nationalist rhetoric. See "Deutsche Gründlichkeit" (Fackelmöbel advertisement), *Constanze*, no. 11, May 15, 1957, 119.

69. "So wohnen wir heute," *Frankfurter Allgemeine Zeitung*, June 29, 1960, 18.

70. Margarete Richter, "Neu-Barock oder sachliche Linie: Betrachtungen zur neuen Wohnkultur," *Frankfurter Allgemeine Zeitung*, July 4, 1950, 11.

71. No author, no title, *Frankfurter Allgemeine Zeitung*, February 16, 1957, 37.

72. Dieter Conrads, "Die Nächsten kennt man am wenigsten: Schwedische Eindrücke," *Brigitte*, no. 22 (October 1954): 7–8, 44, here 8, 44.

73. "Ein Haus mit viel Charme," *Constanze*, no. 21, October 14, 1959, 111.

74. This quantitative analysis could be done on the basis of a full-text search in the digitalized archive of the magazine, made publicly available by the University Library in Heidelberg at https://digi.ub.uni-heidelberg.de/diglit/innendekoration.

75. As an example of the discussion in the 1920s, see Heinrich Ritter, "Die Gemeinsame Sprache: Gedanken über europäisches Wohnen," *Innen-Dekoration*, no. 5 (1925): 159.

76. "Kulturgeschichtliche Randbemerkungen," *Innen-Dekoration*, no. 11, 1938, 386.

77. Michel, "Vom 'Stil'"; "Das Heim und die Lebensaufgabe," *Innen-Dekoration*, no. 5 (1939): 147–49.

78. M. O. Florenz, "Die 'Mailänder Triennale,'" *Innen-Dekoration*, no. 9 (1936): 304–13, 308, 310, 313; "Raumkunst auf der VI. Triennale in Mailand," *Innen-Dekoration*, no. 1 (1937): 26–29. On modern design in Fascist Italy, see Ignacio G. Galán, "Building Simultaneity in Fascist Italy: Film, Furniture, and the Reframing of the Nation," *Journal of the Society of Architectural Historians* 80, no. 2 (2021): 182–201. On aesthetic modernism and Fascism more broadly, see Francesca Billiani, *Fascist Modernism in Italy: The Arts under Dictatorship* (London: I.B. Tauris, 2017).

79. "Kunst und Volk," *Innen-Dekoration*, no. 6 (1940): 174–78, 175.

80. "Stilkräfte der Gegenwart," *Innen-Dekoration*, no. 9 (1940): 248–50.

81. See, for instance, a remark in Hugo Lang, "Landhausbau in England," *Innen-Dekoration*, no. 38 (1927): 94–98, 95. See also Gregor Paulsson, "Neue Gestalten des gedeckten Tisches," *Innen-Dekoration*, no. 46 (1935): 34–40, 35.

82. Hans Henniger, "Neue finnische Raumkunst," *Innen-Dekoration*, no. 12 (1941): 362–67, 363–64. See also Frederik F. Ørskov, "From Nordic Romanticism to Nordic Modernity: Danish Tourist Brochures in Nazi Germany, 1929–39," *Journal of Contemporary History* 55, no. 1 (2020): 29–51; Friedrich Ege, "Finnische Wohnungskultur," *Innen-Dekoration*, no. 11 (1936): 387–89, 387; "Wohnräume der Ausstellung 'Vi Kan' in Oslo," *Innen-Dekoration*, no. 12 (1938): 410–16.

83. See, for instance, Wilhelm Michel, "Zweckform und Kunstform," *Innen-Dekoration*, no. 6 (1940): 166–68; "Stilkräfte der Gegenwart," *Innen-Dekoration*, no. 9 (1940): 248–50; Heinrich Ritter, "Landhausmöbel," *Innen-Dekoration*, no. 2 (1941): 54–55.

84. Gustav Neckel, "Das Nordische und die deutsche Bildung," *Nordische Rundschau*, no. 1–2 (1934): 1–13. See also Joachim Joesten, "The Nazis in Scandinavia," *Foreign Affairs* 15 (July 1937): 720–28, 720.

85. Christian Leitz, *Nazi Germany and Neutral Europe during the Second World War* (Manchester: Manchester University Press, 2000), 49–84.

86. M., "In alten Schlössern," *Innen-Dekoration*, no. 5 (1942): 124–25.

87. Marieluise Henniger, "Schwedische Raumkunst," *Architektur und Wohnform*, no. 1/2 (1948): 22–27, quote 22; Henniger, "Neue Baukunst in Finnland," *Architektur und Wohnform*, no. 2/3 (1948): 27–28, quote 28.

88. Christopher M. Hutton, *Race and the Third Reich: Linguistics, Racial Anthropology, and Genetics in the Dialectic of the* Volk (Cambridge: Polity Press, 2008), 113–39. Scandinavian countries were also referred to as models for state-sponsored design education. See, for instance, "Bei mir zu Haus," *Das Blatt der Hausfrau*, no. 3 (1952): 4–5, 22; Brigitte Beer, "Kinder lernen wohnen," *Frankfurter Allgemeine Zeitung*, December 28, 1957, Bilder und Zeiten, 6. Education policies on good interior design had been actively pursued during the Third Reich. See H. C. Schmidt, "Beseeltes Wohnen," *Innen-Dekoration*, no. 5 (1941): 152–53; Paul Schlemmer, "Wohnkultur—eine deutsche Aufgabe," *Innen-Dekoration*, no. 5 (1941): 136–44, 136, 138. See also Christopher Hutton, "Racial Ideology as Elite Discourse: Nordicism and the Visual in an Age of Mass Culture," *Social Semiotics* 27, no. 3 (2017): 335–47.

89. Eva Noack-Mosse, "Vier Länder—vier Stilarten: Deutschland, Schweden, Italien, Amerika," *Brigitte*, no. 4 (1954): 12–13; "Wie hat sich die Welt verändert!," *Brigitte*, no. 17, August 1954, 30–31; "Wenn die vier Wände zu eng werden, dann wechseln Sie mal die Tapeten!" *Constanze*, no. 3, January 26, 1955, 64–65.

90. A 1958 special issue on modern living culture published by *Constanze* featured many model houses from Germany, but also examples from "Switzerland, Denmark, England, America and Australia." "Der erste Blick in Constanzes neues Sonderheft: So ist das Wohnen eine Lust," *Constanze*, no. 22, October 29, 1958, 10–12.

91. On Raymond Loewy: "Lochstickerei in Porzellan," *Der Spiegel*, no. 30, 22 July 1953, 30–31; "Der Mann, der Geschmack verkauft," *Brigitte*, no. 6, March 1, 1954, 26–27; Wend Fischer, "Industrie-Form—gestern, heute, morgen," *Frankfurter Allgemeine Zeitung*, November 23, 1955, 11. On Knoll international: Helene Rahms, "Die Anmut der strengen Linie," *Frankfurter Allgemeine Zeitung*, July 4, 1953, Bilder und Zeiten 6; "Knoll: Im Haut- und Knochen-Stil," *Der Spiegel*, no. 16, April 13, 1960, 64–75.

92. "in ulm geht man neue wege," *Brigitte*, no. 13, June 1956, 18–21.

93. Eva Noack-Mosse, "Sie formen unseren Lebensstil," *Brigitte*, no. 11, May 1955, 10–11; no. 12, June 1955, 10–11; no. 15, July 1955, 10–11; no. 16, July 1955, 10–11.

94. Bonnett Hardoy's Butterfly Chair is one example for the internationalization of the modern home. It had been shown in the 1952 Marshall Plan exhibit and subsequently popped up regularly in various German or Scandinavian model interiors. Through its consistent use as an icon of modern internationalism it radiated a cosmopolitan allure.

95. E.M., "Heraus aus der Enge: Wie wir wohnen wollen—Oasen der Ruhe," *Die Zeit*, no. 29, July 22, 1954, 22. See also "Das Brigitte-Zimmer: Sehr modern, aber gemütlich," *Brigitte*, no. 20, September 23, 1958, 82–83.

96. Charlotte Ashby, *Modernism in Scandinavia: Art, Architecture and Design* (London: Bloomsbury, 2017), 186. Helene Rahms, "Europäischer Wohnstil von morgen," *Frankfurter Allgemeine Zeitung*, July 9, 1955, Bilder und Zeiten 1. See also on an international exhibition including Japan organized in Kassel "Ausstellung für Wohnkultur," *Frankfurter Allgemeine Zeitung*, January 10, 1957, 6. Yasuko Suga, "Invention of 'Modern' Japonisme: National representation through 'Sangyo Kogei,'" conference paper, 2008.

97. "Lampen: Verspielt, dekorativ, antic," *Brigitte*, no. 2, Januar 1957, 32; "Das Brigitte-Zimmer: Für die junge Familie," *Brigitte*, no. 21, September 1957, 78–79; "Das Brigitte-Zimmer: Wenig Raum, viel Platz!" *Brigitte*, no. 10, Mai 1958, 86–87; "Das Brigitte-Zimmer: Ihr eigenes Reich," *Brigitte*, no. 3, January 21, 1959, 56–57; "Das Brigitte-Zimmer: Wohnraum mit Erker," *Brigitte*, no. 19, September 8, 1959, 82–82; "Das Brigitte-Zimmer: Ein moderner Wohnraum," *Brigitte*, no. 21, October 7, 1959, 98–99; "Das Brigitte-Zimmer: Eine junge Dame richtet sich ein," *Brigitte*, no. 24, November 17, 1959, 97–98. In *Constanze* Japanese interior objects were comparatively rare. I came across only two mentions: "Wenn die vier Wände zu eng werden, dann wechseln Sie mal die Tapeten!" *Constanze*, no. 3, January 26, 1955, 64–65 and "Finn Juhl entwirft die schönsten dänischen Möbel. In seinem Haus ist: Jeder Stuhl weltberühmt," *Constanze*, no. 5, March 4, 1959, 76–77. See also "Nordische Farbtöne: Sonderschau formschöner Industrieerzeugnisse," *Frankfurter Allgemeine Zeitung*, September 6, 1957, 7. Already 1953, the illustrated magazine *Quick* had introduced its readers to pictures of modern Japanese lamps and sculptures. "Wenn ein altes Kulturvolk modern wird: Abstrakte Japankunst," *Quick*, no. 3, January 18 1953, 29.

98. "The example of Japan," *Life*, December 31, 1951, 58–69, quotes 60–61 and 69.

99. Eva Noack, "Japanisch wird modern," *Brigitte*, no. 13, June 1956, 62–64, 63. See with a similar argument Vilma Sturm, "Die leere Fläche," *Frankfurter Allgemeine Zeitung*, May 20, 1950, 12.

100. Christopher Reed, *Bachelor Japanists: Japanese Aesthetics and Western Masculinities* (New York: Columbia University Press, 2017), Introduction (e-book).

101. Penny Sparke, *Japanese Design* (New York: The Museum of Modern Art, 2009), 13–16; Helena Capková, "Transnational Networkers—Iwao and Michiko Yamawaki and the Formation of Japanese Modernist Design," *Journal of Design History* 27, no. 4 (2014): 370–85. Peter McNeil, "Myths of Modernism: Japanese Architecture, Interior Design and the West, c. 1920–1940," *Journal of Design History* 5, no. 4 (1992): 281–94.

102. Heonik Kwon, *The Other Cold War* (New York: Columbia University Press, 2010), 67.

103. Ricy W. Law, *Transnational Nazism: Ideology and Culture in German-Japanese Relations, 1919–1936* (Cambridge: Cambridge University Press, 2019), especially 172, 175, 193, 197, quote 177.

104. Till P. Koltermann, *Der Untergang Des Dritten Reiches im Spiegel der deutsch-japanischen Kulturbegegnung 1933–1945* (Wiesbaden: Harrassowitz, 2009), 84–107. See also Hans Joachim Bieber, *SS und Samurei: Deutsch-japanische Kulturbeziehungen 1933–1934* (Munich: Iudicum Verlag, 2014).

105. Alan Tansman, "Introduction," in *The Culture of Japanese Fascism*, ed. Tansman (Durham and London: Duke University Press 2009), 1–30, 15.

106. Patrick Rössler, *Das Bauhaus am Kiosk/The Bauhaus at the Newsstand* (Bielefeld and Leipzig: Kerber Art, 2009), quote 69.

107. 4000 copies out of a total of 45000 were distributed in Japan. Rössler, *Das Bauhaus am Kiosk/The Bauhaus at the Newsstand*, 71 and 73; Bieber, Bieber, *SS und Samurei*, 226.

108. Sigmund von Weech, "Auf der Suche nach dem neuen Wohnstil," *die neue linie* no. 5 (January 1937): 40–43.

109. Walter D. Mignolo, "The Many Faces of Cosmo-polis: Border Thinking and Critical Cosmopolitanism," *Public Culture* 12, no. 3 (2000): 721–48, 735.

110. "Wie hat sich."

111. Kyra Stromberg, "Die Woolworth-Karawane: Vom 'Teppich des Lebens' zum Blechkanister—Geschmacksverderb im Orient," *Die Zeit*, no. 41, October 8, 1953, https://www.zeit.de/1953/41/die-woolworth-karawane.

112. Edward Said, *Orientalism* (London: Penguin Books, 2003), 3.

113. Kurt Erdmann, *Europa und der Orientteppich* (Berlin: Florian Kupferberg, 1962), 111.

114. Erdmann, *Europa*, 68–77; Oliver Simons, "Orientteppich und Kunstwerk, 1895: Hugo von Hoffmansthals *Märhen der 672. Nacht*," in *Mit Deutschland um die Welt: Eine Kulturgeschichte des Fremden in der Kolonialzeit*, ed. Alexander Honold and Klaus Rüdiger Scherpe (Stuttgart: Metzler, 2004), 182–89.

115. H. Muth, "Der Osten in unserer Möbelkunst," *Innen-Dekoration*, no. 11 (1921): 353–54; H.R., "Drei Teppiche," *Innen-Dekoration*, no. 10 (1935): 332–33; *Die schöne Wohnung: Wohnräume der Gegenwart in 225 Abbildungen* (Munich: Verlag F. Bruckmann, 1934); Fritz Spannagel, *Unsere schöne Wohnung* (Ravensburg: Otto Maier Verlag, 1937); *Die schöne Wohnung: Wohnräume der Gegenwart in 175 Abbildungen* (Munich: Verlag F. Bruckmann, 1941); "Vereinigte Werkstätten für Kunst im Handwerk," *Innen-Dekoration*, no. 12 (1937): 412–17; "Deutsche Architektur- und Kunsthandwerksausstellung," *Innen-Dekoration*, no. 5 (1938): 159–67, 162–63, here 160, 162–63, 167; "Ein Berliner Vorort Wohnhaus," *Innen-Dekoration*, no. 6 (1940): 159–63, 161, 163; A. E. Schlenker, "Die neue Führerinnen-Schule in Schorndorf," *Innen-Dekoration*, no. 6 (1943): 142–60, 149.

116. "Deutsche Architektur- und Kunsthandwerksausstellung," 163.

117. An interior of the 1949 Werkbund exhibition included an Oriental rug. See Castillo, *Cold War*, 6–7. Another exception is "Liebe Constanze! Bitte, hilf uns doch

einrichten!," *Constanze*, no. 9, April 20, 1955, 96–97. An indication that when it comes to an Oriental rug, popular taste contradicted the "architecture's style" can be found in G. Meyer-Ehlers, *Wohnerfahrungen: Ergebnisse einer Wohnuntersuchung* (Wiesbaden: Bauverlag, 1963), illustrations unpaginated.

118. "Tante Frieda wurde kopflos . . ." (Agfa advertisement), *Constanze*, no. 25, December 5, 1951, 30; "Ein Traum wird wahr! Wir richten uns neu ein," *Constanze*, no. 11, May 18, 1955, 124–25; "Drei richten sich ein Zimmer ein," *Brigitte*, no. 21 (October 1955): 14–15; "Es gibt auch modernen Kitsch! Aber woran ist er zu erkennen?," *Brigitte*, no. 22 (October 1955): 14–15.

119. "Kleine Gesetze für Gardinen, Bilder und Teppiche," *Brigitte*, no. 2 (1953): 4–5. In February 1952 *Constanze* published a long article on Oriental rugs that explained their history and the history of their European appropriation. "Wie sieht ein echter Orientteppich aus? Sprung auf den Teppich," *Constanze*, no. 4, February 13, 1952, 46–47.

120. "Wohninseln," *Brigitte*, no. 18 (August 1955): 8; "Das Brigitte Zimmer: Neues paßt zu Altem," *Brigitte*, no. 18 (August 1957): 58–59; "Wir wohnen im Stall," *Constanze*, no. 2, January 11, 1956, 76–77; "Alt und neu in einer Wohnung," *Constanze*, no. 7, March 21, 1956, 142–43; "Ich bin für alte Möbel," *Constanze*, no. 8, April 4, 1956, 118; "Ein Haus fürs Herz," *Constanze*, no. 8, April 4, 1956, 119; "Wir wohnen gerne altmodisch," *Constanze*, no. 25, December 10, 1958, 58–61; "Unser Haus hat viele Tricks," *Constanze*, no. 6, March 18, 1959, 10–13, 10.

121. "Ein Brigitte-Zimmer für ihn: Hier arbeitet der Hausherr," *Brigitte*, no. 19, September 9, 1958, 66–67. See also "Auf schrägem Grund: Ein Haus mit Anker," *Constanze*, no. 4, February 19, 1958, 62–63.

122. "Repräsentation nach Maß?" (Wehra carpet advertisement), *Brigitte*, no. 4 (February 1958): 32; "Essen und essen ist zweierlei!" (Wehra carpet advertisement), *Brigitte*, no. 6 (March 1958): 62; "Deutschlands größte Teppichfabrik kann ihre Teppichwünsche erfüllen . . . ," (Besmer carpet advertisement), *Constanze*, special issue, "Der ideale Haushalt," no. 3 (1958): 43.

123. "Das Brigitte-Zimmer: Hier wird gefeiert," *Brigitte*, no. 23, November 4, 1958, 98–99.

124. "Bleiben Sie auf dem Teppich!," *Constanze*, no. 12, May 30, 1956, 102–3.

125. "Das muß ein Stück von Schaeffler sein . . . ," *Constanze*, no. 11, May 27, 1959, 96.

126. The image, possibly unwittingly, undermines its own fantasy of domination, however, by showing a couple who, although smiling, do not seem entirely at ease with their position in the sky.

127. "In der Wüste hilft das nicht, doch für die Hausfrau ist die AEG-Vampyrette ein zuverlässiger Helfer" (AEG vacuum cleaner advertisement), *Simplicissimus*, no. 7, November 20, 1954, 8.

128. A short time later, the Muslim veil was redefined in the context of the Algerian War as a potent and internationally recognized symbol of Eastern women's oppression, in contrast to the female role in Western consumer modernity. Elizabeth Perego, "The Veil or a Brother's Life: French Manipulations of Muslim Women's Images during the Algerian War, 1954–1962," *Journal of North African Studies* 20, no. 3 (2015): 349–73.

129. "Beneidenswert!" (BBC refrigerator advertisement), *Constanze*, no. 7, March 23, 1956, 6.

130. Antoinette M. Burton, *Burdens of History: British Feminists, Indian Women, and Imperial Culture, 1865–1915* (Chapel Hill: University of North Carolina Press, 1994), 67.

131. Sunka Simon, "Der vord're Orient: Colonialist Imagery in Popular Postwar German *Schlager*," *Journal of Popular Culture* 34, no. 3 (2000): 87–108; Barbara Mennel, "Returning Home: The Orientalist Spectacle of Fritz Lang's *Der Tiger von Eschnapur* and *Das Indische Grabmal*," in *Framing the Fifties: Cinema in a Divided Germany*, ed. John Davidson and Sabine Hake (New York: Berghahn Books, 2007), 28–43.

132. Brian T. Edwards, "Yankee Pashas and Buried Women: Containing Abundance in 1950s Hollywood Orientalism," *Film & History* 31, no. 2 (2001): 13–24, 15. According to the database imdb.com, most films that Edwards mentions were also released in Germany, for instance, *Bagdad* (1949), *Yankee Pasha* (1954), *The Egyptian* (1954), and *Land of the Pharaohs* (1955).

133. Mennel, "Returning Home," 29–32; Thea von Harbou, *Das indische Grabmal* (Berlin: Ullstein, 1921), 37–38.

134. H. Muth, "Der Osten in unserer Möbelkunst," *Innen-Dekoration*, no. 11 (1921): 353–54; Wilhelm Michel, "Vergänglichkeit und Dauer: Verschiedene Baugesinnungen," *Innen-Dekoration*, no. 1 (1928): 16; Wilhelm Michel, "Das feste Leben," *Innen-Dekoration*, no. 11 (1941): 330–37; Heinrich Hahne, "Kleine Hotels auf Rhodos: Erfahrungen und Bilanzen im griechischen Fremdenverkehr," *Frankfurter Allgemeine Zeitung*, December 27, 1957, 13; "Ich war mit einem Ausländer verheiratet," *Constanze*, no. 19, September 5, 1956, 20–23, 22.

135. "Der Besmer-'Micado' ist ein Meisterstsück" (Besmer carpet advertisement), *Constanze*, no. 6, March 19, 1958, 67.

136. "Keine Angst vor Antiquitäten!," *Constanze*, no. 12, May 30, 1956, 28–20. See also "Kunst muss nicht teuer sein," *Constanze*, no. 6, March 19, 1958, 122–25.

137. In the *Innen-Dekoration* of the Nazi years, exotic objects were also scarce. Occasionally, small non-European artifacts appeared in model interiors, but no discourse accompanied such examples.

138. "Das Brigitte-Zimmer: Ein moderner Arbeitsraum," *Brigitte*, no. 1, December 30, 1958, 62–63. In the early 1960s French design magazines promoted an "association style" that combined objects from "primitive" cultures with contemporary European art and modern furnishing, facilitating, according to Daniel J. Sherman, "the transition from empire to a new imagined community of transnational sophistication" ("Post-colonial Chic: Fantasies of the French Interior, 1957–62," *Art History* 27, no. 5 [2004]: 770–805). See also Sherman, *French Primitivism and the Ends of Empire, 1945–1975* (Chicago: University of Chicago Press, 2011), chap. 3.

139. Susanne Zantop, *Colonial Fantasies: Conquest, Family, and Nation in Precolonial Germany, 1770–1870* (Durham, NC: Duke University Press, 1997); Sebastian Conrad, *German Colonialism: A Short History* (Cambridge: Cambridge University Press, 2012), 186–95; Sara Friedrichsmeyer, Sara Lennox, and Susanne Zantop, eds., *The Imperialist*

Imagination: German Colonialism and Its Legacy (Ann Arbor: University of Michigan Press, 1998).

140. Chris Bongie, *Exotic Memories: Literature, Colonialism, and the Fin de Siècle* (Stanford, CA: Stanford University Press, 1991), 4–5.

141. "Kalte Pracht in Hollywood," *Constanze*, no. 13, June 20, 1951, quote 71.

142. "Zu 'Kalte Pracht in Hollywood': Ist Wohnen eine reine Privatsache?," *Constanze*, no. 22, October 24, 1951, 14.

143. For a discussion of the conspicuous absence of the United States in German images of the modern home, see Natalie Scholz, "The 'Modern Home' during the 1950s: West German Cultural Reconstruction and the Ambivalent Meanings of Americanization," *Tijdschrift voor Geschiedenis* 121, no. 3 (2008): 296–311.

144. On the Africa shows in Germany, see Tina Campt, Pascal Grosse, and Yara-Colette Lemke-Muniz da Faria, "Blacks, Germans, and the Politics of Imperial Imagination, 1920–1960," in *The Imperial Imagination: German Colonialism and Its Legacy*, ed. Sara Friedrichsmeyer, Sara Lennox, and Susanne Zantop (Ann Arbor: University of Michigan Press, 1998), 205–29, here 218–22; Hilke Thode-Arora, "Afrika-Völkerschauen in Deutschland," in *AfrikanerInnen in Deutschland und schwarze Deutsche—Geschichte und Gegenwart*, ed. Marianne Bechhaus-Gerst and Reinhard Klein-Arendt (Münster: Lit Verlag, 2004), 25–40.

145. "Die 'Wilden' wohnen gar nicht so unbequem: Sitzen Sie doch mal afrikanisch!," *Constanze*, no. 6, March 7, 1956, 115.

146. "Unser Weltbild hängt schief! Constanze fotografierte junge Ausländerinnen: Wir kommen direkt aus Afrika," *Constanze*, no. 24, November 14, 1956, 36–39.

147. "Tabu: Erwachende Völker," *magnum*, no. 31 (August 1960): 24.

148. Ahmed, "Affective Economies." The term "colonizing culture" is used by Hall, *Familiar Stranger*, 250.

149. On the anxieties in the postwar period about reversed racial hierarchies in relation to "Jews," "Poles," "Russians," and African American GIs, see Frank Biess, *German Angst: Fear and Democracy in the Federal Republic of Germany* (New York: Oxford University Press, 2020), 66–94.

150. Karl Berbuer, "Wir sind die Einwohner von Trizonesien," Carnival song, published November 11, 1948, accessed November 2022, https://www.golyr.de/karl-berbuer/songtext-trizonesien-song-277557.html. See also Peter Limbach, "Trizonesien Lied sorgte für Aufregung," *Kölner Stadt-Anzeiger*, November 5, 2004, https://www.ksta.de/trizonesien-lied-sorgte-1949-fuer-aufregung-14563906. For an earlier use of the term "Bizonia" for the strange status of Germany as an occupied country, see "Die Hauptstadt von Bizonia: Frankfurt a.M.," *Neue Illustrierte*, no. 21, October 17, 1947, 8–9. A woman in blackface and bast skirt appeared during Carnival season on the cover of *Quick*, no. 3, February 6, 1948.

151. Lester, *"Trivialneger,"* 16, 21, 187–98.

152. Timothy L. Schroer, *Recasting Race after World War II: Germans and African Americans in American-Occupied Germany* (Denver: University Press of Colorado, 2007),

34–35, quote 84. See also Heide Fehrenbach, *Race after Hitler: Occupation Children in Postwar Germany and America* (Princeton, NJ: Princeton University Press, 2005), 6–7.

153. Brauerhoch, *"Fräuleins" und GIs*, 227–72; Fehrenbach, *Race after Hitler*, 67–69, 105, 157.

154. *Der Simpl*, no. 13 (June 1949): cover.

155. David Ciarlo, *Advertising Empire: Race and Visual Culture in Imperial Germany* (Cambridge, MA: Harvard University Press, 2011).

156. This interpretation resonates with various studies of the social function of minstrel culture in the United States. See Thomas C. Holt, "Marking: Race, Race-Making, and the Writing of History," *American Historical Review* 100, no. 1 (1995): 1–20, here 15–16.

157. Lester, *"Trivialneger."* During the 1950s West German newspapers reported on Africa nearly exclusively from the perspective of European power interests and the belief in the superiority of European civilization. See Manfred Paeffgen, *Das Bild Schwarz-Afrikas in der öffentlichen Meinung der Bundesrepublik Deutschland* (Munich: Weltforum Verlag, 1976). Monika Albrecht, who has studied high-brow cultural magazines and *Der Spiegel*, sees a continuation of racist clichés until the middle of the decade and their conspicuous decline after 1955; see *"Europa ist nicht die Welt,"* esp. 34–138.

158. See numerous examples in Joachim Zeller, *Weiße Blicke—schwarze Körper: Afrikaner im Spiegel westlicher Alltagskultur; Bilder aus der Sammlung Peter Weiss* (Erfurt: Sutton Verlag, 2010), 21, 77, 104, 162, 172. There is no systematic study of race in advertising in the postwar period.

159. "Vom hohen Olymp," *Quick*, no. 26, July 1, 1951, 873. See also "Olympia ohne uns," *Neue Illustrierte*, no. 17, August 19, 1948, 15, and no. 18, August 26, 1948, 3.

160. "Wie die Neger!" (SABA radio advertisement), *Constanze*, no. 7, 3rd number in March, 1950: 43.

161. "Auch Monsieur Duval in Paris . . . und Mister Shaw in Bombay" (SABA radio advertisement), *Constanze*, no. 4, 2nd number in February, 1950: 54.

162. "Tierfang in Afrika" (Pelikan advertisement), *Simplicissimus*, no. 4, October 30, 1954, 13.

163. It was the ARWA hosiery factory in Parys. See the note among the business news in *Die Zeit*, no. 10, March 10, 1955 ("Erfolgsbilanz von Siemens"), https://www.zeit.de/1955/10/erfolgsbilanz-von-siemens.

164. Helen Laville, "'Our Country Endangered by Underwear': Fashion, Femininity, and the Seduction Narrative in *Ninotchka* and *Silk Stockings*," *Diplomatic History* 30, no. 4 (2006): 623–44.

165. "Deutsche Strümpfe in Afrika," *Quick*, no. 48, November 26, 1955, 66.

166. Dirk van Laak, *Über alles in der Welt: Deutscher Imperialismus im 19. und 20. Jahrhundert* (Munich: Beck, 2005), 7–8; Clemens Escher, *"Deutschland, Deutschland, du mein alles!": Die Deutschen auf der Suche nach ihrer Nationalhymne 1949–1952* (Paderborn: Ferdinand Schöningh, 2017).

167. "In Südafrika: Deutsche Strumpf-Premiere," *Quick*, no. 50, December 10, 1955, 64–65.

168. Lester, *"Trivialneger,"* 191–93.

169. Anne McClintock, *Imperial Leather: Race, Gender and Sexuality in the Colonial Context* (New York: Routledge, 1995), esp. 207–32.

170. "In Südafrika," 65.

171. Fehrenbach, *Race after Hitler*, 107–31, quote 124.

172. This scene was also noticed by Brauerhoch, *"Fräuleins" und GIs*, 227.

173. Film historian and film archivist Ralf Forster dates the production of the film to 1954. See "Von der Zeichentricksinfonie zum Mischfilm: Zäsuren des bundesdeutschen Werbeanimationsfilms um 1960," *montage A/V*, February 22, 2013, 119–31.

174. The second part of the film is available on YouTube: https://www.youtube.com/watch?v=lCW_6vgLRyk (November 2022).

175. Dennis Meyer, "Entnazifierung," in *Lexikon der "Vergangenheitsbewältigung" in Deutschland: Debatten- und Diskursgeschichte des Nationalsozialismus nach 1945*, ed. Torben Fischer and Matthias N. Lorenz (Bielefeld: transcript, 2007), 18–19.

176. McClintock, *Imperial Leather*, 207–31.

177. Ciarlo, *Advertising Empire*, 241–45, 259–65, quote 245.

178. Filth and dirt famously played a crucial role in the antisemitic Nazi film *Der ewige Jude*. See Jennifer Jansen, "The Art and Science of Reading Faces: Strategies of Racist Cinema in the Third Reich," *Shofar: An Interdisciplinary Journal of Jewish Studies* 28, no. 1 (2009): 80–103.

179. Ciarlo, *Advertising Empire*, 324.

180. Isabel Cserno, "Whiteness Studies and the Colonial Aesthetic: Western Popular Culture and the Representations of Race," *Explorations in Ethnic Studies* 29, no. 2 (2006): 66–85; Cserno, "Race and Mass Consumption in Consumer Culture: National Trademark Advertising Campaigns in the United States and Germany, 1890–1930" (PhD diss., University of Maryland, College Park, 2008), esp. 190–228; Katharina Eggers and Robert Fechner, "'The German Alternative': Nationalism and Racism in 'Afri-Cola,'" in *Colonial Advertising & Commodity Racism*, ed. Wulf D. Hund and Michael Pickering (Münster: LIT Verlag, 2013), 197–217.

181. Swett, *Selling under the Swastika*; Jonathan S. Wiesen, *Creating the Nazi Marketplace: Commerce and Consumption in the Third Reich* (Cambridge: Cambridge University Press, 2011). A large-scale survey conducted in 1947 found that postwar Germans' knowledge about commercial brands was very well developed. See Rainer Gries, *Produkte als Medien: Kulturgeschichte der Produktkommunikation in der Bundesrepublik und der DDR* (Leipzig: Leipziger Universitätsverslag, 2003), 149–57.

182. Pamela W. Swett, S. Jonathan Wiesen, and Jonathan R. Zatlin, introduction to *Selling Modernity: Advertising in Twentieth-Century Germany*, ed. Pamela W. Swett, S. Jonathan Wiesen, and Jonathan R. Zatlin (Durham, NC: Duke University Press, 2007), 1–26, here 10–11.

183. "Heute wie früher" (Junghans timepieces advertisement), *Constanze*, no. 13, June 22, 1949, 28.

184. "Pelikan Füllhalter Tinte" advertisement, *Neue Illustrierte*, no. 2, January 23, 1948, 10; Mauthe clocks advertisement, *Constanze*, no. 24, 2nd number in November, 1949: 46;

Deinhard Kabinett advertisement, *Quick*, no. 17, November 7, 1948, 25; Dr. Oetker advertisement, *Quick*, no. 23/24, December 19, 1948, 18.

185. Maggi advertisement, *Neue Illustrierte*, no. 11, May 28, 1948. Similarly, Bosch advertisement, *Quick*, no. 52, December 24, 1950, 5.

186. To name just a few of many more examples: "Die Weltmarke für Lederwaren" (Goldpfeil advertisement), *Constanze*, no. 17 (November 1948): 15; "Telefunken: Die deutsche Weltmarke," *Quick*, March 6, 1949, 17; "DKW war ein Weltbegriff—DKW wird wieder zum Weltbegriff," *Quick*, special issue, 1900–1950, 121; "Odol: Die Welt gebraucht es jeden Tag," *Der Stern*, no. 28, July 15, 1951, n.p.; "Mehr als 7 Millionen Telefunken-Empfänger gingen in alle Welt" (Telefunken radio advertisement), *Quick*, no. 50, December 14, 1952, 49; "Der Welt ein Begriff—die Laurens hat Weltgeltung" (cigarette advertisement), *Quick*, no. 20, May 16, 1954, 27; "Bewährt in aller Welt" (Togal painkiller advertisement), *Der Stern*, no. 10, March 9, 1957, 51; "Das Zeichen weltweiten Erfolges—Formica Kunststoffplatten," *Constanze*, no. 22, October 28, 1959, 46.

187. See the ads for 4711 cologne in *Constanze*, no. 14 (September 1948): 11; *Constanze*, no. 16 (October 1948): 11; *Constanze*, no. 18 (November 1948): 11. The same ads were published in *Quick*.

188. "Export—eine deutsche Existenzfrage," *Neue Illustrierte*, no. 6, March 7, 1947, 6.

189. "Plakat zur Exportmesse 1947 in Hannover," P 90/12299, Archive Deutsches Historisches Museum, Berlin, the image is available at www.dhm.de/archiv/ausstellungen/erf/raum/erstesog/madeing/bild51.htm.

190. "Plakat zur Exportmesse 1948 in Hannover," P 71/1631.1, Archive Deutsches Historisches Museum, Berlin.

191. "Welterfahren-Weltbekannt" (advertisement for Deutsche Shell Aktiengesellschaft), *Neue Illustrierte*, no. 21, October 17, 1947, 14; "Europol Hochleistungsmotoroel," *Neue Illustrierte*, no. 1, January 9, 1948, 10; "Bobina Besen kehren gut," *Der Simpl*, no. 20 (October 1948); "Borgward 'Hansa 1500': Ein Wagen der um die Welt geht," *Constanze*, no. 11, May 25, 1949, 33; "Mauser Rundform Stahlmöbel: Ein neuer Begriff für vollendete Raumgestaltung," *Quick*, March 27, 1949; "Susa in aller Welt: Ein Begriff für Passform und Qualität" (corselet advertisement), *Constanze*, no. 15, 2nd number in July, 1950: 37; "Der neue 'Tausendzünder' erobert sich die Welt," *Quick*, no. 22, June 3, 1951.

192. "17 Millionen zufriedene Frigidaire-Besitzer in der ganzen Welt" (refrigerator advertisement), *Quick*, no. 27, July 4, 1954, 20; "In 62 Ländern der Welt wird Creme Mouson von vielen Millionen von Frauen aller Berufsstände täglich verwendet" (soap advertisement), *Constanze*, no. 3, January 26, 1955, 8; "Kuba Musiktruhen genießen das Vertrauen der Welt" (stereo console advertisement), *Quick*, no. 49, December 5, 1954; "Ein Seidenfaden der die Welt umspannt" (advertisement for Gütermann sewing silk), *Quick*, no. 7, February 12, 1955, 40; "Einer von 850 000" (Rollei camera advertisement), *Quick*, no. 19, May 7, 1955, 32; "Auf der ganzen Welt anerkannt—Neo-Silvikrin" (hair product advertisement), *Der Stern*, no. 6, February 9, 1957, 25; "Ein Band umschlingt den Erdball" (Gold-Zack advertisement), *Quick*, no. 8, February 22, 1958, 26.

193. "National Global Füllschreiber Deutsche Wertarbeit für den Export," *Der Simpl*, no. 20 (October 1948): 236; "Trilysin" (hair product advertisement), *Quick*, May 29, 1949; "DDT kennt die ganze Welt," *Quick*, August 21, 1949.

194. David Ciarlo developed a similar argument with respect to the visual function of Black people in imperial advertising. See "Advertising and the Optics of Colonial Power at the Fin de Siècle," in *Empires of Vision: A Reader*, ed. Martin Jay and Sumathi Ramaswamy (Durham, NC: Duke University Press, 2014), 189–207.

195. "Briefe aus Indien und Australien" (Kupferberg Gold sparkling wine advertisement), *Der Simpl*, no. 3 (February 1949): 30.

196. "Der neue 'Tausendzünder.'"

197. Angelika Epple, "Das Auge schmeckt Stollwerck: Uniformierung der Bilderwelt und kulturelle Differenzierung von Vorstellungsbildern in Zeiten des Imperialismus und der Globalisierung," *WerkstattGeschichte* 45 (2007): 13–31, quotes 24–26.

198. The following analysis is based on advertisements found in *die neue linie* (from 1933 until its last edition in 1942) and the Nazi periodicals *Arbeitertum* (1940–42) and *NS-Frauenwarte* (1941–44).

199. "In Deutschland und Übersee" (Asbach Uralt advertisement), *die neue linie*, no. 2 (November 1935): 10; "Weltmarke des Porzellan" (Rosenthal advertisement), *die neue linie*, no. 9 (May 1937): 35; Deinhardt Kabinett advertisement, *die neue linie*, no. 12 (August 1937): 1.

200. In March 1938 Shell even anticipated a future invasion of Poland by representing a Germany that included the "Danzic Corridor." See Rainer Gries, Volker Illgen, and Dirk Schindelbeck, *"Ins Gehirn der Masse kriechen!": Werbung und Mentalitätsgeschichte* (Darmstadt: Wissenschaftliche Buchgesellschaft, 1995), 29–44.

201. "Eres: Der Mantel guten Stils," *die neue linie*, no. 2 (October 1938): 4. The bottom of the ad specified "Aryan product."

202. The text contrasted the "unchanging" quality of Mercedes cars with the rapid change in technology and "streets." The latter was a hint at the intensely advertised building of the Autobahn, which had been the central theme of a previous Mercedes campaign. See Mercedes-Benz advertisement, *Arbeitertum*, no. 12, September 15, 1939, 21. On Mercedes-Benz during National Socialism, see Swett, *Selling under the Swastika*, 120–23.

203. "Der Sprung in die Neue Welt" (Söhnlein sparkling wine advertisement), *die neue linie*, no. 3 (November 1940): 51; "Feuertaufe im Lande des Champagners," *die neue linie*, no. 4 (December 1940): 63.

204. "Deutsche FORD-WAGEN waren mit dabei!," *die neue linie*, no. 6 (February 1941): 5. Further examples of car brands with explicitly war-related ad strategies are Borgward and Mercedes-Benz. See "Borgward Wagen aus Bremen für große Aufgaben in großer Zeit," full page ad in *die neue linie*, no. 4 (December 1940): 2; and Mercedes ad from 1940 published in Uwe Westphal, *Werbung im Dritten Reich* (Berlin: Transit, 1989), 155.

205. "Tropische Verhältnisse . . . ," *die neue linie*, no. 6 (February 1942): 6. Other examples for how advertisements linked products to the war effort (but not necessarily to geographic expansion) can be found in Swett, *Selling under the Swastika*, pt. 3.

206. On the special conditions for advertising after 1942, see Swett, *Selling under the Swastika*, 229–52.

207. Esbit dry fuel advertising, *NS-Frauenwarte*, no. 8 (November 1942): 101.

208. Rainer Rutz, *Signal: Eine deutsche Auslandsillustrierte als Propagandainstrument im Zweiten Weltkrieg* (Essen: Klartext Verlag, 2007), 9–10.

209. Adam Tooze, *The Wages of Destruction: The Making and Breaking of the Nazi Economy* (London: Penguin Books, 2006), 388–89, 436.

210. Advertisements for 4711 cologne in *Signal*, no. 6, 2nd number in March 1942. See also *Signal*, no. 10, 1st number in May 1941, no. 11, 1st number in June 1941, no. 14, 2nd number in July 1941, and no. 1, 1st number in January 1942.

211. "Een ster die in de hele wereld bekend is!" (Mercedes-Benz advertisement), *Signal*, no. 11 (1944); Swett, *Selling under the Swastika*, 258. See also "Überall auf dieser Erde" (Mercedes-Benz advertisement), *magnum*, no. 50 (October 1963): 61.

212. "In het nieuwe Europa zal iedereen beter leven" (Geha-Werke advertisement), *Signal*, no. 16 (1944): 33; "Het wereldmerk voor lederwaren" (Goldpfeil advertisement), *Signal*, no. 18 (1944): 24.

213. Rutz, *Signal*, 93–94.

214. For concrete numbers, see Tooze, *The Wages of Destruction*, 517–19.

215. Rutz, *Signal*, 393–416.

216. "Bonsa die Klinge ohne Tadel," (advertisement) *Neue Illustrierte*, no. 2, January 23, 1948, 10; "Nur 1 Tropfen" (mouthwash advertisement), *Der Stern*, no. 10, March 9, 1957, 54; "Vom Nordkap bis zum Bosporus" (Grundig advertisement), *Quick*, no. 46, November 16, 1957, 79.

217. Poiger refers to ads from Nivea. See her "Imperialism and Empire," 136. On the influence of colonial myths in West Germany, see Jason Verber, "Remembering at a Time of Forgetting: Weimar Colonialism in West Germany," in *Weimar Colonialism: Discourses and Legacies of Post-imperialism in Germany after 1918*, ed. Florian Ulrich Krobb and Elaine Martin (Bielefeld: Aisthesis-Verlag, 2014), 209–27.

Epilogue

1. *Das Spukschloss im Spessart*, West Germany, 1960, directed by Kurt Hoffmann, Georg Witt-Film G.m.b.H. My thanks go to Boris Schafgans for bringing this film to my attention.

2. *Jonas*, West Germany, 1956–57, directed by Ottomar Domnick, Dr. Ottomoar Domnick Verlag und Film. See also Michael Althen, "Man muss absolut modern sein: Wie der Arzt Ottomar Domnick vor fünfzig Jahren versuchte, dem deutschen Kino auf die Sprünge zu helfen," *Frankfurter Allgemeine Zeitung*, March 7, 2010, https://www.faz.net/aktuell/feuilleton/kino/momente-des-deutschen-films-iv-jonas-man-muss-absolut-modern-sein-1941579-p2.html.

3. Marie Luise Kaschnitz, *Das Haus der Kindheit* (1956; repr., Munich: Deutscher Taschenbuch Verlag, 1995); Walter Abish, *How German Is It—wie deutsch ist es* (New York: New Directions Books, 1979).

4. Wolfgang Pehnt, "Neunzig Jahre Bauhaus: Quadratisch, praktisch, besser," *Frankfurter Allgemeine Zeitung*, July 22, 2009, https://www.faz.net/aktuell/feuilleton/kunst-und-architektur/neunzig-jahre-bauhaus-quadratisch-praktisch-besser-1831998.html.

5. Hanno Rauterberg, "Bauhaus: Ins Zeitlose entrückt," *Die Zeit*, no. 4, January 17, 2019, https://www.zeit.de/2019/04/bauhaus-architektur-100-jahre-modernismus-mythos-revolution.

6. *Emil Nolde—eine deutsche Legende—der Künstler im Nationalsozialismus*, exhibition at the Hamburger Bahnhof Museum für Gegenwart, Berlin, April 12–September 15, 2019.

7. Julia Friedrich, "Kunst als Kitt: Spuren des Nationalsozialismus in der ersten documenta," and Julia Voss, "Das Werner-Haftmann Modell: Wie die documenta zur Bühne der Erinnerungspolitik wurde," both in *documenta: Politik und Kunst*, catalog of the exhibition of the German Historical Museum, ed. Raphael Gross et al. (Munich: Prestel, 2021), 60–67, 68–76.

8. Nanne Buurman, "Northern Gothic: Werner Haftmann's German Lessons, or A Ghost (Hi)Story of Abstraction," *documenta studien #11* (December 2020), https://documenta-studien.de/media/1/documenta_studies__11_nanne_buurman_1.pdf, accessed January 15, 2022.

9. Frances Tanzer, "European Fantasies: Modernism and Jewish Absence at the Venice Biennale of Art, 1948–1956," *Contemporary European History* 31, no. 2 (May 2022): 243–58.

10. *Time*, February 15, 1954, cover.

11. Priya Satia, *Time's Monster: How History Makes History* (Cambridge, MA: Belknap Press of Harvard University Press, 2020).

12. On the emergence of the Columbus myth in the United States and in Europe, see Trouillot, *Silencing the Past*, chap. 4.

13. Kroen, "Robinson Charley," quotes on 68 and 87.

14. Christoph Schmidt, "Rutte: Diepe excuses voor extreem en stelselmatig geweld in Indonesië," *Trouw*, February 17, 2022, https://www.trouw.nl/binnenland/rutte-diepe-excuses-voor-extreem-en-stelselmatig-geweld-in-indonesie~b2397dd5/.

15. Aimé Césaire, *Discours sur le colonialisme* (1950; repr., Paris: Présence Africaine, 1955), 13. The expression "choc en retour" in the French original was translated into English as "boomerang effect," which lacks the psychological aspect of "shock." See Aimé Césaire, *Discourse on Colonialism*, trans. Joan Pinkham (New York: Monthly Review Press, 2000), 36.

16. Césaire, *Discourse on Colonialism*, 37–38.

17. Lynn A. Higgins observes that "France's wartime position as an occupied territory, and thus the implied ironies and reversals of the Algerian situation, made it particularly imperative that the French government (through its ministry of culture) maintain a clear separation between the two" (*New Novel, New Wave, New Politics: Fiction and the Representation of History in Postwar France* [Lincoln: University of Nebraska Press, 1998], 52).

18. *Le petit soldat*, France, 1960, directed by Jean-Luc Godard, Georges de Beauregard.

19. Richard Neupert, *A History of the French New Wave Cinema* (Madison: University of Wisconsin Press, 2002), 220–25.

20. See also *Le petit soldat: A Film by Jean-Luc Godard*, trans. and description of action by Nicholas Garnham (London: Lorrimer Publishing, 1967), 30, 40.

21. Ross, *Fast Cars*, esp. chap. 2, 71–122.

22. Ross, *Fast Cars*, quotes 77, 115, 176, 196.

23. McClintock, *Imperial Leather*, 223.

BIBLIOGRAPHY

Databases

ANNO Historical Newspaper and Magazines. Austrian National Library (https://anno.onb.ac.at/)

Bpk-Bildagentur. Image Bank of Cultural Institutions. Stiftung Preußischer Kulturbesitz (https://www.bpk-bildagentur.de/)

German Digital Library (https://www.deutsche-digitale-bibliothek.de/)

International Movie Database (www.imdb.com)

Portal to Texas History (https://texashistory.unt.edu)

Archives

Brauner, Artur, Archive. Deutsches Filminstitut e.V., Frankfurt am Main.

Collection of private photo albums. Stadtmuseum München

Käutner, Helmut, Archive. Akademie der Künste, Berlin

Private collection of historical photographs and photo albums. Bernd Stiegler, Konstanz

Primary Sources: Periodicals

Arbeitertum: Amtliches Organ der Deutschen Arbeitsfront

Architektur und Wohnform

Banater Deutsche Zeitung

Baukunst und Werkform: Monatsschrift für alle Gebiete der Gestaltung

Bella: Die Filmillustrierte

Brigitte: Das Magazin für Frauen

Constanze: Die Zeitschrift für Frauen und für jedermann

Das Auto: Motor und Sport

Das Blatt der Hausfrau: Illustrierte Monatsschrift für Haushalt, Mode und Unterhaltung

Der Führer: Das Hauptorgan der NSDAP Gau Baden

Der Simpl: Kunst, Karikatur, Kritik

Der Spiegel
Der Stern: Das deutsche Magazin
Der Tag
Deutsche Tagespost: Katholische Zeitung für Deutschland
Die Gegenwart: Eine Halbmonatzsschrift
die neue linie
Die Wandlung: Eine Monatsschrift
Die Zeit: Wochenzeitung für Politik, Wirtschaft, Wissen und Kultur
Filmblätter: Fachzeitschrift für Film, Fono, Foto, Fernsehen, Funk
Film-Echo: Offizielles Organ des Zentralverbandes der Deutschen Filmtheater e.V.
Filmpost-Magazin
Film-Telegramm: Unabhängiger Informationsdienst über Film und Fernsehen
Filmwelt: Das Film- und Fotomagazin
Filmwoche: Der neue Film
Frankfurter Allgemeine Zeitung
Frankfurter Hefte: Zeitschrift für Kultur und Politik
Fränkische Landeszeitung
Fränkisches Volksblatt: Tageszeitung für Unterfranken
Gute Fahrt: Die Zeitschrift für den Volkswagenfahrer
Innen-Dekoration: Mein Heim, mein Stolz, die gesamte Wohnungskunst in Bild und Wort
Jeversches Wochenblatt
Journal of the Royal Society of Arts
Kasseler Zeitung: Überparteiliche Tageszeitung für Nordhessen
Life
magnum: Die Zeitschrift für das moderne Leben
Mittelbayerische Zeitung
Motor-Rundschau für das gesamte Kraftfahrwesen
Neue Illustrierte: Eine aktuelle politische Bilderzeitung
Neue Warte am Inn: Unabhängiges Wochenblatt
New York Times
NS Frauenwarte: Zeitschrift der NS-Frauenschaft
Passauer Neue Presse
Quick: Illustrierte für Deutschland
Rheinische Post: Zeitung für Politik und christliche Kultur
Signal (Dutch edition)
Simplicissimus
Star-Revue: Die Funk- und Fernseh-Illustrierte
Südostdeutsche Tageszeitung: Organ der Deutschen in Rumänien
Sydney Morning Herald
Taunusbote
Times (London)
Völkischer Beobachter: Kampfblatt der national-sozialistischen Bewegung Großdeutschland
Vossische Zeitung: Berlinische Zeitung von Staats- und gelehrten Sachen

Primary Sources: Books and Articles

Abish, Walter. *How German Is It—wie deutsch ist es*. New York: New Directions Books, 1979.

Arendt, Hannah. "The Aftermath of the Nazi Rule: Report from Germany." *Commentary* 10, no. 4 (October 1950): 342–53.

Bammer, Angelika. *Born After: Reckoning with the German Past*. New York: Bloomsbury Academic, 2019.

Benedict, Ruth. *Race: Science and Politics*. New York: Viking Press, 1945.

Berbuer, Karl. "Wir sind die Einwohner von Trizonesien." Carnival song, published November 11, 1948. Accessed January 15, 2023. https://www.golyr.de/karl-berbuer/songtext-trizonesien-song-277557.html.

Boberach, Heinz, ed. *Meldungen aus dem Reich: Die geheimen Lageberichte des Sicherheitsdienstes der SS 1938–1945*. Vol. 9. Herrsching: Pawlak Verlag, 1984.

Bronnen, Barbara, ed. *Geschichten vom Überleben: Frauentagebücher aus der NS-Zeit*. Munich: C. H. Beck, 1998.

Césaire, Aimé. *Discourse on Colonialism*. Translated by Joan Pinkham. New York: Monthly Review Press, 2000.

———. *Discours sur le colonialisme*. 1950. Reprint, Paris: Présence Africaine, 1955.

Deutscher Werkbund Berlin, ed. *Wohnen in unserer Zeit: Wohungsgestaltung der Interbau*. Published on the occasion of Interbau Berlin 57. Darmstadt: Verlag Das Beispiel, 1957.

Deutscher Werkbund, ed. *Werkbund-Ausstellung neues Wohnen: Deutsche Architektur seit 1945, Köln 1949, 14. Mai bis 3. Juli*. Cologne: Lang, 1949.

Deutschland-Berichte der Sozialdemokratischen Partei Deutschlands (Sopade) 1934–1940. Vol. 6, 1939. Frankfurt am Main: Zweitausenteinds, 1980.

Die schöne Wohnung: Wohnräume der Gegenwart in 225 Abbildungen. Munich: Verlag F. Bruckmann, 1934.

Die schöne Wohnung: Wohnräume der Gegenwart in 175 Abbildungen. Munich: Verlag F. Bruckmann, 1941.

Erdmann, Kurt. *Europa und der Orientteppich*. Berlin: Florian Kupferberg, 1962.

Fallada, Hans. *Der Alpdruck*. 1947. Reprint, Berlin: Aufbau, 2015.

Gateway to Germany. Publication on behalf of the German Federal Ministry of the Marshall Plan. Bonn: Verlag für Publizistik of MBH Bonn, 1952.

Großkinsky, August, comp. *Schönheit des Wohnens*. 2nd ed. Freiburg: Otto Kehrer, 1948.

———, comp., in cooperation with the Reichsheimstättenamt der Deutschen Arbeitsfront (Imperial Bureau of Homesteads of the German Labor Front). *Schönheit des Wohnens: Ein Bildwerk über deutsche Wohnmöbel*. Freiburg im Breisgau: Karl Popp Verlag, [1941].

Harbers, Guido. *Die schöne Wohnung*. 6th ed. Munich: F. Bruckmann, 1952.

Harbou, Thea von. *Das indische Grabmal*. Berlin: Ullstein, 1921.

Heining, Heinrich. *Auf Wiedersehen, Franziska!* Berlin: Ufa-Buchverlag G.m.b.H., n.d.

Heuss, Theodor. "Notizen und Exkurse zur Geschichte des Deutschen Werkbundes." In *50 Jahre Deutscher Werkbund*, edited on behalf of the German Werkbund by the Landesgruppe Hessen, 19–26. Berlin: Alfred Metzner, 1958.

———. *Was ist Qualität? Zur Geschichte und Aufgabe des Deutschen Werkbundes*. Tübingen: Rainer Wunderlich Verlag Hermann Leins, 1951.

Joesten, Joachim. "The Nazis in Scandinavia." *Foreign Affairs* 15 (July 1937): 720–28.

Kaschnitz, Marie Luise. *Das Haus der Kindheit*. 1956. Reprint, Munich: Deutscher Taschenbuch Verlag, 1995.

———. *Von Menschen und Dingen*. Schriften der Wandlung 2. Heidelberg: Lambert Schneider, 1946.

———. *Von Menschen und Dingen: Zwölf Essays mit einem Nachwort von Karl Krolow*. Frankfurt am Main: Insel Verlag, 1995.

Kästner, Erich. *Das Blaue Buch: Kriegstagebuch und Roman-Notizen*. Edited by Ulrich von Bülow and Silke Becker. 2nd ed. Marbach: Deutsche Schillergesellschaft, 2007.

———. *Notabene 1945: Ein Tagebuch von Erich Kästner*. Zurich: Atrium, 1961.

Kempowski, Walter. *Das Echolot: Abgesang '45; Ein kollektives Tagebuch*. Munich: Albrecht Knaus, 2005.

Klemperer, Victor. *LTI: Notizbuch eines Philologen*. 1947. Reprint, Stuttgart: Reclam, 2010.

Koch, Alexander. *Praktisch Bauen + schön Wohnen = glücklich Leben*. Stuttgart: Alexander Koch, 1955.

Kräfte sammeln, Kräfte lenken, Kräfte sparen: Drei Reden zur Internationalen Automobil- und Motorrad-Ausstellung Berlin 1939. Reichsverband der Automobilindustrie e.V. Berlin, June 1939.

Kuby, Erich. *Alarm im Werk: Der Junge mit dem Volkswagen*. Munich: F. Schneider, 1955.

———. *Thomas und sein Volkswagen*. Munich: F. Schneider, 1956.

Le petit soldat: A Film by Jean-Luc Godard. Translation and description of action by Nicholas Garnham. London: Lorrimer Publishing, 1967.

Lützeler, Heinrich, and Marga Lützeler. *Unser Heim*. Bonn: Verlag der Buchgemeinde, 2nd ed. 1940 and 4th ed. 1950.

Meyer-Ehlers, G. *Wohnerfahrungen: Ergebnisse einer Wohnuntersuchung*. Wiesbaden: Bauverlag, 1963.

Mönnich, Horst. *Die Autostadt*. Frankfurt am Main: Deutscher Jugendbuchverlag, 1951.

———. *Geboren Neunzehn-Hundert-Achtzehn: Von einem Ende zum Anderen*. Munich: Franz Schneekluth Verlag, 1993.

Neckel, Gustav. "Das Nordische und die deutsche Bildung." *Nordische Rundschau*, no. 1–2 (1934): 1–13.

Noelle, Elisabeth, and Erich Peter Neumann. *Jahrbuch der öffentlichen Meinung, 1947–1955*. Allensbach: Verlag für Demoskopie, 1955.

———. *Jahrbuch der öffentlichen Meinung 1947–1955*. 2nd ed. Allensbach: Verlag für Demoskopie, 1956.

———. *Jahrbuch der öffentlichen Meinung, 1957*. Allensbach: Verlag für Demoskopie, 1957.

———. *Jahrbuch der öffentlichen Meinung, 1958–1964*. Allensbach: Verlag für Demoskopie, 1965.

Padover, Saul K. *Experiment in Germany: The Story of an American Intelligence Officer*. New York: Duell, Sloan and Pearce, [1946].

Paepcke, Lotte. *Unter einem fremden Stern*. Frankfurt am Main: Verlag der Frankfurter Hefte, 1952.

Posener, Julius. *In Deutschland: 1945 bis 1946*. Berlin: Siedler, 2001.

Schelsky, Helmut. *Die skeptische Generation: Eine Soziologie der deutschen Jugend*. Cologne: Diederichs, 1957.

Spannagel, Fritz. *Unsere schöne Wohnung*. Ravensburg: Otto Maier, 1937.

Steiner, George. *Language and Silence: Essays on Language, Literature, and the Inhuman*. New York: Athenaeum, 1986.

Tabori, George. *Theaterstücke 2*. Translated from English by Ursula Grützmacher-Tabori. Munich: Hanser, 1994.

Todtmann, Heinz, and Alfred Tritschler. *Kleiner Wagen auf großer Fahrt*. Offenburg: Verlag Dr. Franz Burda, 1949.

Wantzen, Paulheinz. *Das Leben im Krieg 1939–1946: Ein Tagebuch*. Homberg: Verlag Das Dokument, 2000.

"Wie schnell wandelt sich der Geschmack? Der Weg zur modernen Innenausstattung." Press release of the opinion research institute Allensbach, March 23, 1959.

Primary Sources: Films

Air of Freedom. West Germany, 1951. Produced by HICOG Film Section for ECA Germany.

Alltag in einer Siedlung. Germany, 1942. Abteilung Film Propagandaamt der Deutschen Arbeitsfront.

Auf Wiedersehen, Franziska! Germany, 1941. Directed by Helmut Käutner. Terra-Filmkunst G.m.b.H.

Aus eigener Kraft. West Germany, 1953–54. Directed by Franz Schroedter. Franz Schroedter-Studio KG for the Volkswagen factory.

Aus gutem Holz. Germany, 1938. Döring-Film. Educational film.

Das Spukschloss im Spessart. West Germany, 1960. Directed by Kurt Hoffmann. Georg Witt-Film G.m.b.H.

Deutschland im Jahre Null / Germania Anno Zero. Germany and Italy, 1948. Directed by Roberto Rossellini. Tevere Film.

Die Landärztin. West Germany, 1958. Directed by Paul May. KG Divina Film, Munich.

Die Mörder sind unter uns. Germany, 1946. Directed by Wolfgang Staudte. Deutsche Film AG, East Berlin.

Die Welt huldigt dem Volkswagen. West Germany, 1955. Produced by Walter Knoop.

Eine Frau von heute. West Germany, 1954. Directed by Paul Verhoeven. Fama F.A. Mainz Film.

Film ohne Titel. Germany, 1948. Directed by Rudolf Jugert. Camera Filmproduktion Hamburg.

Franziska / Auf Wiedersehen, Franziska! West Germany, 1957. Directed by Wolfgang Liebeneiner. CCC Filmkunst.

Heimat und Boden. Germany, 1942. Imperial Bureau of Homesteads. Documentary.

In jenen Tagen. (West) Germany, 1946–47. Directed by Helmut Käutner. Camera-Filmproduktion G.m.b.H. Hamburg.

Jonas. West Germany, 1956–57. Directed by Ottomar Domnick. Dr. Ottomar Domnick Verlag und Film.
"Kleiner Wagen . . . große Liebe": Ein Film für Autofreunde. West Germany, 1949. Directed by Ulrich Kayser. UKA Film-Produktion.
Le petit soldat. France, 1960. Directed by Jean-Luc Godard. Georges de Beauregard.
Natürlich die Autofahrer. West Germany, 1959. Directed by Erich Engels. Deutsche Film Hansa, Hamburg.
Sinfonie eines Autos. West Germany, 1949. Directed by Ulrich Kayser and Werner Liesfeld. UKA Film-Produktion Freiburg.
Volkswagen-Geschichten. West Germany, 1950. Directed by Herbert Kruchen. Melodia-Film Produktion Werner Grünbauer Hamburg.
Wir Wunderkinder. West Germany, 1958. Directed by Kurt Hoffmann. Filmaufbau Göttingen.
Zwischen gestern und morgen. Germany, 1947. Directed by Harald Braun. Neue Deutsche Filmgesellschaft, Munich.

Reference Works

Allgemeines Künstlerlexikon—Internationale Künstlerdatenbank—Online
Deutsche Biographie
Munzinger Personen—Internationales Biographisches Archiv
Neue Deutsche Biographie
Oxford English Dictionary

Secondary Sources

Ahmed, Sarah. "Affective Economies." *Social Text* 22, no. 2 (2004): 117–39.
Ahonen, Pertti. "Germany and the Aftermath of the Second World War." *Journal of Modern History* 89, no. 2 (2017): 355–87.
Albrecht, Monika. *"Europa ist nicht die Welt": (Post)Kolonialismus in Literatur und Geschichte der westdeutschen Nachkriegszeit*. Bielefeld: Aisthesis, 2008.
Aly, Götz. *Hitler's Beneficiaries: Plunder, Racial War, and the Nazi Welfare State*. New York: Metropolitan Books, 2008.
Arnold, Jörg. *The Allied Air War and Urban Memory: The Legacy of Strategic Bombing in Germany*. New York: Cambridge University Press, 2016.
Ashby, Charlotte. *Modernism in Scandinavia: Art, Architecture and Design*. London: Bloomsbury, 2017.
Auslander, Leora. "Beyond Words." *American Historical Review* 110, no. 4 (2006): 1015–45.
———. *Cultural Revolutions: The Politics of Everyday Life in Britain, North America and France*. New York: Berg, 2009.
———. *Taste and Power: Furnishing Modern France*. Berkeley: University of California Press, 1996.
Bade, Klaus J., and Jochen Oltmer. "Einwanderungsland Niedersachsen: Zuwanderung und Integration seit dem Zweiten Weltkrieg." In *Zuwanderung und Integration in*

Niedersachsen seit dem Zweiten Weltkrieg, edited by Klaus J. Bade and Jochen Oltmer, 11–36. Osnabrück: Universitäts-Verlag Rasch, 2002.

Baer, Hester. *Dismantling the Dream Factory: Gender, German Cinema, and the Postwar Quest for a New Film Language*. New York: Berghahn Books, 2009.

Bajohr, Frank. "'Arisierung' und Restitution: Eine Einschätzung." In *"Arisierung" und Restitution*, edited by Constantin Goschler and Jürgen Lillteicher, 39–59. Göttingen: Wallstein, 2002.

———. *"Aryanisation" in Hamburg: The Economic Exclusion of Jews and the Confiscation of Their Property in Nazi Germany*. New York: Berghahn Books, 2002.

———. *Unser Hotel ist judenfrei: Bäderantisemitismus im 19. und 20. Jahrhundert*. Frankfurt am Main: Fischer Taschenbuchverlag, 2003.

Baranowski, Shelley. *Strength through Joy: Consumerism and Mass Tourism in the Third Reich*. Cambridge: Cambridge University Press, 2004.

Barnhisel, Greg. "*Perspectives USA* and the Cultural Cold War." *Modernism/Modernity* 14, no. 4 (2007): 729–54.

Barnstone, Deborah. "Nomina Sunt Omina—Capital City Bonn: Inventing an Image for the Federal Republic of Germany." *Journal of Design History* 27, no. 2 (2014): 148–66.

Baron, Lawrence. "Kristallnacht on Film: From Reportage to Reenactments, 1938–1948." In "The Space Between: Literature and Culture 1914–1945." Special issue, *International Cinema and the Space Between: The Long Decade of the 1930s* 16 (2020). https://scalar.usc.edu/works/the-space-between-literature-and-culture-1914-1945/vol16_2020_baron.

Barthes, Roland. *Mythologies*. Selected and translated by Annette Levers. London: Vintage Books, 2009.

Baumann, Angelika, and Andreas Heusler. *München "arisiert": Entrechtung und Enteignung der Juden in Der NS-Zeit*. Munich: C. H. Beck, 2004.

Becker, Franziska. *Gewalt und Gedächtnis: Erinnerungen an die nationalsozialistische Verfolgung einer jüdischen Landgemeinde*. Göttingen: V. Schmerse, 1994.

Becker, Michael, Dirk Braunstein, and Fabian Link. "Postnazistisches Sprechen: Einführung in Peter von Haselbergs Beitrag zum Gruppenexperiment." In *Schuldgefühle: Postnazistische Mentalitäten in der frühen Bundesrepublik; Eine Studie aus dem Gruppenexperiment am Institut für Sozialforschung*, by Peter von Haselberg, edited by Michael Becker, Dirk Braunstein, and Fabian Link, 11–32. Frankfurt am Main: Campus Verlag, 2020.

Becker, Wolfgang, and Norbert Schöll. *In jenen Tagen: Wie der deutsche Nachkriegsfilm die Vergangenheit bewältigte*. Opladen: Leske und Budrich, 1995.

Beek, Gosewijn van. "On Materiality." *Etnofoor* 9, no. 1 (1996): 5–24.

Berghahn, Volker. "German Colonialism and Imperialism from Bismarck to Hitler." *German Studies Review* 40, no. 1 (2017): 147–62.

Bessel, Richard. *Germany 1945: From War to Peace*. London: Simon & Schuster, 2009.

Betts, Paul. *The Authority of Everyday Objects: A Cultural History of West German Industrial Design*. Berkeley: University of California Press, 2004.

———. "The Bauhaus as Cold-War Legend: West German Modernism Revisited." *German Politics and Society* 14, no. 2 (1996): 75–100.

———. "The *Nierentisch* Nemesis: Organic Design as West German Pop Culture." *German History* 19, no. 2 (2001): 185–217.

———. *Ruin and Renewal: Civilising Europe after the Second World War*. London: Profile Books, 2020.

Bhabha, Homi. "The World and the Home." *Social Text*, no. 31/32 (1992): 141–53.

Bieber, Hans Joachim. *SS und Samurei: Deutsch-japanische Kulturbeziehungen 1933–1934*. Munich: Iudicum, 2014.

Biess, Frank. *German Angst: Fear and Democracy in the Federal Republic of Germany*. New York: Oxford University Press, 2020.

———. "Survivors of Totalitarianism: Returning POWs and the Reconstruction of Masculine Citizenship in West Germany, 1945–1955." In *The Miracle Years: A Cultural History of West Germany, 1949–1968*, edited by Hanna Schissler, 57–82. Princeton, NJ: Princeton University Press, 2001.

Billiani, Francesca. *Fascist Modernism in Italy: The Arts under Dictatorship*. London: I.B. Tauris, 2017.

Billig, Michael. *Banal Nationalism*. London: SAGE, 1995.

Birdsall, Carolyn. *Nazi Soundscapes: Sound, Technology and Urban Space in Germany, 1933–1945*. Amsterdam: Amsterdam University Press, 2012.

Black, Monica. *A Demon-Haunted Land: Witches, Wonder Doctors, and the Ghosts of the Past in Post-WWI Germany*. New York: Metropolitan Books, 2020.

Bliersbach, Gerhard. *Nachkriegskino: Eine Psychohistorie des westdeutschen Nachkriegsfilms 1946–1963*. Gießen: Psychosozial-Verlag, 2014.

Bongie, Chris. *Exotic Memories: Literature, Colonialism, and the Fin de Siècle*. Stanford, CA: Stanford University Press, 1991.

Bonnett, Alastair. *The Idea of the West: Culture, Politics, and History*. Houndmills: Palgrave Macmillan, 2004.

Brauerhoch, Annette. *"Fräuleins" und GIs: Geschichte und Filmgeschichte*. Frankfurt am Main: Stroemfeld Verlag, 2006.

Brenner, Michael. *After the Holocaust: Rebuilding Jewish Life in Postwar Germany*. Princeton, NJ: Princeton University Press, 1997.

Brockhaus, Gudrun. "Die Lederhose—ein verkanntes Emblem der 50er." In *Von Dingen und Menschen: Funktion und Bedeutung materieller Kultur*, edited by Hans A. Hartmann and Rolf Haubl, 37–60. Wiesbaden: Westdeutscher Verlag, 2000.

———. *Schauder und Idylle: Faschismus als Erlebnisangebot*. Munich: Antje Kunstmann, 1997.

Buck-Morss, Susan. "Benjamin's *Passagen-Werk*: Redeeming Mass Culture for the Revolution." *New German Critique*, no. 29 (Spring–Summer 1983): 211–40.

———. *Dreamworld and Catastrophe: The Passing of Mass Utopia in East and West*. Cambridge, MA: MIT Press, 2000.

Buettner, Elizabeth. *Europe after Empire: Decolonization, Society, and Culture*. Cambridge: Cambridge University Press, 2016.

Burton, Antoinette M. *Burdens of History: British Feminists, Indian Women, and Imperial Culture, 1865–1915*. Chapel Hill: University of North Carolina Press, 1994.

Buurman, Nanne. "Northern Gothic: Werner Haftmann's German Lessons, or A Ghost (Hi)Story of Abstraction." *documenta studien #11* (December 2020). Accessed January 15, 2022. https://documenta-studien.de/media/1/documenta_studies__11_nanne_buurman_1.pdf.
Campbell, Joan. *The German Werkbund: The Politics of Reform in the Applied Arts*. Princeton, NJ: Princeton University Press, 1978.
Campt, Tina, Pascal Grosse, and Yara-Colette Lemke-Muniz da Faria. "Blacks, Germans, and the Politics of Imperial Imagination, 1920–1960." In *The Imperialist Imagination: German Colonialism and Its Legacy*, edited by Sara Friedrichsmeyer, Sara Lennox, and Susanne Zantop, 205–29. Ann Arbor: University of Michigan Press, 1998.
Capková, Helena. "Transnational Networkers: Iwao and Michiko Yamawaki and the Formation of Japanese Modernist Design." *Journal of Design History* 27, no. 4 (2014): 370–85.
Carter, Erica. *How German Is She? Postwar West German Reconstruction and the Consuming Woman*. Ann Arbor: University of Michigan Press, 1997.
———. "Sweeping Up the Past: Gender and History in the Postwar German Rubble Film." In *Heroines without Heroes: Reconstructing Female National Identities in European Cinema, 1945–1951*, edited by Ulrike Sieglohr, 91–110. London: Cassell, 2000.
Castillo, Greg. *Cold War on the Home Front: The Soft Power of Midcentury Design*. Minneapolis: University of Minnesota Press, 2010.
———. "Domesticating the Cold War: Household Consumption as Propaganda in Marshall Plan Germany." *Journal of Contemporary History* 40, no. 2 (2005): 261–88.
———. "East as True West: Redeeming Bourgeois Culture; From Socialist Realism to *Ostalgie*." In *Imagining the West in Eastern Europe and the Soviet Union*, edited by György Péteri, 87–104. Pittsburgh, PA: University of Pittsburgh Press, 2010.
———. "Marshall Plan Modernism in Divided Germany." In *Cold War Modern: Design 1945–1970*, edited by David Crowley and Jane Pavitt, 66–71. London: Victoria and Albert Museum, 2008.
Cserno, Isabel. "Race and Mass Consumption in Consumer Culture: National Trademark Advertising Campaigns in the United States and Germany, 1890–1930." PhD diss., University of Maryland, College Park, 2008.
———. "Whiteness Studies and the Colonial Aesthetic: Western Popular Culture and the Representations of Race." *Explorations in Ethnic Studies* 29, no. 2 (2006): 66–85.
Ciarlo, David. "Advertising and the Optics of Colonial Power at the Fin de Siècle." In *Empires of Vision: A Reader*, edited by Martin Jay and Sumathi Ramaswamy, 189–207. Durham, NC: Duke University Press, 2014.
———. *Advertising Empire: Race and Visual Culture in Imperial Germany*. Cambridge, MA: Harvard University Press, 2011.
Cohen, Lizabeth. *A Consumer's Republic: The Politics of Mass Consumption in Postwar America*. New York: Knopf, 2003.
Confino, Alon. "Traveling as a Culture of Remembrance: Traces of National Socialism in West Germany, 1945–1960." *History and Memory* 12, no. 2 (2000): 92–121.
———. *A World without Jews: The Nazi Imagination from Persecution to Genocide*. New Haven, CT: Yale University Press, 2014.

Confino, Alon, and Rudy Koshar. "Régimes of Consumer Culture: New Narratives in Twentieth-Century Germany." *German History* 19, no. 2 (2001): 135–61.

Conrad, Sebastian. *German Colonialism: A Short History*. Cambridge: Cambridge University Press, 2012.

———. *Globalisation and the Nation in Imperial Germany*. Cambridge: Cambridge University Press, 2012.

Copley, Claire. "'Stones Do Not Speak for Themselves': Disentangling Berlin's Palimpsest." *Fascism* 8, no. 2 (2019): 219–49.

Courtade, Franzis, and Pierre Cadars. *Geschichte des Films im Dritten Reich*. Munich: Carl Hanser, 1975.

Cowan, Michael. *Walter Ruttmann and the Cinema of Multiplicity: Avant-Garde—Advertising—Modernity*. Amsterdam: Amsterdam University Press, 2014.

Crew, David F., ed. *Consuming Germany in the Cold War*. Oxford: Berg, 2003.

Crowley, David, and Jane Pavitt, eds. *Cold War Modern: Design 1945–1970*. London: Victoria and Albert Museum, 2008.

Darnton, Robert. *The Great Cat Massacre and Other Episodes in French Cultural History*. New York: Basic Books, 1984.

Dekker, Laura. "Niet gelijk, wel gelijkwaardig?" Master's thesis, University of Amsterdam, 2017.

Dobryden, Paul. "Good Germans, Humane Automobiles: Redeeming Technological Modernity—*In Those Days*." *Film & History* 40, no. 1 (2010): 7–24.

Droste, Magdalena. "Bauhaus-Designer zwischen Handwerk und Moderne." In *Bauhaus-Moderne im Nationalsozialismus: Zwischen Anbiederung und Verfolgung*, edited by Winfried Nerdinger, 85–101. Munich: Prestel-Verlag, 1993.

Dundes, Alan, and Thomas Hauschild. "Auschwitz Jokes." *Western Folklore* 42, no. 4 (1983): 249–60.

———. "Kennt der Witz kein Tabu? Zynische Erzählformen als Versuch der Bewältigung nationalsozialistischer Vergangenheit." *Zeitschrift für Volkskunde* 83, no. 1 (1987): 21–31.

Edwards, Brian T. "Yankee Pashas and Buried Women: Containing Abundance in 1950s Hollywood Orientalism." *Film & History* 31, no. 2 (2001): 13–24.

Eggers, Katharina, and Robert Fechner. "'The German Alternative': Nationalism and Racism in 'Afri-Cola.'" In *Colonial Advertising & Commodity Racism*, edited by Wulf D. Hund and Michael Pickering, 197–217. Münster: LIT Verlag, 2013.

Eisen, Markus. "Wilhelm Wagenfeld und Hermann Gretsch." In *100 Jahre Deutscher Werkbund 1907–2007*, exhibition catalog, edited by Winfried Nerdinger, 206–7. Munich: Prestel, 2007.

Ellwood, David W. "The Propaganda of the Marshall Plan in Italy in a Cold War Context." *Intelligence and National Security* 18, no. 2 (2003): 225–36.

———. *Rebuilding Europe: Western Europe, America and Postwar Reconstruction*. Harlow, Essex: Longman House, 1992.

Epple, Angelika. "Das Auge schmeckt Stollwerck: Uniformierung der Bilderwelt und kulturelle Differenzierung von Vorstellungsbildern in Zeiten des Imperialismus und der Globalisierung." *WerkstattGeschichte*, no. 45 (2007): 13–31.

Escher, Clemens. *"Deutschland, Deutschland, du mein alles!": Die Deutschen auf der Suche nach ihrer Nationalhymne 1949–1952*. Paderborn: Ferdinand Schöningh, 2017.

Eser, Willibald. *Helmut Käutner "Abblenden": Sein Leben, seine Filme*. Munich: Moewig, 1981.

Evans, Jennifer V. *Life among the Ruins: Cityscape and Sexuality in Cold War Berlin*. Basingstoke: Palgrave Macmillan, 2011.

Fehrenbach, Heide. *Cinema in Democratizing Germany: Reconstructing National Identity after Hitler*. Chapel Hill: University of North Carolina Press, 1995.

———. *Race after Hitler: Occupation Children in Postwar Germany and America*. Princeton, NJ: Princeton University Press, 2005.

Fernandez, Karen V., and John L. Lastovicka. "Making Magic: Fetishes in Contemporary Consumption." *Journal of Consumer Research* 38, no. 2 (2011): 278–99.

Fischer, Jan Otakar. "Memento Machinae: Engineering the Past in Wolfsburg." In *Beyond Berlin: Twelve German Cities Confront the Nazi Past*, edited by Gavriel D. Rosenfeld and Paul B. Jaskot, 89–115. Ann Arbor: University of Michigan Press, 2007.

Fisher, Jaimey. "Bombing Memories in Braun's *Zwischen Gestern und Morgen* (1947): Flashbacks to the Recent Past in the German Rubble-Film." In *Bombs Away! Representing the Air War over Europe and Japan*, edited by Wilfried Wilms and William Rasch, 329–43. Amsterdam: Rodopi, 2009.

———. "Wandering in/to the Rubble-Film: Filmic Flânerie and the Exploded Panorama after 1945." *German Quarterly* 78, no. 4 (2005): 461–80.

Floré, Fredie, and Mil de Kooning. "The Representation of Modern Domisticity in the Belgian Section of the Brussels World's Fair of 1958." *Journal of Design History* 16, no. 4 (2003): 319–40.

Föllmer, Moritz. *Individuality and Modernity in Berlin: Self and Society from Weimar to the Wall*. Cambridge: Cambridge University Press, 2013.

Forster, Ralf. "Von der Zeichentricksinfonie zum Mischfilm: Zäsuren des bundesdeutschen Werbeanimationsfilms um 1960." *montage A/V*, February 22, 2013, 119–31.

Frank, Stefanie Mathilde. *Wiedersehen im Wirtschaftswunder: Remakes von Filmen aus der Zeit des Nationalsozialismus in der Bundesrepublik 1949–1963*. Göttingen: Vandenhoeck & Ruprecht, 2017.

Frei, Norbert. *Vergangenheitspolitik: Die Anfänge der Bundesrepublik Deutschland und die NS-Vergangenheit*. Munich: C. H. Beck, 1996.

Friedländer, Saul. *Nazi Germany and the Jews, 1939–1945: The Years of Extermination*. New York: HarperCollins, 2007.

Friedrich, Julia. "Kunst als Kitt: Spuren des Nationalsozialismus in der ersten documenta." In *documenta: Politik und Kunst*, edited by Raphael Gross, Lars Bang Larsen, Dorlis Blume, Alexia Pooth, Julia Voss, and Dorothee Wierling, 61–64. Munich: Prestel, 2021.

Friedrichsmeyer, Sara, Sara Lennox, and Susanne Zantop, eds. *The Imperialist Imagination: German Colonialism and Its Legacy*. Ann Arbor: University of Michigan Press, 1998.

Fritsche, Christiane. *Vergangenheitsbewältigung im Fernsehen: Westdeutsche Filme über den Nationalsozialismus in den 1950er und 1960er Jahren*. Munich: Martin Meidenbauer Verlag, 2003.

Fritzsche, Peter. *Life and Death in the Third Reich*. Cambridge, MA: Belknap Press of Harvard University Press, 2008.

Fulks, Barry. "Walter Ruttmann, the Avant-Garde Film, and Nazi Modernism." *Film & History* 14, no. 2 (1984): 26–46.

Fünderich, Maren-Sophie. *Wohnen im Kaiserreich: Einrichtungsstil und Möbeldesign im Kontext bürgerlicher Selbstrepräsentation*. Berlin: De Gruyter, 2019.

Galán, Ignacio G. "Building Simultaneity in Fascist Italy: Film, Furniture, and the Reframing of the Nation." *Journal of the Society of Architectural Historians* 80, no. 2 (2021): 182–201.

Geertz, Clifford. "History and Anthropology." *New Literary History* 21, no. 2 (Winter 1990): 321–35.

Geppert, Alexander, and Till Kössler, eds. *Wunder: Poetik und Politik des Staunens im 20. Jahrhundert*. Berlin: Suhrkamp, 2011.

Geyer, Michael. "Die eingebildete Heimkehr: Im Schatten der Niederlage." In *Demokratie im Schatten der Gewalt: Geschichten des Privaten im deutschen Nachkrieg*, edited by Daniel Fulda, Dagmar Herzog, Stefan-Ludwig Hoffmann, and Till van Rahden, 72–96. Göttingen: Wallstein Verlag, 2010.

Goeschel, Christian. *Suicide in Nazi Germany*. Oxford: Oxford University Press, 2015.

Gogwilt, Christopher L. *The Invention of the West: Joseph Conrad and the Double-Mapping of Europe and Empire*. Stanford, CA: Stanford University Press, 1995.

Gordon, Avery. *Ghostly Matters: Haunting and the Sociological Imagination*. Minneapolis: University of Minnesota Press, 2008.

Goschler, Constantin. "Die Politik der Rückerstattung in Westdeutschland." In *"Arisierung" und Restitution: Die Rückerstattung jüdischen Eigentums in Deutschland und Österreich nach 1945 und 1989*, edited by Constantin Goschler and Jürgen Lillteicher, 99–125. Göttingen: Wallstein, 2002.

Goschler, Constantin, and Jürgen Lillteicher, eds. *"Arisierung" und Restitution: Die Rückerstattung jüdischen Eigentums in Deutschland und Österreich nach 1945 und 1989*. Göttingen: Wallstein, 2002.

Gregor, Neil. *Haunted City: Nuremberg and the Nazi Past*. New Haven, CT: Yale University Press, 2009.

Grieger, Manfred. "Eine Meistererzählung vom Volkswagen und der dazugehörigen Stadt: Der Roman *Die Autostadt* von Horst Mönnich aus dem Jahr 1951." In *Die Wolfsburg-Saga*, edited by Christoph Stölzl, 144–47. Stuttgart: Konrad Theiss, 2008.

Gries, Rainer. *Produkte als Medien: Kulturgeschichte der Produktkommunikation in der Bundesrepublik und der DDR*. Leipzig: Leipziger Universitätsverslag, 2003.

Gries, Rainer, Volker Illgen, and Dirk Schindelbeck. *"Ins Gehirn der Masse kriechen!": Werbung und Mentalitätsgeschichte*. Darmstadt: Wissenschaftliche Buchgesellschaft, 1995.

Groß, Bernhard. *Die Filme sind unter uns: Zur Geschichtlichkeit des frühen deutschen Nachkriegskinos; Trümmer-, Genre-, Dokumentarfilm*. Berlin: Vorwerk 8, 2015.

———. "Wahrnehmen—Observieren—'Checken': Geschichtlichkeit als ästhetische Erfahrung in *Zwischen Gestern und Morgen*." In *Demokratisierung der Wahrnehmung? Das westeuropäische Nachkriegskino*, edited by Hermann Kappelhoff, Bernhard Groß, and Daniel Illger, 115–34. Berlin: Vorwerk 8, 2010.

Gross, Raphael, Lars Bang Larsen, Dorlis Blume, Alexia Pooth, Julia Voss, and Dorothee Wierling, eds. *documenta: Politik und Kunst*. Catalog of the exhibition at the German Historical Museum. Munich: Prestel, 2021.

Grosse, Pascal. "What Does German Colonialism Have to Do with National Socialism? A Conceptual Framework." In *Germany's Colonial Pasts*, edited by Eric Ames, Marcia Klotz, and Lora Wildenthal, 115–34. Lincoln: University of Nebraska Press, 2005.

Grossmann, Atina. "Family Files: Emotions and Stories of (Non-)restitution." *German Historical Institute London Bulletin* 34, no. 1 (2012): 59–78.

———. *Jews, Germans, and Allies: Close Encounters in Occupied Germany*. Princeton, NJ: Princeton University Press, 2007.

———. "A Question of Silence: The Rape of German Women by Occupation Soldiers." *October* 72 (Spring 1995): 43–63.

Gumbrecht, Hans Ulrich. *After 1945: Latency as Origin of the Present*. Stanford, CA: Stanford University Press, 2013.

———. *Nach 1945: Latenz als Ursprung der Gegenwart*. Translated by Frank Born. Frankfurt am Main: Suhrkamp, 2012.

Habermas, Tilman. *Geliebte Objekte: Symbole und Instrumente der Identitätsbildung*. Frankfurt am Main: Suhrkamp, 1999.

Habib, André. "Runies, décombres, chantiers, archives: L'évolution d'une figure dans le cinéma en Allemagne (1946–1993)." *Cinémas: Revue d'études cinématographiques* 18, no. 1 (2007): 29–52.

Haerendel, Ulrike. *Kommunale Wohnungspolitik im Dritten Reich: Siedlungsideologie, Kleinhausbau und "Wohnraumarisierung" am Beispiel Münchens*. Munich: R. Oldenbourg Verlag, 1999.

Hagemann, Karen, Konrad H. Jarausch, and Tobias Hof. "Introduction: Burdens and Beginnings; Rebuilding East and West Germany after Nazism." *Central European History* 53, no. 2 (2020): 275–93.

Hagen, Joshua. "The Most German of Towns: Creating an Ideal Nazi Community in Rothenburg ob der Tauber." *Annals of the Association of American Geographers* 94, no. 1 (2004): 207–27.

Hall, Catherine. "Thinking Reflexively: Opening 'Blind Eyes.'" *Past & Present* 234, no. 1 (February 2017): 254–63.

Hall, Catherine, and Daniel Pick. "Thinking about Denial." *History Workshop Journal* 84, no. 1 (2017): 1–23.

Hall, Stuart. *Familiar Stranger: A Life between Two Islands*. Durham, NC: Duke University Press, 2017.

Hanke, Peter. *Zur Geschichte der Juden in München zwischen 1933 und 1945*. Munich: Stadtarchiv, 1967.

Hardtwig, Wolfgang. "Kunst, liberaler Nationalismus und Weltpolitik: Der Deutsche Werkbund 1907 bis 1914." In *Nationalismus und Bürgerkultur in Deutschland 1500–1914*, edited by Wolfgang Hardtwig, 246–73. Göttingen: Vandenhoeck & Ruprecht, 1994.

Harris, Dianne. *Little White Houses: How the Postwar Home Constructed Race in America*. Minneapolis: University of Minnesota Press, 2013.

Harvey, Elizabeth. "International Networks and Cross-Border Cooperation: National Socialist Women and the Vision of a 'New Order' in Europe." *Politics, Religion & Ideology* 13, no. 2 (2012): 141–58.

———. *Women and the Nazi East: Agents and Witnesses of Germanization*. New Haven, CT: Yale University Press, 2003.

Heineman, Elizabeth. "Gender, Sexuality, and Coming to Terms with the Nazi Past." *Central European History* 38, no. 1 (2005): 41–74.

———. "The Hour of the Woman: Memories of Germany's 'Crisis Years' and West German National Identity." *American Historical Review* 101, no. 2 (1996): 354–95.

Heller, Heinz-B. "'Stählerne Romantik' und Avantgarde: Beobachtungen und Anmerkungen zu Ruttmanns Industriefilmen." In *Triumph der Bilder: Kultur- und Dokumentarfilme vor 1945 im internationalen Vergleich*, edited by Peter Zimmermann, 105–18. Konstanz: Konstanz UVK, 2003.

Herf, Jeffrey. *Reactionary Modernism: Technology, Culture, and Politics in Weimar and the Third Reich*. Cambridge: Cambridge University Press, 1984.

Herlyn, Ulfert, Wulf Tessin, Annette Harth, and Gitta Scheller. *Faszination Wolfsburg, 1938–2012*. Wiesbaden: Verlag für Sozialwissenschaften, 2012.

Herzog, Dagmar. *Sex after Fascism: Memory and Morality in Twentieth-Century Germany*. Princeton, NJ: Princeton University Press, 2005.

Heskett, John. "Art and Design in Nazi Germany." *History Workshop* 6, no. 1 (October 1978): 139–53.

Higgins, Lynn A. *New Novel, New Wave, New Politics: Fiction and the Representation of History in Postwar France*. Lincoln: University of Nebraska Press, 1998.

Hobsch, Manfred. *Film im "Dritten Reich": Alle deutschen Spielfilme von 1933 bis 1945*. Vol. 1, A–E. Berlin: Schwarzkopf & Schwarzkopf Verlag, 2010.

Hoffmann, Stefan-Ludwig. "Gazing at Ruins: German Defeat as Visual Experience." *Journal of Modern European History* 9, no. 3 (2011): 328–50.

Höhn, Maria. *GIs and Fräuleins: The German-American Encounter in 1950s West Germany*. Chapel Hill: University of North Carolina Press, 2002.

Holt, Thomas C. "Marking: Race, Race-Making, and the Writing of History." *American Historical Review* 100, no. 1 (1995): 1–20.

Holzer, Horst. "Selbstverständnis und Inhaltsstruktur aktueller Illustrierten dargestellt an den Zeitschriften *Quick*, *Revue* und *Stern*." PhD diss., University of Munich, 1966.

Hondius, Dienke. *Blackness in Western Europe: Racial Patterns of Paternalism and Exclusion*. London: Routledge, 2014.

Huber, Florian. *Kind, versprich mir, dass du dich erschießt: Der Untergang der kleinen Leute 1945*. Berlin: Berlin Verlag, 2015.

Hughes, Michael. *The Anarchy of Nazi Memorabilia: From Things of Tyranny to Troubled Treasure*. New York: Routledge, 2022.

Hundt, Wulf D. *Wie die Deutschen weiss wurden: Kleine (Heimat)Geschichte des Rassismus*. Stuttgart: J. B. Metzler Verlag, 2017.

Hütter, Hans Walter. *VW Käfer . . . und läuft und läuft und läuft*. Bonn: Stiftung Haus der Geschichte der Bundesrepublik Deutschland, 2005.

Hutton, Christopher M. *Race and the Third Reich: Linguistics, Racial Anthropology and Genetics in the Dialectic of* Volk. Cambridge: Polity Press, 2008.

———. "Racial Ideology as Elite Discourse: Nordicism and the Visual in an Age of Mass Culture." *Social Semiotics* 27, no. 3 (2017): 335–47.

Jackson, Patrick Thaddeus. *Civilizing the Enemy: German Reconstruction and the Invention of the West*. Ann Arbor: University of Michigan Press, 2006.

Jacobsen, Wolfgang, and Hans Helmut Prinzler, eds. *Käutner*. Berlin: Edition Filme, 1992.

James-Chakraborty, Kathleen, ed. *Bauhaus-Culture: From Weimar to the Cold War*. Minneapolis: University of Minnesota Press, 2006.

———. "Beyond Cold War Interpretations: Shaping a New Bauhaus Heritage." *New German Critique*, no. 116 (Summer 2012): 11–24.

Jansen, Jennifer. "The Art and Science of Reading Faces: Strategies of Racist Cinema in the Third Reich." *Shofar: An Interdisciplinary Journal of Jewish Studies* 28, no. 1 (2009): 80–103.

Jarzombek, Mark. "The 'Kunstgewerbe,' the 'Werkbund,' and the Aesthetics of Culture in the Wilhelmine Period." *Journal of the Society of Architectural Historians* 53, no. 1 (1994): 7–19.

Jenkins, Jennifer. "The Citizen at Home: *Wohnkultur* before World War I." In *Citizenship and National Identity in Twentieth-Century Germany*, edited by Geoff Eley and Jan Palmowski, 95–107. Stanford, CA: Stanford University Press, 2008.

———. "Introduction: Domesticity, Design and the Shaping of the Social." *German History* 25, no. 3 (2007): 465–89.

———. "The Werkbund Exhibition 'The New Age' of 1932." In *German Modernities from Wilhelm to Weimar*, edited by Geoff Eley, Jennifer Jenkins, and Tracie Matysik, 283–300. London: Bloomsbury Academic, 2016.

Jones, Siân. "Negotiating Authentic Objects and Authentic Selves: Beyond the Deconstruction of Authenticity." *Journal of Material Culture* 15, no. 2 (2010): 181–203.

Kappelhoff, Hermann. "Kriegerische Mobilisierung: Die mediale Organisation des Gemeinsinns." *Navigationen: Zeitschrift für Medien- und Kulturwissenschaften* 9, no. 1 (2009): 151–65.

———. *Matrix der Gefühle: Das Kino, das Melodrama und das Theater der Empfindsamkeit*. Berlin: Vorwerk 8, 2004.

Kaplan, Marion A. *Between Dignity and Despair: Jewish Life in Nazi Germany*. Oxford: Oxford University Press, 1998.

Kauders, Anthony D. "Juden als Gabe, oder: Eine andere Geschichte der westdeutschen Demokratie." In *Demokratie im Schatten der Gewalt: Geschichten des Privaten im deutschen Nachkrieg*, edited by Daniel Fulda, Dagmar Herzog, Stefan-Ludwig Hoffmann, and Till van Rahden, 152–73. Göttingen: Wallstein Verlag, 2010.

Keilbach, Judith, and Irmgard Zündorf, eds. *Eichmann: Die deutsch-deutsche Berichterstattung über den Eichmann-Prozess*. DVD and booklet. Fridolfing: absolut Medien, 2021.

Kessel, Martina. "Race and Humor in Nazi Germany." In *Beyond the Racial State: Rethinking Nazi Germany*, edited by Devon O. Pendas, Mark Roseman, and Richard F. Wetzell, 380–401. Cambridge: Cambridge University Press, 2017.

King, Anthony. *Spaces of Global Cultures: Architecture, Urbanism, Identity*. London: Routledge, 2004.

Kipp, Michaela. *"Grossreinemachen im Osten": Feindbilder in deutschen Feldpostbriefen im Zweiten Weltkrieg*. Frankfurt am Main: Campus Verlag, 2014.

Kleinberg, Ethan, Joan Scott, and Gary Wilder. "Theses on Theory and History." *History of the Present* 10, no. 1 (2020): 157–65.

Klenke, Dietmar. "Die deutsche Katastrophe und das Automobil: Zur 'Heils'geschichte eines nationalen Kultobjekts in den Jahren des Wiederaufstiegs." In *Moderne Zeiten: Technik und Zeitgeist im 19. und 20. Jahrhundert*, edited by Michael Salewski and Ilona Stölken-Fitschen, 157–73. Stuttgart: Steiner, 1994.

Kluke, Paul. "Hitler und das Volkswagenprojekt." *Vierteljahreshefte für Zeitgeschichte* 8, no. 4 (1960): 341–83.

Koltermann, Till P. *Der Untergang des Dritten Reiches im Spiegel der deutsch-japanischen Kulturbegegnung 1933–1945*. Wiesbaden: Harrassowitz, 2009.

König, Wolfgang. *Volkswagen, Volksempfänger, Volksgemeinschaft, "Volksprodukte" im Dritten Reich: Vom Scheitern einer nationalsozialistischen Konsumgesellschaft*. Paderborn: Schöningh, 2004.

Koshar, Rudy. "Altar, State and City: Historic Preservation and Urban Meaning in Nazi Germany." *History and Memory* 3, no. 1 (1991): 30–59.

———. *From Monuments to Traces: Artifacts of German Memory, 1870–1990*. Berkeley: University of California Press, 2000.

———. *Germany's Transient Pasts: Preservation and National Memory in the Twentieth Century*. Chapel Hill: University of North Carolina Press, 1998.

Krieg, Nina. "'Solang' der alte Peter . . . : Die vermeintliche Wiedergeburt Alt-Münchens nach 1945." In *Geschichte der Stadt München*, edited by Richard Bauer, 394–412. Munich: C. H. Beck, 1992.

Kriegeskorte, Michael. *Automobilwerbung in Deutschland 1948–1968*. Cologne: Dumont, 1994.

Kroen, Sheryl. "Liberal Tales of Origin at the Berlin Industries Fair." Manuscript.

———. "Robinson Charley: The Ideological Underpinnings of Atlantic History." In *Biography and the Black Atlantic*, edited by Lisa A. Lindsay and John Wood Sweed, 66–89. Philadelphia: University of Pennsylvania Press, 2014.

Krüger, Arnd. "Germany: The Propaganda Machine." In *The Nazi Olympics: Sport, Politics, and Appeasement in the 1930s*, edited by Arnd Krüger and William Murray, 17–43. Urbana: University of Illinois Press, 2003.

Kuipers, Giselinde. "The Sociology of Jumor." In *The Primer of Humor Research*, edited by Victor Raskin, 361–98. Berlin: Walter de Gruyter, 2008.

Kwon, Heonik. *The Other Cold War*. New York: Columbia University Press, 2010.

Laak, Dirk van. *Über alles in der Welt: Deutscher Imperialismus im 19. und 20. Jahrhundert*. Munich: C. H. Beck, 2005.

Langfeld, Gregor. *German Art in New York: The Canonization of Modern Art 1904–1957*. Translated by Steven Lindberg. Amsterdam: Amsterdam University Press, 2011.

Laville, Helen. "'Our Country Endangered by Underwear': Fashion, Femininity, and the Seduction Narrative in *Ninotchka* and *Silk Stockings*." *Diplomatic History* 30, no. 4 (2006): 623–44.

Law, Ricy W. *Transnational Nazism: Ideology and Culture in German-Japanese Relations, 1919–1936*. Cambridge: Cambridge University Press, 2019.

Lefort, Claude. *Democracy and Political Theory*. Minneapolis: University of Minnesota Press, 1988.

———. *Essais sur le politique, XIXe–XXe siècles*. Paris: Seuil, 1986.

———. *The Political Forms of Modern Society: Bureaucracy, Democracy, Totalitarianism*. Cambridge, MA: MIT Press, 1986.

Lehmann-Haupt, Hellmut. *Art under a Dictatorship*. New York: Oxford University Press, 1954.

Leitz, Christian. *Nazi Germany and Neutral Europe during the Second World War*. Manchester: Manchester University Press, 2000.

Lester, Rosemarie K. *"Trivialneger": Das Bild der Schwarzen in westdeutschen Illustrierten*. Stuttgart: Akademischer Verlag Hans-Dieter Heinz, 1982.

Lieb, Arne. "Als Hitler 1938 nach Düsseldorf kam." *RP-Online*, November 9, 2013. https://rp-online.de/nrw/staedte/duesseldorf/als-hitler-1938-nach-duesseldorf-kam_aid-9407419.

Limbach, Peter. "Trizonesien Lied sorgte für Aufregung." *Kölner Stadt-Anzeiger*, November 5, 2004. https://www.ksta.de/trizonesien-lied-sorgte-1949-fuer-aufregung-14563906.

Lingohr, Michel. "Die letzte ideologische Bastion? Der nationalsozialistische Angriff auf den Haushalt." In *Entnazifizierte Zone? Zum Umgang mit der Zeit des Nationalsozialismus in ostdeuschen Stadt- und Regionalmuseen*, edited by the Museum Association of the State Brandenburg, 93–110. Bielefeld: transcript, 2015.

Lombardi-Diop, Cristina. "Spotless Italy: Hygiene, Domesticity, and the Ubiquity of Whiteness in Fascist and Postwar Consumer Culture." *California Italian Studies* 2, no. 1 (2011). https://escholarship.org/uc/item/8vt6rovf.

Lupa, Markus. *Das Werk der Briten: Volkswagenwerk und Besatzungsmacht 1945–1949*. Historische Notate. Schriftenreihe des Unternehmensarchivs der Volkswagen AG, Wolfsburg, no. 2. 2nd ed. Wolfsburg, 2005.

Lützen, Wolf Dieter. "Jubiläen, Jubiläen: Die Volkswagen-Annoncen der Jahre 1951 bis 1964." In *Das deutsche Auto: Volkswagenwerbung und Volkskultur*, edited by Knut Hickethier, Wolf Dieter Lützen, and Karin Reiss, 64–88. Gießen: Anabas-Verlag, 1974.

Maase, Kaspar. *BRAVO Amerika: Erkundungen zur Jugendkultur in der Bundesrepublik der fünfziger Jahre*. Hamburg: Junius, 1992.

Maciuika, John. *Before the Bauhaus: Architecture, Politics and the German State, 1890–1920*. Cambridge: Cambridge University Press, 2005.

Martin, Rod A. *The Psychology of Humor: An Integrative Approach*. Burlington, MA: Elsevier Academic Press, 2007.

Marx, Karl. *Das Kapital: Kritik der politischen Ökonomie*. Vol. 1, bk. 1. Berlin: Dietz, 1962.
Mazower, Mark. *Hitler's Empire: Nazi Rule in Occupied Europe*. London: Allen Lane, 2008.
McClintock, Anne. *Imperial Leather: Race, Gender and Sexuality in the Colonial Context*. New York: Routledge, 1995.
McDonald, Gay. "The 'Advance' of American Postwar Design in Europe: MoMA and the Design for Use, USA Exhibition 1951–1953." *Design Issues* 24, no. 2 (2008): 15–27.
———. "The Modern American Home as Soft Power: Finland, MoMA and the 'American Home 1953.'" *Journal of Design History* 23, no. 3 (2010): 387–408.
———. "Selling the American Dream: MoMA, Industrial Design and Post-war France." *Journal of Design History* 17, no. 4 (2004): 397–412.
McKenzie, Brian Angus. *Remaking France: Americanization, Public Diplomacy, and the Marshall Plan*. New York: Berghahn Books, 2005.
McNeil, Peter. "Myths of Modernism: Japanese Architecture, Interior Design and the West, c. 1920–1940." *Journal of Design History* 5, no. 4 (1992): 281–94.
Meng, Michael. *Shattered Spaces: Encountering Jewish Ruins in Postwar Germany and Poland*. Cambridge, MA: Harvard University Press, 2011.
Mennel, Barbara. "Returning Home: The Orientalist Spectacle of Fritz Lang's *Der Tiger von Eschnapur* and *Das Indische Grabmal*." In *Framing the Fifties: Cinema in a Divided Germany*, edited by John Davidson and Sabine Hake, 28–43. New York: Berghahn Books, 2007.
Merritt, Anna J., and Richard L. Merritt, eds. *Public Opinion in Semisovereign Germany: The HICOG Surveys, 1949–1955*. Urbana: University of Illinois Press, 1980.
Meyer, Dennis. "Entnazifierung." In *Lexikon der "Vergangenheitsbewältigung" in Deutschland: Debatten- und Diskursgeschichte des Nationalsozialismus nach 1945*, edited by Torben Fischer and Matthias N. Lorenz, 18–19. Bielefeld: transcript, 2007.
Mignolo, Walter D. "The Many Faces of Cosmo-polis: Border Thinking and Critical Cosmopolitanism." *Public Culture* 12, no. 3 (2000): 721–48.
Miller, Daniel. *The Comfort of Things*. Cambridge: Polity Press, 2008.
Miron, Guy. "'Lately, Almost Constantly, Everything Seems Small to Me': The Lived Space of German Jews under the Nazi Regime." *Jewish Social Studies* 20, no. 1 (2013): 121–49.
Mitscherlich, Alexander, and Margarete Mitscherlich. *Die Unfähigkeit zu trauern: Grundlagen kollektiven Verhaltens*. Munich: Piper, 1967.
Moeller, Robert G. *Protecting Motherhood: Women and the Family in the Politics of Postwar West Germany*. Berkeley: University of California Press, 1992.
———. "The 'Remasculinization' of Germany in the 1950s: Introduction." *Signs* 24, no. 1 (1998): 101–6.
———. *War Stories: The Search for a Usable Past in the Federal Republic of Germany*. Berkeley: University of California Press, 2001.
Moentmann, Elise Marie. "The Search for French Identity in the Regions: National versus Local Visions of France in the 1930s." *French History* 17, no. 3 (2003): 307–27.
Moltke, Johannes von. *No Place Like Home: Locations of Heimat in German Cinema*. Berkeley: University of California Press, 2005.

Mommsen, Hans, and Manfred Grieger. *Das Volkswagenwerk und seine Arbeiter im Dritten Reich*. Düsseldorf: ECON, 1996.

Mueller, Sabine. "Narration, Rubble Film, and Narratability: Helmut Käutner's *In jenen Tagen*." *Modern Language Review* 107, no. 4 (2012): 1168–90.

Myers Feinstein, Margarete. *State Symbols: The Quest for Legitimacy in the Federal Republic of Germany and the German Democratic Republic, 1949–1959*. Boston: Brill, 2001.

Naranch, Bradley D. "Inventing the *Auslandsdeutsche*: Emigration, Colonial Fantasy, and German National Identity, 1848–71." In *Germany's Colonial Pasts*, edited by Eric Ames, Marcia Klotz, and Lora Wildenthal, 21–40. Lincoln: University of Nebraska Press, 2005.

Navaro-Yashin, Yael. *The Make-Believe Space: Affective Geography in a Postwar Polity*. Durham, NC: Duke University Press, 2012.

Nawyn, Kathleen J. "'Ausrottung des "kämpferischen Geistes!"': Zur Beseitigung militaristischer Denkmäler im amerikanisch besetzten Württemberg-Baden, 1945–1947." In *Banal Militarism: Zur Veralltäglichung des Militärischen im Zivilen*, edited by Tanja Thomas and Fabian Virchow, 129–48. Bielefeld: transcript, 2006.

———. "'Striking at the Roots of German Militarism': Efforts to Demilitarize German Society and Culture in American-Occupied Württemberg-Baden, 1945–1949." PhD diss., University of North Carolina at Chapel Hill, 2008.

Nerdinger, Winfried, ed. *Bauhaus-Moderne im Nationalsozialismus: Zwischen Anbiederung und Verfolgung*. Munich: Prestel-Verlag, 1993.

———. *Walter Gropius: Architekt der Moderne 1884–1969*. Munich: C. H. Beck, 2019.

Neupert, Richard. *A History of the French New Wave Cinema*. Madison: University of Wisconsin Press, 2002.

Noack-Mosse, Eva. *Last Days of Theresienstadt*. Translated by Skye Doney and Birutė Ciplijauskaitė. Madison: University of Wisconsin Press, 2018.

Oestereich, Christopher. *"Gute Form" im Wiederaufbau: Zur Geschichte der Produktgestaltung in Westdeutschland nach 1945*. Berlin: Lukas, 2000.

———. "Umstrittene Selbstdarstellung: Der deutsche Beitrag zur Weltausstellung in Brüssel." *Vierteljahrshefte für Zeitgeschichte* 48, no. 1 (January 2000): 127–153.

Olick, Jeffrey K. *In the House of the Hangman: The Agonies of German Defeat, 1943–1949*. Chicago: University of Chicago Press, 2005.

Ørskov, Frederik F. "From Nordic Romanticism to Nordic Modernity: Danish Tourist Brochures in Nazi Germany, 1929–39." *Journal of Contemporary History* 55, no. 1 (2020): 29–51.

Osayimwese, Itohan. *Colonialism and Modern Architecture in Germany*. Pittsburgh, PA: University of Pittsburgh Press, 2017.

Paeffgen, Manfred. *Das Bild Schwarz-Afrikas in der öffentlichen Meinung der Bundesrepublik Deutschland*. Munich: Weltforum, 1976.

Pagenstecher, Cord. "Private Fotoalben als historische Quelle." *Zeithistorische Forschungen / Studies in Contemporary History* 6, no. 3 (2009): 449–63.

Parkinson, Anna M. *An Emotional State: The Politics of Emotion in Postwar West German Culture*. Ann Arbor: University of Michigan Press, 2015.

Paulmann, Johannes. "Representation without Emulation: German Cultural Diplomacy in Search of Integration and Self-Assurance during the Adenauer Era." *German Politics and Society* 25, no. 2 (2007): 168–200.

Pavitt, Jane. "Design and the Democratic Ideal." In *Cold War Modern: Design 1945–1970*, edited by David Crowley and Jane Pavitt, 73–93. London: Victoria and Albert Museum, 2008.

Pence, Katherine, and Paul Betts, eds. *Socialist Modern: East German Everyday Culture and Politics*. Ann Arbor: University of Michigan Press, 2008.

Perego, Elizabeth. "The Veil or a Brother's Life: French Manipulations of Muslim Women's Images during the Algerian War, 1954–1962." *Journal of North African Studies* 20, no. 3 (2015): 349–73.

Petropoulos, Jonathan. "The Art World in Nazi Germany: Choices, Rationalization, and Justice." In *The Arts in Nazi Germany: Continuity, Conformity, Change*, edited by Jonathan Huener and Francis R. Nicosia, 135–63. New York: Berghahn Books, 2006.

Pinkert, Anke. "Can Melodrama Cure? War Trauma and Crisis of Masculinity in Early DEFA Film." *Seminar: A Journal of Germanic Studies* 44, no. 1 (2008): 118–36.

———. *Film and Memory in East Germany*. Bloomington: Indiana University Press, 2008.

Poiger, Uta G. "American Music, Cold War Liberalism, and German Identities." In *Transactions, Transgressions, Transformations: American Culture in Western Europe and Japan*, edited by Uta G. Poiger and Heide Fehrenbach, 127–47. New York: Berghahn Books, 2000.

———. "Imperialism and Empire in Twentieth-Century Germany." *History & Memory* 17, no. 1/2 (2005): 117–43.

———. *Jazz, Rock and Rebels: Cold War Politics and American Culture in a Divided Germany*. Berkeley: University of California Press, 2000.

Rahden, Till van. "Clumsy Democrats: Moral Passions in the Federal Republic." *German History* 29, no. 3 (2011): 485–504.

———. *Demokratie: Eine gefährdete Lebensform*. Frankfurt am Main: Campus, 2019.

Rapaport, Lynn. *Jews in Germany after the Holocaust: Memory, Identity, and Jewish-German Relations*. Cambridge: Cambridge University Press, 1997.

Rashkin, Esther. *Unspeakable Secrets and the Psychoanalysis of Culture*. Albany: State University of New York Press, 2008.

Reagin, Nancy R. *Sweeping the German Nation: Domesticity and National Identity in Germany, 1870–1945*. Cambridge: Cambridge University Press, 2007.

Reed, Christopher. *Bachelor Japanists: Japanese Aesthetics and Western Masculinities*. New York: Columbia University Press, 2017.

Reimer, Robert C. "Turning Inward: An Analysis of Helmut Käutner's *Auf Wiedersehen Franziska*, *Romanze in Moll*, and *Unter den Brücken*." In *Cultural History through a National Socialist Lens: Essays on the Cinema of the Third Reich*, edited by Robert C. Reimer, 214–39. Rochester, NY: Camden House, 2000.

Riederer, Günter. *Auto-Kino: Unternehmensfilme von Volkswagen in den Wirtschaftswunderjahren*. Wolfsburg: Volkswagen Aktiengesellschaft, 2011.

Rieger, Bernhard. "The 'Good German' Goes Global: The Volkswagen Beetle as an Icon in the Federal Republic." *History Workshop Journal* 68, no. 1 (2009): 3–26.

———. *The People's Car: A Global History of the Volkswagen Beetle*. Cambridge, MA: Harvard University Press, 2013.

———. "Schulden der Vergangenheit? Der Mammutprozess der Volkswagensparer, 1949–1961." In *Mit dem Wandel leben: Neuorientierung und Tradition in der Bundesrepublik der 1950er und 1960er Jahre*, edited by Friedrich Kießling and Bernhard Rieger, 185–208. Cologne: Böhlau, 2011.

———. "Was Roland a Nazi? Victims, Perpetrators, and Silences during the Restoration of Civic Identity in Postwar Bremen." *History and Memory* 19, no. 2 (2007): 75–111.

Riemann, Xenia. "Die 'Gute Form' und ihr Inhalt: Über die Kontinuität des sachlichen deutschen Designs zwischen 1930 und 1960." *kritische berichte* 34, no. 1 (2006): 52–62.

Rinn, Gregor M. "Das Automobil als nationales Identifikationssymbol: Zur politischen Bedeutung des Kraftfahrzeugs in Modernitätskonzeptionen des 'Dritten Reichs' und der Bundesrepublik." PhD diss., Humboldt University Berlin, 2008.

Rosenberg, Gavriel D. *Munich and Memory: Architecture, Monuments, and the Legacy of the Third Reich*. Berkeley: University of California Press, 2000.

Ross, Kristin. *Fast Cars, Clean Bodies: Decolonization and the Reordering of French Culture*. Cambridge, MA: MIT Press, 1995.

Rössler, Patrick. *Das Bauhaus am Kiosk / The Bauhaus at the Newsstand*. Bielefeld: Kerber Art, 2009.

———. "Vielfalt in der Gleichschaltung—die 'domestizierte Moderne' am Kiosk: Eine Lifestyle-Illustrierte zwischen Bauhaus-Avantgarde und NS-Propaganda; 'Die neue Linie' 1929–1943." *Jahrbuch für Kommunikationsgeschichte* 9 (2007): 150–95.

Rubin, Eli. "The Form of Socialism without Ornament: Consumption, Ideology, and the Fall and Rise of Modernist Design in the German Democratic Republic." *Journal of Design History* 19, no. 2 (2006): 155–68.

Rutz, Rainer. *Signal: Eine deutsche Auslandsillustrierte als Propagandainstrument im Zweiten Weltkrieg*. Essen: Klartext Verlag, 2007.

Said, Edward. *Orientalism*. London: Penguin Books, 2003.

Santner, Eric. *Stranded Objects: Mourning, Memory, and Film in Postwar Germany*. Ithaca, NY: Cornell University Press, 1990.

Satia, Priya. *Time's Monster: How History Makes History*. Cambridge, MA: Belknap Press of Harvard University Press, 2020.

Schäfer, Hans Dieter. *Das gespaltene Bewusstsein: Vom Dritten Reich bis zu den langen fünfziger Jahren*. Rev. ed. Göttingen: Wallstein, 2009.

Schäfers, Stefanie. *Vom Werkbund zum Vierjahresplan: Die Ausstellung "Schaffendes Volk" in Düsseldorf 1937*. Düsseldorf: Droste Verlag, 2001.

Schanetzky, Tim. *"Kanonen statt Butter": Wirtschaft und Konsum im Dritten Reich. Die Deutschen und der Nationalsozialismus*. Munich: C. H. Beck, 2015.

Scherpe, Klaus R. "Der Orient im Interieur." In *Mit Deutschland um die Welt: Eine Kulturgeschichte des Fremden in der Kolonialzeit*, edited by Alexander Honold and Klaus R. Scherpe, 329–37. Stuttgart: Metzler, 2004.

Schildt, Axel. *Ankunft im Westen: Ein Essay zur Erfolgsgeschichte der Bundesrepublik.* Frankfurt am Main: Fischer, 1999.

Schildt, Axel, and Arnold Sywottek, eds. *Modernisierung im Wiederaufbau: Die westdeutsche Gesellschaft der 50er Jahre*. Bonn: Dietz, 1998.

Schissler, Hanna. "Writing about 1950s West Germany." In *The Miracle Years: A Cultural History of West Germany, 1949–1968*, edited by Hanna Schissler, 3–15. Princeton, NJ: Princeton University Press, 2001.

Schlinkert, Dirk. "Von der Reklame zum Marketing." In *50 Jahre Volkswagenwerbung*, 8–17. Hamburg: Gruner und Jahr, 2002.

Schneider, Falko. "Unfassbares Produzieren: Zur politischen Epistemologie des Wunderbegriffs im 20. Jahrhundert." In *Wunder*, edited by Alexander Geppert and Till Kössler, 305–31. Berlin: Suhrkamp, 2011.

Scholz, Natalie. "The 'Modern Home' during the 1950s: West German Cultural Reconstruction and the Ambivalent Meanings of Americanization." *Tijdschrift voor Geschiedenis* 121, no. 3 (2008): 296–311.

Scholz, Natalie, and Milena Veenis. "Cold War Modernism and Postwar German Homes: An East-West Comparison." In *Divided Dreamworlds? The Cultural Cold War in East and West*, edited by Peter Romijn, Giles Scott-Smith, and Joes Segal, 155–80. Amsterdam: Amsterdam University Press, 2012.

Scholz, Natalie. "'A Final Solution for Humanity'? Modern Design and the Ambivalences of Redemption in Post-war West Germany." *Cultural History* 12, no. 1 (April 2023): 74–97.

———. "Gender and the Morality of Things in Postwar Germany." *Clio. Women, Gender History*, no. 40 (2014): 89–113.

———. "Ghosts and Miracles: The Volkswagen as Imperial Debris in Postwar West Germany." *Comparative Studies in Society and History* 62, no. 3 (2020): 487–519.

Schroer, Timothy L. *Recasting Race after World War II: Germans and African Americans in American-Occupied Germany*. Denver: University Press of Colorado, 2007.

Schütz, Erhard. "Der Volkswagen." In *Deutsche Erinnerungsorte: Eine Auswahl*, edited by Étienne François and Hagen Schulze, 351–68. Munich: C. H. Beck, 2005.

Selle, Gerd. *Geschichte des Design in Deutschland*. Frankfurt am Main: Campus, 1984.

Shandley, Robert R. *Rubble Films: German Cinema in the Shadow of the Third Reich*. Philadelphia, PA: Temple University Press, 2001.

Sherman, Daniel J. *French Primitivism and the Ends of Empire, 1945–1975*. Chicago: University of Chicago Press, 2011.

———. "Post-colonial Chic: Fantasies of the French Interior, 1957–62." *Art History* 27, no. 5 (2004): 770–805.

Simon, Sunka. "Der vord're Orient: Colonialist Imagery in Popular Postwar German *Schlager*." *Journal of Popular Culture* 34, no. 3 (2000): 87–108.

Simons, Oliver. "Orientteppich und Kunstwerk, 1895: Hugo von Hoffmansthals *Märchen der 672. Nacht*." In *Mit Deutschland um die Welt: Eine Kulturgeschichte des Fremden in der Kolonialzeit*, edited by Alexander Honold and Klaus Rüdiger Scherpe, 182–89. Stuttgart: Metzler, 2004.

Sollors, Werner. *The Temptation of Despair: Tales of the 1940s*. Cambridge, MA: Belknap Press of Harvard University Press, 2014.

Sparke, Penny. "'A Home for Everybody?': Design, Ideology and the Culture of the Home in Italy, 1945–1972." In *Modernism in Design*, edited by Paul Greenhalgh, 185–203. London: Reaktion Books, 1990.

———. *Japanese Design*. New York: Museum of Modern Art, 2009.

Spoerer, Mark. "Demontage eines Mythos? Zu der Kontroverse über das nationalsozialistische 'Wirtschaftswunder.'" *Geschichte und Gesellschaft* 31, no. 3 (2005): 415–38.

Stargardt, Nicholas. *The German War: A Nation under Arms, 1939–1945*. London: Vintage, 2015.

Starl, Timm. "Die Bildwelt der Knipser: Eine empirische Untersuchung zur privaten Fotografie." *Fotogeschichte: Beiträge zur Geschichte und Ästhetik der Fotografie* 14, no. 52 (1994): 59–68.

———. "Die Kehrseite der Geschichte. Karl Pawek: Priesterzögling, Zeitschriftengründer, NSDAP-Anwärter, Kriegsverbrecher, Psychopath, Ausstellungsmacher, Kulturpreisträger." *Fotogeschichte* 23, no. 87 (2003): 65–69.

Steege, Paul. *Black Market, Cold War: Everyday Life in Berlin, 1946–1949*. Cambridge: Cambridge University Press, 2008.

Steenkamp, Alta. "The Ideal Homes Competitions of the 1930's: Architectural Setting for a South African White Middle-Class." *Home Cultures* 16, no. 2 (2019): 95–108.

Stern, Frank. "Antagonistic Memories: The Post-war Survival and Alienation of Jews and Germans." In *Memory and Totalitarianism*, edited by Luisa Passerini, 21–43. 1992. Reprint, New Brunswick, NJ: Transaction Publishers, 2009.

———. *The Whitewashing of the Yellow Badge: Antisemitism and Philosemitism in Postwar Germany*. Translated by William Templer. Oxford: Pergamon Press, 1992.

Stern, Fritz. *Verspielte Größe: Essays zur deutschen Geschichte im 20. Jahrhundert*. Munich: C. H. Beck, 1996.

Stern, Lesley. "Paths That Wind through the Thicket of Things." *Critical Inquiry* 28, no. 1 (2001): 317–54.

Stoler, Ann L. "Colonial Aphasia: Race and Disabled Histories in France." *Public Culture* 23, no. 1 (2011): 121–56.

———, ed. *Imperial Debris: On Ruins and Ruination*. Durham, NC: Duke University Press, 2013.

———. "Intimidations of Empire: Predicaments of the Tactile and Unseen." In *Haunted by Empire: Geographies of Intimacy in North American History*, edited by Ann L. Stoler, 1–22. Durham, NC: Duke University Press, 2006.

———. "Introduction: 'The Rot Remains'; From Ruins to Ruination." In *Imperial Debris*, edited by Ann L. Stoler, 1–35. Durham, NC: Duke University Press, 2013.

Stratigakos, Despina. *Hitler at Home*. New Haven, CT: Yale University Press, 2017.

Suga, Yasuko. "Invention of 'Modern' Japonisme: National Representation through 'Sangyo Kogei.'" Conference paper, 2008. https://www.academia.edu/55789680/Invention_of_Modern_Japonisme_national_representation_through_Sangyo_Kogei_.

Swett, Pamela. *Selling under the Swastika: Advertising and Commercial Culture in Nazi Germany*. Stanford, CA: Stanford University Press, 2014.

Swett, Pamela W., S. Jonathan Wiesen, and Jonathan R. Zatlin. Introduction to *Selling Modernity: Advertising in Twentieth-Century Germany*, edited by Pamela Swett, S. Jonathan Wiesen, and Jonathan R. Zatlin, 1–26. Durham, NC: Duke University Press, 2007.

Szeijnmann, Claus-Christian W. "'A Sense of *Heimat* Opened Up during the War': German Soldiers and *Heimat* Abroad." In *Heimat, Region and Empire: Spatial Identities under National Socialism*, edited by Claus-Christian W. Szejnmann and Maiken Umbach, 112–47. Houndmills: Palgrave Macmillan, 2012.

Szejnmann, Claus-Christian W., and Maiken Umbach, eds. *Heimat, Region and Empire: Spatial Identities under National Socialism*. Houndmills: Palgrave Macmillan, 2012.

Szeless, Margarethe. *Die Kulturzeitschrift "magnum": Photographische Befunde der Moderne*. Marburg: Jonas Verlag, 2007.

Tansman, Alan. Introduction to *The Culture of Japanese Fascism*, edited by Alan Tansman, 1–30. Durham, NC: Duke University Press, 2009.

Tanzer, Frances. "European Fantasies: Modernism and Jewish Absence at the Venice Biennale of Art, 1948–1956." *Contemporary European History* 31, no. 2 (May 2022): 243–58.

Taussig, Michael T. *Defacement: Public Secrecy and the Labor of the Negative*. Stanford, CA: Stanford University Press, 1999.

Taylor, Brandon, and Wilfried van der Will, eds. *The Nazification of Art: Art, Design, Music, Architecture and Film in the Third Reich*. Winchester: Winchester Press, 1990.

Thiessen, Malte. "Erinneringen an die 'Volksgemeinschaft': Integration und Exklusion im kommunalen und kommunikativen Gedächtnis." In *"Volksgemeinschaft": Mythos, wirkumgsmächtige soziale Verheißung oder soziale Realität im "Dritten Reich,"* edited by Detlef Schmiechen-Ackermann, 319–34. Paderborn: Schöningh, 2021.

Thode-Arora, Hilke. "Afrika-Völkerschauen in Deutschland." In *AfrikanerInnen in Deutschland und schwarze Deutsche—Geschichte und Gegenwart*, edited by Marianne Bechhaus-Gerst and Reinhard Klein-Arendt, 25–40. Münster: Lit, 2004.

Tofahrn, Klaus W. *Chronologie des Dritten Reiches: Ereignisse Personen, Begriffe*. Darmstadt: Wissenschaftliche Buchgesellschaft, 2003.

Tooze, Adam. *The Wages of Destruction: The Making and Breaking of the Nazi Economy*. London: Penguin Books, 2006.

Treber, Leonie. *Mythos Trümmerfrauen: Von der Trümmerbeseitigung in der Kriegs- und Nachkriegszeit und der Entstehung eines deutschen Erinnerungsortes*. Essen: Klartext, 2014.

Trouillot, Michel-Rolph. *Silencing the Past: Power and the Production of History*. Boston: Beacon Press, 1995.

Tymkiw, Michael. *Nazi Exhibition Design and Modernism*. Minneapolis: University of Minnesota Press, 2018.

Vees-Gulani, Susanne. "From Frankfurt's Goethehaus to Dresden's Frauenkirche: Architecture, German Identity, and Historical Memory after 1945." *Germanic Review* 80, no. 2 (2005): 143–63.

Verber, Jason. "The Conundrum of Colonialism in Postwar Germany." PhD diss., University of Iowa, 2010.

———. "Remembering at a Time of Forgetting: Weimar Colonialism in West Germany." In *Weimar Colonialism: Discourses and Legacies of Post-imperialism in Germany after 1918*, edited by Florian Ulrich Krobb and Elaine Martin, 209–27. Bielefeld: Aisthesis-Verlag, 2014.

Verheyen, Nina. *Diskussionslust: Eine Kulturgeschichte des "besseren Arguments" in Westdeutschland*. Göttingen: Vandenhoeck & Ruprecht, 2010.

Voss, Julia. "Das Werner-Haftmann Modell: Wie die documenta zur Bühne der Erinnerungspolitik wurde." In *documenta: Politik und Kunst*, edited by Raphael Gross, Lars Bang Larsen, Dorlis Blume, Alexia Pooth, Julia Voss, and Dorothee Wierling, 69–76. Munich: Prestel, 2021.

Walch, Teresa. "Degenerate Spaces: The Coordination of Space in Nazi Germany." PhD diss., University of San Diego, 2018.

———. "With an Iron Broom: Cleansing Berlin's Bülowplatz of 'Judeo-Bolshevism.'" *German History* 40, no. 1 (2022): 61–87.

Weckel, Ulrike. *Beschämende Bilder: Deutsche Reaktionen auf alliierte Dokumentarfilme über befreite Konzentrationslager*. Stuttgart: Steiner, 2012.

———. "Die *Mörder sind unter uns* oder: Vom Verschwinden der Opfer." *Werkstatt-Geschichte* 25 (2000): 105–15.

———. "Disappointed Hopes for Spontaneous Mass Conversion: German Responses to Allied Atrocity Film Screenings 1945–46." *Bulletin of the GHI* 51 (Fall 2012): 39–53.

Weißler, Sabine, ed. *Design in Deutschland 1933–45: Ästhetik und Organisation des Deutschen Werkbundes im "Dritten Reich."* Gießen: Anabas-Verlag, 1990.

———. "Worum es geht." In *Design in Deutschland 1933–45*, edited by Sabine Weißler, 8–9. Gießen: Anabas-Verlag, 1990.

Welzer, Harald. *Das soziale Gedächtnis: Geschichte, Erinnerung, Tradierung*. Hamburg: Hamburger Editionen, 2001.

Westphal, Uwe. *Werbung im Dritten Reich*. Berlin: Transit, 1989.

Wichmann, Hans. *Deutsche Werkstätten und WK-Verband: Aufbruch zum neuen Wohnen*. Munich: Prestel, 1992.

Wiesen, Jonathan S. *Creating the Nazi Marketplace: Commerce and Consumption in the Third Reich*. Cambridge: Cambridge University Press, 2011.

———. "Miracles for Sale: Consumer Displays and Advertising in Postwar West Germany." In *Consuming Germany in the Cold War*, edited by David F. Crew, 151–78. Oxford: Berg, 2003.

Williams, Raymond. *The Long Revolution*. Harmondsworth: Pelican Books, 1965.

Winnicott, Donald Woods. *Playing and Reality*. London: Routledge, 2005.

Winstel, Tobias. "Verordnete 'Ehrenpflicht': Wiedergutmachung für jüdische NS-Opfer." In *München "arisiert": Entrechtung und Enteignung der Juden in der NS-Zeit*, edited by Angelika Baumann and Andreas Heusler, 218–36. Munich: C. H. Beck, 2004.

Wolf, René. "'Mass Deception without Deceivers'? The Holocaust on East and West German Radio in the 1960s." *Journal of Contemporary History* 41, no. 4 (2006): 741–55.

Woodham, Jonathan. "Design and Everyday Life at the *Britain Can Make It* Exhibition, 1946: 'Stripes, Spots, White Wood and Homespun versus Chintzy Armchairs and Iron Bedsteads with Brass Knobs.'" *Journal of Architecture* 9 (Winter 2004): 463–76.
Young, Robert J. C. "The Postcolonial Condition." In *The Oxford Handbook of Postwar European History*, edited by Dan Stone, 600–611. Oxford: Oxford University Press, 2012.
Zantop, Susanne. *Colonial Fantasies: Conquest, Family, and Nation in Precolonial Germany, 1770–1870*. Durham, NC: Duke University Press, 1997.
Zeller, Joachim. *Weiße Blicke—schwarze Körper: Afrikaner im Spiegel westlicher Alltagskultur; Bilder aus der Sammlung Peter Weiss*. Erfurt: Sutton Verlag, 2010.
Zentek, Sabine. *Designer im Dritten Reich: Gute Formen sind eine Frage der richtigen Haltung*. Dortmund: Lelesken-Verlag, 2009.

INDEX

George L. Mosse Series in the History of European Culture, Sexuality, and Ideas

STEVEN E. ASCHHEIM, SKYE DONEY,
MARY LOUISE ROBERTS, AND DAVID J. SORKIN

Series Editors

Of God and Gods: Egypt, Israel, and the Rise of Monotheism
JAN ASSMANN

Messengers of Disaster: Raphael Lemkin, Jan Karski, and Twentieth-Century Genocides
ANNETTE BECKER; translated by KÄTHE ROTH

Respectability and Violence: Military Values, Masculine Honor, and Italy's Road to Mass Death
LORENZO BENADUSI; translated by ZAKIYA HANAFI

The Enemy of the New Man: Homosexuality in Fascist Italy
LORENZO BENADUSI; translated by
SUZANNE DINGEE and JENNIFER PUDNEY

The Holocaust and the West German Historians: Historical Interpretation and Autobiographical Memory
NICOLAS BERG; translated and edited by JOEL GOLB

Collected Memories: Holocaust History and Postwar Testimony
CHRISTOPHER R. BROWNING

Contemporary Europe in the Historical Imagination
Edited by DARCY BUERKLE and SKYE DONEY

Cataclysms: A History of the Twentieth Century from Europe's Edge
DAN DINER; translated by WILLIAM TEMPLER with JOEL GOLB

Fascination with the Persecutor: George L. Mosse and the Catastrophe of Modern Man
EMILIO GENTILE; translated by JOHN TEDESCHI and ANNE TEDESCHI

La Grande Italia: The Myth of the Nation in the Twentieth Century
EMILIO GENTILE; translated by SUZANNE DINGEE and
JENNIFER PUDNEY

The Invisible Jewish Budapest: Metropolitan Culture at the Fin de Siècle
MARY GLUCK

Carl Schmitt and the Jews: The "Jewish Question," the Holocaust, and German Legal Theory
RAPHAEL GROSS; translated by JOEL GOLB

Unlearning Eugenics: Sexuality, Reproduction, and Disability in Post-Nazi Europe
DAGMAR HERZOG

Reason after Its Eclipse: On Late Critical Theory
MARTIN JAY

Some Measure of Justice: The Holocaust Era Restitution Campaign of the 1990s
MICHAEL R. MARRUS

The Best Weapon for Peace: Maria Montessori, Education, and Children's Rights
ERICA MORETTI

Confronting History: A Memoir
GEORGE L. MOSSE

Nazi Culture: Intellectual, Cultural, and Social Life in the Third Reich
GEORGE L. MOSSE

Last Days of Theresienstadt
EVA NOACK-MOSSE; translated by SKYE DONEY and BIRUTĖ CIPLIJAUSKAITĖ

What History Tells: George L. Mosse and the Culture of Modern Europe
Edited by STANLEY G. PAYNE, DAVID J. SORKIN, and JOHN S. TORTORICE

The Perils of Normalcy: George L. Mosse and the Remaking of Cultural History
KAREL PLESSINI

Shaping the New Man: Youth Training Regimes in Fascist Italy and Nazi Germany
ALESSIO PONZIO

Propaganda and Persecution:
The French Resistance and the "Jewish Question"
RENÉE POZNANSKI; translated by LENN J. SCHRAMM

The Jews in Mussolini's Italy: From Equality to Persecution
MICHELE SARFATTI; translated by JOHN and ANNE C. TEDESCHI

Redeeming Objects: A West German Mythology
NATALIE SCHOLZ

A History of Italian Fascist Culture, 1922–1943
ALESSANDRA TARQUINI; translated by MARISSA GEMMA

Jews and Other Germans: Civil Society, Religious Diversity, and Urban Politics in Breslau, 1860–1925
TILL VAN RAHDEN; translated by MARCUS BRAINARD

An Uncompromising Generation: The Nazi Leadership of the Reich Security Main Office
MICHAEL WILDT; translated by TOM LAMPERT